IMPROVING THE READING PROGRAM

IMPROVING THE READING PROGRAM

THIRD EDITION

DELWYN G. SCHUBERT
California State College at Los Angeles

THEODORE L. TORGERSON
Emeritus, University of Wisconsin

WM. C. BROWN COMPANY PUBLISHERS
Dubuque, Iowa

Contents

Preface

Improving the Reading Program is the third edition of *Improving Reading Through Individualized Correction*. The present edition retains the same organization of content with its emphasis on hazards to learning, diagnosis, and the use of self-directed corrective material. Readers who have been enthusiastic about the book as a source of self-directed instructional material will be pleased to find much that is completely new.

A diagram which provides the reader with an overview of the book's organization and content appears at the beginning of the volume. Six tenets of learning as they relate to reading are set forth in the first chapter. The hazards to learning presented in the earlier edition have been increased and classified as they pertain to the developmental program, the corrective program, and the administration. Four new chapters with a total of more than 100 pages fully documented have been added. New chapter titles are "The Developmental Program in Reading," "Diagnosis in the Instructional Program," "The Diagnostic Process," and "The Corrective Program in Reading." Many topics have been added or augmented, including reading and the culturally disadvantaged, reading and the gifted, prevention of reading problems, grouping, oral reading, making reading games, and reading in the content fields. A more complete list of problems for discussion accompanies most of the chapters. Several new reading tests are listed in the Appendix, along with a list of screening tests in vision.

Teachers found the earlier editions a valuable source for ordering new material and equipment in the field of reading. The present edition provides a more extensive list accompanied by current prices. Instructors will find this volume very practical for students enrolled in Developmental Reading, Corrective or Remedial Reading, and for teachers in service.

OVERVIEW OF CONTENT AND ORGANIZATION

Tenets of Learning (Chap. 1)	Hazards to Learning	The Instructional Program

Tenets of Learning (Chap. 1)

Learning is the goal of all teaching.

The objective of the reading program is to teach all children to read at capacity level.

Learning is maximized when the school provides adequately for individual differences.

Reading problems are minimized when hazards to learning are identified and corrected.

The teacher's effectiveness in correcting problems in reading is enhanced by the use of self-directed corrective material.

Reading problems are reduced to a minimum when a program of prevention is emphasized.

Educational Hazards (Chap. 2)

Faulty practices in Developmental Reading

Diagnosis in Reading

Correction in Reading

Administrative Policies

Noneducational Hazards (Chap. 3)

Impaired Vision

Impaired Hearing

Impaired Speech

Impaired Health

Neurological Disorders

Mental Immaturity

Emotional Maladjustment

Cultural Deprivation

The Developmental Program (Chap. 4)

Systematic instruction in the skills
Sequential development
Mastery of the skills
Prevention emphasized
Frustration level avoided
Diversified material utilized
Mastery of the reading habits in the primary grades
Exploration of cultural needs

The Diagnostic Program (Chap. 5)

Discovers difficulties in
    word recognition
    word analysis
    comprehension and rate
    study skills
Explores reading expectancy
Identifies hazards to learning

The Diagnostic Process (Chap. 6)

Diagnosis precedes correction
Diagnosis identifies
    problem readers
    nature of the reading problem
    severity of the problem
    reading expectancy
    hazards to learning
    causal factors
    correction needed

The Corrective Program (Chap. 7)

Corrects deficiencies in
    sight vocabulary and word analysis
    comprehension and study skills
    dictionary skills
    meaning vocabulary
    technical vocabulary

The Corrective Material (Chaps. 8-10)

Teacher-made and commercial
    self-directive in nature
    optimum in difficulty
    varied in content and interest
    tailored to meet individual needs

The Improvement Program in Reading (Chap. 11)

Qualified teachers of reading
In-service teacher training
Reading specialists and other consultants
Ample library facilities
Diversified instructional material
Survey of local reading program

1

Reading and the Learning Process

In our culture it is literally true that the roads of knowledge are paved with printer's ink. The ability to read not only differentiates the literate and the illiterate, it is also essential to learning all subjects in school. Although much can be gained through attentive listening, deeper understanding and genuine progress in areas such as science, history, and geography are not possible without the ability to read. Since the reading process permeates the entire curriculum, it is not surprising that the right to read has been considered by some educators as fundamental as the right to life, liberty, and the pursuit of happiness.

Reading specialists such as Durrell,[1] McCallister,[2] Thompson,[3] Witty,[4] and Woodbury[5] estimate that ten to twenty-five percent of children in school have a reading disability. In a recent article by Dempsey,[6] Samuel Sava is quoted as saying that twenty-five percent of the male population is functionally illiterate. Statistical information accumulated by the Office of Education gives the following specifics:

—One out of every four students nationwide has significant reading deficiencies.
—In large city school systems up to half of the students read below expectation.
—There are more than three million illiterates in our adult population.
—About half of the unemployed youth, ages 16-21, are functionally illiterate.
—Three-quarters of the juvenile offenders in New York City are two or more years retarded in reading.
—In a recent U.S. Armed Forces program called Project 100,000, 68.2 percent of the young men fell below Grade Seven in reading and academic ability. [7]

These shocking facts impelled James E. Allen, Jr., former U.S. Commissioner of Education, to spearhead a nationwide attack on reading deficiencies. On September 23, 1969, when addressing the National Association of State Boards of Education in Los Angeles, he stated:

> . . . I am herewith proclaiming my belief that we should immediately set for ourselves the goal of assuring that by the end of the 1970's the right to read shall be a reality for all—that no one shall be leaving our schools without the skill and the desire necessary to read to the full limits of his capability. (7)

The goal set by the former U.S. Commissioner of Education charges the schools of America with the full responsibility for eliminating reading deficiencies. As an aid to understanding and achieving this goal, the authors of this volume set forth the following tenets: *

1. Learning is the goal of all teaching.
   a. Teaching is an educational process and learning is the product.
   b. The chief aim of the school is to promote literacy.
   c. Illiteracy is rampant in the adult population.
   d. The reading skills provide the tools for learning.
   e. A preponderance of pupils in the schools suffer from reading disabilities.

2. The objective of the reading program is to teach all children to read at capacity level.
   a. Nonreaders, disabled readers, underachievers, and dropouts are found in every school system.
   b. A diversified and challenging instructional program adjusted to individual needs must be provided.
   c. A child's reading program must consist of materials that are on an appropriate instructional level and are adapted to his learning needs.
   d. The atypical child will learn when his specific learning problems are corrected and a systematic individualized program of appropriate learning experiences is provided.

3. Learning is maximized when the school provides adequately for individual differences.
   a. Learning is facilitated when the child's favored mode of learning is promoted.

*The tenets listed briefly outline the principles, conditions, and practices in a reading improvement program as presented in this text. A discussion clarifying and implementing this program is provided in subsequent chapters.

b. Learning is enhanced when the teacher promotes a wholesome classroom environment.

c. Learning becomes a challenging experience to the child when he is made aware of his goal, when his interests are aroused, when appropriate incentives are applied, when his learning problems are corrected, and when he recognizes his progress.

4. Reading problems are minimized when hazards to learning are identified and corrected.

   a. The classroom teacher must be a competent and objective observer of child behavior.

   b. The classroom teacher must be alert to behavior symptomatic of a learning problem.

   c. The teacher must be alert to learning hazards.

   d. Reading disabilities must be identified and corrected at an early stage if frustration and failure are to be avoided.

5. The teacher's effectiveness in correcting existing problems in reading is enhanced by the use of self-directed instructional material.

   a. The specific nature and diversity of individual reading disabilities must be determined.

   b. Learning is enhanced when the child understands the nature of his problem and is provided with self-directed corrective material tailored to his needs.

   c. Individualized self-directed instructional material provides an intrinsic incentive for learning, permits all disability cases in the classroom to progress at their own rates of learning, and frees the teacher for effective supervisory activities.

6. Reading problems are reduced to a minimum when a program of prevention is emphasized.

   a. Mastery of the reading skills is a prerequisite to the development of independent reading habits.

   b. Independent reading habits are a prerequisite to successful comprehension.

   c. Wide reading provides the extra practice needed to master the reading skills.

   d. A systematic development program of prevention reduces the need for correction.

Many schools violate the principles and conditions of learning implied in the tenets listed above by promoting practices which tend to inhibit learning and produce problems in reading. The causes of reading disability are complex; usually a constellation of interacting factors is responsible. Although some of these factors are beyond the jurisdiction of the school, the latter still has an obligation to provide a compensating environment whenever possible. While the authors believe it is of fundamental importance to place emphasis on those factors over which the school has direct control, this volume will also delineate hazards and causal factors of reading disability that stem from conditions inherent in the child and his out-of-school environment. It will give suggestions for their alleviation or correction.

A number of widely employed but inefficient or unwholesome practices and policies found in many schools contribute to frustration and failure in reading. *Failure to provide conditions which facilitate learning also becomes a factor which negates an effective reading program.* The educational hazards listed below are discussed in chapter 11.

EDUCATIONAL HAZARDS TO LEARNING

Developmental Program in Reading

1. Beginning formal instruction in reading before a child has attained readiness.
2. Accepting a low level of mastery of word recognition in the primary grades.
3. Employing a round-robin method of teaching oral reading.
4. Failing to develop independent reading habits in all pupils in the primary grades.
5. Failing to use instructional material diversified in difficulty and content in each grade.
6. Requiring retarded readers to use material on a frustration level of difficulty.
7. Relying on group instruction to meet the reading needs of all pupils.
8. Failing to promote a balanced program in reading.
9. Considering reading a mechanical process.
10. Failing to motivate children to read widely.
11. Assuming that teaching is the goal of education.
12. Assuming that reading can be taught effectively as an isolated communicative skill.
13. Failing to recognize that mastery of reading skills differs from mastery of information.
14. Failing to promote wholesome teacher-pupil relationships.

Diagnostic Program in Reading

15. Failing to detect hazards to learning.
16. Failing to estimate the potential of all children.

17. Failing to discover the educational causes underlying individual reading problems.
18. Failing to adequately utilize cumulative records.
19. Failing to provide a systematic and objective testing program.
20. Assuming that retardation is nonexistent when the class average on standardized reading tests reaches or exceeds the norm.

Corrective Program in Reading

21. Failing to provide a systematic longitudinal program of developmental and corrective reading.
22. Failing to eliminate individual difficulties when they first appear.
23. Failing to correct individual difficulties in word analysis in the intermediate grades.
24. Failing to utilize adequate and appropriate corrective material.

Administrative Policies

25. Exposing pupils to fourth-grade materials before they have achieved independent reading habits.
26. Failing to limit the size of classes.
27. Failing to consider competence in the teaching of reading when hiring new teachers.
28. Failing to provide in-service education for all teachers in the area of reading.
29. Failing to provide ample material needed for meeting the wide range of reading ability and interests in each classroom.
30. Failing to interpret the school's reading program to the public.
31. Failing to provide a well-staffed and well-equipped school library.

Learning to read effectively demands systematic developmental instruction and individualized correction. Basal readers form the core of most developmental instructional programs. Basal readers are, however, frequently criticized for having a limited and repetitious vocabulary which provides an unimaginative, uninteresting, and frequently deadly content. The authors contend that while this is sometimes true, instruction will not be dull when in the hands of a skillful teacher who provides meaningful instruction in terms of interesting and attainable goals.

The reading program advocated by the authors recommends employing basal readers for systematic developmental reading in the first four grades with supervised recreational reading. But it does not stop at this point. *Developmental instruction must be accompanied by diagnosis of reading difficulties and an individualized approach for corrective in-*

struction. The authors suggest that simple clinical procedures are an essential and integral part of classroom teaching. The diagnostic, developmental, and corrective procedures described are the result of many years of experience by the authors in directing a reading clinic and helping teachers in the field to improve reading programs.

This book sets forth conditions and practices which are essential to successful learning. It delineates conditions essential to a flexible program of instruction designed to prevent, correct, and eliminate reading failure. It helps teachers to determine individual needs and to meet those needs with a minimum of time and effort. It clarifies the problem of how to modify group instruction to meet the needs of the retarded reader without using out-of-school time for individual tutoring. It resolves the question teachers raise, "Do I dare neglect the bright children by giving extra time for the less able?"

The authors recognize that in spite of the presence of many unwholesome conditions and inefficient instructional practices, from fifty to sixty percent of the pupils in the average school often attain a so-called normal status in reading. *This book describes an improvement program in reading which has as its objective the attainment of true reading potential for all pupils.*

Classroom teachers can streamline their corrective work by moving from individual tutoring into a program of individualized correction utilizing self-directive instructional material. When this is done, pupils can work independently to overcome their difficulties. The required high-level mastery of the basic reading skills of word recognition and word analysis can then be attained. Such mastery will give rise to independent fourth-grade readers, readers who then can cope with the many new and unfamiliar words that are introduced at that level. The authors contend that a primary-grade program which insures total mastery of the basic reading skills of word recognition and word analysis will preclude, in a large measure, later reading failures. Mastery of these basic skills provides a sound foundation for the successful mastery of the vast hierarchy of new reading skills (using the dictionary, finding central thoughts of paragraphs, skimming, summarizing, and so on) which are developed at the fourth-grade level and beyond.

Another essential of reading improvement involves a carefully planned recreational reading program for all pupils. Daily fun reading of this type permits individual choice of books and other reading material under teacher guidance. In order to find the right books for the right children, materials which vary widely in interest appeal and difficulty level must be provided. Pupils do not profit from books that are uninteresting or too difficult.

In summary, the authors emphasize the following essential aspects of an effective program in reading:

1. Systematic developmental instruction in the reading skills in the first four grades (the instructional material utilized for this purpose will be determined largely by the training and experience of the staff). Teachers who are competent to provide systematic instruction which results in a mastery of the reading skills by employing materials other than basal readers should be encouraged to do so.

2. Periodic and systematic parent and pupil interviews and the use of screening tests to discover hazards to learning in the areas of health, hearing, vision, and adjustment.

3. Periodic and systematic evaluation of each child's reading efficiency as a part of the teacher's instructional program so that reading difficulties can be discovered as soon as they develop.

4. Total mastery of the reading skills maintained at all levels, the frustration level of instruction avoided, and all instructional material adapted to the reading level of the pupil.

5. A diagnosis of individual reading problems utilizing school records, oral and silent reading tests of a formal and informal nature, intelligence tests, and listening comprehension tests.

6. Corrective instruction following diagnosis that is individualized through the use of self-directed instructional material.

7. A systematic program of recreational reading for all pupils, permitting free choice of material selected from books adapted to the reading competence of the individual in his fields of interest.

8. A classroom atmosphere which is conducive to learning.

The unwholesome conditions and school practices listed in this chapter are discussed in some detail in chapter 2. The essential aspects of an improvement program in reading, already set forth, are discussed and described in the remaining chapters. Individualized correction in reading that utilizes self-directed material is emphasized throughout the book, with an extensive listing of teacher-made and commercial reading material in chapters 8, 9, and 10. Chapter 11 directs the teacher and administrator to the information, practices, and conditions essential in implementing an improvement program in reading.

PROBLEMS FOR ORAL AND WRITTEN DISCUSSION

1. Evaluate your instructional program in reading in terms of the six tenets set forth in this chapter.

2. Name five or more hazards to learning that you consider to be most critical. Justify your selection.

REFERENCES

1. D. D. DURRELL, *Improvement of Basic Reading Abilities* (New York: Harcourt, Brace and World, Inc., 1940), p. 281.
2. J. M. McCALLISTER, *Remedial and Corrective Instruction in Reading* (New York: Appleton-Century-Crofts, 1936), p. 4.
3. L. J. THOMPSON, *Reading Disability: Developmental Dyslexia* (Springfield, Ill.: Charles C Thomas, Publisher, 1966), p. xvi.
4. P. A. WITTY, *Reading in Modern Education* (Boston: D. C. Heath and Co., 1949), p. 178.
5. C. A. WOODBURY, "The Identification of Underachieving Readers," *Reading Teacher* 16 (1963):218-223.
6. D. DEMPSEY, "The Right to Read," *Saturday Review* 54, no. 16, April 17, 1971, p. 22.
7. J. E. ALLEN, "The Right to Read—Target for the 70's," *Journal of Reading* 13 (1969):95-101.

2

Classroom Conditions and Practices Which Tend to Produce and Aggravate Reading Disabilities

"When I was a boy," writes an editorialist "we all learned how to read. Of course, we didn't have to contend with those new-fangled methods." Statements such as these are found daily in newspapers and magazines throughout the United States. They infer that a return to "the good old days" is the panacea for all educational ills.

Teachers do not share this opinion. Many of them would explain reading problems in terms of out-of-school hazards. They feel that poor readers often are the products of homes where the intellectual, physical, and emotional needs of children have been ignored. Parents, of course, admit no shortcomings and believe that the school alone is responsible for all reading problems. "If the teacher would devote more time to my child, he would be a better reader."

Needless to say, research shows that both home and school can contribute to reading failure; however, when the stigma of reading failure does fall on the school, an honest appraisal of the situation leads to the inevitable conclusion that only a small percentage of handicapped readers are products of schools where teachers did not give them sufficient attention. Most poor readers have received a lion's share of the teacher's time—time which likely as not included individual as well as group attention. How, then, was the school inefficient?

The school was remiss if it failed to provide a wholesome atmosphere conducive to learning and if it failed to recognize and eliminate educational•practices and conditions which inhibit learning. These hazards are listed in chapter 1 and discussed in some detail in this chapter.

1. BEGINNING FORMAL INSTRUCTION IN READING
BEFORE A CHILD HAS ATTAINED READINESS

Reading readiness has been defined as "the level of maturity a child must reach before he can succeed in formal reading under normal instruction. A chronological age of six years and a minimum IQ of 100 is usually implied, with normal health, hearing, vision, etc."(1)

Although reading readiness is of great significance at the first-grade level, it is not a concept that should be limited to beginning reading. This was pointed out by Cole as early as 1938. She wrote:

> Readiness to read is usually thought of as a problem met only in the first grade. On the contrary, it reappears whenever a pupil starts a new level of work. One should therefore investigate a given individual for his readiness to read at the first grade, the fourth, the seventh, the ninth, and at his entrance to college. In each of these grades the pupil meets new types of reading matter; his work will inevitably be below the necessary level of achievement if he is not ready before he starts. (2)

The number of years and months a child has lived does not tell us, with any degree of assurance, the amount and quality of his experiential background, how much native ability or intellectual maturity he possesses, his powers of visual and auditory discrimination, and his emotional and social maturity. Other factors relating to the instructional program itself (specifically, the degree to which it provides for individual differences) are responsible for reading success or failure in the first grade. We cannot, therefore, consider a child's sixth or seventh birthday as optimum to initial reading instruction.(3, 4)

Unfortunately, many parents feel their children are ready to read as soon as they reach school age. Parents are often so ambitious for their children that they will initiate instruction at home at very young ages. Newspaper advertisements and books have added fuel to the fire by advocating the formal teaching of reading to children at two, three, or four years of age.

Most specialists in early childhood education are opposed to early reading instruction.(5, 6) They do not feel young children are sufficiently mature physically and emotionally to take formal reading instruction without undesirable side effects. They believe childhood is the time for many learnings that are needed before formal instruction in reading begins. Finally, they feel that a premature introduction to reading might give rise to permanent antagonism or distaste for the reading process.

2. ACCEPTING A LOW LEVEL OF MASTERY OF WORD RECOGNITION IN PRIMARY GRADES

The majority of children come to school with a wide speaking and meaning vocabulary. Since, as one child stated it, "reading is nothing more than talk writ down," the first-grade teacher's job is primarily one of encouraging and aiding associational learning. The child must learn to match "those little scratches on paper" with their familiar auditory counterpart.

Although reading in its most elementary form involves synthesizing sight and sound, mature reading goes much further. One must never lose sight of the fact that reading is a meaningful process. A child who recites all the words but when asked what he read says "I wasn't listening" is not reading. Reading is a cerebral process that requires comprehension and critical thinking.

There are times when a child's background or experiential maturity is so meager that he can't bring proper meaning to the printed page. He is not ready to comprehend what he is reading. Too often, however, teachers put the cart before the horse by stressing high-level skills of comprehension and interpretation before a child has evolved an adequate sight vocabulary. The first step in learning to read involves mastering word perception. Nothing is more fundamental to all reading skills than an adequate sight vocabulary. Brown and Loper concur in this belief when they state:

A major concern of corrective instruction in reading is growth in word recognition. Although comprehension of reading material is the ultimate purpose of reading, there can be little hope that a student will ever be able to understand a passage unless he has sufficient word recognition skills to identify the printed words which make up the passage. It is not a question of whether word recognition or comprehension is more important; it is simply an understanding that written words cannot convey meaning to a student unless he is able to decipher them.

. . . Since beginning reading instruction is so largely concerned with the skills of word identification, it is not at all peculiar to find that most students who experience difficulty in reading in the first three grades do so because of poor abilities in the area of word recognition rather than comprehension. (7)

3. EMPLOYING A ROUND-ROBIN METHOD OF TEACHING ORAL READING

Round-robin reading with a heterogeneous group is as pedagogically outdated as the dodo. Unfortunately, there are some classrooms where this kind of archaic activity still persists.

Very few children benefit from round-robin reading. When a proficient reader is obliged to follow the slow and halting reading of a disabled reader (most often the former will have read ahead on his own and finished the selection before others are halfway through), he understandably finds the reading lesson an unbearable chore. It is quite conceivable, too, that he might acquire some of the bad habits to which he has been exposed; and when the proficient reader is called upon to read aloud, he covers the material with such ease and fluency that the deficient readers in the room are quickly lost. Round-robin reading has other disadvantages.

As poor readers stumble and stutter their way through their oral reading, embarrassment and misery know no bounds. Often the class is critical and unkind. Even the teacher may share a similar attitude. As a result, poor readers develop emotional problems, and reading becomes a source of aversion.

4. FAILING TO DEVELOP INDEPENDENT READING HABITS IN ALL PUPILS IN THE PRIMARY GRADES

One of the most difficult problems for the intermediate-grade teacher is to promote new reading skills in pupils who have failed to acquire independent reading habits. Achieving new goals in reading becomes extremely difficult if the basic sight vocabulary of the primary grades and the skills of word analysis have not been mastered. Continued sequential development of word-analysis skills, mastery of uncontrolled and technical vocabulary, and the development of new study skills are all a part of normal growth in reading beyond the primary grades. When the basic sight vocabulary and the essentials of phonetic and structural analysis are taught in the primary grades to the point of mastery resulting in immediate recall, pupils will have acquired the tools that permit them to unlock new words with a minimum of hesitancy. Such pupils are ready to pursue a refinement and extension of these skills and to continue growth in meaning vocabulary and the study skills. Sequential developmental instruction resulting in a mastery of the reading skills appropriate to each grade level is the best prevention of later difficulties in reading.

5. FAILING TO USE INSTRUCTIONAL MATERIAL DIVERSIFIED IN DIFFICULTY AND CONTENT IN EACH GRADE

Pupils in the average classroom above the primary grades usually reflect a range of five or more grades in reading ability, with the majority having instructional levels in reading either below or above their current grade placement. This wide disparity in achievement represents a diversity of individual reading difficulties and interests, and it demands instructional material that is diversified in content and difficulty. If frustration is to be avoided and inherent interests are to be challenged, basal readers on several grade levels are needed along with ample supplementary material. Teachers must be free to select widely from the textbook library as well as from the library of resource material that is available for supplementary and recreational reading. A teacher who discovers that the class average on an objective reading test is at the grade norm should recognize that both retardation and acceleration exist in the class. This means that the basal reader for the grade is usually too difficult for some pupils and too easy for others.

Methods that can be used in discovering the optimum instructional levels for retarded readers and the nature of their specific reading difficulties will be discussed in subsequent chapters.

6. REQUIRING RETARDED READERS TO USE MATERIAL ON A FRUSTRATION LEVEL OF DIFFICULTY

One cannot develop his biceps with weights that are too heavy to manipulate. By the same token, a child cannot improve his reading skill when books are too difficult. With books of optimum difficulty, however, practice becomes meaningful and improvement results. Relying on practice with materials of the grade at which a student is experiencing failure is largely a waste of time. When a pupil is asked to read material that is too difficult, he may fidget and squirm, become inattentive, frequently or continuously point with a finger, seem bored or lazy, or become mischievous. If he is actually forced to read material on the frustration level, a deep-seated aversion for reading will usually develop.

Instructional material in reading should be sufficiently challenging to insure progress but not so difficult that frustration results. When a child is expected to work by himself without teacher assistance, easier reading material is needed. Suggestions for ascertaining a child's optimum instructional and independent or free reading levels are set forth in chapter 5.

7. RELYING ON GROUP INSTRUCTION TO MEET THE READING NEEDS OF ALL PUPILS

Undifferentiated group instruction, a common practice in the intermediate and upper grades, tends to be inefficient since all children do not thrive on the same educational diet. When instructional material is of optimum difficulty for the average reader, it is too difficult for some and too easy for others. What results? Poor readers invariably are stymied, while superior readers become bored because they are not challenged. As the superior readers stagnate, reading difficulties continue to accumulate for the disabled reader and resistance to instruction becomes increasingly acute. If this situation persists, all motivation, self-direction, and satisfaction in work well done withers away.

Undifferentiated group instruction also fails to take cognizance of factors that inhibit learning. In addition, resistances to learning which develop are treated frequently as discipline problems rather than attitudes and behavior to be understood and improved through proper guidance.

It is evident that undifferentiated group instruction provides but a partial answer to the multiplicity of learning problems facing the classroom teacher. Only when group practices are augmented by diagnosis and individualized corrective instruction can children's unique needs be met, and only then can effective learning be achieved.

8. FAILING TO PROMOTE A BALANCED PROGRAM IN READING

Many reading programs fail to furnish a sufficient variety of materials. A well-balanced program should include several sets of basal readers to provide systematic instruction in basic reading skills and the techniques of reading. Workbooks accompanying these readers are also needed to minimize the time-consuming activity of creating suitable follow-up work. Commercially-made and teacher-made reading games and activities are valuable in making provision for pupils who need additional practice in word-recognition and word-analysis skills. A classroom library of books and magazines together with picture dictionaries should be found in all primary classrooms. Above the primary grades, reference books such as a world atlas and almanac also have an important place. Other accessories needed to balance a reading program include filmstrips, slides, recordings, and films.

A functional reading program never overemphasizes one aspect of the reading process at the neglect of another. When it does, children's reading skills suffer. Too much emphasis on phonics, for example, tends to destroy interest in reading and results in slow and laborious word-calling. On the other hand, too little emphasis on phonics weakens word-attack skill and makes independent reading difficult. Other aspects of the reading program, such as study-type reading versus recreational reading, oral reading versus silent reading, and independent reading versus group instruction, also require a similar balance. It should be remembered that all readers must have their reading programs fit their individual needs.

If we wish all children to develop into well-rounded and independent readers with a lifetime interest in reading, constant vigilance must be given to both group and individual balancing of the reading program.

9. CONSIDERING READING A MECHANICAL PROCESS

A study entitled "Reading as Reasoning" was published in 1917. The author, Edward L. Thorndike, considered reading as a thinking process. Although reading specialists gave relatively little emphasis to this concept prior to 1950, many reading texts currently in use devote space to it.(8, 9)

Evidence that calling words isn't reading was provided by Smith in relating the case of a fifth-grade boy reading the Gettysburg Address. Parenthetical interpolations indicate what the pupil was thinking when trying to make the words meaningful.

Fourscore (a score is what we have after a baseball game is played) and seven years ago our fathers (this must mean our own and our stepfathers) brought forth on this continent (that's North America, we had that in social studies) a new nation (that's America or the U.S.A. I think) conceived (I wonder what that means) in liberty (that's what a sailor gets) and dedicated (that's what they did to the building on the corner) . . . (10)

It is obvious that reading is more than a process of eye movements and word-recognition skill. Reading is more than "barking at the print." Proper meaning must be brought to printed symbols to insure their understanding and enhance interpretation. Too often students lack the concepts needed to make words live. A student's ability to call words accurately doesn't mean in itself that he comprehends the material. One third-grader read beautifully before the class, but when asked to tell in his own words what he had just read, he hesitated a few moments and said, "Gee, I guess I wasn't listening to myself."

One of the best ways for a teacher to make reading a vital thinking process is to ask stimulating questions that enable the child to project himself into and identify himself with the characters in a story. Teachers who ask questions such as "What is the color of Mary's hat?" are not encouraging a child to think. Reading should not be done for the purpose of regurgitating facts. Reading should be an idea-getting and an idea-stimulating process. Teachers who view reading as a thinking process can do much to help children by employing more questions of the *how* and *why* variety. For example, rather than "What is the color of Mary's hat?" the question "Why would or wouldn't you like to wear a hat the color of Mary's?" would be preferable. This would encourage the child to evaluate what he is reading in terms of himself. In the final analysis, all the meaning a child ever finds in a story comes to him only in terms of his own particular experiences.

Unless we encourage a child to think about and evaluate what is read, he will be unable to evaluate contradictory points of view in the numerous newspapers, magazines and books to which he is exposed later in life. (See pages 147-148 for a discussion of critical reading.)

10. FAILING TO MOTIVATE CHILDREN TO READ WIDELY

Educational psychologists tell us that purposeful practice is essential to the mastery of any complex skill. The pupil who reads only a basal reader and is not induced to do any additional reading does not develop his reading skill to maximum potential. Likely as not, such a student's reading activities outside of school are virtually nonexistent. Without sufficient practice it is difficult for him to develop or even maintain skills taught in the earlier grades. Sooner or later he becomes a nonreader in fact as well as in theory.

Is there danger of our developing a generation of children who can read but will not? Are those who believe that we are in the twilight of the printed page alarmists or realists?(11)

Certainly statistics show that we may be justified in being concerned. More money is spent in the United States each year for the repair of TV sets (not for the purchase, mind you!) than is spent for new books. And what is particularly disconcerting is how we take many of the latest communicative gadgets as a matter of course. For example, when an elderly woman was offered a free plane ride recently she exclaimed, "No thank you. You won't catch me in one of those new-fangled devices. I'm going to stay home and watch television just like the good Lord intended me to do."

It appears that teaching students how to read isn't enough. Today's teachers must be aware of the need to inculcate children with a deep and abiding interest in reading. The ubiquitous query "Why read?" must be replaced by the more productive and forceful "Let's read."

11. ASSUMING THAT TEACHING IS THE GOAL
OF EDUCATION

Instruction is an educational process and learning is the product. Many teachers never evaluate their teaching in terms of learning or desirable changes in their pupils. These teachers are prone to say, "I do a good job of teaching. I work hard with my students—real hard. I have presented the required curricular content. What more can I do?"

Teaching does involve a generous expenditure of time and energy, but it is important that attention be devoted to what is appropriate. The teacher should consider himself successful only when all the children with whom he works are progressing. This criterion of good teaching calls for continuous testing, diagnosing, teaching, testing, and more diagnosing. It calls for individualizing instruction in terms of pupils' levels of achievement, peculiar strengths and weaknesses, rates of learning and learning potential. The answer, then, is not a need to work harder but to work more effectively.

When a teacher can see students forging ahead in the acquisition of reading skills, when he can see interest sparkle, when he can see a noticeable improvement in scholarship, when these changes are taking place in his classroom, then, and then alone, can he say with satisfaction, "I am doing a good job of teaching."

12. ASSUMING THAT READING CAN BE TAUGHT EFFECTIVELY
AS AN ISOLATED COMMUNICATIVE SKILL

It is not by accident that teachers' colleges invariably offer a basic methods course in the language arts rather than having prospective teachers take separate introductory courses in the teaching of reading, writing, listening, and speaking. The reason is that reading is not a skill that can be developed in isolation. Good teachers of reading capitalize on the relationships inherent in the language arts, all of which are means of social communication involving ideas, concepts, and emotions. Children express themselves through writing and speech, while they interpret the expressions of others through listening and reading.

The interrelationship of listening, speaking, reading, and writing is evident when one considers that lack of oral language stimulation in the home, delayed speech, impaired hearing, and speech defects often are associated with reading disability. Handicaps in the areas of listening and speaking are reflected in a child's writing and spelling.

It is probable that the world has known few successful writers who were not proficient readers. Many professional writers point out that they must read a great deal if they are to write. Similarly, a relationship exists between writing skill and oral speech. Cutforth, an English language specialist, says that if what children write is poor the teacher should concentrate on oral language.(12)

Buswell stresses the great similarity between speaking and reading in his definition of the reading process.

Psychologically, the processes of speech and reading are quite similar, the difference being mainly in the sense avenues through which the verbal stimuli are received. . . . The essential difference between knowing how to understand oral speech is the substitution of visual perception of printed verbal symbols for the auditory impression of the same symbols when spoken. The thoughts expressed are the same, the vocabulary is the same, and the word order is the same. The new problem in reading is to learn to recognize the visual symbols with accuracy and reasonable speed. (13)

As a child gains proficiency in one communicative skill, all language skills benefit indirectly. This is reflected in high correlations between reading and spelling, reading and composition. The majority of poor readers are inaccurate spellers. By the same token, the child who reads little is not likely to write well. The language-experience approach, popularized by R. Van Allen, capitalizes on such interrelationships, the basic premise being, "What they can say, they can write, and what they can write, they can read." (See chapter 4 for additional information about the language-experience approach.)

13. FAILING TO RECOGNIZE THAT MASTERY OF READING SKILLS DIFFERS FROM MASTERY OF INFORMATION

Many teachers fail to recognize that learning of skills differs from learning information or developing concepts. Methods of instruction must differ in each instance. For example, information can be imparted orally by a teacher, but improving reading skills is something only the student can do through practice. It is a perfect example of learning through doing.

Demands on the learner are very exacting when skills are being learned. A pupil may acquire new information readily if he has an eighty percent mastery of previously related information; but an eighty percent mastery of the sight vocabulary of a given reader does not provide a student with the readiness he needs to succeed with the more complex comprehension skills and the more challenging vocabulary of a subsequent reader. Word-perception skill must entail at least a ninety-five percent mastery of the sight vocabulary before a student is ready to move into more difficult material.

14. FAILING TO PROMOTE WHOLESOME TEACHER-PUPIL RELATIONSHIPS

Perhaps no condition for learning in the elementary school is more important than wholesome teacher-pupil relations. The child who likes his teacher is the child who likes to learn. Strong emotions of insecurity, hate, fear, or resentment inhibit learning. Motivation must come from within rather than be imposed from without. Pupils resist learning if the teacher exhibits traits of unfairness, sarcasm, or ridicule. When the teacher shows partiality, when she is autocratic and disregards the rights and privileges of her pupils, she destroys confidence, security, and social acceptance. As a result, learning is replaced by loss of interest, emotional tensions, and disciplinary problems.

Mental health, a basic condition of learning, is best fostered in a classroom by a teacher who is warm and understanding, a teacher who has a genuine interest in children. These are teacher qualities that always have and always will have a magical effect in a learning situation.

15. FAILING TO DETECT HAZARDS TO LEARNING

Children from a privileged environment enter first grade eager to learn to read because their parents read widely and have provided them with a cultural environment in which they are exposed to enriched language experiences and a broad experiential background. Although children from a privileged environment do have advantages denied those from underprivileged homes, all children should be carefully studied for any inherent weaknesses in their readiness for learning just as soon as they enter school.

Hazards to learning are present in the home as well as in the school. Noneducational hazards identified with the home may be reflected in physical impairment, unwholesome parent-child relationships, emotional immaturity, and cultural deprivation, all of which can result in a lack of interest in learning. Often the school assumes that every child's experiential background upon entering school is like that of children from a typical middle-class culture. Because of this assumption, the school provides a meager compensatory environment during the preschool and primary grades. As a consequence, children from disadvantaged and bilingual homes resist learning, fail in reading, and enter the intermediate grades as disabled readers.

During the preschool and primary grades, teachers must be alert to individual problems arising as a result of a meager experiential background. They must promote a compensatory school environment which will enrich the dearth of experiences in the life of the disadvantaged. A systematic program of discovery and training is vital to the development of readiness and subsequent learning.

16. FAILING TO ESTIMATE THE POTENTIAL OF ALL CHILDREN

Teachers sometimes are prone to consider poor readers dull. "I do a good job of teaching," they say. "If a child doesn't learn, he's just dumb." The truth is that approximately ninety percent of all poor readers have intelligence quotients in excess of 80, with some reaching well into the 130s and above. In most cases, the poor readers do have potential to do better.

It is unfortunate if teachers believe pupils are working up to capacity because distributions of reading and mental ability in a class are similar. Based on this premise, it is assumed that the poor reader is a slow learner. The school, they feel, is therefore absolved of any responsibility for improving the reading status of its pupils. Needless to say, intelligence test scores are often cited to bolster this contention.

Group intelligence tests should be interpreted warily, since many such tests above the third grade are heavily weighted with items involving reading. This means the intelligence quotient of a poor reader on a verbal intelligence test usually underestimates his true mental ability. It is therefore always important to secure a nonlanguage or performance I.Q. and M.A., along with verbal aspects of a poor reader's intelligence. When this is done, it is not rare to find that for poor readers most verbal I.Q.'s are markedly below nonverbal I.Q.'s. This discrepancy has been widely reported in the educational literature. Records kept at the University of Wisconsin Reading Clinic, where the California Test of Mental Maturity was given to 266 intermediate-grade children who entered the clinic, revealed an average verbal I.Q. for this group of poor readers of 92 and an average nonverbal I.Q. of 99. Twenty-eight percent of the group had verbal I.Q.'s of 100 and above, while forty-one percent had nonverbal I.Q.'s of 100 or above. Almost half (forty-eight percent) had verbal I.Q.'s that were five or more points below their nonverbal I.Q.'s.

When group intelligence tests are employed, results may be invalid. A poor reader who has suffered through years of failure often works at an intelligence test as he would any other school assignment; that is, he guesses or does it in a very perfunctory way. Such a give-up or I-don't-care attitude may result in a low score. The most valid measure of a retarded reader's intellectual capacity can be obtained by the school psychologist who administers an individual test such as the Stanford-Binet or the Wechsler-Intelligence Scale for Children.

Another avenue of appraisal open to the teacher is to read aloud for a child and then quiz him on what was heard. If the child can comprehend material at or above his reading grade level in difficulty, the teacher can be assured that the pupil has normal reading potential. However, the problem of the bilingual child must be given special consideration when listening comprehension is used as a criterion of reading potential. Commercial tests such as the Durrell-Sullivan Reading Capacity Tests and Spache's Diagnostic Reading Scales use listening skill to ascertain a student's potential reading ability.

Underestimating a poor reader's capabilities usually results in neglect of the child. This may prove disastrous to the individual and often results in a distinct loss to society.

17. FAILING TO DISCOVER THE EDUCATIONAL CAUSES UNDERLYING INDIVIDUAL READING PROBLEMS

The role of the school in connection with the how-did-they-get-that-way aspect of reading retardation has been pointed out by many authorities. Some of the educational causes of reading failure of which the teacher should be aware include exposing children to reading before they are ready, overcrowding of classrooms, unpleasant teaching personality, improper methodology, inadequate provision for children who are absent a great deal or who have changed schools frequently, and a lack of emphasis upon prevention or individual correction.

Children who lack the requisite social, emotional, mental, and physical maturity suffer frustration when forced into reading prematurely. A poor start often is accompanied by frustration and emotional disturbances which augur poorly for reading development.

Overcrowding of classrooms makes it difficult, if not impossible, for a teacher to get to know her pupils and to make adequate provision for them as individuals.

Sarcastic and inconsiderate teachers hinder the reading development of boys and girls by making remarks such as "Why are you so dumb?" and "I don't know why I bother with you." These remarks often affect children undesirably.

Some teachers overemphasize one method of instruction to the exclusion of others. Many children learn best when a look-and-say method is used; others are in need of a kinesthetic or auditory approach. A few may require an idiosyncratic method designed to meet their individual needs. Teachers should not adhere slavishly to just one method.

Children who have missed school a great deal or have been shifted from one school to another need understanding teachers. When teachers discover that a child's schooling was characterized by much absenteeism, efforts need to be made to plug the gaps in his educational background. And when a child who has changed schools many times is transferred to their classroom, teachers should make an effort to learn what materials and methods have previously been used in teaching him.

Reading difficulties are unique with each pupil, and early discovery and correction prevent an accumulation of problems which will lead to severe disability.

What syndrome or constellation of factors, educational and noneducational, reflects the critical hazards that destroy an individual's desire to succeed and therefore inhibits learning? The steps involved in a diagnosis which discovers causal factors in a reading problem are discussed in detail in chapter 6.

18. FAILING TO ADEQUATELY UTILIZE CUMULATIVE RECORDS

Above the primary grades, all pupils will have attended school for three or more years. A number of teachers will have had extensive opportunities to observe, confer, and evaluate their growth in learning. Perhaps, too, certain physical, emotional, and intellectual problems impeding the success of normal progress will have been detected. All this information, together with the results of developmental and corrective programs, should be recorded on cumulative school records. When this responsibility is faithfully discharged by each teacher, a gold mine of useful information about each child can be made readily available when needed.

All teachers should study cumulative records very carefully at the beginning of each school year. They should add additional information to these records whenever anything of significance arises. The dividends resulting from this practice would be tremendous. The gap that too frequently exists because of the yearly break in continuity of instruction as a child moves from one teacher to another would disappear.

19. FAILING TO PROVIDE A SYSTEMATIC AND OBJECTIVE TESTING PROGRAM

In terms of individual needs, both developmental and corrective instruction in reading assumes that these needs have been discovered through careful evaluation. Observation and informal testing are useful techniques to identify the more obvious problem cases. However, to evaluate an individual's reading problem more precisely, to determine its nature and severity, it becomes necessary to utilize objective tests of known validity and reliability. (See Appendix C.) Accuracy of evaluation is essential for a valid diagnosis on which an effective corrective program may be based.

A systematic objective testing program administered at least twice each year and employing reliable survey tests will serve as an important method of identifying classroom problem readers, and test records will set forth their longitudinal development in reading. Diagnostic tests, both oral and silent, are needed to determine the nature of the disabled reader's problem. These tests are useful instruments to the teacher in spelling out the nature and extent of the corrective program needed.

In summary, a systematic objective testing program alerts the teacher to preventive needs, provides data for longitudinal records, suggests appropriate instructional levels, and enables him to chart individual corrective programs.

20. ASSUMING THAT RETARDATION IS NONEXISTENT WHEN THE CLASS AVERAGE ON STANDARDIZED READING TESTS REACHES OR EXCEEDS THE NORM

Norms on achievement tests are averages of the performance of pupils in each of several grades throughout the nation. What is true of the country at large isn't, however, always applicable to an individual grade or class. What is more, national norms do not constitute standards of excellence or even satisfactory achievement. Most students fail miserably to measure up to their full potential.

The teacher who consults norms is dealing with averages. It must not be overlooked that fifty percent of the scores fall below the norm. In a typical fourth grade, for example, approximately one-third of the children are reading on third-, second-, and even first-grade levels. By the same token, approximately one-third of the children in the average fourth grade are reading on the fifth-, sixth-, and seventh-grade levels.

The teacher who accepts norms as the standard for her grade and expresses satisfaction with the results overlooks the retarded readers in her class who are in dire need of corrective instruction. A teacher should convert individual scores on a standardized reading test to grade scores and group these scores in a way that highlights those children who are retarded one, two, three, or more years in their reading skills. She should make a similar tabulation of those who are accelerated. The teacher thus becomes aware of the retardation and acceleration in her grade. This gives her a more realistic view of the problems to be faced in terms of the number of atypical readers in the class and the nature of their problems.

21. FAILING TO PROVIDE A SYSTEMATIC LONGITUDINAL PROGRAM OF DEVELOPMENTAL AND CORRECTIVE READING

In most elementary schools a child is assigned a new teacher each year. Teachers who wish to make maximum contributions to continued development of a new group of children must avail themselves of all pertinent information contained in previous school records. If the new teacher does not study and profit from the developmental and corrective instruction provided by previous teachers, weeks and months will elapse before she is in a position to provide appropriate instruction. Thus valuable time is lost, student morale is impaired, and annual growth is hindered.

The school record should reveal a child's longitudinal progress in reading. Specifically, it should include the child's yearly instructional level, a description of his reading difficulties, the results of formal and informal methods of evaluation, and any corrective measures that were employed. Also included should be known hazards to learning and methods that were employed to alleviate them.

Cumulative records are often incomplete. Under these circumstances, interviews with parents and previous teachers should take place in an effort to augment school records. Children with learning problems must be challenged by new and more efficient methods and materials. Therefore, evaluation should seek to reveal the most appropriate instructional techniques to pursue. Uninterrupted growth in learning from year to year demands keeping and utilizing the results of past and current diagnostic and corrective practices.

22. FAILING TO ELIMINATE INDIVIDUAL DIFFICULTIES WHEN THEY FIRST APPEAR

It should be recognized that prevention is the key that will insure normal progress in reading. The teacher who is keenly aware of the importance of preventive measures will be alert to individual difficulties when they first arise. She will correct these difficulties immediately by providing suitable instruction. She will not introduce new and more difficult material until the child is prepared for it. When difficulties first arise they are few in number, and a minimum of correction is needed to overcome or eliminate them. When inadequate or partial learning is permitted to go unheeded and uncorrected, the cumulative effect results in frustration, failure, and feelings of inadequacy characteristic of retarded readers.

The golden era for prevention is in the primary grades. In these grades the teacher should adopt a goal of complete mastery of reading skills taught at each level. This is the key to prevention. Introducing new and more difficult material to a primary-grade child before he has mastered the current sight vocabulary ignores the first step in a program of prevention. This common practice results in a rapid accumulation of difficulties which cause loss of interest, absence of growth, lowered mastery, and ultimate failure.

23. FAILING TO CORRECT INDIVIDUAL DIFFICULTIES IN WORD ANALYSIS IN THE INTERMEDIATE GRADES

Children who have failed to acquire independent reading habits when they reach the intermediate grades are usually weak in word-analysis skills. Usually, too, they are reading below the fourth-grade level. They find it difficult to master the new skills needed to comprehend the texts that emphasize content material containing an uncontrolled and technical vocabulary. A diagnostic study of each retarded reader's mastery of a basic sight vocabulary and the primary-grade skills of word analysis is essential to an effective corrective program. Mastery of the skills in which there are deficiencies provides the background needed to become a normal reader.

24. FAILING TO UTILIZE ADEQUATE AND APPROPRIATE CORRECTIVE MATERIAL

Reading difficulties are unique with each child. Three children in a class who are disabled in their reading skills usually present three distinct problems in need of specific corrective material that is designed to alleviate the difficulties peculiar to each.

After a child's reading problem has been diagnosed, the teacher is ready to initiate correction. The material selected can make the difference between success and failure. It is essential, therefore, that instructional material should be appropriate in terms of the child's reading or instructional level, his interests, and his skills. Too often material is chosen simply because there happens to be much of it available or because it worked with another child who had trouble last year. Material should be chosen to accomplish a specific purpose. Such material may be available commercially or may be evolved by the teacher. Sometimes, too, the child can actively participate in the construction and design of it.

When materials are being designed, those of a self-corrective nature should be given much consideration. With disabled readers, group instruction often becomes inappropriate, and individual tutoring is impractical. The use of self-directive material enables each pupil to correct his difficulties at his own rate with a minimum of supervision from the teacher.

The reader will find that chapters 8, 9, and 10 provide descriptions of specific instructional materials—both commercial and teacher-made—that are designed to meet specific reading needs.

25. EXPOSING PUPILS TO FOURTH-GRADE MATERIALS BEFORE THEY HAVE ACHIEVED INDEPENDENT READING HABITS

The skills of word analysis emphasized in grades two and three become the open sesame whereby a child continues to acquire an extended sight vocabulary of new and unfamiliar words when he reaches the fourth grade. This is evident when one learns that of the 2,000 words the average pupil can identify readily at this level, one-half of them are gained through the skills of word analysis. For example, one representative reading series presents 1,778 different words in its basal readers for the primary grades. Of these 1,778 different words, 863 are to be learned as a sight vocabulary and the remaining 915 through the skills of word analysis.

The fourth-grade pupil who is an independent reader has acquired an introduction to dictionary usage. His stock of sight words prepares him for recognizing and understanding almost all words except new technical ones. Pronunciation of unfamiliar words is accomplished independently through his knowledge of word analysis. The dictionary is of further assistance in arriving at the correct pronunciation of the most difficult words and proves an authoritative source for checking their meaning.

Students who have an adequate sight vocabulary and possess independence in word-analysis skills are ready to do recreational reading. They are eager to use these skills as tools in exploring new and interesting content. In guiding the reading growth of such pupils, teachers should shift instructional emphasis to comprehension skills since unfamiliar words and concepts are encountered more frequently by these students.

The fourth-grade pupil who lacks mastery of word-perception skills cannot use reading as a tool in the content areas. Since the uncontrolled vocabulary he meets includes many words foreign to his own speaking and listening vocabularies, he readily becomes confused. Limitations of time make it extremely difficult for his teachers to help him overcome his deficiencies. The problem is further complicated by the pupil's resistance to corrective work involving lower-grade materials.

Students with I.Q.'s between 70 and 80 are found in regular classrooms. If these slow learners are promoted to the fourth grade (a rigid grade standard of achievement is not tenable in such cases), teachers must continue to strive for high levels of sight vocabulary mastery and word-analysis skill. The slow-learning child who is introduced to fourth-grade material before these foundational skills are well in hand will experience a hopeless sense of failure.

A basic cause of failure in reading in the intermediate grades stems from an administrative policy of promoting a child from the third grade into the fourth when his basic sight vocabulary is at a level of mastery of ninety percent or less. Teachers in the primary grades should strive for one hundred percent mastery of word-recognition and word-attack skills. Similarly, intermediate-grade teachers should give retarded readers corrective work in these skills before moving into more difficult material. Reading progress would take place more rapidly, and there would be considerably less failure if administrators encouraged teachers to adhere religiously to this basic principle.

26. FAILING TO LIMIT THE SIZE OF CLASSES

A good school administrator knows that no teacher, regardless of her capabilities, can do an adequate job of teaching with a classroom of forty or more children. There is no doubt that a primary cause of reading failure could be eliminated if class size in the elementary school were limited to twenty-five children. Even smaller classes on the primary-grade level can prove trying, since children in these grades have short attention spans and find it difficult to work independently.

A positive relationship exists between reading growth among students and provision for their individual needs. When classes are too large, it is a physical impossibility for a teacher to become well acquainted with the reading needs of all her pupils. Students who develop difficulties go unheeded. And when they are brought to the attention of the teacher, she is so harassed by demands on her time that corrective work is not attempted. There is little doubt that large classes are fertile breeding grounds for poor readers.

27. FAILING TO CONSIDER COMPETENCE IN THE TEACHING OF READING WHEN HIRING NEW TEACHERS

The problems of developmental and corrective reading found in the average classroom are numerous, diverse, and frequently very complicated. In order to recognize and resolve these problems, the teacher must be a competent and sympathetic observer of pupil behavior and a student of the psychology of learning. She must understand the reading process and be sensitive to the needs of a program which will prevent reading problems from arising or accumulating. She must be alert to optimum methods of learning and their application to individual needs. She must have achieved skill in analyzing reading problems and be adept at selecting techniques and materials involved in correction.

The foregoing understandings and skills may be acquired in accredited courses in the teaching of reading and in the related fields of psychology and child development. Preservice minimum standards set by the International Reading Association for classroom teachers in the field of reading consists of a bachelor's degree including a minimum of six semester hours in the teaching of reading.*

Administrators have the responsibility of requiring that these minimum standards be met by those who are added to the teaching staff each year. Recommendations for a further improvement of the effectiveness of the existing staff of teachers is discussed in some detail in chapter 11.

28. FAILING TO PROVIDE IN-SERVICE EDUCATION FOR ALL TEACHERS IN THE AREA OF READING

In-service training in reading is the primary responsibility of the administrator. Through a good in-service program, a staff of teachers who vary in training, experience, interest, and philosophy can develop into a concerted action unit. The in-service program takes many forms: It may involve individual consultation with a faculty member who has pupils in need of special reading help, or it may entail workshops, conferences, extension courses, and summer school courses in reading. (See chapter 11 for a fuller discussion of this.)

IRA Bulletin of Minimum Standards for Professional Preparation in Reading for Classroom Teachers (Newark, Del.: International Reading Association).

Teachers' meetings can be devoted to the subject of reading improvement. An administrator may also encourage department heads on the junior and senior high school levels to have subject matter teachers devote time to a discussion of reading and a sharing of effective methods and materials.

In-service programs are a boon to intermediate- and upper-grade teachers who have had little or no training in primary reading methods. These teachers feel frustrated in their attempt to provide correction for their severely retarded readers because they are unable to discover the nature or the extent of their reading difficulties. In some instances, intermediate- and upper-grade teachers place the blame on primary teachers by accusing them of not doing a thorough job of teaching. Passing the buck solves no problems and is not commendable professionally.

A superintendent is needed to coordinate the efforts of teachers by working with the principals whose schools are involved in reading improvement programs. For example, intermediate-grade teachers should know what reading instruction is given to boys and girls in the primary grades. Similarly, they need to know the exact nature of reading demands at the junior and senior high school levels. Insights such as these are provided by the alert administrator.

29. FAILING TO PROVIDE AMPLE MATERIAL NEEDED FOR MEETING THE WIDE RANGE OF READING ABILITY AND INTERESTS IN EACH CLASSROOM

The school budget is frequently a deterrent to the purchase of supplementary reading material, both developmental and corrective. Administrators must be adamant, therefore, about the need for providing ample instructional material for their school. Teachers should not be expected to make bricks without straw. Without a variety of materials on hand, they cannot begin to meet the diversified reading needs and levels within their classrooms. This diversification must encompass multi-level instructional material including easy reading material with a high level of interest.

30. FAILING TO INTERPRET THE SCHOOL'S READING PROGRAM TO THE PUBLIC

Above all else, a good administrator must be a good public relations man. The administrator who fails to sell the lay public on the value of the school's reading program will face taxpayers who are reluctant to support needed budgetary demands. Every effort should be made, therefore, to interpret to the public the corrective, remedial, and developmental reading programs of the school.

Because reading problems are often related to physical and emotional problems, the school administrator particularly needs to seek the cooperation of various medical and paramedical groups in the community. Included in these groups are psychiatrists, psychologists, neurologists, otologists, ophthalmologists, optometrists, pediatricians, and general practitioners.

These specialists can diagnose and treat children who are referred by the school. They also can provide the school with valuable information which enables teachers to be of maximum assistance to a handicapped child. Without such cooperation, teachers may unknowingly negate the efforts of the out-of-school specialist.

31. FAILING TO PROVIDE A WELL-STAFFED AND WELL-EQUIPPED SCHOOL LIBRARY

Without a good librarian, no library can function well. It is the responsibility of the school administrators to hire competent librarians for their school and not be satisfied with individuals who lack training and experience in library work.

A good school library needs funds if it is to acquire an ample supply of books, magazines, films, and recordings. Money must be found to purchase these materials. When money is not available, the administrator should investigate the possibility of getting financial support from PTA's and other civic groups. Perhaps he can make arrangements with the local public library which will permit the school to borrow books and other reading materials when needed. Some school principals have encouraged librarians to avail themselves of the vast amount of free materials made available by commercial firms and government agencies.*

The degree to which a library is used in a school is a valid index of the success of the school's reading program. An administrator should be alert to ways of increasing library usage. He can encourage and help the teachers avoid conflicts by having them schedule library periods at different times. Under no circumstances should the principal authorize the use of the library for study hall purposes. Such a practice

---

*An excellent source of free reading material is Gordon Salisbury's *Catalog of Free Teaching Materials*, P.O. Box 1075, Ventura, California, 93001. The selling price of the book is $2.50. Include fifteen cents for mailing charges.

often negatively conditions students to the library and raises havoc with the librarian's effectiveness.

SUMMARY

The inference that a return to "the good old days" will solve all reading problems is erroneous. There is a natural tendency for parents to feel that the school is to blame for all reading problems. The school, on the other hand, points to the important role which the home and parents play in readying a child for reading. In the final analysis, it is evident that the home and school must share responsibility for reading failure. It is important for the latter to recognize the serious consequences of certain practices and conditions over which it has control. These may be found in the developmental program, the diagnostic program, or the corrective program. In addition, administrative policy may be inimical to the success of a school's reading program.

Undifferentiated group instruction using the same basic reader for all pupils makes no provision for individual differences and violates the principle of readiness. Many pupils in the lower grades who are subjected to this practice become victims of a low level of mastery in the skills of word recognition and word analysis. This prevents their becoming independent readers when they reach the intermediate grades. Unless a comprehensive diagnosis is made of individual reading difficulties followed by intensive corrective instruction, these pupils soon become severely retarded readers or even nonreaders.

Many individuals vary in their attainment of reading goals in spite of a balanced developmental program of instruction for the class. Unless the corrective and recreational reading program is adjusted to individual needs in learning, reading difficulties multiply, learning is inhibited, and academic achievement suffers.

PROBLEMS FOR ORAL AND WRITTEN DISCUSSION

1. Why is it important to correct reading difficulties when they first appear?
2. What educational hazards are frequently overlooked by teachers? Why?
3. Select two or more hazards to learning that you have corrected and indicate the corrective measures you have taken.
4. Observe a class for thirty minutes and describe the hazards to learning you were able to identify.

REFERENCES

1. D. G. SCHUBERT, *A Dictionary of Terms and Concepts in Reading*, 2nd ed. (Springfield, Ill.: Charles C Thomas, Publisher, 1969), p. 258.

2. L. COLE, *The Improvement of Reading* (New York: Farrar and Rinehart, Inc., 1938), p. 281.
3. I. H. ANDERSON et al., "Age of Learning to Read and Its Relation to Sex, Intelligence and Reading Achievement in the Sixth Grade," *Journal of Educational Research* (February, 1956):447-453.
4. R. S. HAMPLEMAN, "A Study of the Comparative Reading Achievements of Early and Late School Starters," *Elementary English* (May 1959):331-334.
5. N. B. SMITH, "Shall We Teach Formal Reading in the Kindergarten?" *The Compass* (February 1964).
6. S. MOSKOWITZ, "When Should Reading Instruction Begin?" *IRA Conference Proceedings* (1963):218-222.
7. D. A. BROWN and D. J. LOPER, "Word Recognition in the Elementary School," *Corrective Reading in the Elementary Classroom* (Newark, Del.: International Reading Association, 1968), p. 91.
8. R. STRANG, C. McCULLOUGH, and A. TRAXLER, *The Improvement of Reading* (New York: McGraw-Hill Book Co., 1961), p. 3.
9. G. SPACHE, *Reading in the Elementary School*, 2nd ed. (Boston: Allyn and Bacon, Inc., 1969), p. 27.
10. N. B. SMITH, "Reading: Concept Development," *Education* (May 1950): 540-558.
11. D. H. RUSSELL, "Reading for Effective Personal Living," in *Readings in Reading*, D. G. Schubert and T. L. Torgerson, eds. (New York: Thomas Y. Crowell Co., 1968), pp. 3-10.
12. J. A. CUTFORTH, *English in the Primary School* (Oxford: Basil Blackwell, 1954).
13. G. T. BUSWELL, "The Process of Reading," *The Reading Teacher* (December 1959):108.

SELECTED READINGS

BOND, GUY, and MILES TINKER. *Reading Difficulties: Their Diagnosis and Correction.* 2nd ed. New York: Appleton-Century-Crofts, 1967, ch. 6.

CARTER, HOMER, and DOROTHY McGINNIS. *Diagnosis and Treatment of the Disabled Reader.* New York: The Macmillan Co., 1970, ch. 4.

DeBOER, JOHN, and MARTHA DALLMANN. *The Teaching of Reading.* Rev. ed. New York: Holt, Rinehart & Winston, Inc., 1970, chs. 4A, 4B.

DECHANT, EMERALD. *Diagnosis and Remediation of Reading Disability.* West Nyack, N.Y.: Parker Publishing Co., Inc., 1968, ch. 3.

HARRIS, ALBERT. *Effective Teaching of Reading.* New York: David McKay Co., Inc., 1962, pp. 317-340.

HEILMAN, ARTHUR. *Principles and Practices of Teaching Reading.* Columbus, O.: Charles E. Merrill Books, Inc., 1961, ch. 1.

SCHELL, LEO, and PAUL BURNS. *Remedial Reading.* Boston: Allyn and Bacon, Inc., 1968, ch. 12.

SCHUBERT, DELWYN, and THEODORE TORGERSON. *Readings in Reading.* New York: Thomas Y. Crowell Co., 1968, selections 12-14, 16, 70.

SPACHE, GEORGE, *Toward Better Reading.* Champaign, Ill.: Garrard Publishing Co., 1963, ch. 1.

WITTY, PAUL; ALMA FREELAND; and EDITH GROTBERG. *The Teaching of Reading.* Boston: D. C. Heath and Co., 1968, ch. 5.

3

Noneducational
Hazards to Learning

CAUSAL FACTORS

Noneducational problem areas with which the teacher should be concerned may be categorized briefly as follows: visual, auditory, and speech defects; immaturity and sex differences; general health; dominance problems and neurological impairment; emotional maladjustment; home environment and intellectual development. (See chapter 2 for a discussion of educational factors.)

No one factor can be singled out to explain reading failure. While one cause or hazard may be of more consequence than another when an individual case is studied, several factors usually are involved. This is particularly true when serious disability cases are encountered. The principle of multiple causation has been stressed by many authorities in reading. One of the most thorough research studies corroborating the principle of multiple causation was done by Robinson.(1) Her investigation involved thirty cases of severe disability that were studied by a group of specialists. These included a psychiatrist, a psychologist, a pediatrician, a neurologist, an ophthalmologist, an otolaryngologist, a social worker, a speech pathologist, and an endocrinologist. Causal factors uncovered were categorized in order of frequency. The most frequent were visual difficulties and social problems, followed by emotional maladjustment, neurological difficulties, speech difficulties, school methods, auditory problems, endocrine disturbances, and general physical difficulty.

VISUAL IMPAIRMENT

Approximately eighty percent of the children in a typical school have normal vision. The remaining twenty percent can be expected to suffer from visual anomalies. On causal inspection one would expect to find a marked positive relationship between visual defects and reading skills because reading of printed symbols involves the eyes. But the literature is not conclusive. Some investigators find that visual defects contribute to reading failure while others do not. Why aren't visual-reading relationships consistent?

Flax(2) believes that poor research is the prime reason for inconsistent findings. He feels that the majority of existing research studies are guilty of inherent deficiencies in research design which preclude the emergence of any meaningful relationships. Betts(3) discusses a number of factors which investigators have not held constant: age of subjects, readiness to learn to read, and methods and quality of teaching. Other factors which may explain the discrepancy of findings are the lack of a universal definition of reading disability, differing methods of measuring visual deficiencies, and a lack of agreement as to what constitutes a visual problem.

There are many kinds of visual defects, some of which appear to have more etiological significance in connection with reading problems than others. Certain visual defects—errors of refraction—result from malformation of the eyeball. These include myopia, hyperopia, astigmatism, and aniseikonia. The myopic (nearsighted) eye has a posterior-anterior axis that is too long in relation to the focusing apparatus. As a consequence, the myope experiences difficulty when looking at distant objects (the blackboard, for example) because the image focuses in front of the retina. At near point however, myopia, if not too marked, is an asset rather than a liability to efficient reading. Since the slightly nearsighted eye requires less accommodative effort to maintain proper focal distance when book reading, the viewer experiences little or no strain. A few of the investigators who report significantly higher percentages of myopia among good readers in comparison to unselected cases includes Eames,(4) Farris,(5) and Bartlett.(6)

The hyperopic (farsighted) eye has a posterior-anterior axis that is too short in relation to the focusing apparatus. A small amount of farsightedness is often conducive to eagle-eye vision at far point. But the hyperope is likely to experience some difficulty at near point (when book reading, for example) because the image tends to focus behind the retina. This requires additional accommodative effort which can be fatiguing. Research by Eames,(7) Robinson,(8) Hulsman,(9) and Hirsch (10) support the contention that hyperopia is not compatible with good reading.

Astigmatism is caused by unequal curvature of the surface of the cornea and/or the crystalline lens of the eye. The astigmatic individual experiences blurring because of these irregularities. Betts(11) found astigmatism among many of his severe cases of reading disability and felt that the defect was one of the causes involved. Eames,(12) on the other hand, found a greater incidence of the defect among good readers than among unselected ones. Many researchers(13, 14, 15) report an inability to differentiate groups of good and poor readers on the basis of astigmatism. Several specialists have voiced the opinion that severe astigmatism might prove quite detrimental to efficient reading in individual cases. Romaine(16) states, "It would seem most important to correct any marked degree of astigmatism." Cleland,(17) sharing the same view, states, ". . . in severe cases of astigmatism it was found to be closely allied with reading failure." In a 1968 study involving induced astigmatism, Schubert and Walton(18) state that astigmatism was a cause of eyestrain. Blur and distortion, headaches, and adverse psychological effects were reported by the thirty subjects participating in the experiment. Since mild astigmatism, if uncorrected, can result in eyestrain, it was thought prudent to correct the defect whenever it was present.

Aniseikonia is a condition in which the images of the two eyes differ in size or shape, making fusion difficult and often resulting in headaches and other manifestations of discomfort. It is believed that differences in size or shape of retinal images exceeding five percent are serious. Individuals vary considerably, however, in their tolerance of this condition. Therefore, in some cases smaller discrepancies in the two images might cause difficulty. Research by Anderson and Dearborn(19) led them to the conclusion that aniseikonia must be considered in about one-half the serious cases in reading.

Normal binocular vision is dependent on proper alignment of the eyes. They must be focused accurately on the object of regard. When this occurs, the two retinal images which are transmitted simultaneously to the vision centers (occipital lobe) can be integrated into a single ocular image (fusion). Fusion problems vary in their degree of severity. Mild, latent cases of muscular imbalance resulting in fusion difficulties are termed phorias. The more extreme and manifest types of imbalance are termed tropias. Prefixes are employed to indicate the direction in which one eye turns or tends to turn in relation to the other. These are *exo-* (out), *eso-* (in), *hyper-* (up), and *hypo-* (down). When fusion is not complete, the subject experiences blurred imagery even though each eye, individually (as in the case of aniseikonia), sustains a clear image. There are also cases of slow fusion which may prove a handicap in reading because very precise focusing is required. Some individuals overcome their fusion defects through sheer effort and experience, blurring only after prolonged use of the eyes when fatigue begins to develop. As a result of blurring, or possibly diplopia (seeing double), suppression may take place. The suppressed eye frequently weakens (becomes amblyopic) if continuous disuse is involved.

Numerous research studies have indicated that there is a positive relationship between reading difficulties and fusion irregularities. Statements regarding this relationship have been made by specialists in reading and vision. Romaine(20) states: "In my opinion muscular imbalances themselves, more definitely than any other ocular defect, are a factor in poor reading." In reference to reading clinic cases, Cleland(21) says: "I sincerely believe that slow or sluggish fusion is the direct or indirect cause of more reading failures than the records show." Park and Burri(22) of the Northwestern University Medical School gave thorough ophthalmological examinations to 225 first- through eighth-grade children. The ocular defects which they felt were most closely related to poor reading were exophoria, esophoria, and fusion difficulties. Of the many specialists who concur in the belief that fusion problems are of importance in connection with reading difficulties, a number of them believe that exophoria, in particular, is the principal offender. Park(23) says: "Phorias are significant, especially exophoria for reading distance." In comparing the eye movements of normal and exophoric students, Sabatini(24) found that the latter showed greater divergent movements at the beginning of lines. He felt that this resulted in greater reading fatigue and was a factor of considerable importance. Eames(25) reports finding significantly greater incidence of exophoria among reading disability cases than among unselected ones. In summarizing his study, Hulsman(26) says that exophoria, along with hyperopia, ". . . seemed to be the eye defects most commonly found in poor readers."

Of the various types of immaturity that relate to reading success or failure, there is strong evidence that visual immaturity is highly significant.(27, 28, 29, 30) A sizable percentage of six- and seven-year-old children have eyes that haven't had sufficient time to develop fully. Such eyes are likely to be so farsighted that seeing objects like printed words on a page proves troublesome. Another problem stems from the inability of some children's eyes to work together as a team. When near-point binocular vision is not properly developed, a child sees printed words that are fuzzy and indistinct. Needless to say, such a situation does not augur well for reading success.

The well-known optometrist and educator Dr. A. M. Skeffington advocates the use of convex spherical lenses in the first grade.(31) These "learning lenses," as he terms them, would protect the vision of young children and would make it easier for them to engage in near-point work. According to Harmon, near-point tasks give rise to an avoidance response: a physiological urge to escape. The use of convex spheres "allows the organism to continue at the near-centered visual task; but it provides satisfaction of the avoidance urge, that of avoiding or getting away from the containing task. Thus, the organism can 'achieve' and 'avoid' at the same time."(32)

Apropos, here, is the reported success of the New Castle, Pennsylvania, system of teaching reading in the first grade.(33) The New Castle approach minimized near-point reading and used filmstrips intensively. All first graders (even some with low I.Q.'s) are reported to have learned how to read and to have achieved unprecedented reading scores on standardized tests at the end of the year.

Another solution to the problem of visual immaturity is to omit formal reading from the programs of children who demonstrate this shortcoming. Although some children may feel excluded and suffer emotionally when this is done, it is more desirable than forcing them into near-point activity before they are ready.

It is well known that practice lags behind research a decade or two in most areas. It nevertheless is unfortunate that many schools fail to recognize the relationship between visual immaturity and first-grade reading failure. Schools should employ the proper near-point tests or seek cooperation of visual specialists who can do a competent job of determining which children are visually immature.

In summarizing the findings regarding visual-reading relationships, the following conclusions seem warranted:

1. Many studies show that certain visual anomalies (e.g., exophoria, hyperopia) are found more often among retarded readers; but they also show that among good readers there are children who suffer from exactly the same visual defects.

2. It is necessary to consider reading problems as a result of multiple causation if contradictions such as the preceding are to be explained. For example, the intelligence of a child as well as numerous other factors (physical or environmental) may make compensation for his defect possible or impossible.

3. Visual disorders may retard both good and poor readers so that comparison between groups doesn't give an accurate picture of the problem.

4. Findings based on group studies are not always applicable to individual cases.

5. Some visual defects like myopia may be conducive to good reading; while other defects like hyperopia or aniseikonia seem more detrimental to reading progress.

6. Lack of visual maturity rather than visual defect is a factor to consider in first-grade reading difficulty.

7. Although there is no consensus as to the exact relationship between the many specific defects of vision and the reading problem, authorities do agree that a thorough visual examination is an essential part of individual diagnosis.

8. To help insure the possibility of children achieving their maximal efficiency in reading, it would seem wise to correct all possible visual anomalies.

How can one determine the visual condition of a child's eyes? It can be done as follows: Hold the child's glasses before your sighting eye, approximately one foot away. Look through one lens at a spot on the wall. Continue to watch the spot while you move the lens vertically. If the spot moves with the movement of the lens, the lens is concave (a minus lens) and indicates myopia. If the spot at which you are looking moves in the opposite direction of the moving lens, the lens is convex (a plus lens) and indicates farsightedness. If the movement of the target viewed through the lens is very slow in comparison to the speed at which the lens is moved, then a stronger prescription, possibly a plus or minus 2.00 diopters or more, is involved. If the movement of the target is relatively fast, then the power of the lens is less, perhaps a half-diopter (0.50) or one diopter (1.00) lens. By moving the lens horizontally in front of the target it is possible to determine if astigmatism is involved. If the target moves faster or slower in one meridian than it does in another, then the two meridia differ in power and one can be assured that the child is wearing glasses that correct for astigmatism. By repeating the procedure with the remaining lens, the teacher can determine whether the two eyes are equally astigmatic or different in that regard. These kinds of information are of value to the teacher who wishes to understand the visual status of a child.

DETECTING VISUAL DEFECTS

All screening tests* for vision used by the school have shortcomings. This is particularly true of the Snellen chart. Often the chart is ad-

*See pages 152-155 for additional information about vision screening.

ministered in a way that permits a child to cheat. For example, some children simulate good vision by memorizing the chart; others squint, a practice helpful to the myope since the size of the pupil is reduced. It is important to recognize that the Snellen chart checks vision only at far point and fails completely to detect severe cases of poor fusion and muscular imbalance. It also fails to detect most cases of astigmatism and farsightedness. Nearsightedness is the only defect adequately screened by the Snellen chart, and this defect, ironically, is the one most often associated with good reading and good scholarship.

The Snellen chart can be made more effective by employing a plus 1.00- or 1.50-diopter spherical lens for purposes of retesting. The farsighted child will see as well or better when the lens is used, but the child who has normal vision or who is myopic will be hindered by use of the lens. It is desirable to also have the child read the chart with both eyes after typical monocular testing has taken place. If the child sees less well with both eyes than he did when each eye was tested individually, a fusion problem may be suspected.

There are a number of visual screening tests that are superior to the Snellen chart. Among these are the Keystone School Visual Survey Tests (Keystone View Company, Meadville, Penn.), the Orthorater (Bausch and Lomb Optical Company, Rochester, N. Y.) and the Eames Eye Test (Harcourt Brace Jovanovich, New York City). Additional information about these tests can be found in Appendix C.

Other visual screening tests include the A O Sight Screener (American Optical Company, Kansas City, Mo.), Atlantic City Eye Test (Freund Brothers, 1514 Pacific Avenue, Atlantic City, N. J.), Massachusetts Eye Test (Welch-Allyn Inc., Skanteateles Falls, N. Y., or American Optical Company, 62 Mechanic Street, Southbridge, Mass.), New York School Vision Tester (Bausch and Lomb, Inc., Rochester, N. Y.), Prism Reader (Educational Developmental Laboratories, Huntington, N. Y.), Spache Binocular Reading Test (Keystone View Company, Meadville, Penn.), Stereotests (Titmus Optical Company, Petersburg, Va.), and the T/O Vision Testers (Titmus Optical Company, Inc., Petersburg, Va.).

The use of informal tests such as the cover test, ocular motility test, near point of convergence test, and the physiological diplopia test is helpful in screening children for muscular imbalances. (See chapter 5 for a detailed discussion of these tests.)

The most valuable vision-screening technique is known as the Modified Clinical Technique. According to the Orinda Study (University of California Press, 1959), it is by far the most efficient means of identifying children who are in need of professional vision attention.

Some modern school systems enlist the cooperation of vision specialists who employ the Modified Clinical Technique. These specialists provide complete and competent visual-screening testing for all the children at a very nominal cost. One such program is conducted by the Los Angeles College of Optometry in Los Angeles, California,* where eight thousand children are examined yearly. In the typical school where testing takes place, all first graders, all referrals, all new transfer students, and all children placed in a borderline category the previous year are tested.

The screening team consists of fourteen to fifteen students in their clinical year, together with two faculty members who are licensed optometrists and hold Health and Development Credentials.

The tests given are essentially those of the Modified Clinical Technique and include the following:

1. Skiametry (retinoscopy) to determine the refractive state of the eye;
2. Visual acuity using the illiterate E test;
3. Phoria tests at 20 feet and 16 inches to measure muscle imbalance or binocular coordination;
4. The Cover Test or objective and quantitative determination of binocular coordination;
5. Convergence and vision tests to determine ocular motility;
6. Internal (ophthalmoscopic) and external inspection for pathology or organic anomalies.

All children are given all tests. These are performed by the student clinicians, and the record is then evaluated by one of the supervising staff before a disposition is made. The dispositions are *pass, borderline, fail,* and *under care.* The record is given to the nurse, and consultation on individual cases is held at the time of testing. If necessary, retesting is done. The nurse then makes the referral by notifying parents of the results. Since the teachers are usually present while their classes are screened, it is frequently possible to correlate the visual test results with teacher observation and/or scholastic achievement. This often results in more accurate and meaningful referrals.

Programs such as the foregoing are very successful and pay unprecedented dividends to the school districts employing them.

Careful observation by the classroom teacher can do much to improve the results of a school's visual testing program. The reader is

*The writers are indebted to Frank A. Brazelton, O.D., Visual Survey Director, Los Angeles College of Optometry, for information about the College's vision-screening program.

referred to chapter 5 for a listing of observable symptoms of visual problems. Observation of any symptoms should be reported to the school nurse or doctor for further screening. If no school nurse or doctor is available, the matter should be brought to the attention of the parents who have the responsibility of taking their child to the proper medical specialist for an examination.

In certain instances, the school nurse may report negative findings while the teacher continues to feel great concern about the child's vision because of a chronic symptomatology. When this happens, parents should be informed of the teacher's concern. On occasions, well-meaning nurses fail to detect a visual problem because their skill in specialized areas is limited or because the instruments and tests at their disposal are not sufficiently refined. Sometimes only a thorough examination by a competent visual specialist can pinpoint the problem.

EYE MOVEMENTS

In 1879, a Frenchman named Javal observed that an individual's eyes do not move smoothly along lines of print during reading, but make a number of starts and stops. These are called saccadic movements. Although the stops (fixations) last but one-fourth to one-half second, they are the pauses that inform. During these pauses the reader reacts to words and phrases. The number of fixations he makes is dependent on the difficulty of the material and his knowledge of it, his purpose, the vocabulary encountered, and the format of the printed page. Dividing the number of fixations by the words read is an index of recognition span, the amount a reader sees per fixation. The average span of recognition, according to Spache, (34) is .45 of a word in the first grade to 1.11 words in college. This is much smaller than is generally realized.

If a reader's attention fluctuates or if he does not comprehend the text, his eyes may backtrack. These reverse movements of the eyes are called regressions. Most often, regressions serve a useful purpose. If, however, they become an unnecessary habit, they can impede reading speed.

The movement of the eyes from the end of one line to the beginning of another is called a return sweep. Unless muscular imbalances such as exophoria are present, the return sweep is accurate and quick, taking about 1/25 of a second.

Today, oculomotor behavior is regarded as a reflection or a symptom of reading efficiency. Poor eye movements are not considered the cause of poor reading. The eyes are servants of the brain. When a reader is confused, it is mirrored in his eye-movement patterns. The poor reader, therefore, doesn't need eye-movement training to reduce the number of fixations he makes; he needs training to improve his word-recognition, phrasing, and comprehension skills.

HEARING

Most hearing losses fall into two categories: perception (nerve) loss and conduction loss. The latter is a loss in loudness due to sound that is blocked in its transmission to the inner ear. Examples of the causes for conduction losses are wax in the ear, otitis media damage, and otosclerosis. Nerve loss is the result of deterioration of or lesions within the inner-ear structure. Vowel sounds usually are heard when a nerve loss is present, but many or all the voiceless consonants are not heard. These include *f, h, th, p, t, sh,* and *ch.* Difficulties with voiced consonants also are likely. These involve *b, d, g, v, th, z, zh, j,* and *w.* Lastly, the nerve-deaf child tends to confuse nasal sounds such as *m, n,* and *ng.*

Since learning to read involves making visual auditory associations, the student having a hearing loss is readily confused and is at a distinct disadvantage.(35) He sees letters which he has been unable to hear and finds that words which sound the same to him have different letters in them.

The degree to which a given auditory loss impedes a child's progress in reading is dependent on many factors. These include the age at which the child suffered the loss, the extent and configuration of the loss, the extent of language development and comprehension prior to the loss, and the level of the child's intelligence. It should also be remembered that a constellation of factors usually is involved in reading retardation. A child with a marked visual problem, for example, would be more encumbered by a hearing loss than a child who had normal vision.

Children who cannot detect the presence of sound are said to lack *auditory acuity.* Some children, however, can hear the presence of sound but have great difficulty discriminating between sounds that are similar. These children lack powers of *auditory discrimination.* They might find it impossible, for example, to hear the differences between the words *bat, bet, bit, but.* Their inability to discern small differences between sounds often manifests itself in their speech and spelling. Phonic training proves difficult, and word-recognition skill fails to develop at a normal rate. Some writers consider poor auditory discrimination an important cause of reading deficiency.(36)

Spache states that poor auditory discrimination is often associated with pitch discrimination, recognition of auditory rhythms and beat, discrimination of tonal quality, timbre, and loudness.(37) If this is true, it would appear obvious that children with poor auditory discrimination would not show normal musical aptitude. The administration of the Seashore Musical Aptitude Test to such a group might prove interesting.

Regardless of causation, it would seem valuable to expose children with poor auditory discrimination to simple poems and nursery rhymes as well as commercial games such as Consonant Lotto and Go Fish. Such exposure would bring to their attention both alliteration and rhyme and would motivate them to sharpen their auditory discrimination.

Once the presence of a hearing defect is known, classroom teachers at all levels can take measures to minimize its effects. Some of these are listed:

1. Assign to the child a front seat which favors his better ear and give him a roving-seat privilege so that he may always move close to the source of sound.
2. Liberally repeat oral directions.
3. Write directions being given orally on a small card or piece of paper and place it in front of the child.
4. Give the child additional speech clues by letting him see your face in good light when you speak.
5. Summarize the day's happenings periodically.

A number of formal and informal tests can be employed in auditory screening. (See chapter 5 for a description of these.) It is important, too, that classroom teachers be familiar with the symptoms of auditory impairment. A list of these can be found in chapter 5.

SPEECH

Speech development and reading ability are positively correlated. The child who has a limited vocabulary and finds it difficult to express himself in sentences is likely to experience reading difficulty. It should come as no surprise to learn that de Hirsch(38) found high correlations between reading failure in the primary grades and several measures of language proficiency in kindergarten.

Sometimes children with speech defects suffer from actual malformation of the speech organs. In most instances, however, the causal factors of the disorder are almost identical to those which give rise to reading problems. Emotional problems seem particularly potent as a cause of speech defects. This is especially true of stuttering. It must be remembered that a child with a speech defect is often embarrassed when reading by real or imagined laughter from his classmates and teacher. In subsequent reading situations greater feelings of insecurity and a flooding of the emotions build up inside of him. This in turn results in more articulatory difficulty, and a vicious circle is perpetuated.

Children with speech problems (see page 132 for a suitable inventory) should be referred to a speech specialist if possible. The teacher will want to do what is possible, however, to prevent the emotional difficulties that accompany speech defects from affecting reading. Scott and Thompson's book will prove valuable to the teacher who is unable to enlist the aid of a speech specialist.(39)

A child with a speech defect is likely to find phonic analysis difficult because of his inability to sound individual phonemes. Patience is needed. The teacher should make a special effort to assist the child in his word-attack skills.

MATURITY AND SEX DIFFERENCES

Superficially, seven- or eight-year-olds in a group look very much alike, but closer scrutiny soon reveals differences. Children enter every school grade showing wide disparities in their mental, emotional, and physical maturities. The reasons for these variations are multiple. They involve inheritance, parental training, school environment, the child's chronological age, and his sex. Although it is not fair to blame reading retardation on sex, it is a known fact that two and three times as many boys as girls are found in reading disability groups.

Some authors(40) have tried to explain the difference in terms of hormones. There probably are simpler explanations, however. Boys are far more active physically than girls and find it difficult to adjust to sedentary classroom activity. Besides, they are interested in cowboys, Indians, and jet airplanes. Dick, Jane, and the little red hen prove lifeless and unstimulating. On a Saturday afternoon, it is not unusual to find a group of little girls playing school. But little boys—they would sooner be caught embroidering than playing school. As a matter of fact, many boys feel strongly that reading is sissy stuff. Add to all these explanations the basic fact that boys at age six lag behind girls about six months in physical maturity, and we have some good reasons why the distaff side of life fares so well in reading.

Criscuolo(41) states that the development of girls' visual acuity and their fine motor skills are more advanced at early school age. There also is a difference in the metabolic rate between the sexes. Since boys consume more oxygen and their energy output is greater, sedentary activity is affected.

Sexton(42) emphasizes the disadvantage of having boys taught by female teachers. She refers to the "female school." She observes that school culture is typically "polite, prissy, and puritanical" and that there is little place in this female culture for some of the high-ranking values of boy-culture—courage, loyalty, independence—or the high-ranking interests of boys—sports (except in gym class), outdoor life, popular music, adventure, sex, and action. It is interesting to note, in this regard, that in Germany, a country where male teachers dominate the primary grades, more girls than boys fail in reading.

Schools which abide by research findings often require a minimum mental age of six to six and one-half for beginning reading. Of course, children with much lower mental ages can be taught to read when conditions are favorable. It is well known, however, that most children taught by an average teacher in an average classroom using conventional material need mental ages of six to six and one-half if they are to prove successful in learning to read. Schools which base entrance solely on chronological age, therefore, expose many first-grade children to inevitable failure.

Although intelligence tests are not without error, intelligence quotients and mental ages derived from them have value if one bears in mind that a child's reading ability can be expected to approximate his intelligence only when all conditions are optimum. It must be recognized that intelligence test scores are influenced by a child's experiences, language development, and interest.

Teachers should recognize that a retarded reader (one reading below grade level) who has an intelligence quotient below ninety may be doing as well as can be expected for an individual of limited mental ability. When a child's mental grade placement is below his actual grade placement, he cannot be expected to attain the grade status of his class; however, it must not be assumed that all handicapped readers are mentally slow. Retarded and disabled readers are found at every level of intelligence. The child whose reading grade placement is below his mental grade placement should be considered a disabled reader. Such a reader is achieving below his potential and is likely to profit from appropriate remediation. (See chaper 5.)

GENERAL HEALTH

Part of a teacher's detective work must concern children's general health. Research in reading has shown that, to a degree, the ancient

Greeks were right in believing that a good body and a good mind go hand in hand.

Eames(43) compared 875 reading failures with 486 nonfailing students as to their physical status and found that the reading failure group exhibited 21.1 percent more frequency of disease than did the control group.

Physical malnutrition has been found prevalent among some groups of poor readers. In cataloging physical findings among 215 poor readers, Park(44) classed a sizeable percentage of them as suffering from disturbed nutrition. The seriousness of poor nutrition has been highlighted by Scrimshaw(45) who states that an inadequate diet, especially one low in proteins, can result in smaller brain size and damage to the central nervous system.

Several investigators have found that endocrine disturbances and poor reading are related. Park(46) reported that of 215 poor readers, twenty-seven percent of them suffered from hypothyroidism while four percent had hyperthyroidism. Posner(47) found hypothyroidism occurred frequently among reading disability cases he studied. When given thyroid extract, they showed great improvement in "understanding, remembering, and reading. Some gained one and one-half years in reading ability in one semester without any change in teaching methods. . . ."

Freedom from disease, proper rest, and good nutrition give rise to the alertness and attention-sustaining power conducive to good reading. Children who are ill are more likely to react phlegmatically to intellectual tasks or easily become irritable and tense when things do not go well. Many times, too, children who are ill miss out on basic reading instruction because of excessive absence. When such children do attend school, they often lack the zest and enthusiasm to profit from instruction.

Teachers should remain alert to the symptoms of poor health at all grade levels. They should be aware of symptoms indicative of underactivity and overactivity of the thyroid gland as well. (See page 130 for appropriate list of symptoms.)

DOMINANCE

The terms *dominance* and *laterality* refer to the consistent choice or superior functioning of one side of the body over the other. This is believed to result from a dominant cerebral hemisphere which is on the side opposite the preferred hand, eye, or foot.

Those who relate dominance to reading skill believe that not being completely one-sided in handedness, eyedness, and footedness constitutes a condition wholly or partially responsible for reading disability.

A number of theories involving dominance have been evolved through the years to explain reading disability. Two of the better known are by Orton and Dearborn.

Orton believed that visual records, or engrams, found in the dominant hemisphere of the brain are used in making symbolic associations.(48) Engrams in the nondominant hemisphere, he reasoned, would be opposite in sign, or mirrored in nature. Most often these mirrored engrams are elided or unused in the language function. When, however, an individual fails to develop consistent dominance, these latter engrams evince themselves in the form of reversals. Since, according to Orton, the making of reversals was the foremost characteristic of the poor reader, he suggested the word *strephosymbolia*, meaning "twisted symbols," as a suitable label for the difficulty.

Dearborn believed that movements away from the center of the body are more easily made than those in the opposite direction.(49) The right-handed and right-eyed individual would find it easier, therefore, to write and read since both skills necessitate left-to-right progressions. Sinistrads and those with a mixed or inconsistent preference for either side would be prone to make reversals and, in general, experience word-recognition confusions.

A current proponent of unilateral cortical control is Delacato. He states: "Right-handed humans are one-sided, i.e., they are right-eyed, right-footed and right-handed, with the left cortical hemisphere controlling the organism."(50)

What Delacato and other theorists in this area fail to recognize is that *anatomically eye preference and handedness are unrelated.*(51, 52) Although the nerve fibers pass from each hand to the opposite hemisphere of the brain, *both hemispheres are involved in the control of each eye.*(53) When the nerve fibers from each retina pass through the optic chiasma, they decussate. Fibers from the nasal side of the retina pass onto the opposite hemisphere, while the others terminate on the same side. Crider found that individuals who were right-handed had retinas which were more sensitive on the right side.(54) Since the right hemisphere is involved in controlling the right side of the retinal field, one would expect such individuals to be left-handed. It is neurologically sound, it would seem, to be right-handed and left-eyed or vice versa. Ironically, this is a condition deplored by Dearborn, Orton, and Delacato.

Delacato's use of occlusion to change eyedness and his advocacy of the Stereo-Reader (a device designed to encourage suppression of vision in one eye which in itself is considered by specialists in vision to be an unhealthy condition) would seem fruitless. As stated by Flax: "Since neither eye can send all of its incoming visual information to a single side of the brain, attempts to equate uniocular function with unilateral cortical dominance are incompatible. The success reported by Delacato must stem from factors other than visual dominance."(55)

Spache, a leading reading authority, states that reading disability cannot be cured or prevented by imposing one-sided motor preferences on an individual.(56) In reference to dominance tests, he says:

The time spent in futile tests of these functions might better be devoted to discovering children whose perceptual-motor development is inadequate. These children exhibit problems of confusion in left-right orientation, in directionality, in form perception and spatial perception and in concepts of body image. Their lack of development results also in ocular inco-ordinations and lack of hand-eye co-ordination with consequent difficulties in reading and writing. (57)

Since 1960, a number of researchers have reported no significant relationships between dominance preferences or inconsistency and difficulties in reading. Among these are Balow and Balow,(58) Beck,(59) Belmont and Birch,(60) Capobianco,(61) and Coleman and Deutsch. (62)

Because we live in a right-handed society, left-handed children are subjected to many pressures and sometimes develop emotional problems which may account for confusions thought attributable to left-handedness per se. There have been instances, for example, where teachers and parents, with misplaced zeal, have tied a child's left hand behind his back so he would be unable to use it.

Another frustration is that a left-handed child often is forced to use a desk designed for right-handers. Under these circumstances, writing proves a chore even though the child slants his paper in the appropriate direction. One elementary school principal has spent much time observing and studying left-handedness. He himself is a sinistral. He believes left-handed children, on the average, write more slowly than right-handed children, because a left-handed child must push rather than pull his pencil across the paper when writing from left to right. The latter, he contends, is easier.

In summary, the evidence that left-handedness or mixed dominance is directly involved in bringing about reading disability is insufficient to warrant such a conclusion. Dramatically new research approaches are needed before a definite relationship between laterality and reading disability can be established. Secondary conditions such as those described in the two foregoing paragraphs undoubtedly may contribute to a left-handed child's maladjustment and should not be overlooked.

NEUROLOGICAL IMPAIRMENT

There is no doubt that severe injury to the brain can cause loss of reading ability. For example, some individuals who are victims of an apoplectic stroke lose the ability to read. Dattner, Davis, and Smith(63) tell of a fifty-year-old coast guard officer who lost his ability to read as the result of an accident. The man was able to write, however, and showed no other loss in the area of language. This kind of aphasia is usually referred to as word blindness, or acquired alexia.

The man to whom use of the terms "word blindness" and "acquired alexia" is often attributed was an English opthalmologist named Hinshelwood.(64) Hinshelwood examined children who had not succeeded in learning how to read. Since the symptoms of these young nonreaders were similar to those who were victims of acquired alexia, he hypothecated the presence of a congenital variety of alexia. This was due, he said, to an abnormality of the angular and supramarginal gyri of the dominant hemisphere.(65)

Evidence that word blindness stems from an abnormality of a localized area of the brain (specifically the occipital lobe) isn't conclusive. Hallgren feels that reading difficulty resulting from a localized lesion in the dominant hemisphere is exceedingly rare.(66) Goldstein views every mental performance as a dynamic process which involves the entire cortex.(67)

Gesell placed emphasis on minimal brain damage as a cause of reading disability and singled out birth injuries as frequently responsible. (68) In support of Gesell's views, several studies employing electroencephalography report that abnormal EEG's appear in high concentration in children with reading disabilities.(69, 70)

Contrary to the opinions of the foregoing theorists and researchers, a number of today's leading reading specialists feel that there is too much concern over neurological impairment as a cause of reading disability. Bond and Tinker state: "It is likely that there is an over-emphasis upon brain damage as a cause of reading disability."(71)

The terminology used to describe severely retarded readers, many of whom are thought to be neurologically impaired, is a matter of concern. For example, Herman(72) employs the terms "congenital word blindness" and "congenital alexia." Spache is dubious about the use of these labels. He states:

The group is clearly identified in Dr. Herman's mind despite his recognition that there is not "one symptom nor one straightforward objective finding on which to base the description."(73)

Similarly, Money,(74) editor of a series of papers, uses the terms "specific reading disability" or "dyslexia" in referring to certain children. Spache says the following about Money's designation of a group of readers as dyslexic:

It is difficult for this reviewer to recognize clearly the small group of severely retarded readers who are assumed to be dyslexic. This is particularly true since, as repeated frequently in these papers, there is *not a single*, consistent symptom or reading behavior which distinguishes the syndrome called "specific reading disability," from among the clinical population of severely retarded readers. Perhaps it is naive to expect that a recognizable syndrome would be composed of a group of interrelated symptoms or behaviors which collectively have diagnostic significance and aid in differential diagnosis and treatment. Symptoms of dyslexia are mentioned by the dozens in these various papers, but no coherent or distinguishing syndrome appears. In fact, every symptom or behavior mentioned as characteristic of this "specific reading disability" has been observed in many retarded readers by this writer and other reading clinicians, who then, in naive ignorance of the incurability of the condition, proceeded to repair the retardation and restore the clients to apparent normalcy. We cannot help but wonder what the course of clinical reading would have been during the past three or four decades if this pessimistic theory had been offered earlier. (75)

A number of other writers have expressed concern over the use of the word *dyslexia*. Adams states: "Its sound is noxious, its meaning is obscure, it has divided the efforts of honest men when collaboration would have been the better course."(76) In a similar vein, Dauzat writes: "The term has become so ambiguous, however, that educators as well as laymen have become confused."(77)

From the evidence available at the present time, it would seem prudent for teachers to be cautious about attributing reading disability to neurological impairment. They should be careful, too, about labeling a child "word blind," or "dyslexic." It is obvious that there is no consensus as to what is meant by such terms, and the application of an imposing label is not synonymous with diagnosis.

Symptoms of neurological impairment with which reading specialists and teachers should be familiar are—

1. Awkwardness, clumsiness, or poor coordination when walking, running, or writing.
2. Difficulties in sucking and swallowing.
3. Delayed speech or articulation difficulties.
4. Paralysis or weakness of the extremities.
5. Abnormalities of the head.
6. Persistent headaches.
7. Convulsive seizures or lapses in consciousness.
8. Overactivity and concentration difficulties.

Causes of neurological impairment with which reading specialists and teachers should be acquainted are—

1. Familial neurological dysfunction.
2. Congenital defects of the central nervous system.
3. Complications of pregnancy.
   a. German measles, mumps, virus pneumonia, scarlet fever, and encephalitis.
   b. Rh incompatibility.
   c. Toxemia.
   d. Threatened abortion.
4. Complications of birth or labor.
   a. Caesarean section.
   b. Premature birth.
   c. Prolonged labor—breech presentation, high forceps delivery.
   d. Dry birth.
   e. Precipitous birth.
   f. Improper use of anesthesia.
   g. Asphyxia from various causes, e.g., prolapse of the cord. (Most of the foregoing in this group can result in oxygen deprivation.)
5. Childhood diseases.
   a. Encephalitis (particularly measles encephalitis).
   b. Meningitis.
   c. High fever with delirium.
6. Head injury involving unconsciousness (particularly before the age of three).
7. Miscellaneous.
   a. Poisons resulting in unconsciousness.
   b. Burns involving large areas of the body surface.
   c. Excessive crying or head-banging during the first year of life.

A NEUROCHEMICAL THEORY

One of the most fascinating and provocative studies of the last fifteen years was carried out by Smith and Carrigan(78) who offered a neurochemical explanation of synaptic transmission problems which they felt related to reading disability.

To make normal neural transmission possible, a delicate balance between two substances—acetylcholine (ACH) and cholinesterase (CHE) —is essential. ACH is needed if an impulse is to bridge the junction (synapse) between neurons. Repetitive firing of a neuron continues until

ACH is neutralized by CHE. The latter, it appears, acts as a circuit breaker.

An overabundance of ACH makes it difficult for an individual to change his fixation point. This, in turn, results in slow reading and an inability to blend phonemes. Too much CHE, on the other hand, makes it difficult for an individual to sustain fixation and brings about rapid shifts in attention. When ths condition exists, inaccurate reading characterized by substitution of one sound for another results.

Smith and Carrigan identified endocrine disorders as having a bearing on synaptic transmission and neural activity. In a number of experiments, a variety of medications were prescribed to correct metabolic as well as synaptic abnormalities. Involved were vitamins, hormones, stimulants, and tranquilizers. Unfortunately, groups that received treatment did not make statistically significant gains. At the present time the organic approach to reading difficulties advocated by Smith and Carrigan remains unproved.

If a child's developmental history or behavior indicates possible neurological impairment, a neurological examination is needed. Psychological tests also are helpful in uncovering neurological defects. Many of these tests involve items or subtests of the Stanford-Binet and/or Wechsler Intelligence Scale for Children. Included in these are Repetition of Digits, Copying a Diamond, Kohs Block Design, Memory for Designs, Object Assembly, and Coding or Digit Symbol. Additional tests include the Goodenough Draw-a-Man Test, Bender Visual Motor Gestalt, Archimedes Spiral Test, Ellis Visual Designs, Knox Cube Test, Peabody Picture Vocabulary Test, and others as preferred by the psychologist involved.

EMOTIONAL MALADJUSTMENT

"I don't feel so good," the child said when a strange and inexperienced therapist asked him to begin reading an oral reading test.

"Try, please try," repeated the therapist.

"Gee, I don't feel so good in my stomach, I'm real sick."

"Read this!" the examiner insisted.

Minutes later, it was too late for regret. The child had meant it. The session was at an end.

Pathological illness such as this is not unknown among retarded readers. Some children complain of nausea when faced with a reading situation; others suffer pains, headaches, or dizziness. These psychosomatic manifestions are used by the child to escape or temporarily avoid a disagreeable situation.

Pathological illness is one of the many symptoms of personality maladjustments shown by poor readers. Gates has cataloged the symptoms manifested by one hundred cases of reading disability in the following way:

1. Nervous tensions and habits such as stuttering, nail biting, restlessness, insomnia, and pathological illness—ten cases;
2. Putting on a bold front as a defense reaction, loud talk, defiant conduct, sullenness—sixteen cases;
3. Retreat reactions such as withdrawal from ordinary association, joining outside gangs and truancy—fourteen cases;
4. Counterattack such as making mischief in school, playing practical jokes, thefts, destructiveness, cruelty, bullying—eighteen cases;
5. Withdrawing reactions including mind wandering and daydreaming—twenty-six cases;
6. Extreme self-consciousness, becoming easily injured, blushing, developing peculiar fads and frills and eccentricities, inferiority feelings—thirty-five cases;
7. Give-up or submissive adjustments as shown by inattentiveness, indifference, apparent laziness—thirty-three cases. (79)

The full import of the relationship between emotional disturbances and reading problems is evident when one considers its frequency. Over three decades ago, Witty reported that about half the children coming to the psychoeducation clinic at Northwestern University suffered from "fears and anxieties so serious and so far-reaching that no program of re-education could possibly succeed which did not aim to re-establish self confidence and to remove anxieties."(80) Gates' estimate was still higher. He believed that seventy-five percent of poor readers show evidence of personality maladjustment.(81) More recently, Harris stated that close to one hundred percent of the children seen in the Queens College Educational Clinic show some kind of emotional difficulty.(82)

Many reading authorities concur in the belief that most of the emotional disturbance seen among disabled readers is a result of reading failure rather than the cause of it. The child who reads poorly not only feels inadequate because he knows he is not doing as well as his classmates, but often is subjected to numerous social pressures. Teachers may unwittingly remark, "I don't think you'll ever learn" or "Why must you be so lazy?" Classmates don't hesitate to label him a dumbbell, and his parents may make home life intolerable by their unsympathetic reactions to his failure. Preston, for example, reports that parents of one hundred poor readers of normal intelligence called their children lazy, stupid, dumb, boob, dunce, simp, bonehead, big sissy, blockhead, fool, idiot and feebleminded.(83) Certainly it is not difficult to see why disabled readers become emotionally disturbed.

Although most disabled readers are emotionally disturbed because of their frustrations and failure, one must not overlook those children whose emotional difficulties came from other sources. For example, a child who is labeled lard, fats, slats, or beanpole because of his physical stature is subjected to stress. Worse still is the emotional scarring suffered by the youngster born with crooked teeth, facial birthmarks, or strabismus. These conditions and many others can have an adverse effect on the emotional health of a child.(84)

Those of us who have sat through a movie when the picture was out of focus can appreciate the emotional disturbance children with visual defects experience when they constantly have to contend with distorted images. On occasion, all of us have heard a defective sound track that proved intolerable after only a few minutes of unintelligibility. Think of what the auditorily impaired child experiences.

Endocrinologists tell us that hyperthyroidism frequently manifests itself in nervousness and emotional instability. Similarly, it is not unusual to find irritability and irascibility accompanying brain damage. Certainly a child suffering from undernourishment, lack of rest, chronic infections, and the like, finds nothing in his poor health to improve his disposition.

Many emotionally disturbed children are victims of unfortunate home conditions. A child may be rejected because he was unwanted. Such a child may fail in reading as a means of securing attention from parents who otherwise are indifferent to him. On the other hand, a child may be the victim of oversolicitousness. Since busy teachers are not able to give undivided attention to a child who was babied and pampered, reading failure is inevitable. Certain children do not want to learn how to read since they realize that learning how to read is associated with growing up. The last thing they want to do is to grow up.

Youngsters who come from broken homes or homes in which dissension and inconsistent discipline are prevalent are in a perpetual state of emotional turmoil. Very often unwitting parents subject children to invidious comparisons. If a child is forced to compete with a superior sibling or neighborhood prodigy, he frequently develops feelings of inferiority resulting in a give-up or submissive attitude which spells defeat before he begins.

Because the home plays such an important role in the emotional life of a child, teachers of emotionally unstable children will want to visit with parents. Once a teacher pinpoints a possible cause, or causes, of the problem, he should not hesitate to talk to the parents about it. More often than not, parents will initiate changes if they believe their children will benefit. (See Appendix D for a letter of suggestions which can be given to parents.)

Teachers, too, may be guilty of some of the same shortcomings characterizing parents. They may reject certain children or make unfavorable comparisons between brothers and sisters. Sarcastic remarks by the teacher, such as "How can you be so stupid?" and "I don't know why I waste my time on you," may have traumatic effects on a child. An unpleasant teaching personality accompanied by uninspired teaching and the use of deadening drills has driven many children into maladjustment. Other children suffer maladjustment because they are forced into reading before they have the requisite readiness. Frustration and failure do not augur well for future mental health.

There are many ways for classroom teachers to detect emotionally disturbed children. Perhaps the most simple and practical way is daily observation of the child's overt behavior. In this connection the teacher would find a listing of the symptoms of emotional difficulty helpful. (See pages 130-132 for this listing.) When employing such a list, however, the teacher should realize that he is dealing with a whole child. Consequently, each symptom must be considered in light of the child's total personality.

A question employed by Paul A. Witty which frequently helps in uncovering the causes of an emotional problem is "If you had one wish which might come true, what would be your wish?"(85) Older students can be asked to write responses to questions such as "What Bothers You?" and "What Things Do You Worry About?"

Psychologists are trained to employ a number of methods and techniques for studying personality. Most clinical psychologists give projective tests such as the Rorschach and the Thematic Apperception Test. Other tests that may be given include the Michigan Picture Test, the Children's Apperception Test, and the Fehrenbach Sentence Completion Test.

Certain personality tests can be used by classroom teachers who wish to supplement their subjective judgment of children's personality patterns. These include Mental Health Analysis Test,(86) California Test of Personality,(87) and Aspects of Personality.(88) When employing such tests teachers should realize that children often answer questions in a way they feel will be pleasing to parents or teachers. Teachers also should consider that poor readers may misinterpret questions. Reading the questions aloud for the child is not recommended either, since tests are not standardized in this way and the norms would be inapplicable.

HOME ENVIRONMENT

As early as 1933, Ladd(89) reported that homes of lower socio-economic status were associated with retarded readers. Current research shows that reading retardation among culturally disadvantaged children, many of whom are from homes of low socioeconomic status, is massive. This is understandable. Since reading is a process of bringing meaning to the printed page, a child needs a good home environment, one that is experientially enriching. The disadvantaged child knows no such home. His home provides few, if any, stimulating experiences. His parents do not read, and the language he hears is inadequate. He is not read to, he has no opportunity to take trips, to attend a nursery, or go to summer camp. Children from a home such as this have not learned to think verbally and to express themselves with fluency. Reading for them is a formidable task.

A number of unfavorable parent-child relationships (ambitious and dominating parents, overly solicitous parents, parents who reject the child or make invidious comparisons, etc.) which were discussed in connection with emotional maladjustment on pages 52-55 are also part of the total picture. Research by Stewart,(90) Missildine,(91) Seigler and Gynther,(92) and many others, support the thesis that the emotional climate of the home has a pronounced effect on a child's academic success. (See Home Inventory, chapter 5.)

INTELLECTUAL DEVELOPMENT

Thorndike(93) regarded reading as a thinking process. Consider the following: A child who reads well must be capable of sustaining attention, he must be able to remember what he has read, he must discern likenesses and differences, he must have a good meaning vocabulary, he must be able to follow a sequence of events and anticipate outcomes, he must be able to evaluate what he has read, etc. There is little doubt that intelligence and reading are positively related.

According to Witty and Kopel,(94) children who have I.Q.'s under fifty are generally regarded as unable to learn how to read. Those with I.Q.'s between fifty and seventy are limited to fourth-grade achievement at best. Most readers, according to these same authors, "are sufficiently bright to read satisfactorily if appropriate and attainable goals are provided and if there is sound motivation."

With children in the elementary grades, the following correlations between reading test scores and the California Test of Mental Maturity have been reported.

language factors with Thorndike-McCall Reading Test .... .824
nonlanguage factors with Thorndike-McCall Reading Test .... .557

language factors with Gates Silent Reading Test, type A .... .805
nonlangauge factors with Gates Silent Reading Test, type A .... .359

language factors with Gates Silent Reading Test, type B .... .799
nonlanguage factors with Gates Silent Reading Test, type B .... .413

language factors with Gates Silent Reading Test, type D .... .844
nonlanguage factors with Gates Silent Reading Test, type D .... .514 (95)

From these and other investigations, it is obvious that although the correlation between reading comprehension tests and group intelligence tests is positive, a one-to-one ratio does not exist. No two abilities are perfectly correlated. What is more, reading and intelligence test scores invariably are standardized on samples drawn from different populations, a factor making valid comparison impossible.

Care must be exercised in selecting an intelligence test for a poor reader. As stated in chapter 2, many intelligence tests are heavily weighted with verbal elements and therefore are not valid for a retarded reader. Another factor worth considering, particularly with group intelligence tests, is that a poor reader often becomes completely discouraged because of continued failure and frustration. He develops a defeatist attitude which easily can invalidate intelligence test scores. Many disabled readers with this attitude take tests in a perfunctory manner. This is particularly true when group measurements are used; therefore, pupils with intelligence quotients of seventy-five or lower, and those showing a variability of ten or more points on successive administrations, should be given an individual intelligence test by a trained examiner.

Even with individual intelligence tests like the Stanford-Binet and Wechsler Intelligence Scale for Children, caution is still necessary. Bond and Fay report that retarded readers do considerably poorer on the Stanford-Binet than do children of equal ability who have no reading problem.(96) Notwithstanding this indictment, Clymer's study suggests that the best measure of mental ability to be used with retarded readers is the Stanford-Binet.(97)

Minimum mental ages also have been set up for success in first-grade reading. Early researchers, Morphett and Washburne,(98) believed that six to six years six months was optimum. A few years later, Gates(99) challenged these figures. He contended that determination of an optimum mental age for beginning reading was difficult to arrive at because teachers vary in their ability to meet individual differences. They also differ widely in the methods, procedures, and materials they employ.

Recent studies support the contention that no one mental age can be considered as the criterion for beginning reading with all children. Although mental age is one of the major growth factors which contribute to success in beginning reading, it must be remembered that physical, emotional, and social growths are as important as mental development.

There is need for caution when using intelligence tests. Some of the reasons that are given by Strang(100) are—

1. Intelligence tests measure the results of an interaction between a pupil's heredity and his environment. They do not measure an innate learning ability but represent developed ability. Malnutrition, lack of intellectual stimulation, and low reading achievement can affect intelligence test results adversely.
2. Intelligence tests show how an individual functioned at the time he took the test.
3. The scores an individual attains on an intelligence test fluctuate from test to test. Between the ages of three and ten I.Q. scores may change more than fifteen points. The reliability of intelligence tests is not high enough for individual diagnosis.
4. Intelligence tests may have a serious lack of validity, especially above the age of thirteen.
5. Errors in interpretation may result if students' cultural background is not considered. Especially questionable is the suitability and validity of intelligence tests for Negroes and other minority groups.
6. Language proficiency must be considered in interpreting intelligence tests. Students' cultural background and educational experiences must not be overlooked when interpreting test results. Children from non-English-speaking homes are likely to show retarded language development.
7. Practice and/or coaching may raise scores attained on intelligence tests.

SUMMARY

The causes of reading failure are many and complex. Almost always a matrix of factors is involved. Good teachers, as a result, must be good detectives. They must be alert to any and all symptoms indicating the presence of factors that are inimical to learning. Questions such as the following provide teachers with the proper orientation. Are these children sufficiently mature to be exposed to formal reading instructions?

Do my pupils have the interest that is essential to reading growth? Do they have normal vision and hearing? How is their general health? Are they alert and full of life? Are they suffering from any emotional disturbances?

The teacher must always do what he can to minimize any hazards to learning as soon as he uncovers them. He makes, for example, special seating arrangements for a nearsighted or auditorily impaired child. He provides special understanding and warmth when an emotionally disturbed child is involved. He often calls on other school specialists for help. Perhaps the school has a speech therapist, a psychologist, or a doctor who can render valuable assistance. When these measures are not sufficient, parents should be alerted and the assistance of out-of-school specialists solicited.

PROBLEMS FOR ORAL AND WRITTEN DISCUSSION

1. Discuss emotional maladjustment and its relationship to a reading disability.
2. Summarize and evaluate one or more of the references listed at the end of the chapter.
3. Describe the services a teacher could receive from a special teacher of reading, a school psychologist, an optometrist, a social worker.
4. Discuss the uses of group intelligence tests by the classroom teacher in relation to reading.
5. Describe the compensatory school environment a teacher can provide for each of the noneducational hazards described in this chapter.

REFERENCES

1. HELEN ROBINSON, *Why Pupils Fail in Reading* (Chicago: University of Chicago Press, 1946).
2. NATHAN FLAX, "Problems in Relating Visual Function to Reading Disorder," *American Journal of Optometry* 47 (1970):366-371.
3. EMMETT A. BETTS, "Visual Aids in Remedial Reading," *Educational Screen* 15 (1936):108-110.
4. THOMAS EAMES, "A Frequency Study of Physical Handicaps in Reading Disability and Unselected Groups," *Journal of Educational Research* 29 (1936):2.
5. L. P. FARRIS, "Visual Defects as Factors Influencing Achievement in Reading," *California Journal of Secondary Education* 10 (1934):51.
6. L. M. BARTLETT, *The Relation of Visual Defects to Reading Ability*, doctor's dissertation, University of Michigan, 1954.
7. THOMAS EAMES, "Comparison of Eye Conditions among 1000 Reading Failures, 500 Ophthalmic Patients and 150 Unselected Children," *American Journal of Ophthalmology* 31 (1948):717.
8. ROBINSON, op. cit., p. 136.

9. H. L. HULSMAN, "Visual Factors in Reading with Implication for Teaching," *American Journal of Ophthalmology* 36 (1953):1585.
10. M. J. HIRSCH, "The Relationship of School Achievement and Visual Anomalies," *American Journal of Optometry* 32 (1955):262-70.
11. EMMETT BETTS, *The Prevention and Correction of Reading Difficulties* (Evanston, Ill.: Row, Peterson, 1936), p. 156.
12. EAMES, "A Frequency Study of Physical Handicaps in Reading Disability and Unselected Groups," op. cit., p. 3.
13. EAMES, "Comparison of Eye Conditions among 1000 Reading Failures, 500 Ophthalmic Patients and 150 Unselected Children," op. cit., pp. 713-717.
14. D. E. SWANSON and J. TIFFIN, "Betts' Physiological Approach to the Analysis of Reading Disabilities as Applied to the College Level," *Journal of Educational Research* 29 (1936):447-448.
15. PAUL WITTY and DAVID KOPEL, "Factors Associated with the Etiology of Reading Disability," *Journal of Educational Research* 29 (1936): 449-459.
16. H. ROMAINE, "Reading Difficulties and Eye Defects," *Sight Saving Review* 19 (1949):98.
17. D. L. CLELAND, "Seeing and Reading," *American Journal of Optometry* 30 (1953):476.
18. DELWYN SCHUBERT and HOWARD WALTON, "Effects of Induced Astigmatism," *The Reading Teacher* 21 (1968):547-551.
19. W. F. DEARBORN and I. H. ANDERSON, "Aniseikonia as Related to Disability in Reading," *Journal of Experimental Psychology* 23 (1938): 559-577.
20. ROMAINE, op. cit., p. 98.
21. CLELAND, op. cit., p. 477.
22. G. E. PARK and C. BURRI, "The Relationship of Various Eye Conditions and Reading Achievement," *Journal of Educational Psychology* 34 (1943):290-299.
23. G. E. PARK, "Reading Difficulty (Dyslexia) from an Ophthalmic Point of View," *American Journal of Ophthalmology* 31 (1948):34.
24. R. W. SABATINI, "Behavior of Vision," *Optometric Weekly* 44 (1953): 1727.
25. THOMAS EAMES, "A Comparison of the Ocular Characteristics of Unselected and Reading Disability Groups," *Journal of Educational Research* 25 (1932):214.
26. HULSMAN, op. cit., p. 1585.
27. LUELLA COLE, *The Improvement of Reading* (New York: Farrar and Rinehart, 1938), p. 282.
28. GEORGE BERNER and DOROTHY BERNER, "Reading Difficulties in Children," *Archives of Ophthalmology* 20 (1938):830.
29. GEORGE PARK and CLARA BURRI, "Eye Maturation and Reading Difficulties," *Journal of Educational Psychology* 34 (1943):538-539.
30. O. NUGENT and VIVIENNE ILG, "Newer Developments in Orthoptics with Reference to Reading Problems," *Archives of Physical Therapy* 22 (1941):225-232.
31. A. M. SKEFFINGTON, "What 'Learning Lenses' Mean in the Beginning School Grades—and Why," *The Optometric Weekly* (September 6, 1962).

32. DARELL HARMON, *Notes on a Dynamic Theory of Vision* (privately published, 1958).
33. GLENN MCCRACKEN, "New Castle Reading Experiment," *Elementary English* 30 (1953):13-21.
34. GEORGE SPACHE, *Toward Better Reading* (Champaign, Ill.: Garrard Publishing Co., 1963), p. 111.
35. DOROTHEA EWERS, "Relations Between Auditory Abilities and Reading Abilities," *Journal of Experimental Education* 18 (1950):239-262.
36. SPACHE, op. cit., p. 43.
37. Ibid., p. 43.
38. J. A. FIGUREL, ed., "Challenge and Experiment in Reading," *Proceedings of the International Reading Association*, 1962, p. 7.
39. LOUISE SCOTT and J. THOMPSON, *Talking Time* (Manchester, Mo.: Webster Publishing, 1951).
40. GEORGE PARK ET AL., "Biologic Changes Associated with Dyslexia," *Archives of Pediatrics* 72 (1955):71-84.
41. NICHOLAS CRISCUOLO, "Sex Influences on Reading," *The Reading Teacher* 21 (1968):762.
42. PATRICIA C. SEXTON, *Education and Income* (New York: Viking Press, 1961).
43. THOMAS EAMES, "Incidence of Diseases among Reading Failures and Non-Failures," *Journal of Pediatrics* 33 (1948):615.
44. GEORGE PARK, "Dyslexia from a Physical Viewpoint," *Illinois Medical Journal* 97 (1950):31
45. NEVIN SCRIMSHAW, "Infant Malnutrition and Adult Learning," *Saturday Review* 84 (1968):64-66.
46. PARK, "Dyslexia from a Physical Viewpoint," op. cit., p. 31.
47. "Slow Thyroid Can Slow Child's Reading Ability," *Science News Letter* 68 (1955):8.
48. SAMUEL ORTON, *Reading, Writing and Speech Problems in Children* (New York: Norton, 1937).
49. WALTER DEARBORN, "Structural Factors Which Condition Special Disability in Reading," *Proceedings of the American Association of Mental Deficiency* 38 (1933):266-283.
50. CARL DELACATO, *The Treatment and Prevention of Reading Problems* (Springfield, Ill.: Charles C Thomas, Publisher, 1959), p. 6.
51. DELWYN SCHUBERT, *The Doctor Eyes the Poor Reader* (Springfield, Ill.: Charles C Thomas, Publisher, 1957), p. 24.
52. LOIS BING, "A Critical Analysis of the Literature on Certain Visual Functions Which Seem To Be Related to Reading Achievement," *Journal of American Optometric Association* 22 (1951):454-463.
53. BLAKE CRIDER, "Ocular Dominance: Its Nature, Measurement and Development," unpublished doctor's dissertation, Western Reserve University, reported in *Why Pupils Fail in Reading* by H. Robinson (Chicago: University of Chicago Press, 1946), p. 42.
54. Ibid., p. 42.
55. NATHAN FLAX, "The Clinical Significance of Dominance," *American Journal of Optometry* 43 (1966):566-580.
56. SPACHE, op. cit., p. 117.
57. Ibid., p. 116.

58. I. H. BALOW and B. BALOW, "Lateral Dominance and Reading Achievement in the Second Grade," *American Educational Research Journal* 1 (1964):139-143.

59. HARRY BECK, "The Relationship of Symbol Reversals to Monocular and Binocular Vision," *Peabody Journal of Education* 38 (1960):137-142.

60. LILLIAN BELMONT and H. G. BIRCH, "Lateral Dominance, Lateral Awareness and Reading Disability," *Child Development* 36 (1965): 57-71.

61. R. J. CAPOBIANCO, "Ocular-Manual Laterality and Reading in Adolescent Mental Retardates," *American Journal of Mental Deficiency* 70 (1966):781-785.

62. R. I. COLEMAN and CYNTHIA P. DEUTSCH, "Lateral Dominance and Right-Left Discrimination: A Comparison of Normal and Retarded Readers," *Perceptual and Motor Skills* 19 (1964):43-50.

63. BERNHART DATTNER, VERNAM DAVIS, and CHARLES SMITH, "A Case of Subcortical Visual Verbal Agnosia," *Journal of Nervous and Mental Disorders* 116 (1952):808-811.

64. JAMES HINSHELWOOD, *Congenital Word Blindness* (London: Lewis, 1917).

65. Ibid., p. 53.

66. BERTIL HALLGREN, *Specific Dyslexia* (Copenhagen, Denmark: Munksgaard, 1950), p. 53.

67. KURT GOLDSTEIN, *Aftereffects of Brain Injuries in War* (New York: Grune and Stratton, Inc., 1942), p. 82.

68. ARNOLD GESELL and C. AMATRUDA, *Developmental Diagnosis: Normal and Abnormal Child Development* (New York: Hoeber Medical Books, 1947), p. 248.

69. J. HUGHS, R. LEANDER and G. KETCHUM, "Electroencephalographic Study of Specific Reading Disabilities," *Electroencephalographic and Clinical Neurophysiology* 1 (1949):377-378.

70. MARGARET KENNARD, RALPH RABINOVITCH, and DONALD WEXLER, "Abnormal Electroencephalogram," *Canadian Association Journal* 67 (1952): 332.

71. BOND, op. cit., p. 118.

72. KNUD HERMAN, *Reading Disability: A Medical Study of Word-Blindness and Related Handicaps* (Springfield, Ill.: Charles C Thomas, Publisher, 1961).

73. GEORGE SPACHE, "Interesting Books for the Reading Teacher," *The Reading Teacher* 11 (1962):374.

74. JOHN MONEY, *Reading Disability: Progress and Research Needs in Dyslexia* (Baltimore: Johns Hopkins Press, 1962).

75. GEORGE SPACHE, "Interesting Books for the Reading Teacher," *The Reading Teacher* 18 (1964):239. Reprinted with permission of the author and the International Reading Association.

76. RICHARD B. ADAMS, "Dyslexia: A Discussion of Its Definition," a paper prepared for the Second Meeting of the Federal Government's Attack on Dyslexia (Washington, D. C.: Bureau of Research, U. S. Office of Education, August 9, 1967).

77. SAM V. DAUZAT, "Good Gosh! My Child Has Dyslexia," *The Reading Teacher* 22 (1969):630-633.

78. DONALD SMITH and PATRICIA CARRIGAN, *The Nature of Reading Disability* (New York: Harcourt, Brace and World, Inc., 1959).
79. ARTHUR GATES, "Failure in Reading and Social Maladjustment," *Journal of the National Education Association* 25 (1963):205-206.
80. PAUL WITTY and DAVID KOPEL, *Reading and the Educative Process* (Boston: Ginn and Company, 1939), p. 231.
81. ARTHUR GATES, "The Role of Personality Maladjustments in Reading Disability," *Journal of Genetic Psychology* 59 (1941):77-83.
82. HARRIS, op. cit., p. 264.
83. MARY PRESTON, "The Reaction of Parents to Reading Failure," *Child Development* 10 (1939):173-179.
84. Parts of this section are drawn from D. G. SCHUBERT's "Understanding and Handling Reading-Personality Problems," *Elementary English* (December 1960): 537-539.
85. WITTY and KOPEL, op. cit., 339.
86. CALIFORNIA TEST BUREAU, Monterey, California.
87. Ibid.
88. Ibid.
89. MARGARET LADD, *The Relation of Social, Economic, and Personal Characteristics to Reading Disability* (New York: Bureau of Publications, Teachers College, Columbia University, 1933), p. 81.
90. ROBERT S. STEWART, "Personality Maladjustment and Reading Achievement," *American Journal of Orthopsychiatry* 20 (1950):415.
91. WHITNEY MISSILDINE, "The Emotional Background of 30 Children with Reading Disabilities with Emphasis Upon Its Coercive Elements," *The Nervous Child* 5 (1946):271.
92. HAZEL SEIGLER and MALCOLM GYNTHER, "Reading Ability of Children and Family Harmony," *Journal of Developmental Reading* 4 (Autumn 1960):17-24.
93. EDWARD L. THORNDIKE, "Reading as Reasoning: A Study of Mistakes in Paragraph Reading," in *Readings in Reading*, Delwyn G. Schubert and Theodore L. Torgerson, eds. (New York: Thomas Y. Crowell Co., 1968), pp. 47-57.
94. WITTY and KOPEL, op. cit., p. 228.
95. RUTH STRANG, CONSTANCE McCULLOUGH, and ARTHUR TRAXLER, *Problems in the Improvement of Reading* (New York: McGraw-Hill Book Co., 1955), pp. 74-75.
96. GUY BOND and MILES TINKER, *Reading Difficulties: Their Diagnosis and Correction* (New York: Appleton-Century-Crofts, 1967), p. 90.
97. THEODORE CLYMER, "The Influence of Reading Ability on the Validity of Group Intelligence Tests," unpublished Ph.D. thesis, University of Minnesota, Minneapolis, 1952.
98. MABEL MORPHETT and C. WASHBURNE, "When Should Children Begin to Read?" in *Readings in Reading*, Delwyn G. Schubert and Theodore L. Torgerson, eds. (New York: Thomas Y. Crowell Co., 1968), pp. 90-97.
99. ARTHUR GATES, "The Necessary Mental Age for Beginning Reading," in *Readings in Reading*, Delwyn G. Schubert and Theodore L. Torgerson, eds. (New York: Thomas Y. Crowell Co., 1968), pp. 98-100.
100. RUTH STRANG, *Diagnostic Teaching of Reading*, 2nd ed. (New York: McGraw-Hill Book Co., 1969), pp. 216-218.

SELECTED READINGS

BOND, GUY, and MILES TINKER. *Reading Problems: Their Diagnosis and Correction.* 2nd ed. New York: Appleton-Century-Crofts, 1967, chs. 4-6.

CARTER, HOMER, and DOROTHY McGINNIS. *Diagnosis and Treatment of the Disabled Reader.* New York: The Macmillan Co., 1970, ch. 4.

DECHANT, EMERALD. *Diagnosis and Remediation of Reading Disability.* West Nyack, N. Y.: Parker Publishing Co., Inc., 1968, ch. 3.

FREIRSON, EDWARD, and WALTER BARBE. *Educating Children with Learning Disabilities: Selected Readings.* New York: Appleton-Century-Crofts, 1967, Part IIB.

HARRIS, ALBERT. *How to Increase Reading Ability.* 5th ed. New York: David McKay Co., Inc., 1970, ch. 10.

KARLIN, ROBERT. *Teaching Elementary Reading.* New York: Harcourt Brace Jovanovich, 1971, ch. 10.

OTTO, WAYNE, and RICHARD McMENEMY. *Corrective and Remedial Teaching.* Boston: Houghton Mifflin Co., 1966, ch. 2.

ROBINSON, HELEN. *Why Pupils Fail in Reading.* Chicago: University of Chicago Press. 1946.

STRANG, RUTH. *Diagnostic Teaching of Reading.* 2nd ed. New York: McGraw-Hill Book Co., 1969, ch. 9.

WILSON, ROBERT. *Diagnostic and Remedial Reading.* Columbus, O. Charles E. Merrill, Publisher, 1967, ch. 3.

4

The Developmental Program in Reading

A number of authors have written about developmental reading,(1, 2) but a clear-cut definition of the term *developmental reading* is difficult to find. It is not easy to define something that has as many facets as developmental reading. A brief definition by Schubert is as follows:

> Reading instruction designed to develop systematically the skills and abilities considered essential at each grade level; at the junior and senior high school levels it may involve giving all students one or more courses in reading or giving all students reading instruction in every subject matter area.(3)

Inherent in the foregoing definition is the assumption that every child should develop flexible reading habits that will enable him to read at his maximum potential. Since students vary in ability and rate of learning, a developmental program inescapably includes diagnosis and correction or remediation.

Corrective reading entails "remedial activities carried on by a regular classroom teacher within the framework of regular class instruction."(4) Corrective reading ordinarily is provided for those who have mild difficulties and may involve one pupil, a group of pupils, or the entire class.

Remedial reading instruction consists of "activities taking place outside the framework of class instruction, usually conducted by a special teacher of reading."(5) Since pupils falling into this category are generally those who experience more severe difficulty in reading, the remedial specialist would more likely employ an individual approach to their problems.

BASIC ELEMENTS OF A DEVELOPMENTAL PROGRAM IN READING

1. Reading is not a subject but a process that cuts across the entire curriculum. All teachers regardless of grade level or subject are teachers of reading.

2. The developmental program requires cooperation among all persons involved in pupils' growth. Parents, teachers, counselors, psychologists, medical specialists, etc., must work together as a team.

3. Reading continues throughout the educational life of the individual. It starts during the preschool years and continues into high school and college. Many individuals continue to develop their reading skills throughout their adult life.

4. The developmental program involves the whole child. It must take cognizance of all skills, attitudes, personal, social, and intellectual factors that are directly or indirectly related to learning and the reading process.

5. The developmental program should capitalize on the interrelationships between reading and other communicative skills. It must not treat reading as an isolated activity.

6. The developmental program should employ a variety of methods and approaches to learning, at all times striving to meet the needs of the learner in the most efficient way.

7. The developmental program should employ a vast variety of materials that are designed to meet the needs of the learner in terms of his interests and abilities.

8. The developmental program must strive to develop independent readers who are capable of reading critically.

9. The developmental program must strive to develop independent readers who, throughout their lives, will use reading both as a learning tool and as a recreational activity.

10. The developmental program must strive to help all students reach their maximum reading potential. In this regard, it must take particular cognizance of the culturally disadvantaged and must provide appropriate correction to meet the needs of this group.

11. The developmental program entails continuous evaluation of pupils so that prevention and correction can be given immediately to those experiencing difficulties.

12. The developmental program involves a structured and logical sequence of instruction in the basic reading skills.

THE PRESCHOOL PERIOD

A child is on the road to reading just as soon as he begins to distinguish similarities and differences in the world about him. A baby's excitement when he sees his mother's face, his parents' joy when he listens to their speech, the thrill of baby's first words—all these things are steps leading to the day when printed symbols representing auditory symbols will become meaningful to the child.

There is little doubt that a child's early experiences with printed matter have an influence on his attitude toward books and reading during his early school years. Monroe and Rogers believe that as early as one year a child may give books and magazines attention as objects to be mouthed, manipulated, and dropped.

A year-old infant spends many happy moments of the day in his playpen tearing out magazine pages, crumpling, mouthing, stamping them with his feet until he has surrounded himself with a litter of shredded paper. During such activity he may give momentary attention to a portion of a picture attracted primarily by its brightness. (6)

According to Monroe and Rogers,(7) a child from twelve months to fifteen months of age realizes that books contain pages to be turned and that pictures resemble familiar objects. From fifteen months to eighteen months, he begins to appreciate that books are to be taken care of and that pictures represent both familiar and unfamiliar objects. From eighteen months to twenty-four months, the child learns to turn pages without tearing them. He also recognizes the front and back of a book and that pictures have a top and a bottom. At this age the child derives more and more pleasure from books. He attends to adults who tell stories about the pictures in books, and he begins to appreciate that the language used relates to specific pictures and that one picture leads to another. Gradually, true awareness and appreciation of reading develops.

READING IN THE PRIMARY GRADES

Reading Readiness

In 1931, a carefully controlled study by Washburne and Morphett(8) led them to the conclusion that a mental age of six to six and one-half years was essential for success in beginning reading. In 1962, a study by Roche provided evidence indicating that children who were not ready for reading profit from being given appropriate readiness experiences and that any delay resulting from such training does not affect their later school progress. In spite of these and other studies, the trend has been toward teaching reading to younger and younger children. Many schools are introducing formal reading instruction in kindergarten, and others have urged that reading instruction be given to two-, three-, and four-year-old children. Sipay,(9) with tongue in cheek, has written an entertaining article suggesting that reading instruction be given prenatally.

Most reading specialists agree that there is a substantial correlation between mental age and success in beginning reading. But as pointed out by Gates,(10) one cannot set a specific minimum mental age for beginning reading. Too many factors are involved. Some mature and capable children are ready to read at four or five years of age. The majority are not. Forcing a child into reading prematurely can result in an antipathy for reading. Since delaying initial reading instruction does not appear to be harmful, it would seem better for schools to err on the side of waiting too long to introduce reading than to err on the side of introducing reading too soon.

A good kindergarten experience is of inestimable value to children who might otherwise lack readiness for beginning reading.(11) In a study by Fast(12) it was shown that there is a definite relationship between attending kindergarten and reading progress in the first grade. Children who have had the benefit of kindergarten experiences are better able to sustain attention, follow directions, and adjust to group situations in the primary grades. Such training is particularly vital to children who come from homes that have failed to provide needed verbal stimulation and an appropriate background of experience. Culturally deprived children fall into this category. They may be wise in the ways of street gangs, but beyond this, their cultural horizons come to an abrupt halt. What, then, is more fundamental to a program in reading for this group than the filling in of experiential gaps? If the home has failed to provide the stimulation needed to develop the background requisite to successful reading, the school must do the job— and the earlier this can be done the better. Some of the ways to accomplish the task are as follows:

1. Take pupils on trips and excursions to places of interest.
2. Give experience with concrete objects.
3. Expose pupils to lively bulletin boards and other displays.
4. Label objects.
5. Have pupils make picture collections.
6. Use marionette and puppet shows and other dramatic activities.
7. Expose pupils to choice movies and TV shows.
8. Use filmstrips, slides, and charts.

9. Familiarize pupils with picture dictionaries and illustrated books.
10. Have the pupils guess rhyming words and repeat words and experiences.
11. Read choice selections orally.
12. Discuss experiences and stimulate informal conversation.
13. Use oral directions.

Teachers working with culturally deprived children should make extensive use of experience charts, capitalizing on the children's oral communication. Use also can be made of the Peabody Language Development Kit and the Ginn Language Kit. To enhance visual and auditory perception the *Michigan Successive Discrimination Listening Program* (13) and the *Frostig Program for the Development of Visual Perception*(14) may prove valuable. The latter material, however, should be used with reservations. A study by Rosen indicates that perceptual training with the Frostig material contributes very little to reading achievement. The following is an abstract of the Rosen study:

To investigate the effects, if any, of perceptual training upon selected measures of reading achievement in first grade, 12 experimental classrooms of first-grade pupils, randomly selected, received a 29-day adaptation of the Frostig Program for the Development of Visual Perception while 13 control classes added comparable time to the regular reading instructional program. Analysis of the data revealed statistically significant differences between the treatment groups in most of the post-perceptual capabilities, favoring the experimental groups, without concomitant effects on reading criterion measures. While the total score from the Frostig Developmental Test of Visual Perception appeared to have a strong predictive function regarding first-grade reading, the training of visual perception subskills did not appear to have a significant effect on reading ability at the end of the first-grade year. Additional findings are reported that strongly suggest the need for further research. (15)

In support of the Rosen study, a recent article by Balow(16) evaluates research in this area by stating, "Fully consistent with most of the other experimental investigations reported in the professional literature is the finding that the application of Frostig work sheets for development of visual perception did not produce particular change in reading skills."

Readiness workbooks are still recommended by many teachers, but they no longer enjoy the universal favor they did at one time. Readiness workbooks have been severely criticized as being of limited value in contributing to children's reading readiness. Durrell and Nicholson state:

Although the lessons of the reading readiness books may develop desirable abilities such as language fluency, motor skills and attention to nonword forms and sounds, it is doubtful that they contribute greatly to reading readiness. (17)

In a similar vein Spache states that "despite the widespread dependence upon readiness workbooks, there has been extremely little research demonstrating their supposed values."(18)

Although some forms of immaturity such as myelination of nerve fibers require time, and time alone, teachers need not sit back and wait for readiness to develop. To help immature children develop the motor skills that underlie perceptual ability, teachers will want to acquaint themselves with the unique approaches described by Kephart,(19) Radler and Kephart,(20) and Getman and Kane.(21) However, according to Balow,(22) "While motor and perceptual skills weaknesses are frequently found in learning disabled pupils, there is great likelihood that these are most often simply concomitants without causal relevance; thus the argument cannot depend upon assumed etiologies for learning disabilities." Balow (23) also states, "No experimental study conforming to accepted tenets of research design has been found that demonstrates special effectiveness for any of the physical, motor, or perceptual programs claimed to be useful in the prevention or correction of reading or other learning disabilities."

Immature children can be the bane of a first-grade teacher's existence. It is difficult, if not impossible, to teach reading to children who cannot give sustained attention, cannot get along with others in group situations, cry easily, have temper tantrums, and cannot and will not remain seated. One can appreciate why research has shown it is better to err on the side of waiting too long for reading readiness to develop than to force a child into reading before he profits from it. (See pages 134-135 for a Reading Readiness Checklist.)

Better schools of today employ sensitive screening procedures to detect children who lack the requisite readiness for reading. Informal day-by-day observations by kindergarten and first-grade teachers, combined with reading readiness and intelligence tests, yield valuable data in determining a child's readiness for reading. (See Appendix C for a description of readiness tests.)

The Culturally Disadvantaged

Every year the incidence of cultural deprivation increases. Estimates run as high as one deprived child for every two enrolled in the schools of the fourteen largest cities in the United States.(24) This is a matter of great concern for teachers because teaching reading to the culturally deprived is quite different from teaching reading to the culturally advantaged. Middle-class children, as a whole, do well in school, and retarded reading among the gifted is frequently overlooked because they are likely to score above the norm on reading tests. But the disadvantaged child is destined to experience failure from the very beginning.

Teachers who are trying to improve the reading ability of the culturally disadvantaged should keep in mind that culturally disadvantaged children—

1. have a meager background of experience and are retarded in their conceptual development;
2. possess negative or weak self-concepts;
3. come from homes that have not internalized many of the customs, values, and elements of the majority-group culture;
4. have limited or unrealistic aspirations;
5. tend to have an excess of health and physical problems;
6. are likely to consider doing well in school "sissy stuff" and are in need of strong motivational approaches;
7. are deficient in their speech and language development (this is an especially important factor if bilingualism or inner-city dialects are involved);
8. are deficient in their visual and auditory perception;
9. are, from the first year of school, likely to fall back in their reading until they are a year or more below grade level by the intermediate grades;
10. are likely to read two or three years below grade by the time they reach the secondary schools.

The language of the educationally disadvantaged child is generally informal and restricted. His vocabulary is small, and words are pronounced in a way that makes it difficult for an "outsider" to understand. By the same token, the formal and more complex speech of the teacher is not understood by the child.

Helping the disadvantaged build a vocabulary requires a special technique. The teacher must build a bridge between the child's primary language and that of the school. How this is done is crucial. The you-must-not-say-that approach is not the answer, since it forces the student to reject his nonstandard primary language. Riessman has stated:

One's primary language, because it is primary, is not to be denied lightly, for it is, in very basic ways, one's own self. Asking the disadvantaged child to suppress the language he brings to the learning situation is equivalent to demanding that he suppress his identity, and all the defenses that go with it. . . . (25)

Riessman suggests the Dialect Game. The teacher takes a word she has heard students use—*cool*, for example. She asks them to explain its meaning in their language. They may reply with "You play it cool" and "When the cops are coming you cool it." The teacher then asks how the same things might be said on the radio or TV. Replies may include words such as *calm, casual,* and *collected.* Students react enthusiastically to this approach.

It is evident that the successful teacher of the culturally disadvantaged builds on what the pupil brings to the learning situation rather than taking something away from him. When a first-grade pupil refers to a dog as "bow-wow," the teacher says, "Yes, this is a dog. Dogs say "bow-wow," rather than "No, this is not a 'bow-wow,' it is a dog."

Poor auditory discrimination is a serious impediment to the language development of the culturally disadvantaged. Unfortunately, auditory discrimination does not respond to training as easily as visual discrimination.(26) Feldman and Deutsch report accomplishing very little in their attempts to improve the auditory discrimination of Negro children who were reading disability cases.(27)

It is important for teachers to realize that reading materials found in many schools are completely foreign to culturally disadvantaged children. They care little about Dick and Jane and the little red hen. What interest them are stories that relate to their own experiences and backgrounds. Needless to say, many teachers have found the language experience approach helpful in this regard. Other teachers have had success with commercial materials designed to meet the needs of the culturally disadvantaged. Among these are: *Lift Off to Reading* (Science Research Associates), *Reading in High Gear* (Science Research Associates), and the *Miami Linguistic Readers* (D. C. Heath and Co.). *Reading in High Gear* is written for the junior or senior high school student; *Lift Off to Reading* and the *Miami Linguistic Readers* are designed for younger children.

Following is a list of professional publications that are of value to teachers of the culturally disadvantaged:

BEREITER, CARL, and SIEGFRIED ENGLEMANN. *Teaching Disadvantaged Children in the Preschool.* Englewood Cliffs, N. J.: Prentice-Hall, Inc., 1966.

FROST, JOE L., and GLENN R. HAWKES. *The Disadvantaged Child: Issues and Innovations.* Boston: Houghton Mifflin Co., 1966.

GOWAN, JOHN C., and GEORGE D. DEMOS, eds. *The Disadvantaged and Potential Dropout.* Springfield, Ill.: Charles C Thomas, Publisher, 1966.

HORN, THOMAS. *Reading for the Disadvantaged: Problems of Linguistically Different Learners.* Newark, Del.: International Reading Association, 1970.

LORETAN, JOSEPH O., and SHELLEY UMANS. *Teaching the Disadvantaged.* New York: Teachers College, Columbia University, 1966.

REISMAN, FRANK. *The Culturally Deprived Child.* New York: Harper and Row, 1962.

SPACHE, GEORGE D. *Good Reading for the Disadvantaged Reader.* Champaign, Ill.: Garrard Publishing Co., 1970.

STROM, ROBERT D. *Teaching in the Slum School.* Columbus, O.: Charles E. Merrill, Publisher, 1965.

TABA, HILDA, and DEBORAH ELKINS. *Teaching Strategies for the Culturally Disadvantaged.* Skokie, Ill.: Rand McNally & Co., 1966.

WEBSTER, S. W., ed. *The Disadvantaged Learner: Knowing, Understanding, Educating.* San Francisco: Chandler Publishing Co., 1966.

ZINTZ, MILES. *Education Across Cultures.* Dubuque, Ia.: Kendall/Hunt Publishing Co., 1969.

METHODS

There is no one best method for teaching beginning reading. However, one method may have some features that are more effective with certain children. Among the more widely used programs are the language experience, linguistics, alphabet approaches, words in color, individualized reading, and the basal reading approach.

Language-Experience Method

The language-experience approach is based on the interrelationship and interdependence between listening, speaking, writing, and reading. As R. Van Allen,(28) the chief proponent of the approach, has phrased it:

What I can think about, I can talk about.
What I can say, I can write.
What I can write, I can read.
I can read what I write and what other people can write for me to read.

Since the language-experience approach does not separate reading instruction from the development of listening, speaking, and writing skills, it is possible to capitalize on children's backgrounds of experience in developing instructional materials. From the very beginning, children are encouraged to express themselves orally while working with various media—paint, clay, drawing, etc. Initially, the teacher records thoughts as dictated by the child. After reading his own stories, the child moves naturally into reading other children's stories. The teacher works with individual children and with small groups of children. Soon they express a desire to write their own stories. This is encouraged by the teacher who gives all the help needed. The stories (some of these may be very short) are illustrated and are bound together into a book. Sometimes several students contribute materials which become books devoted to things such as airplanes, pets, and summer vacations. Books become everyone's reading property.

Stauffer(29) and Spache(30) have written about the limitations of the language-experience approach. Some of the limitations discussed by the latter are (1) Continuing the language-experience approach beyond the primary grades may retard a child's reading development; (2) There is doubt regarding children's ability to make a transition from reading their own language to reading the language of others; (3) Since children's listening, speaking, writing, and reading vocabularies vary in size and depth, there is some doubt as to the truth of the assumption "What I can think about, I can talk about. What I say, I can write. What I can write, I can read"; (4) Organizational problems are significant: How do teachers record and evaluate the various materials used? How do teachers measure and evaluate the development of children's reading skills? What checklists of reading skills do teachers use?; (5) Many educational experiments refute the assumption inherent in the language-experience approach that incidental learning of skills is equal to or superior to direct or planned presentations.

Linguistics

Linguists are concerned with grapheme-phoneme relationships. They believe that children find meaning when they learn to associate sounds (phonemes) with appropriately matched printed symbols (graphemes). Learning to read consists of responding to patterns of letters. In other words, reading is a matter of turning graphic symbols into speech sounds.

The ideas of the late Leonard Bloomfield, an outstanding linguist, were published in 1961.(31) It was Bloomfield's belief that teachers should begin reading instruction by teaching the sounds of the letters in the alphabet, both upper- and lower-case. In his book *Let's Read*, initial reading experiences exclude English words that are not phonetic, that is, those for which the grapheme-phoneme relationship is unreliable. Later, as the child develops competence, words that represent inconsistencies in the English writing system are introduced. In Part I of *Let's Read*, words that fit a consonant-vowel-consonant pattern are found: *man, pin, but,* and so on. These evolve into lists of words. In the case of *man*, the list becomes *man, ran, fan, van*. Accompanying *pin*, the words which appear are *bin, din, fin, kin*. Simple sentences employing learned words are provided: A man ran a tan van. In Part II of *Let's Read,* consonant blends are introduced. Subsequent parts and lessons are devoted to carefully planned modifications of a sequential nature. As instruction continues, meaningful usage of words that have been learned changes from short sentences to paragraphs; and paragraphs eventually become stories which are eight to ten pages in length.

A number of basal reading series based on linguistic principles have been introduced since 1961. In commenting on these, Harris states:

> They have in common agreement that "decoding" or translating the printed forms into their spoken equivalents is the first and most important goal of a reading program. Most of them also agree on using whole words and the principle of minimal variation, rather than a synthetic sounding-blending procedure. It is difficult to discern an important difference between a linguistic reading program and a whole-word phonics program. (32)

Alphabet Approaches

It should be common knowledge that inconsistencies in English spelling complicate the reading process. English might be classed paradoxically as an unphonetic, phonetic language. It has twenty-six letters to represent some forty-four sounds. And three of the twenty-six letters—*c, q,* and *x*—have little or no value.

According to Hildreth,(33) of the 350 commonest words in the English language, fewer than 200 can be written as they sound, e.g., *again, always, before, where,* and so forth. Approximately one-third of all the words in an unabridged dictionary have one or more silent letters in them. Is it any wonder that there have been attempts to develop and promote a phonetically regular alphabet? Benjamin Franklin proposed one. In more recent years it was George Bernard Shaw who strongly advocated a more (fonetic) approach to spelling because of the time and trouble it would save. It was he who humorously pointed out that the word *fish* could be spelled "ghoti." His reasoning was as follows: The letters *gh* have the sound of an *f* in the word *enough;* the vowel *o* has a short-*i* sound in the word *women;* and the letters *ti* sound like the consonant digraph *sh* in the word *nation.*

Initial teaching alphabet

The alphabetic scheme that has had the largest following was introduced in Great Britain during the early 1960s by Sir James Pitman. Initially, it was referred to as the Augmented Roman Alphabet (ARA). More recently, the name has been changed to Initial Teaching Alphabet (ITA).

ITA recognizes forty-four phonemes in the English language, and it provides one symbol for each of these sounds. To minimize confusion between capital and lowercase letters such as *B* and *b* it employs capitals that are enlarged versions of lowercase letters. With the exception of *q* and *x* (these letters are completely eliminated), the beginning reader of ITA is introduced to only lowercase letters of our alphabet plus twenty augmentations. Primarily, the augmentations involve two conventional letters that have been linked together with most of the changes occurring in the bottom or middle parts. Since the tops of letters provide more clues to recognition than the lower parts, reading ITA doesn't prove very difficult. As soon as children have learned the sounds of the forty-four symbols, they are on their way. There is no silent-*e* rule to remember or no double-vowel rule to apply. Rules or generalizations are not needed.

In a study reported by Downing,(34) British children exposed to ITA were, after two years, significantly better readers than children who were taught by exposure to traditional orthography. The ITA groups learned to read more easily; they were better spellers; and they were more creative and fluent in their writing. In a later report, Downing and Rose(35) pointed out the following advantages of ITA: It lightens the load of learning to read; it requires fewer whole-word representations to be learned; it simplifies spelling and reduces the complexity of phonic symbols. Hilaire and Thompson(36) reported that children participating in their ITA study "conceptualized stories better, developed more imaginative story lines and showed more original and flexible use of the words they selected."

Cutts,(37) who was not convinced of the merits of ITA, pointed to several factors that make appraisal of its validity doubtful: not knowing the long-range effects of ITA; the role of the Hawthorne effect in ITA experiments; difficulties some children may have in making a transition from ITA to traditional orthography; and the fact that studies show that the importance of an early start in reading is not particularly advantageous.

Words in Color

Words in Color, designed by Gattengo,(38) uses a color scheme (thirty-nine different colors are involved) to represent forty-seven different sounds, twenty of which are vowel sounds, and the remainder, consonant sounds. Regardless of the spelling used to represent a given sound (phoneme), the same color is used consistently. For example, the *ph* in the word *phone* would have the same color as the *f* in the word *fox*. It is the color, therefore, and not the grapheme that is of greatest help to a beginner. Unfortunately, the only color printing that a child sees is found on twenty-nine wall charts, twenty-one of which contain words but no sentences. No sustained reading material in the color code is available, and it is rather improbable that a teacher would write a story on the board since it would require a tremendous array of multicolored chalk. At the time of this writing, no controlled research is available to determine the value of this system.

Diacritical marking system

Edward Fry evolved a marking scheme to help in the pronunciation of graphemes. His Diacritical Marking System (DMS) is felt to be superior to the ITA because of greater consistency in phoneme-grapheme relationships. Also, transfer problems are minimized. Fry's system uses letters found on a standard typewriter so that basic orthography is retained. In 1964, Fry compared ITA with two basal approaches, both identical except for his diacritical marking system which was employed with one of them. No significant differences in reading were found among the three first-grade groups involved in the experiment.(39)

Individualized Reading

Individualized reading is based on the concepts evolved by Willard C. Olson.(40) These include self-seeking behavior, self-selection, and self-pacing. Olson contends that children have an inherent maturational drive and pattern of development which enable them to select wisely materials suited to their needs, interests, and maturational level. As children proceed at their own rate with materials and instruction provided by the teacher, pacing is achieved.

The following outline provides a brief description of some of the more important aspects of individualized reading.

1. The teacher secures a wide variety of reading materials. These materials vary in level of difficulty and in interest appeal. Trade books, basals, newspapers, pamphlets, magazines, and reference books may be included.
2. Children choose what they want to read.
3. The teacher holds individual conferences with the children. During the conference (the time involved usually is five to ten minutes), the teacher discusses with the child the material being read. By having the pupil read aloud, the teacher is able to note reading errors. Phonic principles are taught, and comprehension is checked by previously prepared questions. Some teachers suggest other books to be read in an effort to help the child's reading progress.

4. The teacher and the child keep detailed records. For the teacher these may include things such as the date, the name of the book being read, the particular page involved, etc.
5. Special needs and interest groupings are utilized. All groups are temporary and are dissolved when they have served their function.
6. Evaluation is made in terms of quantity and quality of the books read. Attitudinal changes about books and reading are considered. Standardized tests are not used very extensively.

Those who are enthusiastic about individualized reading contend that it has the following advantages. Children read more and their interests are given consideration; the teacher discovers the needs of each child and provides a reading skills program designed to meet those needs; the plan is equally successful with classes of differing size and with classes having children of differing abilities; and parents as well as their children are pleased with the plan.(41)

Sartain(42) lists certain dangers in the approach. These include (1) A lack of opportunity for teaching new words and concepts needed before reading is begun; (2) Teaching a systematic and complete program of skills and identifying individual difficulties is hardly possible when the teacher has only a few working minutes weekly with each child; (3) Skills taught for short periods and not systematically reviewed may lack permanence; (4) Limited group interaction lessens the opportunity for critical thinking and literary appreciation; (5) Slow-learning pupils who do not respond to independent work become restless and waste their time; (6) Working with individuals rather than groups of children with similar needs is inefficient timewise; and (7) Conscientious teachers are frustrated by individual-conference demands, while careless teachers are provided with no direction.

Basal Readers

This is the most widely used approach to the teaching of reading in the United States. Recent surveys reveal that the basal reader is used in more than ninety percent of the schools. In general, basal readers are designed for grades one through six, although some have been developed for the secondary school. The typical series starts with a readiness book, preprimers, primers, and a first reader. At the second- and third-grade levels, two texts a year are provided. At grade four and beyond, one text a year is furnished. Workbooks accompany each textbook. A teacher's manual and additional supplementary materials, such as filmstrips and recordings, are available.

Basal programs provide a logical and sequential development of material that seeks to achieve mastery of basic reading skills. Strict vocabulary control, especially at the primary level, is adhered to. As a result, the language of basal readers has been considered colorless, boring, and unduly repetitious. Humorous stories of the "look, look, look" and "see, see, see" variety are widely circulated.

Using basal readers and workbooks in a stereotyped manner fails to meet individual differences present within a classroom. But even if used intelligently (many teachers admit that they never bother reading the teacher's manual), one cannot expect basal readers that are limited to one grade level to prove effective with all pupils in the class. Special methods and special supplementary materials are also needed in a sound reading program.

Because of their wide acceptance, it is interesting and valuable to learn exactly how schools employ basal readers. In a questionnaire study titled "How Are Basal Readers Used?" Ralph Staiger(43) found that of the 474 schools responding, roughly half were using a single series of readers. About 17 percent were varying their procedures so it was doubtful if a one-series plan was being used. Two series of readers were used cobasally by 20 percent of the schools; 5.7 percent used three series cobasally; and 5.1 percent used more than three series.

Workbooks accompanying basal readers were used widely. According to Staiger, of those schools employing a single basal, 91.4 percent of them used workbooks, while only 76.3 percent of schools employing cobasals and 49.0 percent of schools employing tribasals used workbooks.

Some of the most widely used basal reading programs have been by Allyn and Bacon, Incorporated; American Book Company; Ginn and Company; Harper and Row, Publishers; Holt, Rinehart and Winston, Incorporated; J. B. Lippincott Company; Lyons and Carnahan; The Macmillan Company; and Scott, Foresman and Company.

According to Spache,(44) those who support the basal reading program (most reading specialists do) agree on advantages such as the following: Basal reading series provide systematic guidance in the development of reading skills; use materials based on children's interests and common experiences; offer a program greatly superior to what most teachers could create; give techniques and provide materials for determining initial reading readiness and for proceeding step-by-step through easy stages; use a basic or core vocabulary essential to beginning or subsequent reading; provide materials carefully scaled in difficulty and sequentially arranged to facilitate learning; use material that is exemplary in terms of typography, format, and physical readability; and include a variety of different kinds of reading experiences—recreational and work-study reading, poetry and prose, factual and fictional, and so on—that extend children's ideas and knowledge in many areas.

Spache(45) and various writers he quotes mention the following limitations of the basal reader approach: Basal reading series fail to inform teachers of the true purposes of the reading readiness program; they offer readiness training materials that are of doubtful validity; they contain many stories that are uninteresting; they fail to prepare children for reading in the content fields; they have workbooks of questionable value; and they are too restrictive in their control of vocabulary. Other limitations, according to Sartain,(46) are a result of teacher misuse. For example, all children are expected to read the same stories at the same rate; the reading program is limited to one series of basal readers; whole groups of children are expected to follow in their books while individual pupils read aloud; teachers fail to utilize the skills program of the teacher's manual to meet children's varying needs.

PRIMARY READING SKILLS

Phonics

Everyone agrees that phonics, or phonetic analysis,* should be emphasized in the primary grades. However, there is disagreement as to how early this instruction should begin and the emphasis it should receive. In 1937, Dolch and Bloomster(47) correlated mental age with the ability to apply phonic principles. They concluded that a mental age of seven was minimal to phonic success.

The influence of the Dolch-Bloomster research was widespread. For many years basal readers placed major emphasis on phonics in the second and third grades, minimizing it in the first grade. Today, however, the situation is somewhat different. Many reading specialists are favoring an early introduction of phonics.

Synthetic and analytic phonics

Phonic methods fall into two categories: the synthetic and the analytic.† Synthetic phonics involves building up words from their parts; analytic phonics (sometimes called intrinsic phonics) involves discovering natural sound units within words.

---

*For definition of phonics and related terminology, see Appendix A1.
†Also see pages 202-224.

Synthetic phonics is begun by teaching the child a large number of letter sounds and other isolated phonetic elements. After these are mastered, the child is expected to sound out words by recognizing and blending the parts in a left-to-right manner.

The greatest weakness of letter-by-letter sounding is that the extraneous *schwa* sound is appended to voiced sounds and, often, to voiceless sounds as well. Thus the word *man* becomes *muh-a-nuh*. To circumvent this problem of unwanted distortion, some reading specialists recommend sounding the initial consonant and the vowel following it as a single unit. By employing this suggestion, the word *man* now becomes *ma-nuh*.

Synthetic phonics has other disadvantages. Drill on isolated sounds is uninteresting and can easily dampen a child's enthusiasm for reading. It must be recognized, also, that *l, st, cl, ed,* and so forth, are meaningless to a child and are unrelated to his listening and speaking vocabularies.

Analytic phonics uses meaningful words that are presented as wholes. The child does not learn to sound isolated elements of words. Instead, he is led to identify the elements in whole words. He is encouraged to use letter substitution techniques. For example, if the child encounters a new word such as *rake*, he may reason as follows: It begins like *run* and ends like *take*. Why, it must be *rake*.

Analytic phonics is preferred by most reading authorities. Although there is no experimental proof of the superiority of analytic phonics, the following advantages seem apparent.(48)

1. The whole-word approach capitalizes on children's interest in words.
2. The whole-word approach enables children to discover letter sounds by themselves. Because of this, they are more likely to understand and use what they learn in reading situations.
3. Blending problems are avoided.
4. The whole-word approach results in practice in "reading through" words. This is the skill needed when a child encounters new words in contextual setting.
5. The analytic method is conducive to learning words so that they are likely to become familiar sight words.

Phonic sequence

Teachers are interested in the sequence in which children should learn phonic elements. In 1948, Dolch(49) recommended the following order:

1. Single-consonant sounds.
2. Consonant blends and digraphs
3. Short vowel sounds
4. Long vowel sounds

5. Final *e* rule
6. Double vowels
7. Diphthongs

8. Soft *c* and *g*
9. Number of syllables in a word
10. Dividing words into syllables.

More recently, Spache(50) recommended a phonics syllabus that is similar to the early one proposed by Dolch. The order is—

1. Simple consonants
2. Harder consonants
3. Consonant blends and digraphs
4. Short vowel sounds
5. Long vowel sounds

6. Silent letters
7. Vowel digraphs (double vowels)
8. Vowel diphthongs
9. Vowels with *r*
10. Phonograms

There are those who attribute all reading failure to a lack of phonic training. By the same token, there are those who attribute reading failure to an overemphasis on phonics. To attribute all reading failure to too little or too much phonics is unrealistic. The reasons why children do poorly in reading are multiple. Lack of phonic skill could at best be only one of the factors contributing to a child's disability.

ORAL READING

At the time of the Pilgrims, reading was synonymous with reading the Bible, and this meant reading aloud. Few people could read, and those who were able to do so were expected to share the contents of The Good Book with others. It was common practice, for example, to find families gathered around the dinner table each evening while father read aloud from the Bible. Under these circumstances, it is understandable why the school stressed oral reading.

There were complaints about the practice of oral reading, but they were few and far between. In 1838, Horace Mann pointed out that there was too much emphasis on pronouncing words and that children "do not understand the meaning of the words they read. . . ."(51) In the early 1900s Huey registered a similar complaint.(52) And in the 1920s, Judd and Buswell(53) called for a change in reading instruction which would shift emphasis to silent rather than oral reading. The pendulum finally did begin to swing. It swung so far, in fact, that in many schools oral reading was minimized to the degree that inaccurate word recognition and poor spelling resulted.

Today it is recognized that oral reading is not passé. It does have a place in the total reading program. Children do benefit from oral reading. Some of these benefits are—

1. Oral reading helps in the removal of speech defects that may stem from the presence of another language in the home or from a culturally deprived background.

2. Oral reading before a group helps a shy child gain self-confidence and poise.
3. Oral reading gives the child practice in oral communication which can result in improved conversational skill.
4. Oral reading provides the teacher with opportunities to diagnose reading problems and to evaluate reading progress.
5. Oral reading provides opportunities for dramatizing stories and results in increased motivation.

Teachers who wish to improve their oral reading instruction will find the following suggestions helpful:

1. Provide children with a model of good oral reading. This can be done by having them listen to radio and TV programs, commercial or teacher-made recordings of exemplary readers, or to the teacher's reading.
2. Give children opportunities to read material silently before reading it aloud.
3. Minimize round-robin reading activity and substitute meaningful reading before an audience. This can be accomplished in a number of ways.
   a. Children can turn a story into a play by reading aloud suitable parts.
   b. Children can read aloud sections from a story as others act out what they have heard.
   c. Children can simulate a radio or TV program (the latter can be done by having children illustrate parts of a story or play with pictures or slides) by reading before a microphone over station READ.
   d. Children can read, in proper sequence, numbered parts of a story that has been cut and divided. It is advisable to mount the story on oaktag before cutting it into parts.
   e. Children can read aloud announcements, directions, or instructions before the group or class.
   f. Children can provide general information relating to a topic or subject under consideration by reading aloud before the group or class.
   g. Children can read poetry or poetic prose in unison or in groups or by parts. Choral reading of this kind has many values.
      (1) It develops a feeling of belongingness and helps build self-confidence among shy children.
      (2) It teaches cooperation because the children participating must work together if the speaking choir is to produce results that are pleasing.

(3) It motivates children to improve the quality of their speech.

(4) It enhances children's appreciation of poetry.

The tape recorder is a very valuable device for improving children's oral reading and should not be overlooked by the teacher. Some of the advantages of using the tape recorder are—

1. The teacher who records the oral reading of children can rehear the recording and analyze carefully the kinds of errors made.
2. By giving pupils an opportunity to hear themselves they are likely to become aware of their own weaknesses.
3. The use of a tape recorder motivates better oral reading.
4. Tapes are easily stored and do not wear out readily. They can be used and reused.
5. Sections of tape can be replayed whenever the teacher wishes to emphasize a point illustrated by the reading.

In writing about the value of the tape recorder, Strang, McCullough, and Traxler state that it

. . . can be used to record book discussions, dramatic interpretations of books, reactions to newspaper or magazine articles, and the like. The play-back of such recordings helps the students evaluate their organization of ideas, their reasoning, and the effectiveness of dramatic presentations or arguments. Interest in reading is contagious; through a well-presented re-corded discussion which is sent to other classes or schools, the interest can spread. (54)

WORD RECOGNITION

How does the teacher add words to a child's sight vocabulary? The simplest approach is to pronounce words for the child at the time he is looking at them. In other words, "talking the print" is helpful. On the other hand, a pupil may learn a word because it has been used to label an object or picture in the classroom. Or he may learn a word because it is incorporated in an experience chart with which he has been working individually or as a member of a group.

The amount of repetition required to have a word become part of a child's sight vocabulary varies tremendously. Some pupils are able to recall words with a minimum of practice. Others fail to recognize words even though they have been exposed to them many times. At one time, Arthur Gates said that twenty to forty repetitions are nec-essary before mastery takes place. Other things being equal, the highly intelligent child adds new words to his sight vocabulary more rapidly than a dull child. But many factors unrelated to intelligence have a bearing on the speed of sight vocabulary development. For example, words are easier to learn if they are meaningful to the child and familiar to him through everyday conversation, if they have distinctive shapes or features, and if they are emotionally pleasing. In the case of the latter, a child may learn to recognize the word *cookie* after one repetition, but the word *where* may require weeks of repetition before he responds to it correctly.

Gates(55) set forth a number of principles to observe in developing word-form perception in children. Some of these involved—

1. Inducing pupils to react actively and vigorously to word forms.
2. Providing guidance in discovering the most significant features of printed words.
3. Displaying words in many different forms.
4. Avoiding the introduction of too many words in a single lesson.
5. Helping pupils utilize a variety of clues.
6. Helping pupils see and use those parts of words which are most helpful for word recognition.
7. Encouraging pupils to try different ways of analyzing words instead of repeating the same one.
8. Comparing new words with other words. Such comparisons should involve words which have been previously encountered.

Basal readers in the primary grades contain a controlled vocabulary based on the spoken and hearing vocabularies of children in these grades. Investigations reveal that six-year-old children who do not have a language handicap have a speaking vocabulary of at least three to five thousand words. A first-grade reader containing a vocabulary of a thousand words or less, therefore, does not present a problem in comprehension to the vast majority of children. In this connection, it is significant that problems of comprehension which seem apparent when children read orally or silently are usually nonexistent when the same material is read aloud to the children by the teacher. In the lower grades problems of comprehension during silent and oral reading usually are the result of an inadequate sight vocabulary coupled with an inability to attack new words.

When a child experiences sight vocabulary problems, he is in distress. An immediate halt should be called. He should not be exposed to more difficult readers until he can demonstrate at least a ninety-five percent mastery of the words listed in back of his present reader. Daily and weekly evaluations of word mastery are essential. The teacher can help a child acquire this mastery by giving him other books and materials of parallel difficulty and by employing suitable individualized corrective procedures. If a child is exposed to a new and more difficult reader before he has acquired the requisite sight vocabulary, his reading ceases to be meaningful and enjoyable. Independent reading habits and skills become an unattainable goal.

It is true that a few stories entail settings that may be foreign to the experiential backgrounds of some pupils. When these stories are involved, a resourceful teacher provides appropriate learning experiences. By taking pupils on field trips, using pictures, films, and the like, and by employing oral discussion, the teacher can furnish the orientation needed.

STRUCTURAL ANALYSIS

A knowledge of phonics is very helpful in structural analysis. However, structural analysis involves the discernment of larger, more meaningful units (morphemes) than phonics, which deals with phonograms (a letter or letters representing speech sounds) and their matching phonemes (units of sound). Included in structural analysis are inflectional endings, compound words, roots, syllables, prefixes, and suffixes. By studying the structure of unknown words pupils may note the following:

1. Variant endings based on common roots

look	looking	looked
talk	talking	talked
wash	washes	washed

2. Compound words consisting of two familiar words

sunshine	milkman	sometimes

3. Root words to which prefixes have been added

unhappy	export	recount

4. Root words to which suffixes have been added

blackness	dangerous	sinful

5. Root words to which both prefixes and suffixes have been added

unkindly	distrustful	repayable

Current basal reader series introduce all of the foregoing structural units in the primary grades. During the intermediate grades, pupils' knowledge is extended as additional prefixes, suffixes, and roots are taught. Syllabication, introduced at the third-grade level, becomes increasingly valuable as a method of word analysis in the intermediate and upper grades. In spite of this fact, a number of reading authorities are dubious about the teaching of syllabication rules. Spache(56) questions their values and cites a number of studies to corroborate his opinion. Deighton,(57) for example, advocates teaching only three principles: (1) Each syllable has a vowel sound; (2) Prefixes are separate syllables; (3) Doubled consonants may be split. Too many other rules, he says, are of doubtful value because of exceptions.

Teachers who are convinced that principles of syllabication have value will be interested in Clymer's study.(58) After analyzing the phonic principles found in the manuals, workbooks, and readers of four basal series, Clymer singled out forty-five for evaluative purposes. Each phonic generalization was checked against words found in a composite list of all the words introduced in the four basic series from which the generalization was drawn, plus words from the Gates Reading Vocabulary for the Primary Grades. The eight principles which pertained to syllabication are as follows:

Generalization	Number of Words Against Which Generalization Was Tested	Percent of Utility
1. In most two-syllable words, the first syllable is accented.	971	85
2. If *a, in, re, ex, de,* or *be* is the first syllable in a word, it is usually unaccented.	99	87
3. In most two-syllable words that end in a consonant followed by *y,* the first syllable is accented and the last is unaccented.	105	96
4. If the first vowel sound in a word is followed by two consonants, the first syllable usually ends with the first of the two consonants.	563	72
5. If the first vowel sound in a word is followed by a single consonant, that consonant usually begins the second syllable.	427	44
6. If the last syllable of a word ends in *le,* the consonant preceding the *le* usually begins the last syllable.	64	97
7. When the first vowel element in a word is followed by *th, ch,* or *sh,* these symbols are not broken when the word is divided into syllables and may go with either the first or second syllable.	30	100
8. In a word of more than one syllable, the letter *v* usually goes with the preceding vowel to form a syllable.	73	73

Since Clymer sets his criterion of acceptance at a seventy-five percent level of utility, generalizations 4, 5, and 8 would be eliminated. It should be noted, however, that rule 8 was tested against a small number of words when comparisons were made with the samples involved in the testing of the fourth and fifth rules. Considerable credence can be given to the value of the first three rules (these deal with accenting of syllables) since a more recent study by Winkley corroborates Clymer's findings in connection with them. As a matter of fact, Winkley's thorough evaluation of eighteen accent generalizations placed the aforementioned rules among eight that were rated as most significant.(59) Two other studies confirming Clymer's findings regarding the utility of syllabication principles have been done by Bailey(60) and Emans. (61)

CLASSROOM ORGANIZATION

Grouping refers to organization of the class to reduce heterogeneity and to facilitate instruction. It is not an instructional procedure. Grouping in and of itself does not result in more effective learning.

Through the years various grouping plans have been proposed. These plans fall into two categories: interclass grouping and intraclass grouping.

Interclass, or administrative, grouping is designed to make teaching easier by reducing the range of ability within classes. According to Clymer,(62) the following criteria have been applied in an attempt to achieve homogeneity: intelligence, chronological age, sex, achievement, and interest or vocational goal. Unfortunately, studies have shown that homogeneous grouping does not accomplish a great deal. In studying the reading of intermediate-grade pupils, Russell(63) found no differences in achievement between homogeneous and heterogeneous groups. In another investigation, Hollingshead(64) found that ability grouping did not substantially reduce the range of achievement in reading within the group.

It seems obvious that selecting individuals on the basis of one criterion does not insure similarity in other respects. For example, several readers may have almost identical reading test scores and yet differ tremendously in their reading comprehension or specific word-attack skills. Similarly, students who have almost identical sight vocabularies may not be at all comparable in their reading speed or level of comprehension. Homogeneity in one respect or trait cannot eliminate individual differences in other respects or traits.

To the classroom teacher, intraclass grouping is an economical way to individualize instruction. Various types of grouping within the classroom have been identified. These are achievement grouping, research grouping, interest grouping, special-needs grouping, team grouping, and tutorial grouping.

The efficient teacher is adept at employing several kinds of grouping in a flexible manner. He may employ one kind today and a different kind tomorrow. On occasion, he may have several kinds of grouping taking place simultaneously.

Achievement Grouping

Grouping by reading level is common practice. Customarily, three groups are organized, but there are times when a teacher may wish to divide his class into two groups: those who can read normally for the grade and those who cannot. For an average class, Harris(65) suggests placing two-thirds of the class in the upper group and one-third in the lower group. This kind of grouping, he feels, is best for the teacher who is learning the technique. Later, as the teacher gains experience, the number of groups can be increased.

Since there is a greater spread in reading ability in the intermediate grades than there is in the primary grades, one would expect to find fifth- and sixth-grade teachers employing four or five groups rather than the traditional three. But quite to the contrary, very often there is less grouping at these levels. Are intermediate-grade teachers less interested than primary teachers in meeting individual reading needs?

Teachers who employ ability grouping should exercise care in naming their reading groups. Designations such as "bluebirds, robins, and sparrows; oaks, willows, and saplings," are likely to dampen the enthusiasm of many children. Also, teachers should be cautious of their demeanor. Too often they are animated when working with their top group, somewhat somber with the middle group, and downright depressing with the low group.

Ability grouping need not be limited to the elementary grades. It can be employed very profitably at the junior and senior high school levels. For example, when studying the short story, an English teacher can assign poor readers a simple short story; average readers, one of medium difficulty; and the able readers, a difficult one. Likewise, ability grouping might find application in a social studies or even a science class.

Research or Interest Grouping

When a group of children have a common interest or wish to find answers to a common problem, the opportunities for interest and research grouping present themselves. With the help of the librarian, the teacher can provide an array of appropriate reading material on several levels of difficulty. Good readers brush elbows with poor readers. The group is held together by a common interest or problem. Later, when a report is made to the class, everyone has an opportunity to contribute, regardless of his reading level. Research and interest groupings have the advantage of not stigmatizing the students involved.

Special-Needs Grouping

Very often a teacher discovers that several pupils have a weakness in common. If, for example, a sixth-grade teacher finds that a half dozen pupils cannot break polysyllabic words into syllables, she can bring them together to play a suitably designed syllable game and have them receive special instruction in the principles of syllabication. As soon as the pupils develop the needed skill, the group is disbanded.

If used judiciously, special-needs grouping can be extremely helpful in reducing the need for remedial reading, since the classroom teacher can correct students' difficulties just as soon as they appear.

Team Grouping

As the saying goes, "Two heads are better than one." So when two pupils have a common interest or need, they can be encouraged to work together. What they cannot accomplish individually, they may be able to do as a team. To facilitate this kind of grouping, sociometric techniques may be used.(66)

Teachers who employ team grouping will find the following advice helpful.

To be successful a team must have a definite job to do and know exactly what is expected. Requiring a concrete result—such as a written report or filled-in blanks—and a reasonable but not too generous time limit will hold the partners down to business. They must discover that teamwork is a privilege that can be lost through horseplay. (67)

Tutorial Grouping

When one student knows a skill and another does not, the teacher can assign the two students to work together. As with team grouping, the teacher may wish to use the sociogram to minimize personality clashes.

Because there is a strong desire on the part of a student to please his peers, tutorial grouping is likely to pay dividends. But what about the helper? How does he benefit? The following quote answers this question:

As teachers all know, one understands better the things he has had to teach. Martin reinforces his learnings by teaching them. He will spend a large part of his life explaining his ideas to other people. If education is preparation for life, he can learn how to get along with different kinds of people. So Martin's teaching benefits him while it releases the teacher for other instructional tasks which only he can perform. (68)

PREVENTION IN READING

Better than being cured of a disease is never to have had it at all. Prevention is far more desirable than remediation. But prevention is not easy, and for too many years we have been satisfied with an emphasis on the cure. We need to look for ways to prevent reading problems.

The Parents' Role in Prevention

The seeds of reading failure may be sown long before the child comes to school. Any program of prevention, therefore, must begin with parents because it is they who guide the child during his most formative years. It is the duty of the school to reach parents and provide them with needed preventive information. Newspaper articles, TV programs, PTA conferences, letters to parents,* and conferences— all these means and media should be utilized to do the job.

Parent-child relationships

Just as surely as plants need fresh air and sunshine, children need love and affection. Parents who neglect or reject their children will find that the resulting insecurity and lack of confidence spell failure in school at a later date. If, on the other hand, parents are overly solicitous, the child may become so accustomed to being spoon-fed that his first-grade teacher finds it impossible to give him the attention to which he is accustomed. Again, he is destined to a poor start in reading.

Parents who employ corporal punishment when a child does poorly in reading fill the child with seething emotions which block any and

---

*See Appendix D, *Letter to Parents of Disabled Readers.*

all attempts to improve. Often this is especially true of parents who invidiously compare one child with another. Parents must accept each child as an individual and avoid comparisons with other children. Other don'ts for parents include bribing the child with money for getting good grades or denying him any TV privileges because he fails to measure up to expectations.

The need for a TV viewing schedule is evident when one considers that children spend more time learning from television than from church and school combined. One author(69) states, "by the time they enter first grade they will have received more hours of instruction from television networks than they will later receive from college professors while earning a bachelor's degree." It would seem advisable for parents and child to work out together a reasonable TV viewing schedule which should be followed.

Cultural background

Reading is a meaningful process which capitalizes on a child's background of experience. Unless the child can bring proper meaning to printed symbols, he cannot understand what the author is trying to convey to him. Answering a child's questions, reading to him, taking him on trips, excursions, picnics, boat rides, car rides, and so forth— all these things will add to his background of experience and will enlarge his speaking and listening vocabularies. Few things are more valuable to a child in a beginning reading situation.

Physical health

Reading clinics usually report a high incidence of physical defects among reading disability cases. It is essential that parents provide their children with physical examinations (annually, if possible) so that sources of physical difficulty can be detected and treated before they interfere with learning. It is especially important for parents to attend to their child's vision by making doubly sure that the specialist to whom they go is interested in near-point visual functions. Parents must realize that a 20/20 Snellen chart rating does not mean freedom from visual defects.

Because children cannot meet classroom demands when they are sleepy, parents must make sure that their child has an adequate amount of rest. Good nutrition is another must. Morning school hours are too demanding for the child who has left home without a good breakfast. A good hot breakfast (preferably a high-protein breakfast) is what is needed. Such a breakfast will see him through the morning hours when metabolic demands on the body are great.

THE TEACHER'S ROLE IN PREVENTION

"A stitch in time saves nine." And so it is with reading disabilities. Often they are the product of accumulated neglected needs. Reading failures could be minimized if teachers would employ corrective measures whenever small problems were uncovered. Consider children such as these: Jim was absent for three weeks and missed instruction of short vowel sounds; Mary habitually makes mistakes involving little words such as *the* and *it*; Harry points at each word; Roger fails to group words into meaningful phrase units but plods along one word at a time.

Are the foregoing serious? Perhaps not in and by themselves, but as other difficulties arise and they begin to coalesce, a reading-disability case is born. It must be remembered that reading skill is dependent on a hierarchy of related and sequential skills. One difficulty leads to another. The child who has not mastered his initial consonant sounds cannot be expected to cope with consonant blends; the child whose sight vocabulary is meager cannot read in thought units. Early diagnosis and immediate remediation are the only answers. Teachers who fail a child in this regard are exposing him to certain reading failure.

Promoting a systematic program of prevention and mastery of the reading skills in the primary grades leads to the development of independent reading habits. This goal is attained when difficulties in word recognition and word analysis are detected, corrected, and maintained.

In certain ways, there is considerable overlap between parents' and teachers' roles in prevention. One of these areas centers around early detection of physical problems that are inimical to learning. Success in reading demands energy, attention, and alertness. A child may lack these if he is in poor health. One cannot expect maximum learning by the mind when there is not maximum efficiency of the body.

Although teachers do not have the responsibility of providing yearly physical examinations for all their pupils, they must become a first line of defense by developing a seismographic sensitivity to any symptoms of physical difficulties that are likely to interfere with reading skills. They should be well acquainted with the overt manifestations of visual defects, auditory impairment, glandular malfunction, and poor general health. (See chapter 5 for lists of symptoms.) When teachers are aware of such symptoms, they should bring the child to the attention of the school nurse or doctor.

Emotional problems

Emotional problems often are a concomitant of learning problems. With reading disability it is a moot question whether emotional maladjustment, in an individual case, was the cause or the effect of the disorder. Nevertheless, it is important for teachers to become aware of emotional disturbances which inhibit learning. The teacher who spots symptoms of such a disturbance (see pages 130-132) should refer the child to the school psychologist or counselor for help. In working with an emotionally disturbed child the teacher can abide by the following principles: (70)

1. Provide a warm, accepting atmosphere.
2. Provide opportunities for the poor reader to talk with you.
3. Determine the poor reader's interests and use them to motivate reading.
4. If the pupil's attention span is limited, keep instructional periods short.
5. Have each pupil begin at the level and stage of reading growth at which he can achieve success.
6. Provide each retarded reader with concrete evidence of his gains and give him honest praise when it is earned.
7. Give the poor reader instruction and practice in advance of required oral reading so that he can perform well and gain greater self-respect.
8. Define clearly the purpose of each reading assignment.
9. Give the poor reader recognition when he makes oral contributions and performs satisfactorily in tasks which do not involve reading.
10. Cooperate with the home.

READING IN THE INTERMEDIATE GRADES

The intermediate grades are those in which previously learned skills are refined and improved. Word-analysis skills become more automatized, and the pupil is given systematic instruction in the use of the dictionary. The latter is particularly important in helping the student develop his meaning vocabulary.

During this period more and more expository or factual reading is encountered (reading for knowledge becomes increasingly important), and many comprehension skills are consolidated or added to the pupil's repertoire: anticipating outcomes; following directions; reading for different purposes; spotting central thoughts of paragraphs; remembering important details; outlining; summarizing; reading graphs, charts, and tables; and locating information.

In the fourth, fifth, and sixth years in school, very rapid growth takes place in the rate of comprehension and the extension of reading interests. Witty and Kopel(71) report that the amount and variety of reading activity of typical boys and girls reach their peak at twelve or thirteen years.

Strang indicates that the intermediate grades are good ones in which to teach techniques of locating information such as using the card catalog, table of contents, index, headings, and italics.

. . . After learning to locate sources of information, the pupil is ready to begin examining them for accuracy, authenticity, and relevancy. He takes useful notes, organizes the facts, and writes a readable report which he presents in an interesting way. It is here that he receives instruction in the special skills of reading maps, graphs, and tables. (72)

READING IN THE CONTENT FIELDS

Intermediate and upper-grade pupils find reading subject matter textbooks more difficult than storybook reading. The reasons for this are (1) a lack of a technical vocabulary and the needed background of experience may stand in the way of comprehension; (2) a limited mastery of the skills of word analysis; and (3) lack of a definite purpose in reading.

The field of mathematics includes such unusual words as *cone, root,* and *integer.* The reader of scientific material encounters *watt, spectrum,* and *oxidation.* Not knowing one of these key words and not having in mind the concepts involved can make comprehension of a sentence or paragraph rather difficult. It is important, therefore, that all subject matter teachers assume the responsibility of helping pupils learn new words basic to understanding the subject.

There are instances when a student is familiar with certain technical words when he hears them. But if he has not mastered the skills of word analysis (for example, he does not know how to break a word into syllables or cannot interpret diacritical markings in the dictionary), the words remain unknown to him until someone pronounces them. If he is not given this kind of assistance, he is quickly inundated and frustrated by the numerous polysyllabic words encountered in content field reading.

A good reader of content field material varies the way he reads according to the purpose for which he is reading. For example, reading technical material requires a slow, meticulous rate, while reading an exciting short story permits faster reading. A student reads a laboratory manual for the purpose of following directions; he reads a problem in mathematics to discover what facts are given that will facilitate his solving it. Different types of materials require different mental approaches as well as various reading rates. Pupils need guidance in learning how to adjust to the purpose for which they are reading.

Mathematics

Everyone knows that when reading mathematical materials, one must read slowly and exactly. A problem in mathematics seldom contains a great deal of superfluous or unnecessary information. Fast or cursory reading is likely to result in confusion and many mistakes and should be discouraged.

In solving a written problem the reader should go through a number of steps. First he reads the problem quickly to learn what it is about. During a second reading he locates exactly what is being asked. Just what is the problem? Is it the cost of a dozen eggs or the number of ten cent stamps that can be purchased with a given amount of money? Once the reader knows what he is supposed to find out, he then reads the problem again, looking for relevant details which will provide the facts needed to solve it. When he is completely familiar with the facts, he works out an answer. Finally, he rereads the problem a last time to check the answer and to make doubly sure the solution is complete.

Science

Science, like mathematics, makes reading demands on pupils that are similar in many respects. Pupils must read carefully and give full attention to details. Rereading is often necessary because the material is too difficult to be understood in one reading.

The technical vocabulary of science is heavy. During the assignment period, the science teacher should introduce pertinent words by writing them on the chalkboard. Each word should be pronounced so that pupils will become acquainted with the spoken word as well as with the printed symbol. Familiarizing students with the technical vocabulary of science is time well spent. Only when a pupil understands scientific terminology can he begin to understand scientific language patterns.

In addition to a technical vocabulary, equations, formulas, graphs, diagrams, and drawings frequently appear. Since understanding and mastery of these are essential, the wise teacher takes time to discuss and clarify them.

The pages of science books often are filled with sentences and paragraphs that are heavily ladened with facts, many of which are beyond the child's realm of experience. Through the use of visual aids (especially motion pictures), discussion, and demonstration, a teacher can help build a background of experience which will make comprehension of the text easier.

Social Studies

The volume of reading required in the social studies area makes heavy demands on students. Efficient reading in this area involves an emphasis on informational reading. Some of the specific skills entailed include finding central thoughts of paragraphs, locating related details, detecting a sequence of events, discerning cause and effect relationships, reading graphs and charts, and map-reading ability.

The intelligent reader of social studies is in need of a broad general vocabulary. He also needs to be acquainted with various technical vocabularies: politics, government, religion, sociology, law, and so forth.

When reading social studies material, there is a need to react critically to what is read. The reader must be sensitive to the presence of propaganda and should not hesitate to compare the viewpoints of several authors before accepting what he reads as true. He must decide if statements are facts or opinions, and he must become acquainted with sources which generally are thought to be reliable.

If pupils are to become discerning citizens and intelligent voters of the future, teachers of social studies must assume the responsibilities of teaching needed reading skills.

READING SKILLS

Context Clues

As stated by Hildreth, "inferring the meaning of a word from what went before, and deliberately reading ahead for clues to meaning, is an essential technique for word recognition."(73)

Because of its importance to word recognition, practice in utilizing context clues begins very early. Continued instruction and constant practice during the primary grades and beyond result in continuous improvement of the skill.

Children who read a great deal learn many words by using context clues. Typically, the following occurs when a child encounters an unknown word. He tries phonics and structural analysis to arrive at a pronunciation. If the result is unfamiliar to his learning vocabulary, he guesses at the word from the context and moves on. By the end of the fourth grade, the average reader becomes quite adept at helping himself through a combination of context clues and sounding. And if he is unhappy with the tentative pronunciation or supposed meaning of a word, he may consult a dictionary.

Dictionary Usage

Although picture dictionaries are introduced in the primary grades, formal dictionary training is reserved for the intermediate grades. Once a pupil knows how to use this important tool, he has acquired true independence in word attack. He then has a source for assistance in the pronunciation, spelling, and meaning of words. Unfortunately, many readers have a distinct aversion for the dictionary. This antipathy is undoubtedly an outgrowth of their lack of skill in using it. In any event, it is necessary for a teacher to exercise all of his ingenuity when trying to instruct students in dictionary usage.

Subskills which are essential to locating words, pronouncing them, and defining them are as follows:

1. Location Skills

   a. Knowing alphabetical sequence;
   b. Determining what letters precede and follow a given letter;
   c. Alphabetizing words according to their beginning letters;
   d. Alphabetizing words according to beginning two- and three-letter patterns;
   e. Using guide words intelligently;
   f. Knowing the value of thumb indexes;
   g. Learning to open the dictionary that lacks thumb indexes at a point near the word.

2. Pronunciation Skills

   a. Using key words to interpret diacritical markings;
   b. Recognizing syllables;
   c. Understanding and interpreting primary and secondary accent marks;
   d. Understanding and appreciating the *schwa* sound;
   e. Reading phonetic spelling.

3. Definition Skills

   a. Realizing that a word may have multiple meaning;
   b. Comprehending definitions provided;
   c. Choosing from several definitions given the one that gives the best explanation of the meaning of the unknown word.

Reading Comprehension

Reading comprehension, the goal of reading instruction at all levels, is usually thought of as understanding the meaning of what is read. At the intermediate-grade levels, reading comprehension includes more than getting the meaning of a story or selection. Thinking should be encouraged. And with thinking comes interpretation, an aspect of reading which goes beyond comprehension. For example, a child may read a story about elephants. He compares what he has just read with what he has actually observed elephants do at the zoo. Or he may compare two stories about elephants to see if they agree or disagree in the facts presented. This is interpretive and critical reading, the kind of thoughtful reading teachers should endeavor to develop in their pupils. It is begun in the primary grades but receives greater emphasis at the intermediate level.

Comprehending and interpreting what is read is dependent on concepts acquired through past experiences. These may be direct or vicarious. Early sensory experiences—tasting, touching, smelling, hearing, seeing—are basic and fundamental. Later, listening to the radio, watching television, traveling, and hearing the conversation of older people increase the tempo of concept development.

Understanding the meaning of individual words is requisite to meaningful reading. Mastery of a technical vocabulary is often synonymous with concept development. If the reader does not know the meaning of words used by an author, he cannot comprehend the author's thoughts.

The ability to group words into units of thought rather than reading word-by-word is another requisite to reading comprehension. For example, the sentence "The boy / hit the ball / over the fence" contains three thought units. Proficiency in perceiving thought units leads naturally to sentence comprehension. And when a pupil learns to discern the difference between topical sentences and those which provide examples, details, or support the main idea, he is comprehending paragraphs. Skills of these kinds require greater emphasis in the intermediate grades than in the primary grades.

Other comprehension skills that are important to develop or expand during the intermediate grades include (1) reading to follow more complex directions, (2) reading to remember, (3) reading to anticipate outcomes, (4) learning to outline, (5) learning to summarize, and (6) critical reading. (For a more detailed discussion and specific recommendations pertaining to these skills see pages 248-265.)

Since study-type reading begins to have importance during the intermediate grades, many teachers introduce the SQ3R method of study. The method was evolved by Francis Robinson(74) several decades ago and has proved particularly effective in aiding comprehension and retention. A simplified version of Robinson's SQ3R method of study follows.

Survey: Have the pupil read quickly all the headings in the chapter or article to see the big points that are to be developed. This survey should not take more than two or three minutes. Darkened paragraph headings, italicized headings, pictures, graphs, and summary statements should receive attention. This orientation will help the pupil organize ideas as he reads them later.

Question: Now have the pupil begin to work. Tell him to turn the first heading into a question. This can be done by using *what, why, where, when,* or *how.* The question will arouse his curiosity and increase his comprehension. It will bring to his mind information already known and will help him understand the section more quickly. Most important, the question will make important points stand out while explanatory details will be recognized as such. Turning a heading into a question should be done immediately when reading the heading.

Read: The pupil now reads to find the answer or answers to the question. This is not a passive plowing along but an *active search* for answers.

Recite: (This is the most important step in the Survey Q3R Method.) The pupil now looks away from the book and briefly recites the answer in his own words. If he can't do this, he glances at the book again. A second attempt is made to recite. He continues to read and recite as long as necessary. An excellent way to do this reciting from memory is to have the pupil jot down, under the question he writes out, cue phrases in outline form.

When he is satisfied he knows what he has read, he repeats steps 2, 3, 4 on each succeeding headed section. That is, he turns the next heading into a question, reads to answer that question, and then recites the answer by jotting down cue phrases in outline form. He reads in this way until the lesson is completed.

Review: When the lesson has thus been read through, the pupil looks over his notes to get a bird's-eye view of the lesson and checks his memory again by quickly reciting the subpoints under each heading. He can do this by covering up his notes and trying to recall the main points and by covering the main points while he tries to recall the subpoints under them.

Speed of Reading

It is definitely an advantage to get desired information from books quickly and efficiently. By the time the average student has reached the fourth grade, articulation during silent reading is minimal, phrasing ability has improved, and he should be able to read faster silently than orally. Special emphasis on reading speed at this time can pay dividends.

Teachers who are interested in increasing the reading speed of intermediate-grade students should keep in mind the following points.

1. Reading speed without comprehension is not reading. The most adequate definition of reading speed is *rate of comprehension.*
2. Rapid, average, or slow readers who comprehend poorly should not be pressured to read more rapidly. With all poor comprehenders, major emphasis should be given to training that stresses accurate reading.
3. Slow readers who comprehend well are the most likely candidates to profit from an increased emphasis on speed.
4. Flexibility in reading rate is more important than speed per se. Good students vary their reading speed in accordance to their purposes and the difficulty of the reading material.
5. Mechanical devices are not needed to improve students' rate of comprehension. (See pages 256-257.)

Teachers may give periodic tests of an informal nature to encourage students to develop acceptable reading rates for different kinds of material. (See chapter 5 for additional information about such tests.)

READING IN THE UPPER GRADES

Junior and senior high school students face heavy reading demands. A great deal of this reading is centered around assignments which students are expected to complete independently. The reading is not easy. Specialized nomenclature is encountered in different subject matter areas accompanied by more involved sentence and paragraph structure. Many secondary teachers assume that their students can analyze words, read interpretively and critically, and study effectively. The truth is, however, that reading deficiencies are all too prevalent.

In a report by Donovan,(75) it was shown that almost one-quarter of 45,000 New York City freshman and sophomore high school students were reading two to five or more years below grade. In terms of mental ability, 42.3 percent were reading below their potential.

What can be done? Some secondary schools have reading specialists who offer developmental reading courses for all students regardless of their reading status. Other schools provide developmental or remedial courses which can be taken by students as an elective. English teachers frequently are asked to assume the responsibility of teaching reading even though they have little background and/or interest in the area. Ideally, all subject matter teachers should be involved in the reading program, since reading skills differ in science, history, mathematics, and other subjects. Few high schools have developed a well-coordinated, concerted action approach.

Study Skills

Upper-grade students are expected to study independently a number of hours each week, but few of them receive instruction from their teachers that proves helpful. Students who are exposed to study-skills instruction often fail to employ it properly, either because they were not given sufficient practice or because they find a haphazard approach easier to use.

Since reading at the junior and senior high school levels is not taught as a separate subject, content field teachers must assume additional responsibility in giving students how-to-study tips. For example, getting-to-know-your-textbook sessions can prove very profitable in bringing to students' attention ways in which their textbooks can help them study. The following questions are offered as a guide.

Knowing your textbook

1. What is the title of your text and when was it published?
2. Why is the date of publication important?
3. What can you learn about the author?
4. What does the author tell you about the features of his book which will help you in your studies?
5. If the book has a glossary or an appendix, how will these help you in your studies?
   a. How does a glossary differ from a dictionary?
   b. What type of material is found in an appendix and how does it help you?
6. Does the author furnish study helps to aid you in comprehending the book?
   a. Are there questions at the beginning or end of each chapter?
   b. Is there an introductory statement at the beginning of each chapter?
   c. Are summaries or conclusions provided at the end of each chapter?
   d. Does the author list additional references which you might consult?

e. Are division or section headings set forth clearly in dark or italicized print?

Survey Q3R method

Students in the upper grades need to become acquainted or re-acquainted with Robinson's SQ3R method of study. (See pages 99-100 for more detailed information.) It is a very efficient and effective method which can be used in studying practically any subject. Students who use the method will find that their comprehension and retention of studied material is markedly improved. Because of its positive effects on scholarship, subject matter teachers should take time to show how it can be applied to their particular area of specialization.

Skimming

Skimming, the first step of the SQ3R method of study, should be given special attention because it is a valuable skill for streamlining reading. There are two types of skimming: one is skimming to get a general impression of a selection, and the other is skimming to locate a specific bit of information. (The latter is referred to by some authors as scanning.)

When skimming for a general impression, the reader gets a bird's-eye view of the material by reading headings, first and last sentences of paragraphs, pictures, graphs, diagrams, and summaries or conclusions. It is this type of skimming a student uses when there isn't sufficient time to read an article or chapter conscientiously. Skimming may also be used when the title of a selection suggests to the student that he possesses a considerable amount of advance information about the material and that it will contain little that is new to him.

In skimming to locate a specific piece of information, the student lets his eyes travel down the page without actually reading, stopping once or twice on each line of print. By looking at the white space between the lines rather than at the lines themselves, a student can spread his attention more evenly throughout his field of vision. Thus, with the proper mind set, he is able to locate quickly the precise fact or bit of information he is seeking.

Outlining

Pupils who learn to outline (initial instruction begins in the intermediate grades) have mastered the technique of locating main ideas and related details. This means, of course, that comprehension is taking place—and comprehension is the crux of the reading process.

Good outliners are invariably good comprehenders; but not all good comprehenders are able to outline. Since planned exercises in outlining are needed, every subject matter teacher has the responsibility of improving reading through teaching students to outline.

Teachers should use the blackboard for outlining several pages from a class text to furnish students with a good example of what should be done. In this connection, students should become familiar with the following lettering and numbering system: Roman numbers (I, II, III, . . .) for the highest-order headings, capital letters (A, B, C, . . .) for the second order, Arabic numerals (1, 2, 3, . . .) for the third order, and lowercase letters (a, b, c, . . .) for the fourth order. If additional orders are needed, parentheses can be used to enclose Arabic numerals, for example, (1), for the next order, and parentheses can enclose lowercase letters, for example, (a), for a still lower order. Accompanying this lettering and numbering system with consistent indention results in a nicely structured outline.

It is important to point out to students that they need more than one item under any subdivision. For example, should there be a "1" there also should be a "2." Should only one item exist, subordination of the point involved is unnecessary.

Note-taking

Outlining skill provides the needed organizational training to take notes more efficiently when reading or hearing a speech. Taking notes when reading, of course, is quite different from taking notes from a speech. With the former, a student can take his time; but when taking lecture notes, time is of the essence. A student must remain very attentive and critical and must learn to record ideas clearly and succinctly. Students will find the following points helpful in developing note-taking skill during lectures:

1. Take notes in your own words whenever possible. You will remember and understand better by not writing verbatim the words of the lecturer.
2. If you miss an important point, speak to the lecturer at the end of the period. Perhaps, too, a fellow student might be consulted for the needed information.
3. Write as legibly as circumstances permit and look at your notes before they become too cold. If too much time does not pass, you more likely will be able to decipher your hieroglyphics. What's more, additional points you were unable to record may occur to you, and these can be incorporated into the outline.

4. If you have the time, it is very desirable to rewrite and reorganize your notes. Use a colored pencil or pen to highlight certain important points.
5. Review your notes with regularity.

Summarizing

The ability to express in brief the essential ideas of a lengthy selection is a valuable study skill. Several subskills are involved in learning to summarize.

Pupils who have learned how to locate the main ideas of paragraphs have mastered the skill that is most basic to writing good summaries. Another skill that is important is the ability to put information in sequential order. Lastly, a pupil must be able to put the writer's statements into his own words as succinctly as possible. This means deleting unnecessary adjectives, adverbs, and other padding words that contribute little to the thought of a selection.

Pupils will find summarizing a chapter or lengthy selection somewhat easier if they outline the material first. Then, after checking the outline and using it as a guide, they can write briefly a series of paragraphs summarizing the material.

INTEREST AND MOTIVATION

"No" is the answer a retarded reader invariably gives when asked if he enjoys reading. Needless to say, pupils who are not interested in reading read few books. Any pupil who curtails his reading activities becomes more and more retarded in reading skill. Just as it is impossible to become a good swimmer without swimming, it is not possible to become a proficient reader without extensive reading. This fact is undoubtedly fundamental to many cases of reading retardation.

Why do so many children become uninterested in reading? It is much like the well-known fact that mixing cod-liver oil with a child's orange juice is a sure way to bring about an aversion for the latter. The child who experiences frustration and displeasure when he reads soon begins to avoid the process. Sometimes this Pavlovian conditioning is a direct outgrowth of being forced into first-grade reading before adequate readiness has been developed. Often, too, instructional material chosen for the child throughout the grades is far above or below (usually the former) his reading level. Still another explanation could be overemphasis on isolated word drill and old-fashioned phonics which results in a "reading isn't fun" attitude.

The interest factor also relates to the limited experiential background characterizing many poor readers. After the primary grades, much of a child's background of experience is acquired vicariously through reading. These vicarious experiences stand the child in good stead when he is attempting to read new material. The printed page is always more meaningful when proper concepts are brought to the word symbols involved. The retarded reader often has great voids in his experiential background because he has not read a great deal. These voids make successful reading comprehension difficult.

Although a teacher can find many studies that do an excellent job of furnishing him with a knowledge of the general trends of children's interests,(76, 77, 78) he finds no rule of thumb for determining the exact interests of specific children. This requires detective work, the most fruitful of which involves observation, questionnaires, and interviews.

Since motivation is the indispensable ingredient of all learning activity, a wise teacher should be a good merchandiser of reading material. Often a child is fascinated by a story in the basal reader and wishes he could read more stories like it. The teacher should be able to "strike while the iron is hot" by immediately supplying him with additional stories dealing with the same subject. This can be done by using the school library which is always a most valuable adjunct to the classroom.

Teachers should surround children with reading stimuli. A classroom library with books of all kinds and descriptions should be provided. Poor readers should be furnished books adapted for them, and superior readers should be given books having a wide variety of content at grade level and above. In this connection, the special motivational appeal of paperbacks should not be overlooked.

In a controlled study at the elementary school level, Lowery and Grafft(79) concluded that the use of paperback books brought about significant increases in the number of pleasant or positive attitudes the groups had toward reading and a decrease in the number of negative attitudes.

Another experiment employing paperbacks was initiated with sophomores at the Lincoln High School in Manitowoc, Wisconsin. The students were given a chance to read paperbacks in class two to three hours a week. They were subjected to no lectures, no discussion, no tests, no homework, and no book reports. The paperbacks included quality novels, plays, biographies, and collections of essays and poems. In one semester, slow readers completed twenty books; fast readers completed fifty books. At the end of the experiment, the 286 sophomores involved reacted enthusiastically. Most of them stated that it was the best way to study literature.

Paperbacks have many advantages: They are inexpensive and, unlike hard-cover books, are not associated as readily with study, examinations, and other unpleasantries. Since they are not bulky, they can be slipped into a purse or pocket for ready accessibility whenever opportunities for reading present themselves.

One ingenious teacher used paperbacks in connection with the initiation of a familiarization period for twenty nonreaders. Attractive paperbacks were distributed, and after each two-minute interval, a whistle was blown. The blowing of the whistle was a signal for the pupils to exchange paperbacks. After it had been blown three or four times, several students gave the teacher unfriendly looks. (Already they had found a book they wished to read.) But the whistle-blowing continued until the class period ended. At that point, the teacher informed the students that the paperbacks with which they had become familiar were available for checkout. Within a few short minutes all paperbacks disappeared.

Teachers who wish to locate appealing paperbacks for their pupils should send for free and annotated catalogs such as the following:

Bantam Pathfinder Editions for Young People (Bantam Books, Inc., Educational Division, 271 Madison Avenue, New York, N. Y. 10016).

Bantam Books—Junior and Senior High Schools (666 Fifth Avenue, New York, N. Y. 10019).

Berkley Highland School Catalog (Kable News Company, 777 Third Avenue, New York, N. Y. 10017).

Complete Guide to Tempo Books (Select Magazines, 229 Park Avenue South, New York, N. Y. 10003).

Educational Paperbacks—Junior and Senior High Schools (Simon and Schuster, Inc., Educational and Library Department, 1 West 39th Street, New York, N. Y. 10018).

Paperback Classroom Libraries and Learning Units (Educational Reading Service, East 64 Midland Avenue, Paramus, New Jersey 07652).

Paperbacks for Junior and Senior High Schools (Dell Publishing Company, Inc., 750 Third Avenue, New York, N. Y. 10017).

Readers' Choice Catalog (Scholastic Book Services, Scholastic Magazines, 904 Sylvan Avenue, Englewood Cliffs, New Jersey 07632; also, 5675 Sunol Boulevard, Pleasanton, California 94566).

Stereotyped and laboriously detailed book reports destroy reading interest. Imaginative teachers are capable of devising book-reporting procedures that are both enjoyable and motivational. For example, a California teacher* has great success employing a bimonthly book-court session which she describes as follows:

> We hold court session in our room every other Friday. The court consists of a judge, the defendant (the person who is making the book report), and a jury, consisting of class members who also have read the book being reported on.
>
> The defendant who is seated to the left of the judge is sworn in with his hand on a dictionary. After he is sworn in, the judge asks some leading questions about events in the story, about the characters, etc. During this examination, the judge and defendant are very serious. When the questioning is concluded, the jury decides whether the defendant has read and understood the book, or was trying to bluff. If the jury decides he was just bluffing, the judge sentences him to read the book and to appear in court in two weeks to report on it again.
>
> "Next case!" The gavel bangs on the desk, and a new defendant and a new jury take their places for the next book report. All is done in good spirit, and no one becomes angry. As a matter of fact, the children love this form of book reporting and look forward to it avidly.

Another teacher had book reports take the form of a "Tell the Truth" panel. This is based on the television show bearing the same name. A moderator introduces three students who are seated behind a table as numbers one, two, and three. The title and the author of the book in question are then introduced by the moderator. Class members ask questions of the panel members by addressing them by number. Each member is supposed to pretend he has read the book or, conversely, each member can fabricate vague replies so the class wonders if anyone has read the book. After a few minutes of questioning, the moderator asks the class, by a show of hands, to decide who is the real reader of the book. The person who really read the book then stands and gives the rest of his report.

Many students enjoy supplementing the reading of a book by writing a follow-up story of their own. Other students can be encouraged to write a letter to the author of the book read. By addressing the letter to the author in care of the publisher, an answer is very often assured. (It is important, however, not to write to authors who are no longer living.) The author's reply can be posted on the bulletin board for all to see.

Students who are artistically inclined should be encouraged to design posters or book jackets as a form of book reporting. Other pupils

*Mrs. Leah Rawson, Grendel School, Azusa, California.

can model clay figures or dress dolls in costumes to depict characters in stories.

It is evident that book reports can be used to motivate and stimulate pupils to read. They need not incur negative reactions. If handled properly, book reporting can be a rewarding experience serving to interest all students in the joys of reading.

A systematic recreational reading program is essential for the reading improvement of all pupils. Children in the elementary grades should be given some time every day to read for fun. This makes learning to read worthwhile and can do more than anything else to inculcate children with a lifetime interest in reading.

Recreational reading is a tremendous boon for superior readers. They are not forced to follow, in lock-step fashion, a standard curriculum. Free reading permits superior readers to move ahead as fast as they wish and gives them the opportunity to develop rapidly along the lines of their special interests and talents.

Care must be exercised when selecting books for poor readers. These pupils will not benefit from books that are too difficult. On the other hand, they do not like baby books. They must be given books that are especially adapted so as to have high interest appeal and a difficulty level that facilitates easy reading. Preferably, grade markings or designations should be absent.

INSTRUCTIONAL MATERIAL

Subject matter teacher involvement is basic to a good developmental reading program. Unfortunately, many secondary teachers object to being part of a developmental reading program even though they recognize a need for it. The reason? They know little about the teaching of reading and they are afraid to attempt it.

A good in-service program can do much to alleviate any concern a subject matter teacher has about teaching reading. (See chapter 11 for details regarding in-service training programs.) Once teachers have seen some demonstrations and are provided with time to learn about some practical reading techniques they really can use, much of their apprehension will disappear.

If subject matter teachers are going to help all students develop their reading skills, special materials are needed. Too often only one textbook is provided, and every student, regardless of his reading ability, is expected to read it. When this is the situation, many students are destined to failure. Consider, for example, an eighth-grade social science class that has a single textbook. About fifty to sixty percent of the students will be able to read the book. Of the remaining students, many of them will find the text absolutely impossible.

What can the teacher do to help? She can locate another text (better still, two other texts) that are organized in somewhat the same way as the class text. These easier texts can be assigned to students who are unable to fathom the more difficult book for the course. Naturally, this may mean using materials written by different authors because, at the present time, there are few multilevel subject matter texts available. But publishers are responsive to the demands of teachers. If they know a market exists for multilevel texts, these kinds of books will be forthcoming. Teachers should make their needs known.

Another procedure that can be employed has been termed the multilevel unitary teaching method.(80) This works well with certain broad areas of learning and proves superior to a two- or three-textbook approach. In English, for example, when a unit on the short story is introduced, all students are not required to read the same short story. Instead, a number of short stories ranging from easy to very difficult are made available. When this is done, no student need be exposed to reading levels that are beyond him. Social studies, too, is amenable to the multilevel unitary teaching method. If the "Western Movement" is the unit under consideration, the teacher begins by rounding up all kinds of materials that relate directly or indirectly to the unit. Trade books, magazine articles, newspaper articles, pamphlets, reference books, textbooks, and so on, are included. During an exploratory session, students decide on what aspects of the unit interest them and the activities in which they wish to participate. Then they begin to work individually, in teams, or in small groups. Some of the work is done in the library and some in the classroom. The teacher acts as a resource person, moving from group to group and individual to individual, whenever problems arise or advice is sought. As students and groups complete their work, they get ready for a sharing period. This reporting, or sharing, may take many forms. Students may paint a mural, design a bulletin board display, make a tape recording, write a play, design a quiz game or a crossword puzzle, engage in a panel discussion, design a poster, and many other things.

For the teacher, the multilevel unit approach requires a greater expenditure of thought and energy than the use of a single textbook. But it pays tremendous dividends. By working independently at optimum levels, students accomplish more than they would with a traditionally structured program.

When the administration insists that all students read the same textbook, all is not lost. The teacher can do certain things to make the procedure tolerable. Making sure that students are familiar with the vocabulary of a section or chapter before they read it is helpful. Differentiated assignments are also helpful. Good readers can be given more inference-type questions—those involving implication and deduction; poor readers are held to questions that are more factual. Lastly, students should not be required to memorize the language of the text, but should be encouraged to put things into their own words.

When it is impossible for a student to read the text independently, the teacher may assign an able reader to read the material aloud while the poor reader follows silently. The teacher may also provide a tape recording of the text. This recording may be of the teacher's voice or may carry the voice of another student. It can be interspersed with helpful remarks such as "Just in case you don't know the meaning of that word, it means . . ." or "We read about this on page 83. You might want to turn off the recorder and review what was said right now."

READING AND THE GIFTED

Intellectually gifted students are in need of guidance in reading. A reading program for the gifted should be designed to develop and expand their interests and tastes and provide enriched experiences. Such a program

1. should give freedom of library usage and provide opportunities for the self-selection of books;
2. should impose no grade ceiling on students' book choices as long as they can read them;
3. should provide instruction in the use of the library;
4. should educate students in the mechanics of research and the use of reference sources;
5. should instruct students in good study habits and skills (the SQ3R method would be especially valuable);
6. should not bore students with instruction not needed;
7. should avoid giving unnecessary drill beyond the attainment of mastery;
8. should emphasize *how* and *why* questions that are designed to stimulate critical thinking and critical reading;
9. should provide special assignments which permit students to move ahead at their own pace;
10. should help students achieve a balance in their daily activities— reading, television viewing, socializing, rest, and family time.

The foregoing points are predicated on the contention that if gifted students are to measure up to their full potential and make true contributions to society, they must develop the ability to discipline themselves and to expand their own educational horizons.

SUMMARY

A developmental reading program begins at birth and continues throughout the life of an individual. Parents and teachers both have important roles to play in preventing reading problems. An effective program of developmental reading must encompass such factors as readiness, appropriate instructional level, diversification of instructional material, motivation, diagnosis of reading problems and individualized correction. Mastery of the reading skills and the development of independent reading habits in the primary grades are the indispensable goals to be sought. A number of approaches to instruction, including such methods as linguistics, language experience, ITA, and individualized reading, are in various stages of experimentation. The most widely accepted method involves the use of basal readers. Traditional ability or achievement grouping should be supplemented by other kinds of grouping plans: research grouping, interest grouping, team grouping, tutorial grouping, and special-needs grouping. Although proficiency in silent reading is an ultimate goal of reading instruction, teachers should not overlook the value and place of oral reading. As a pupil encounters more and more expository reading material, it is important that content field teachers—science, history, mathematics, and so on—assume responsibility for teaching reading skills peculiar to their area of specialization.

PROBLEMS FOR ORAL AND WRITTEN DISCUSSION

1. Describe a program of reading readiness in the first grade, indicating the use of tests, teacher judgments, and other criteria.
2. Describe your use of experience charts in the first grade.
3. Describe your use of basal readers, indicating strengths and weaknesses of materials used.
4. Summarize and evaluate the contents of the manual accompanying a series of basal readers.
5. Outline a program of phonics you would use in the primary grades, indicating emphasis and materials.
6. Discuss prevention in the reading program, indicating its importance and methods of attainment.

7. Discuss the importance of acquiring independent reading habits in the primary grades and its impact on learning and promotion.

8. How can a special teacher of remedial reading or other specialist help the classroom teacher with her reading problems?

9. What new reading skills must be developed in the intermediate grades?

10. Why is a knowledge of primary reading methods and materials important for intermediate- and upper-grade teachers of reading?

11. What study skills must be mastered by pupils in the intermediate and upper grades?

12. Outline a program for developing meaning vocabulary.

13. Describe and evaluate the use of workbooks in reading for a particular grade.

14. Discuss the importance of recreational reading, indicating materials and methods of promotion.

15. Determine the rate of oral and silent reading at each grade level by consulting the norms appearing in reading test manuals.

REFERENCES

1. ROBERT KARLIN, *Teaching Reading in High School* (New York: Bobbs-Merrill Co., Inc., 1964), ch. 12.

2. HENRY A. BAMMAN, URSULA HOGAN, and CHARLES E. GREENE, *Reading Instruction in the Secondary Schools* (New York: Longmans, Green and Co., 1961), pp. 9-10.

3. DELWYN G. SCHUBERT, *A Dictionary of Terms and Concepts in Reading*, 2nd ed. (Springfield, Ill.: Charles C Thomas, Publisher, 1968), p. 263.

4. Ibid., 262.

5. Ibid., 268-269.

6. MARION MONROE and BEATRICE ROGERS, *Foundations for Reading* (Chicago: Scott, Foresman and Co., 1964), p. 6.

7. Ibid., pp. 7-11.

8. MABEL MORPHETT and CARLTON WASHBURNE, "When Should Children Begin to Read?" in *Readings in Reading*, Delwyn G. Schubert and Theodore L. Torgerson, eds. (New York: Thomas Y. Crowell Co., 1968), pp. 90-97.

9. EDWARD R. SIPAY, "The Effect of Prenatal Instruction on Reading Achievement," *Elementary English* (April 1965):431-432.

10. ARTHUR I. GATES, "The Necessary Mental Age for Beginning Reading," in *Readings in Reading*, Delwyn G. Schubert and Theodore L. Torgerson, eds. (New York: Thomas Y. Crowell Co., 1968), pp. 98-100.

11. M. C. ALMY, *Children's Experience Prior to First Grade and Success in Beginning Reading*, Contributions to Education, No. 954 (New York: Bureau of Publications, Teachers College, Columbia University, 1949).

12. R. FAST, "Kindergarten Training and Grade I Reading," *Journal of Educational Psychology* (January 1947):52-57.

13. Ann Arbor Publishers, 711 North University, Ann Arbor, Mich.
14. Consulting Psychologists Press, Palo Alto, Calif.
15. CARL L. ROSEN, "An Investigation of Perceptual Training and Reading Achievement in the First Grade," *American Journal of Optometry* 45 (May 1968):322-332.
16. BRUCE BALOW, "Perceptual-motor Activities in the Treatment of Severe Reading Disability," *The Reading Teacher* (March 1971):521.
17. DONALD D. DURRELL and ALICE K. NICHOLSON, "Preschool and Kindergarten Experience," in *Readings in Reading*, Delwyn G. Schubert and Theodore L. Torgerson, eds. (New York: Thomas Y. Crowell Co., 1968), pp. 122-133.
18. GEORGE D. SPACHE and EVELYN B. SPACHE, *Reading in the Elementary School* (Boston: Allyn and Bacon, Inc., 1969), p. 191.
19. NEWELL C. KEPHART, *The Slow Learner in the Classroom* (Columbus: Charles E. Merrill Books, Inc., 1960).
20. D. RADLER and N. KEPHART, *Success Through Play* (New York: Harper and Row, Publishers, 1960).
21. G. N. GETMAN and ELMER KANE, *The Physiology of Readiness* (Minneapolis P.A.S.S., Inc., 1964).
22. B. BALOW, op. cit., p. 523.
23. Ibid., p. 523.
24. FRANK RIESSMAN, *The Culturally Deprived Child* (New York: Harper and Row, Publishers, 1962), p. 1.
25. FRANK RIESSMAN and FRANK ALBERTS, "Digging the Man's Language," *Saturday Review*, September 17, 1966, p. 80.
26. GEORGE D. SPACHE et al., "A Longitudinal First Grade Readiness Program," *The Reading Teacher* (May 1966):580-584.
27. SHIRLEY C. FELDMANN and CYNTHIA P. DEUTSCH, *A Study of the Effectiveness of Training for Retarded Readers in Auditory Perception Skills Underlying Reading*, U.S.O.E. Title VII Project 1127 (New York: Institute for Developmental Studies, Department of Psychiatry, New York Medical College, 1965).
28. R. VAN ALLEN, "Three Approaches to Teaching Reading," *Challenge and Experiment in Reading*, International Reading Association Conference Proceedings, Vol. 7 (1962):153-156.
29. RUSSELL G. STAUFFER, "The Language-Experience Approach," in *First Grade Reading Programs*, James F. Kerfoot, ed., Perspectives in Reading, No. 5. (Newark, Del.: International Reading Association, 1965).
30. GEORGE SPACHE and EVELYN SPACHE, op. cit., pp. 179-182.
31. LEONARD BLOOMFIELD and CLARENCE L. BARNHART, *Let's Read: A Linguistic Approach* (Detroit: Wayne State University Press, 1961).
32. ALBERT J. HARRIS, *How to Increase Reading Ability*, 5th ed. (New York: David McKay Co., Inc., 1970), p. 71.
33. GERTRUDE HILDRETH, *Teaching Reading* (New York: Henry Holt and Co., 1958), p. 162.
34. JOHN DOWNING, "The I.T.A. (Initial Teaching Alphabet) Reading Experiment," *The Reading Teacher* (November 1964):105-110.
35. JOHN DOWNING and IVAN ROSE, "The Value of ITA: We're Enthusiastic," in *Readings in Reading*, Delwyn Schubert and Theodore Torgerson, eds. (New York: Thomas Y. Crowell Co., 1968), pp. 506-508.
36. PHILIP G. HILAIRE and LOIS THOMPSON, "ITA: A Review and Assessment," *Occasional Papers*, Oakland Schools, Pontiac, Michigan.

37. WARREN G. CUTTS, "The Value of ITA: It's Too Soon to Know Definitely," in *Readings in Reading*, Delwyn Schubert and Theodore Torgerson, eds. (New York: Thomas Y. Crowell Co., 1968), pp. 508-510.

38. CALEB GATTENGO, *Words in Color* (New York: Xerox Educational Division).

39. EDWARD FRY, "A Diacritical Marking System to Aid Beginning Reading Instruction," *Elementary English* 41 (Fall 1964):15-17.

40. WILLARD C. OLSON, *Child Development* (Boston: D. C. Heath and Co., 1949).

41. HARRY W. SARTAIN, "Individualized Reading—An Evaluation" in *Readings in Reading*, Delwyn Schubert and Theodore Torgerson, eds. (New York: Thomas Y. Crowell Co., 1968), pp. 517-523.

42. Ibid., p. 520.

43. RALPH STAIGER, "How Are Basal Readers Used?" in *Readings in Reading*, Delwyn Schubert and Theodore Torgerson, eds. (New York: Thomas Y. Crowell Co., 1968), pp. 302-306.

44. GEORGE SPACHE and EVELYN SPACHE, op. cit., pp. 91-92.

45. Ibid., pp. 93-103.

46. SARTAIN, op. cit., p. 519.

47. EDWARD DOLCH and M. BLOOMSTER, "Phonic Readiness," *Elementary School Journal* 38 (1937):201-295.

48. Hildreth, op. cit., pp. 341-342.

49. EDWARD DOLCH, *Problems in Reading* (Champaign, Ill.: Garrard Press, 1948).

50. GEORGE SPACHE and EVELYN SPACHE, op. cit., p. 395.

51. HORACE MANN, *Second Annual Report Covering the Year 1838 to the Board of Education, Massachusetts* (Boston: Dutton & Wentworth, State Printer, 1839), p. 40.

52. EDMUND HUEY, *The Psychology and Pedagogy of Reading* (New York: The Macmillan Co., 1908), p. 10.

53. CHARLES H. JUDD and GUY T. BUSWELL, *Silent Reading: A Study of the Various Types.* Supplementary Educational Monographs, No. 76. (Chicago: The University of Chicago Press, 1922).

54. RUTH STRANG, CONSTANCE McCULLOUGH, and ARTHUR TRAXLER, *The Improvement of Reading* (New York: McGraw-Hill Book Co., Inc., 1961), p. 421.

55. ARTHUR GATES, *The Improvement of Reading* (New York: The Macmillan Co., 1947), ch. 9.

56. GEORGE SPACHE and EVELYN SPACHE, op. cit., p. 412.

57. LEE DEIGHTON, *Vocabulary Development in the Classroom* (New York: Bureau of Publications, Teachers College, Columbus University, 1959).

58. THEODORE CLYMER, "The Utility of Phonic Generalizations in the Primary Grades," *The Reading Teacher* (January 1963):252-258.

59. C. WINKLEY, "Which Accent Generalizations Are Worth Teaching?" *The Reading Teacher* (December 1966):219-224.

60. MILDRED BAILEY, "The Utility of Phonic Generalizations in Grades One Through Six," *The Reading Teacher* (February 1967):413-418.

61. ROBERT EMANS, "The Usefulness of Phonic Generalizations Above the Primary Grades," *The Reading Teacher* (February 1967):419-425.

62. THEODORE CLYMER, "Criteria for Grouping for Reading Instruction," *Proceedings of the Annual Conference on Reading* 21 (December 1959) University of Chicago Press.

63. DAVID RUSSELL, "Interclass Grouping for Reading Instruction in the Intermediate Grades," *Journal of Educational Research* (February 1946): 462-470.
64. ARTHUR HOLLINGSHEAD, *An Evaluation of the Use of Certain Educational and Mental Measurements for Purposes of Classification,* Contribution to Education, No. 302, Bureau of Publications.
65. HARRIS, op. cit., p. 116.
66. MARVIN D. GLOCK, "Discussion: Classroom Techniques of Identifying and Diagnosing the Needs of Retarded Readers in High School and College," in *Better Readers for Our Times,* William S. Gray and Nancy Larrick, eds., International Reading Association Conference Proceedings, vol. 1 (New York: Scholastic Magazines, 1956), pp. 132-133.
67. RUTH STRANG, CONSTANCE MCCULLOUGH, and ARTHUR TRAXLER, *The Improvement of Reading,* 4th ed. (New York: McGraw-Hill Book Co., 1967), p. 50.
68. Ibid., p. 50.
69. NICHOLAS JOHNSON, "What Do We Do About Television?" *Saturday Review,* July 11, 1970, p. 44.
70. HELEN M. ROBINSON, "Some Poor Readers Have Emotional Problems," *The Reading Teacher* (May 1953):25-33.
71. PAUL WITTY and DAVID KOPEL, *Reading and the Educative Process* (New York: Ginn and Co., 1939), p. 27.
72. RUTH STRANG, CONSTANCE MCCULLOUGH, and ARTHUR TRAXLER, *The Improvement of Reading,* 4th ed. (New York: McGraw-Hill Book Co., 1967), p. 127.
73. HILDRETH, op. cit., p. 155.
74. FRANCIS ROBINSON, *Effective Study* (New York: Harper, 1946), p. 28.
75. BERNARD E. DONOVAN, *Survey of Reading Abilities of Pupils Entering the Academic High Schools in September 1955* (New York: Board of Education, 1955), pp. 1-3.
76. GEORGE NORVELL, *The Reading Interests of Young People* (Boston: D. C. Heath and Co., 1950).
77. HERBERT RUDMAN, "The Informational Needs and Reading Interests of Children in Grades IV Through VIII," *Elementary School Journal* 55 (1955):502-512.
78. ROBERT THORNDIKE, *Interests* (Bureau of Publications, Teachers College, Columbia University, 1941).
79. L. F. LOWERY and W. GRAFFT, "Paperbacks and Reading Attitudes," *The Reading Teacher* (April 1968):618-623.
80. J. R. NEWTON, *Reading in Your School* (New York: McGraw-Hill Book Co., 1960), p. 138.

SELECTED READINGS

BERGER, ALLEN. "Reading Readiness: A Bibliography." *Elementary English* 45 (February 1968):184-189.

DAVIS, ALLISON. "Teaching Language and Reading to Disadvantaged Negro Children." *Elementary English* 42 (November 1965):791-797.

DURKIN, DOLORES. *Children Who Read Early.* New York: Teachers College Press, Columbia University, 1966.

DURR, WILLIAM. *Reading Instruction: Dimensions and Issues.* New York: Houghton Mifflin Co., 1967, secs. 2-10, 12.

GOODMAN, KENNETH. "Linguistics in Reading." *Elementary School Journal* 64 (April 1964):355-364.

HARRIS, ALBERT. *How to Increase Reading Ability.* 5th ed. New York: David McKay Co., Inc., chs. 1-7.

KARLIN, ROBERT. *Teaching Elementary Reading.* New York: Harcourt Brace Jovanovich, 1971, ch. 5.

LEE, DORIS, and R. V. ALLEN. *Learning to Read Through Experiences.* New York: Appleton-Century-Crofts, 1963.

RIESSMAN, FRANK. "Styles of Learning." *NEA Journal* 55 (March 1966):15-17.

ROBINSON, H. ALAN. *The Underachiever in Reading.* Chicago: University of Chicago Press, 1962.

SCHUBERT, DELWYN, and THEODORE TORGERSON. *Readings in Reading.* New York: Thomas Y. Crowell Co., 1968, selections 20-32, 37-40, 43, 44, 72-77.

SPACHE, GEORGE, and EVELYN SPACHE. *Reading in the Elementary School.* Boston: Allyn and Bacon, Inc., 1969, chs. 2-6, 12, 13.

STANCHFIELD, JO. "Boys' Reading Interests as Revealed Through Personal Conferences." *The Reading Teacher* 16 (October 1961):41-44.

STAUFFER, RUSSELL, ed. *Reading Teacher* 18 (April 1965). An issue devoted entirely to the problems of the disadvantaged learner.

STRANG, RUTH. "Teaching Reading to the Culturally Disadvantaged in Secondary Schools." *Journal of Reading* 10 (May 1967):527-535.

—————, CONSTANCE MCCULLOUGH, and ARTHUR TRAXLER. *The Improvement of Reading.* 4th ed. New York: McGraw-Hill Book Co., 1967.

WITTY, PAUL, ALMA FREELAND, and EDITH GROTBERG. *The Teaching of Reading.* Boston: D. C. Heath and Co., 1966.

5

Diagnosis in the Instructional Program

THE IMPORTANCE OF DIAGNOSIS

Reading diagnosis has been defined as follows:

A scientific analysis and description of a reading disability designed: (a) to identify the nature of the difficulty such as reading errors, faulty reading habits, and level of the reading competence; (b) to locate underlying causal factors, and (c) to prescribe corrective or remedial treatment. The process encompasses both formal and informal techniques involving interviews, observations, oral reading, silent reading, and intelligence tests along with an assessment of personal and environmental factors conditioning learning. (1)

The major purpose of a reading diagnosis is to gather data and acquire insights which will be helpful in planning an effective corrective program. Without diagnosis a teacher can make only hit or miss decisions regarding materials and procedures that should be used with a reading problem case.

Effective treatment is impossible without diagnosis. When someone visits a physician and complains of chills and muscular aches, he isn't plunged into a tub of ice water to break his fever or given rubbing liniment to assuage his pain. A physician knows too well that the elimination of symptoms does not cure a disease. If he finds a syndrome that indicates bacterial invasion, antibiotics may be prescribed to attack the infection at its source and thereby restore good health.

A perusal of the literature on reading reveals that all too often corrective work in reading parallels the ice-water and rubbing-liniment analogy. Methods, techniques, and gadgets are used which are primarily concerned with manifestations of symptoms rather than amelioration of causal factors.

Although diagnosis should precede prescription, it is not necessary to delay corrective work until absolutely all data about a child's problem are collected. Diagnosis and corrective procedures should be combined. As instruction continues and more testing and observation take place, the teacher gains additional insights into the problem. Diagnosis does not end until correction is completed.

When the elementary teacher in a typical school meets a new class, she can expect that ten to twenty-five percent of the pupils will be retarded one or more years in reading. If the school is located in a culturally depressed area, the retarded group may exceed fifty percent of the class. The reading problems in this instance not only become more numerous but more severe because the children involved are often from bilingual and/or culturally deprived homes which have provided them with meager intellectual stimulation and limited cultural experiences. The children have known nothing but failure, and they no longer have a zest for learning.

Identifying retarded readers, determining the nature and severity of their problems, and locating causal factors and specific reading difficulties become the paramount problems for every elementary school teacher at the beginning of the school year. Appropriate developmental and corrective work cannot be planned for the ensuing year without the information gained from an efficient diagnostic program.

Some of the many questions that can be answered in a reading diagnosis are as follows:

1. What learning problems, if any, does each pupil have? (See chapter 2 for a discussion of learning problems.)
2. What are his oral- and silent-reading grade levels?
3. What is the nature of his reading problem? Do the difficulties encompass faulty word recognition, faulty word analysis, or faulty comprehension?
4. What faulty reading habits has he acquired, and what specific reading skills and abilities has he failed to master?
5. Is the difficulty of the present developmental material on his frustration level, instructional level, or independent reading level?
6. What grade level of difficulty is recommended for developmental instruction?
7. What is the pupil's present independent reading level?
8. What is his potential reading level?
9. What sequence of corrective instruction seems advisable?
10. What reading level should the pupil seek to attain this year?

Many of the foregoing questions can be answered by employing silent and oral reading tests. These tests (particularly the latter) will demonstrate objectively what deficiencies in the basic reading skills have led many pupils into scholastic doldrums. In order to eliminate the individual difficulties indicated by a detailed diagnosis, individualized self-directed corrective instruction should be provided.

NATURE AND EXTENT OF A READING DIAGNOSIS

It is almost axiomatic that the more a teacher knows about a child and his reading problem, the more likely he will be able to help the child overcome his difficulties. But a teacher must stop data-gathering at some point. Where and when he stops will depend on a number of factors: the diagnostic equipment and materials available, the teacher's background of experience and training, the severity of the problem, and the amount of time he has at his disposal. The latter often is the primary factor that limits the depth of a teacher's diagnosis. The chief means of gathering information involves the following: cumulative records, observation, interviews with teachers and parents, informal testing, reading inventories, screening tests, and reading test scores. It also becomes important to recognize when a child's reading problem is sufficiently complicated and severe to warrant referral to a reading specialist.

The reading specialist, because of his training and smaller student load, is able to delve more profoundly into a child's reading problem. Not only is the reading specialist interested in cataloging the symptoms of reading disability, but he is concerned with uncovering the etiological or causal factors of the disorder. In addition to diagnostic approaches used by the classroom teacher, therefore, he may employ individual intelligence and personality tests, in-depth diagnostic reading tests, and additional physical screening tests. This often involves a case-study approach.

PRINCIPLES OF DIAGNOSIS

Classroom teachers as well as reading specialists can profit from the following principles of diagnosis:

1. Diagnosis is continuous. It does not stop until reading disability ceases to exist.
2. Standardized tests do not determine instructional or independent reading levels. Most often a frustration level is represented.

3. Reading test scores are not valid indicators of achievement or potential unless a child has put forth his best efforts. Therefore, the child should be free from undue tension in the testing situation. Rapport is essential.
4. Test scores are not sacrosanct. They are not fixed and immutable. They are measures of status attained and must not be considered unerring indicators of future performance.
5. Causal factors of reading disability do not operate in isolation. Although there may be a primary cause, a constellation of causes is usually involved. Therefore, each cause must be interpreted and evaluated as part of the total pattern.
6. The diagnostic process should be as objective and scientific as possible. Diagnostic prejudice (the tendency to attribute all reading disability to a pet cause or causes) should be avoided.
7. When causality of reading disability is being considered, a team approach is desirable. Specialists in differing areas—social worker, speech correctionist, school psychologist, psychiatrist, endocrinologist, optometrist, otolaryngologist, neurologist, and others—are likely to discern cause-and-effect relationships which escape the generalist.
8. A syndrome or pattern of symptoms is more important in diagnosis than isolated symptoms.
9. Data must be analyzed and evaluated so as to establish cause-and-effect relationships. Care must be exercised. Symptoms can easily be confused with causes; causes can be confused with symptoms.
10. An early diagnosis has greater value than a belated one. It can do much to prevent reading difficulties from becoming serious, and it can help children avoid failure and personality maladjustment.

INFORMAL TOOLS AND PROCEDURES

Cumulative Records

A vast amount of valuable information can be gleaned from cumulative records. Routinely, cumulative records should be studied by all classroom teachers at the beginning of the school year. When a child is given remedial help, the teacher should avail himself of existing school records. Questions that may be answered by consulting them are as follows: What was the nature of the difficulty when it first manifested itself? What was the age and grade of the child at that time? What corrective work was provided? Does the child have a history of frequent absences? Has he attended a number of different schools? What is the nature of his achievement record? What are the results of past and current standardized achievement tests? What intelligence test scores are available? Do data on the child's past and present physical status indicate the presence of any defects that are significant? Are there anecdotal records that might prove helpful in understanding the child's problem?

Observation

As an impartial observer, a classroom teacher can readily identify many reading problems. A retarded reader is often disinterested in reading and cannot, even if he tries, do the reading required. The child may read in a slow, halting manner and demonstrate a limited sight vocabulary. He fails to understand what he reads, and when he encounters an unfamiliar word, he does not know how to analyze it.

Through observation, a teacher may detect habits which are detrimental to a child's reading. These include lip movements and subvocalization during silent reading, unnecessary head movements, and finger pointing. By observing a reader's eyes during silent reading, the teacher may learn about eye-movement patterns, span of recognition, regressive tendencies, and other reading idiosyncrasies that interfere with reading efficiency.

During silent reading periods, the teacher can answer a number of important questions about a pupil's reading. Does he seem to enjoy reading? Does he appear to be able to use reference books? What seem to be his reading preferences? Can he read for long periods without losing interest?

One of the ways to learn about a pupil's interests is through observation. What does he like to talk about? What does he do when he has free time? Does he draw? If so, what does he draw? A child who draws airplanes, for example, may find books such as *Sabre Jet Ace* or *Pilot Jack Knight* very interesting reading.

To improve the reliability and validity of observations, Carter and McGinnis(2) offer suggestions such as the following: Study all school records (teacher reports, test information, physical reports), family history, and academic history; establish rapport with the child observed; have a flexible and original approach—one that can be modified; develop hypotheses implicitly, use your intuitive powers, substantiate hypotheses by observation of the pupil in different settings; do not infer too much, be explicit, stick to facts and simple interpretation whenever possible, judgments should be tentative and not too technical and profound; be aware that individuals and surroundings change, don't assume an individual's responses will be the same in all situations;

physical, psychological, and environmental factors are involved; observed facts are valid and reliable to the degree that the observer is aware of his own prejudices, preconceptions, and emotional bias.

A perceptive and impartial observer is dependent on a rich background of information and experience. Without an adequate background and experience he would not know what to look for nor would he appreciate the significance of what he observes. Since the psychology of reading problems embraces many fields, some knowledge of opthalmology, otology, neurology, endrocrinology, psychology, pediatrics, and education is needed. The more an observer can learn about reading and its related areas, the better he will perform in his role as an observer.

Classroom teachers and reading specialists who are sensitive to significant symptoms of overt pupil behavior in the areas of hearing, vision, health, social and emotional behavior, and speech can readily identify pupils who require special attention or are in need of referral. The use of the inventories in this chapter will alert teachers to many symptoms of learning problems and will provide a record of systematic observational data. Intelligent use of these inventories will serve to make observation more objective and impartial.

Interviews

Most teachers and reading specialists find the interview or conference a simple and direct approach which can provide information useful in the diagnosis and treatment of a disabled reader.

Interviews may serve a variety of purposes: to acquaint the interviewer with the subject and his reading problem; to produce pertinent information; to disclose developmental aspects of the problem; and to permit cooperative planning between the interviewer and the pupil for a program of correction. Frequently, answers that a pupil has given to questions on a reading test or any other test can be verified or enlarged upon during an interview. The interview is particularly useful in helping the teacher or reading specialist to secure developmental history, beginning with the onset of the problem, which may reveal the causes of the pupil's present reading difficulty.

The skilled interviewer gives the subject full opportunity to relate his experiences and express his feelings. It is advisable to avoid as many direct questions as possible and to elicit information through conversation in which the interviewer tells the story about himself, his problems, his successes and failures. Pertinent facts to be gained will depend upon the function of the interview, the subject's age, and the nature of the problems. The interviewer must be kind, sympathetic, and very adept at placing the subject at ease, at eliciting pertinent data, at recognizing whether or not the responses are genuine, and at evaluating the importance of the information gained. Throughout the interview he must be alert to significant behavior on the part of the subject.

It is frequently necessary to hold several interviews. The function of the first may be to become better acquainted with the subject and to establish rapport. This lays the groundwork for further study of the pupil.

When the objective of the interview is to help the interviewee understand himself and his problem better and to plan cooperatively appropriate therapy, it is known as a therapeutic interview. The therapy must seek to eliminate or ameliorate the causal factors and to promote a constructive program under conditions which will insure a normal emotional life, happiness, and success.

Information about the home and the family can be gathered best by visiting the parents in their home. When access to the home is not feasible or possible, the parents should be persuaded to come to the school for a conference. During the interview, information about the existing parent-child relationship should be obtained indirectly. This information should be verified by actual observation whenever possible.

The Home Environment Inventory found in this chapter lists those aspects of the home life important for the observer to study. The inventory should serve to direct the observations and to indicate important information to be gathered during the interview. The items checked on the inventory should reveal the conditions in the home which are hazards and may exert an unwholesome influence on the development of the child.

The present status of the child can be understood best in the light of his developmental history. The sum of his experiences in and out of school is largely responsible for his present status and must be evaluated so that the teacher can locate the causes of his reading problem. When and where did the symptoms of his difficulty first appear? What environmental factors which could be considered causal were present at that time? Are these factors still present? Has the child been living in an environment conducive to normal physical, emotional, and social development? What therapeutic measures have already been attempted by parents and teachers? How can the human relationships which the child experiences be measured and evaluated? These are some of the important problems to be considered.

It is obvious that inferences or hear-say evidence about the pupil's home should not be countenanced. The teacher or reading specialist must obtain such information from the parents themselves. Conferences held with them will permit the teacher to gather much data about the child's reading problem from the parents' point of view. The general objectives of the school and the reasons for taking a special interest in the child must be made evident to the parent. The parent interview will enable the interviewer to gather vital information relative to the pupil's early developmental history. The conditions surrounding the child's birth, the age at which he began to walk and talk, the ease or difficulty in his early training, his childhood diseases, and the onset of the reading problem are some of the important aspects of the developmental history that can be acquired by the teacher or social worker.

It is necessary to gain wholesome rapport with the parents so that needed facts will not be distorted or withheld. How many children are there in the home? How do they get along with one another? How does the pupil compare with his sisters and brothers (if any) in school work, interest in the home, and in general behavior? What duties or chores do the children have? How much spending money do they receive? What do they do to earn money? How do they spend their weekends? How do they spend their summer vacation? How much time is spent in watching television? Do the older children have any responsibility in caring for the younger siblings? How much time do the parents share with their children?

If the child is the only child, do the parents provide normal social opportunities for him to play with other children? Does he get along well with other children, and how does he compare in age with his companions? What does he like to do when he is at home? Does he have pets and does he look after them? Does he put away his toys and take care of his own room? Is he responsible in performing his duties?

Do the parents show favoritism and do they compare the duller child unfavorably with the more fortunate siblings? Is the child adopted? Are there relatives or boarders in the home? Does the father share responsibility in training the children? Is he a real companion to them? How are the children disciplined? Are the parents consistent in their correction? What situations in the home give rise to problem behavior? Is the child rejected?

Several conferences may be required to gather the desired information. After rapport has been established and the parent is eager to convey information that will help the interviewer understand the child better, arrangements should be made for a visit to the home when the children are present. The father should be there if at all possible. Keen observation will disclose pertinent facts and conditions. The adequacy of the home and the neighborhood can be ascertained. Parent-parent relationship and parent-child relationship can be determined by observing the routine of the home under normal conditions. Observation in the home during a meal or at bedtime is especially helpful. The "atmosphere" of the home and methods used in handling the children will serve to verify, modify, or discount the parents' own analysis.

The influence of the home on the adjustment of a child cannot be overemphasized. The experiences gained during the preschool period, the most formative years, result in well-developed modes of adjustment and well-defined levels of emotional and social maturity. The child comes to school with an acquired personality and a pattern of habits which encourage learning, if normal, but retard learning if the development has been unwholesome. If he is socially and emotionally immature, he has not acquired the habit of following directions, a sense of responsibility, nor the cooperation and concentration necessary for learning to read in a formal school environment. Extreme negativism and emotionality likewise are hazards to a successful reading experience. Maladjustment in the home reappears in the school and interferes with all learning. In these cases, the home and school must cooperate in planning a program of home and school responsibilities for the pupil.

Pupil Reports of Interest

Many teachers have discovered that they can involve a pupil in reading if they capitalize on his interests. As early as 1939, Witty and Kopel(3) designed comprehensive inventories of interests and activities for both elementary and secondary students. Many aspects of living and adjustment other than activities relating to reading were included in these early inventories. Some of the questions were answerable by a *yes* or *no,* while others called for more lengthy answers. Although more than three decades have passed since Witty and Kopel introduced their inventories, most of the questions are as useful and valid now as they were then.

Interest inventories and questionnaires are readily available. They can be found in professional books by Bond and Tinker,(4) Harris,(5) and many others. After looking over a number of these inventories, some teachers feel that they would like to evolve their own, one more suited to the kinds of pupils with whom they work. The authors recommend this. They have seen a number of teacher-made inventories that are excellent.

BEHAVIOR INVENTORIES

The following inventories will prove valuable to observing teachers who wish to relate specific symptoms of difficulty to areas of concern.*

Home Environment

PARENTAL RELATIONSHIP
1. Parents are incompatible
2. Parents quarrel
3. Broken home
4. One or more relatives live in the home

CHILD TRAINING
1. Parents disagree on methods of child training
2. Parents dominate the child
3. Parents are inconsistent in disciplining the child
4. Parents are too severe in their discipline
5. Parents are overindulgent or oversolicitous
6. Parents are neglectful
7. Child's spending money is inadequate or excessive
8. Child has no home duties or responsibilities
9. Child's food habits are undesirable
10. Child's rest is inadequate
11. Child's moral and ethical training is inadequate

PARENT-CHILD RELATIONSHIP
1. Parents reject the child
2. Father seems unconcerned about the child's problem
3. Father seems unconcerned about the child's future
4. Father disapproves of the child's choice of a career
5. Father shows no concern for the child's education
6. Mother seems unconcerned about the child's problem
7. Mother seems unconcerned about the child's future
8. Mother disapproves of the child's choice of a career
9. Mother shows no concern for the child's education

*All inventories and forms appearing in this book may be reproduced by teachers for their own use.

CHILD-TO-CHILD RELATIONSHIP

1. Children are quarrelsome in the home
2. Child is jealous of a sibling
3. Child is an only child
4. Child has too few contacts with other children

SOCIOECONOMIC STATUS

1. Parents do not speak English
2. Parents have few if any cultural interests
3. Parents do not read to the children
4. Parents do not use the public library
5. There are no worthwhile books or magazines in the home
6. There are no books for children in the home
7. Father tends to be shiftless
8. Mother tends to be shiftless
9. Family is insecure economically
10. Home is inadequate

COMMUNITY

1. Neighborhood is undesirable
2. Companions are undesirable
3. Playgrounds are lacking or unsupervised
4. Home-community relationship is unwholesome

Hearing

ACUITY

1. Questions must be repeated
2. Imitates other pupils
3. Seems confused
4. Daydreams
5. Faulty speech
6. Unintelligible speech
7. Speaks in a monotone
8. Voice abnormally loud or soft
9. Symbolic gestures in lieu of words
10. Language handicap
11. Strained expression on face when listening
12. Ignores verbal directions
13. Reads lips
14. Tilting or turning head as if to favor better ear
15. Cupping a hand behind the ear
16. Blank expression on face

EAR TROUBLE
1. Spells of dizziness
2. Noises in the ears
3. Excess of wax in ears
4. Discharge from ears
5. Earaches or mastoid pains
6. Previous middle-ear problems

Vision

1. Squinting when reading from or looking at the blackboard
2. Excessive blinking, scowling, or facial distortion when reading at near point
3. Holds book too close to eyes
4. Holds head too close to desk
5. Confuses words and letters
6. Tilts head to one side
7. Closes or covers one eye when reading
8. Irritability evidenced when reading
9. Has inflamed, swollen eyelids
10. Has inflamed eyeballs
11. Has discharge from eyes
12. Pain in and about eyes
13. Pain in the back of the neck
14. Has headaches after reading, seeing a movie, or viewing television
15. Eyes sensitive to light
16. Eyes tire when reading
17. Unwilling to wear glasses prescribed
18. One eye turns in (squint)
19. Eyes tremble or twitch
20. Frequent rubbing of the eyes
21. Watering of the eyes with close work
22. Dizziness or nausea after much close work

Observable Pupil Behavior Symptomatic of Underlying Problems When Frequently Displayed

Physical Development

1. Obese, overweight
2. Thin, underweight
3. Excessive height
4. Retarded stature

Health

1. Mouth breather
2. Frequent severe colds
3. Frequent sore throat
4. Chronic cough
5. Poor teeth
6. Sore gums
7. Swollen or enlarged neck glands
8. Dry, scaly skin
9. Protruding eyeballs
10. Frequent itching
11. Convulsions, seizures
12. Blank spells
13. Fainting spells
14. Frequent headaches
15. Persistent pain
16. Nervous mannerisms, tics
17. Puffiness of eyes and face
18. Swollen hands or feet
19. Sallow complexion
20. Flushing of the skin
21. Listless, tired
22. Falls asleep in school
23. Frequent absence due to illness

Handicaps

1. Faulty posture
2. Awkward gait
3. Crippled, physical handicap
4. Partially paralyzed
5. Has had scarlet fever
6. Has had rheumatic fever
7. Not immunized against disease

Social and Emotional Behavior

AGGRESSIVE

1. Angers easily
2. Temper tantrums
3. Uncooperative
4. Sex irregularities

5. Uncontrolled bladder or bowels
6. Enuresis (bed wetting)
7. Truancy, unexcused absences
8. Cheats
9. Resents correction
10. Destructive
11. Overcritical of others
12. Irresponsible
13. Impudent, defiant
14. Quarrelsome
15. Cruel to animals
16. Irritable
17. Belligerent, bossy
18. Bully
19. Vindictive
20. Steals
21. Dishonest, untruthful
22. Marked change in personality
23. Negativistic

RECESSIVE
1. Runs away from home
2. Seeks attention
3. Overconscientious
4. Emotionally inadequate
5. Overexuberant
6. Whiner
7. Pessimistic
8. Suspicious
9. Plays by himself
10. Avoids others, unfriendly
11. Shunned by others
12. Overreligious
13. Daydreams, preoccupied
14. Plays with younger children
15. Physical coward
16. Selfish
17. Feigns illness
18. Too submissive
19. Depressed
20. Overdependent
21. Sullen
22. Nervous tensions, tics

23. Bites fingernails
24. Fearful, timid, shy
25. Worries
26. Jealous
27. Cries easily

Speech

VOCAL
1. Remains silent because of his speech handicap
2. Speaks too loudly
3. Has to be reminded frequently to speak louder
4. Quality of voice annoying
5. Voice lacks variety
6. Inflections of voice are tiresomely repetitious
7. Voice suggests a person of different age or sex

ARTICULATORY
1. Speaks too slowly
2. Speaks too rapidly
3. Omits or slides over sounds
4. Adds superfluous words
5. Difficult to understand pronunciation of certain words
6. Clumsy speech
7. Speech requires undue effort
8. Speech is accompanied by distractive movements of the lips or tongue

RHYTHMIC
1. Speech is blocked at times
2. Speech is blocked by stopping the air flow
3. Speech is blocked by restricting movements of the tongue or lips
4. Repeats certain sounds unnecessarily
5. Distractive movements of head, face, or hands during speech block

LINGUISTIC
1. Shows difficulty in understanding simple oral directions
2. Although words are clear, difficult to understand the meaning of his thought
3. Resorts to signs and gestures to express his wants
4. Has difficulty in recognizing simple words when spelled for him orally.

Children who are identified by inventories as having a physical or speech problem should be brought to the attention of the proper specialist. The school nurse or doctor, the psychologist, and the speech specialist can be helpful with such cases.

A school psychologist may be of assistance with children who have been identified as emotional and social behavior problems. Teachers can help by employing an anecdotal method. By concentrating on a pupil's problem and recording his behavior in situations as they arise, the teacher gains an insight into the pupil's attitudes, feelings, and conflicts. Insight and understanding make it possible for the teacher to apply proper therapy. A series of objective behavior descriptions which reveal the pupil's manner of adjusting to others and to problem situations in general will provide valuable information to the school psychologist as well.

READINESS TESTS AND CHECKLISTS

Besides intelligence tests, kindergarten or first-grade teachers find that reading readiness tests are helpful in deciding whether children are ready for formal instruction in beginning reading. They are also of value to teachers of children who have failed beginning reading.

Although there is some overlap between intelligence tests and reading readiness tests, the latter focus attention on items that are dependent to some degree on training and are less likely, therefore, to be measures of aptitude or learning potential. They include items such as letter discrimination and word matching, selecting an appropriate picture from several presented, remembering a story, detecting rhyming words, and writing one's name.

Some representative readiness tests are Gates Reading Readiness Tests (Bureau of Publications, Teachers College), Harrison-Stroud Reading Readiness Test (Houghton Mifflin Company), Lee-Clark Reading Readiness Test (California Test Bureau), Metropolitan Readiness Test (Harcourt Brace Jovanovich, Inc.), and the Murphy-Durrell Diagnostic Reading Readiness Test (Harcourt Brace Jovanovich, Inc.).*

Combining intelligence test data with what has been learned from a reading readiness test and informal observation gives the teacher a fairly broad basis for determining reading readiness of a given child. To objectify informal observation a checklist such as the following is recommended.

*See Appendix C for additional information regarding these tests.

READING READINESS CHECKLIST

	Evaluation of Factor Involved				

Vision:

Acuity at near point 1 2 3 4 5
Acuity at far point 1 2 3 4 5
Binocular skill 1 2 3 4 5
Eye-hand coordination 1 2 3 4 5
Directional sense 1 2 3 4 5

Hearing:

Auditory acuity 1 2 3 4 5
Auditory discrimination 1 2 3 4 5
Clarity of enunciation 1 2 3 4 5

Speech:

Absence of baby talk 1 2 3 4 5
Absence of a lisp 1 2 3 4 5
Absence of stuttering 1 2 3 4 5
Overall clarity of speech 1 2 3 4 5

General Health:

Absence of fatigue 1 2 3 4 5
Well-nourished body 1 2 3 4 5
Bodily coordination 1 2 3 4 5
Freedom from physical defects 1 2 3 4 5

Social and Emotional Status:

Leadership ability 1 2 3 4 5
Ability to work with others 1 2 3 4 5
Ability to carry on independently 1 2 3 4 5
Absence of infantile behavior 1 2 3 4 5
Feelings of security 1 2 3 4 5

Home Environment:

Quality of English spoken in home 1 2 3 4 5
Parental interest in books 1 2 3 4 5
Parental sharing of books with child 1 2 3 4 5
Parental harmony 1 2 3 4 5
Parental agreement on disciplinary measures 1 2 3 4 5
Parental acceptance 1 2 3 4 5
Travel opportunities 1 2 3 4 5

READING READINESS CHECKLIST (*Continued*)

Evaluation of
Factor Involved

Language Skill:

Listening skill 1 2 3 4 5
Speaking vocabulary 1 2 3 4 5
Use of complete sentences 1 2 3 4 5
Ability to tell a story 1 2 3 4 5

Intelligence:

Ability to recognize relationships 1 2 3 4 5
Ability to think sequentially 1 2 3 4 5
Ability to memorize with ease 1 2 3 4 5
Ability to sustain attention 1 2 3 4 5
Ability to make good judgments 1 2 3 4 5

DIAGNOSING DIFFICULTIES IN WORD RECOGNITION AND WORD ANALYSIS

Informal Reading Inventory

An informal reading inventory provides a means whereby a teacher can evaluate a child's reading as he reads aloud materials on different levels of difficulty. By administering an informal reading inventory a teacher can determine the level at which a child can read independently, the level at which he needs instructional aid, the level at which he encounters failure and frustration, and his hearing comprehension level.

As a child reads materials that vary in difficulty, the teacher can learn much about his strengths and weaknesses. He can pinpoint the specific kinds of errors that characterize the child's reading. An analysis of this kind enables the teacher to provide a suitable instructional program.

Knowing the difficulty level of reading material which a pupil can read without any special help is of great value to a teacher. Much of the work a child does in school must be carried out by him independently. If the material presented is too difficult, the pupil fails and cannot be expected to develop an interest in reading nor can he develop a high standard of performance.

Instructional material that is too easy results in little or no intellectual stimulation. By the same token, instructional material that is too difficult not only proves intellectually stultifying, but develops in the pupil a distaste for learning.

If a teacher is to read aloud to his pupils or engage them in other kinds of listening activity, it is important for him to know the pupils' listening comprehension level.

Teachers who wish to locate the right book for a child's independent, instructional, or listening comprehension level should be aware of the specific criteria to be applied in determining them. These are as follows:

Independent Reading Level: This is the highest reading level at which a child can read easily and fluently, without help, with few word-recognition errors and very good comprehension and retention. Word-recognition errors do not exceed more than one per 100 words of running text and comprehension scores are ninety percent or higher. It is the level of optimum difficulty for recreational reading material.

Instructional Reading Level: This is the highest level at which a child reads satisfactorily, provided he receives teacher preparation and supervision. Word-recognition errors do not exceed more than five per 100 words of running text, and comprehension scores are seventy percent or above. It is the level of optimum difficulty for textbook reading.

Frustration Reading Level: This is the lowest level at which a child's reading skills break down. Fluency disappears, word-recognition errors are common, comprehension is defective, retention is poor, and evidence of emotional tension and discomfort manifests itself. Word-recognition errors exceed ten per 100 words of running text, and comprehension scores are fifty percent or below. It is the level that usually reflects the difficulty of textbooks used by retarded readers.

Listening Comprehension Level: This is the highest level at which a child can comprehend seventy percent of what is read aloud to him. This level can serve as an index of the child's capacity for reading achievement.

What kind of material should be used in an informal reading inventory? Betts suggests—

. . . any type of material, especially when the level of reading ability can be ascertained. To be most helpful, however, the inventory should be made with materials used in classroom reading activities. When an approximation of general level of reading achievement is needed, a well-graded series of basal readers is probably appropriate. (6)

The steps in giving an individual reading inventory have been described by Strang, McCullough, and Traxler.(7) These authors suggest that the teacher begin by deciding on a series of graded paragraphs which may be obtained from an unfamiliar basal reader series or may be specially written for the students being tested. Each paragraph should be mounted on a separate card. When working with the student, the teacher begins by asking a few friendly questions about his interests and reading habits. Then a word-recognition test such as the Wide Range Achievement Test should be given. The results from this test indicate the level at which the student should begin to read orally. As he reads, the teacher records the errors made, noting whether he answers briefly or at length; whether he does so in his own words or uses the words of the book; and whether he embellishes what the author said. After the first oral reading, the teacher should let the student read silently, then reread orally, and note any improvement. The student continues to read the graded series of paragraphs until he reaches his frustration level. The teacher then reads aloud a paragraph on the same level of difficulty and asks the same kinds of questions about it. Finally, the teacher records the student's independent, instructional, and frustration levels. He checks evidences of poor phrasing, comprehension, vocalization, and methods of word attack. He makes notes on other significant indications of reading ability, attitudes, and interests.

No informal reading inventory is included in this volume. Teachers who wish to avail themselves of already prepared inventories or material lending itself to constructing an inventory will find the following list of value.

ARONOW, MIRIAM S., and J. W. WRIGHTSTONE. *The Informal Appraisal of Reading Abilities.* Educational Research Bulletin No. 10, May 1949. New York: Board of Education of the City of New York.

BETTS, EMMETT A., and CAROLYN WELCH. *Informal Reading Inventory.* New York: American Book Co., 1964.

BOTEL, MORTON. *Botel Reading Inventory.* Chicago: Follett Publishing Co., 1961.

Group Informal Reading Inventory. Language Arts Supplement to Suggestions for the Teaching of Reading. Philadelphia: Curriculum Office.

JOHNSON, MARJORIE S., and ROY A. KRESS. *Informal Reading Inventories.* Newark, Del.: International Reading Association, 1965.

McCRACKEN, ROBERT A. "The Development and Validation of the Standard Reading Inventory for the Individual Appraisal of Reading and Performance in Grades One Through Six." *Improvement of Reading Through Classroom Practice.* Proceedings of the IRA Annual Convention, vol. 9 (1964):310-313.

Macmillan Reader Placement Test. New York: The Macmillan Co., 1967.

SILVAROLI, NICHOLAS J. *Classroom Reading Inventory.* Dubuque, Ia.: Wm. C. Brown Co. Publishers, 1969.

SMITH, NILA B. *Graded Selections for Informal Reading: Diagnosis for Grades 1 Through 3.* New York: New York University Press, 1959.

SMITH, NILA B. *Graded Selections for Informal Reading: Diagnosis for Grades 4 Through 6.* New York: New York University Press, 1963.

ORAL READING TESTS

Filling in blanks at random as in silent reading tests of the recognition type is not possible when a pupil is given an oral reading test. Guessing or bluffing is quickly discerned, and the teacher is able to locate specific difficulties in word recognition and word analysis. Faulty reading habits also become apparent.

Information particularly relevant to an analysis of each pupil's weaknesses in word-recognition and word-analysis skills can be obtained through the child's oral reading performance.

1. What is the size of his sight vocabulary?
   a. Does he skip words?
   b. Does he add words?
   c. Does he substitute words?
   d. Does he repeat words?
   e. Does he reverse words?
   f. Does he read word by word?
   g. Does he point to words?
   h. Does he lose his place?
2. Does he know the names of the consonants and their sounds?
3. Does he know the sounds of common blends and consonant digraphs?
4. Does he know the long and short sounds of the vowels? Diphthongs?
5. Is he aware of any generalizations or so-called rules pertaining to vowel sounds?
6. Does he utilize context clues?
7. Can he blend parts of a word into a whole?
8. Does he recognize common prefixes and suffixes?
9. Is he aware of word roots?
10. Can he break long words into syllables?

Unlike silent reading tests, oral reading tests must be administered individually. From ten to twenty minutes is usually ample time for administration. Commonly used oral reading tests include the Gray (Bobbs-Merrill) and Gilmore (Harcourt Brace Jovanovich, Inc.).

The teacher who uses an oral reading test soon becomes adept at employing a shorthand system for recording reading errors. A code such as the following (Gilmore Oral Reading Test)(8) can prove valuable when making assessments of a pupil's reading needs through informal reading tests. Teachers have many opportunities for informally evaluating children's oral reading in the classroom and through individual conferences.

Type of Error	Rule for Marking	Examples
Substitutions A sensible or real word substituted for the word in the paragraph.	Write in substituted word.	black The boy is back of the girl. girl See the girls.
Mispronunciations A nonsense word which may be produced by (1) false accentuation; (2) wrong pronunciation of vowels or consonants; or (3) omission, addition, or insertion of one or more letters.	Write word in phonetically (if time permits) or draw a line through the word.	sĭm'-bŏl-ĭk (1) symbolic (or) ~~symbolic~~ blĕs'-fŏͦl (2) blissful (or) ~~blissful~~ blĕnt (3) bent (or) ~~bent~~
Words Pronounced by Examiner A word on which the subject hesitates for 5 seconds. (The word is then pronounced by the examiner.)	Make two checks above word pronounced.	✓✓ It is a fascinating story.
Disregard of Punctuation Failure to observe punctuation.	Mark punctuation disregarded with an "x."	x Jack, my brother, is in the navy.
Insertions (including additions) A word (or words) inserted at the beginning, middle, or end of a sentence or line of test.	Write in inserted word or words.	the The dog and ∧ cat are fighting.
Hesitations A pause of at least 2 seconds before pronouncing a word.	Make a check above the word on which hesitation occurs.	✓ It is a fascinating story.
Repetitions A word, part of a word, or group of words repeated.	Draw a wavy line beneath word (words) repeated.	He thought he saw a whale.
Omissions One or more words omitted. (If a complete line is omitted, this is counted as one omission error.)	Encircle the word (or words) omitted.	Mother does all ⦅of⦆ her work with great care.

Most standardized oral reading tests are similar to the Gilmore. The 1968 revision of the test has four forms and consists of ten paragraphs of increasing difficulty which range from preprimer to high school. A child taking the test reads from a booklet of heavy cardboard in which single paragraphs appear on individual pages. In a separate booklet, the examiner records the errors made according to the code already described. He also records reading time in seconds and the answers to the five comprehension questions following each paragraph. A manual provides directions for errors, norms for accuracy, comprehension, and rate of reading. Although designed for pupils in grades one through eight, it can be employed most profitably with disabled readers in high school.

Through the use of a tape recorder, teachers will learn how to score an oral reading test objectively.* An individual record sheet will enable the teacher to record errors made by the pupil as he reads. After the scoring has been completed, the significant errors should be entered on a reading checklist. (See fig. 1 in chapter 6. A descriptive list of oral reading tests appears in Appendix C.)

WORD LISTS

Teachers may acquire information about a child's sight vocabulary and word-attack skill by the use of informal tests. Selecting the fifteenth or twentieth word from several representative pages from an unfamiliar reader or textbook provides a useful word-recognition test. When this is done, two copies should be prepared. One is placed before the child and the other is used by the teacher for recording responses. A small card can be employed to expose words tachistoscopically. When a child misses a word that has been flashed, it can be presented a second time without any time limit. Such a procedure will give the teacher a useful insight into a child's word-analysis skill. Mastery is indicated when a pupil responds immediately; lack of mastery is indicated when a pupil shows delayed recall. Usually, a flash recognition vocabulary of ninety-five percent indicates an adequate sight vocabulary for fluent reading.

Teachers who wish to avail themselves of already prepared word lists will find the following of value:

BOTEL, MORTON. *Bucks County 1185 Common Words.* A list of 41 preprimer words, 67 primer words, 124 first-grade words, 359 second-grade words,

---

*Teachers can get practice and become proficient in objectively scoring oral reading tests by listening to tape recordings of children who have taken such tests. When teachers agree as to errors made, they have acquired the necessary objectivity in their scoring.

and 594 third-grade words. *How to Teach Reading.* Chicago: Follett Publishing Co., 1959, pp. 103-113.

DOLCH, EDWARD W. *A Basic Sight Vocabulary.* A list of 220 words said to make up more than fifty percent of the running words in elementary school reading materials. Printed cards useful in teaching these words are available from Garrard Publishing Co., Champaign, Ill. *The Elementary School Journal* 36 (1936):456-460.

—————. *Ninety-five Nouns Common to the Three Word Lists.* A list of nouns common to three first-grade vocabulary lists. Picture word cards for teaching these are available from Garrard Publishing Co., Champaign, Ill., 1941.

DURRELL, DONALD. A list of words according to intermediate grade levels: fourth, fifth, sixth. *Improving Reading Instruction,* New York: World Book Co., 1956, pp. 367-392.

FRY, EDWARD. "Teaching a Basic Reading Vocabulary." A list of 100 first-grade words, 100 second-grade words, and 100 third-grade words. *Elementary English* 37 (1960):38-42.

GATES, ARTHUR. *A Reading Vocabulary for the Primary Grades.* A list of 1,811 words, arranged in three levels of 500 words each and a supplementary list of 311 words. Bureau of Publications, Teachers College, Columbia University, 1935.

KEARNEY, NOLAN C. "An Analysis of the Vocabulary of First Grade Reading Material." A list of the 441 most common words found in 121 preprimers, primers, and first readers. *Journal of Educational Research* 43 (1950): 481-493.

KNIPP, HELEN. *Basic Vocabulary Phrases and Sentences for Early Reading Instruction,* Meadville, Pa.: Keystone View Co., 1952.

KRANTZ, L. L. *The Author's Word List for Primary Grades.* A graded list of words based on the study of vocabulary of 84 preprimers, 69 primers, 84 first readers, 85 second readers, and 47 third readers. Minneapolis, Minn.: Curriculum Research Co., 1945.

RINSLAND, HENRY. *A Basic Vocabulary of Elementary School Children.* A list of 14,571 words which is based upon words used in writing by children in grades 1-8. New York: The Macmillan Co., 1945.

STONE, CLARENCE. *Word Lists by Reading Levels.* A list of 100 preprimer words, 225 primer words, 455 first-reader words, 1,101 second-reader words, and 1,916 third-reader words. Manchester, Mo.: Webster Publishing, 1950.

THORNDIKE, EDWARD L. *A Teachers Wordbook of 30,000 Words.* A list based on a count of 10,000,000 words from both adult and children's books. Each word is categorized with a symbol denoting the thousand in which it belongs. Words in the first 5,000 are designated as first half or second half of the thousand. Bureau of Publications, Teachers College, Columbia University, 1944.

SILENT READING TESTS: SURVEY

Most silent reading survey tests provide a meaning vocabulary score and a comprehension score and are helpful in determining the level at which pupils can read. Although most of these tests have a working time of only thirty to forty-five minutes and enable a teacher to locate retarded readers quickly, they do have limitations.

A teacher must recognize that a child's reading level, as indicated by a silent reading survey test, is often an overestimate of his instructional level. Silent reading tests are group tests and are usually of the recognition type. They permit guessing which often results in grade scores, especially for retarded readers, that average one grade or more above their effective reading level. For example, a sixth-grade boy could recognize only two or three words on sight. His word-analysis skill was nonexistent. Yet, on a standardized silent reading test for the intermediate grades, he achieved a 2.7 grade score. Investigation revealed that this had been accomplished by filling in blanks at random.

When silent reading tests of the survey type are employed, it must not be assumed that several pupils in a given grade share the same difficulties because they received the same low score on the test. Further study will show that these pupils usually do not suffer from the same reading handicaps. The reading grade score on a silent reading test is based on the total correct responses. Each pupil has his own constellation of strengths and weaknesses of which an effective corrective program must take cognizance and be designed to meet. For example, in the skills of word analysis some pupils may be weak in beginning sounds and blends while others need help with vowel sounds and the principles of syllabication. Seldom do pupils in a class have identical weaknesses in many of the basic reading skills.

Most survey tests provide grade norms which the teacher may use as a rough measure of a child's reading level. Other norms frequently found include age norms and percentile norms. When a comparison is made between intelligence and reading, it is advisable to use age rather than grade scores.

A descriptive list of silent reading tests appears in Appendix C.

SILENT READING TESTS: DIAGNOSTIC

Group diagnostic silent reading tests are more analytical than survey tests since they provide measures of such silent reading abilities as noting important details, discovering central thoughts, following directions, using reference skills, summarizing, outlining, organizing and reading maps, graphs, and charts. (See Appendix C.)

Although most diagnostic reading group tests do not provide sufficient information regarding sight vocabulary deficiency and word-analysis skill, several tests are very helpful in these respects. One of these,

The Silent Reading Diagnostic Test,* is especially valuable because it can be administered and interpreted by a classroom teacher who has not had special training in clinical reading. By employing the test, a teacher can learn a great deal about pupils' word-recognition vocabulary and word-attack skills. The following description of the eleven subtests involved will give the reader an understanding of what kinds of information *The Silent Reading Diagnostic Tests* yield.

TEST I: Word Recognition. This test has fifty-four items. Each consists of a picture accompanied by five words. A line is drawn around the word that tells about the picture. The choices are arranged so a child can commit initial, middle, final, or reversal errors.

TEST II: Recognition of Words in Context. The test consists of twenty-eight items, each of which involves a child's choosing one of five words to complete a sentence.

TEST III: Recognition of Reversible Words in Context. The list consists of a short story in which twenty-three words can be reversed, each of which involves the possibility of making a full or partial reversal.

TEST IV: Word-Recognition Techniques, Visual Analysis, Locating Usable Elements. This is a thirty-six item test involving a picture that is accompanied by a long word containing the shorter word identified by the picture. For example, the word *addressing* would be accompanied by a picture of a dress.

TEST V: Word-Recognition Techniques, Visual Analysis, Syllabication. This is a twenty-four-item test requiring the child to draw lines between the syllables of lengthy words.

TEST VI: Word-Recognition Techniques, Visual Analysis, Locating Root Words. A thirty-item test consisting of words containing word roots around which the child draws a circle.

TEST VII: Phonetic Knowledge, General Word Elements. A thirty-item test which involves a child's encircling one of five word elements pronounced by the examiner.

TEST VIII: Recognition of Beginning Sounds. A thirty-item test which involves a child's encircling one of five words that begins with the same sound as the word pronounced by the examiner.

*Authored by Bond, Clymer and Hoyt and published by Lyons & Carnahan. For a more complete description see Bond, G. L., and M. A. Tinker, *Reading Difficulties: Their Diagnosis and Correction* (New York: Appleton-Century-Crofts, 1967), pp. 221-227.

TEST IX: Rhyming Words. A thirty-item test which involves a child's encircling one of five words that rhymes with the word pronounced by the examiner.

TEST X: Letter Sounds. A thirty-item test which involves a child's encircling one of four letters that stands for the sound uttered by the examiner.

TEST XI: Word Synthesis. A test which measures a child's ability to blend parts of a word into a whole, both visually and phonetically.

Although the Bond, Clymer, and Hoyt tests just described were designed for use in grades three through six, they can be used to great advantage with disabled readers on the junior and senior high school levels.

Other group reading tests which provide diagnostic data relevant to sight vocabulary and word analysis include the Doren Diagnostic Reading Test and the McCullough Word Analysis Test. See Appendix C for additional information regarding these and other tests.

IN-DEPTH TESTS IN READING

Several individually administered tests of a more detailed nature are available when such data are needed. One such test is *The Diagnostic Reading Scales*. These scales provide the examiner with a wide range of diagnostic information.

The first unit of *The Diagnostic Reading Scales* is devoted to three word lists designed to test a pupil's skills at word recognition and analysis and to determine the level of reading passages to which he should be introduced. According to the author, these reading passages (they number twenty-two and are of graduated difficulty) simulate the type and range of material that might be found in classroom reading assignments at levels ranging from mid-first-grade to eighth grade. The materials include narrative, expository, and descriptive selections from the natural and physical sciences, social sciences, and children's literature. The passages yield three levels for each pupil. These are the instructional level, the independent level, and the potential level. The latter is determined by ascertaining the auding level.

The battery closes with six supplementary phonic tests which furnish information about a child's knowledge of consonant sounds, vowel sounds, consonant blends, common syllables, blends, and letter sounds.

One of the authors has employed the foregoing test in a reading clinic setting with excellent results. Other tests which merit attention include the *Durrell Analysis of Reading Difficulty* and the *Gates-*

McKillop Reading Diagnostic Test. (See Appendixes C and C1 for additional information regarding these tests.)

DIAGNOSING DIFFICULTIES IN COMPREHENSION AND THE STUDY SKILLS

Reading is more than "barking at the print." Reading is a meaningful process. Because this is true, the child who fails to bring proper meaning to printed symbols and fails to comprehend what the writer wishes to convey is not reading.

While comprehension is the all-important goal at all grade levels, generally it is not a problem to the average primary-grade child. The narrative material used by authors of basal readers at this level employs well-controlled vocabularies which carefully stay within the average child's background of experience. Consequently, understanding the printed page becomes little more than blending sight and sound. Once the primary grade child has learned to associate familiar sounds with the new and unfamiliar written symbols on the printed page, he is able to understand the story the author wishes to convey. It is obvious, then, that a mastery of the basic reading skills is the "open sesame" to comprehension for most children in the primary grades. Since, however, there is a natural tendency on the part of children to accept what appears in print as sacrosanct, there is always a need for teachers to stimulate children to react critically to what has been read. (See chapter 9 for suggestions as to how reading can be made a thinking process.)

Any weakness in the basic reading skills evidences itself quickly in the fourth grade and beyond. Expository materials are encountered and vocabulary burdens increase with alarming rapidity at these levels. The child whose basic sight vocabulary and word-analysis skills are below par soon is in over his head. Not only is he troubled by high-frequency words which he should have mastered long ago, but he is bewildered by technical words in arithmetic such as *minuend, subtrahend,* and *quotient,* and technical words in geography such as *latitude, longitude,* and *doldrums.* As the number of unknown words increases, comprehension is impossible and mastery of the unknown symbols proves an overwhelming task because of their prevalence.

Evaluating a child's competence in the basic reading skills is an important first step in dealing with comprehension problems in the intermediate and upper grades. Too often teachers expend time and energy on trying to develop high-level comprehension skills when attention should first be devoted to building a basic sight vocabulary and to teaching independence in basic word-attack skills.

Pupils who comprehend material read to them by the teacher but who fail to comprehend when reading silently are often handicapped by basic reading skill deficiencies. Formal and informal listening tests, therefore, prove valuable in diagnosis. (See Appendix C for a description of listening tests.) Further corroboration or verification of sight-vocabulary and word-attack deficiencies that are needed can be had by employing formal and informal oral reading tests. (See chapter 6 for a more complete discussion of this.)

Word Meaning

In intermediate and upper grades, word meaning becomes an important factor in comprehension since students encounter many aurally unfamiliar words at these levels. When a student lacks a good meaning vocabulary, sentence comprehension and paragraph comprehension become difficult because of the many gaps in the continuity of the reading process. It is essential, therefore, to measure the size of a student's meaning vocabulary and to evaluate his ability to use the dictionary when diagnosing comprehension problems. Fortunately, most silent reading tests, both survey and diagnostic, include sections that are devoted to meaning vocabulary.

When a pupil's meaning vocabulary is meager, a teacher will find it profitable to inventory his background of experience. It will be found that some children are products of environments that have provided little or no cultural stimulation. If this is true, the school has the responsibility of giving the kinds of direct and indirect experiences needed to compensate for such impoverishment.

Sentence Comprehension

When expressing complete thoughts, the shortest basic unit is the sentence. The disabled reader who learns to understand sentences can move directly into paragraph comprehension.

A great deal more than meaning vocabulary is involved in sentence comprehension. Many poor readers can call all the words in a sentence and, seemingly, know the meaning of each word, but the overall meaning or concept of the sentence escapes them. Such a difficulty may stem from an inability to group words into meaningful thought units. Consider, for example, how difficult it is to comprehend the following sentence.

(It was a long) (time after the) (big fight had) (taken place by) (the roadside.)

Words go together to make thought units. The child who has not sensed the inherent rhythm within the language structure struggles vainly for meaning. How much easier and more meaningful the sentence becomes when the words are grouped into logical phrases.

(It was) (a long time) (after the big fight) (had taken place) (by the roadside.)

The simplest way to check phrasing ability is to ask a pupil to read aloud. Does he group the words into intelligent phrases? Are there slight pauses in the right places?

Another impediment to sentence comprehension which can be detected by having a child read aloud is his inattention to punctuation. Ignoring commas can result in immediate confusion of sentence sense. Consider, for example, the following:

Jim, too, saw two of them.
Bill said to him, "Today, we shall go to the movies."

Paragraph Comprehension

"The whole is more than the sum of its parts." A disabled reader often is inclined to consider each sentence in isolation from the rest of the sentences in a paragraph. He fails to connect all sentences into a unified whole. He sees the trees but misses the forest.

In order to comprehend a paragraph as a unified whole, it is necessary for the reader to spot the main or central idea of the paragraph. Once he knows what the general idea of the paragraph is, related details fall into place.

Fortunately, most silent reading tests devote sections to paragraph comprehension, enabling teachers to determine if pupils have weaknesses in this regard.

As was true with difficulty in sentence comprehension, inattention to punctuation must be considered as a possible cause of poor paragraph comprehension. Ignoring periods, question marks, semicolons, and colons will result in running together the thoughts of sentences. A pupil's tendency to ignore these landmarks, which an author employs to emphasize the ideas he has organized into a paragraph, can be readily detected by having a pupil read aloud.

Critical Reading

We live in a democracy where it is essential for pupils to discern truth from falsehood and good from evil. Pupils are too prone to accept anything and everything in print as infallible. The statement "I know it is true because I read it" is a familiar refrain.

Two important factors which are associated with a pupil's ability to read critically are intelligence and experiential background.

Children of superior intelligence are more likely to react critically to what they read than children of average or below-average intelligence. Although the relationship between intelligence and critical reading is positive, a high-intelligence quotient doesn't assure high performance in critical reading. Even the very bright may have weaknesses in this regard.

Children who have a reservoir of rich experiences are in a better position to evaluate what is read than are children whose background of experiences is meager. Critical thinking is difficult when one possesses an inadequate frame of reference.

When a pupil reads, understands, and then sanctions material containing contradictions, questionable opinions, or improbable situations which should be obvious, a need for instruction in critical reading exists. Chapter 9 will provide a number of practical suggestions for helping students develop critical reading ability.

Concentration

Some students suffer comprehension difficulties because of mind-wandering tendencies. They read words and lines of print but find on turning a page that although their eyes were going through the mechanical process of reading, their minds were playing hide-and-go-seek. This inability to concentrate makes comprehension difficult and efforts should be made to uncover causes of the problem.

Visual difficulties, poor general health, and emotional disturbances (see chapter 3) are frequently responsible for concentration problems. Other factors that should be investigated when causal factors are probed include difficulty of the material being read, reader interest, lighting, and the presence of distracting influences in the study environment.

Retention

Since many reading comprehension tests are tests of retention,(10) a pupil's ability to remember what he has read has a direct bearing on his comprehension test score.

Although some disabled readers can remember material they do not understand, the opposite is often true. Problem readers show little retention for what has been read. Although infrequent, the authors have encountered children who could not tell in their own words the thought of simple sentences just read.

When a disabled reader is forced to read material that is too difficult, poor retention is understandable. But when the reading material is relatively simple, why should retention be poor? Some children become victims of an unfortunate kind of conditioning brought about by teachers who consistently ask factual questions immediately after silent reading takes place. When this occurs year after year, it isn't surprising to find that children expect and wait to be pumped for information. Means of correcting this situation will be treated in chapter 9.

Following Directions

Standardized reading tests frequently have a section devoted to following directions. There is a very good reason for this. We live in a gadget-filled world. The ability to understand and follow directions is essential to our efficient use of the latest, modern conveniences. Manuals of all kinds containing printed directions are available to the housewife, auto mechanic, radio technician and numerous other specialists who are part of our modern-day world. The inability to follow printed directions leads to frustration and costly errors.

The results of an inability to follow directions may be amusing and, in some instances, tragic. Hovious provides us with two anecdotes to illustrate this point. She tells of a family that went on a two weeks' vacation. "While they were gone, they wanted their house painted white, with green trimmings. When they came back, they found that the workmen had painted the vacant house next door! Naturally, the workers had to come back and paint the right house. They lost money and the house owner was inconvenienced—all because the painters did not follow directions." Another example involved a woman who was cleaning some clothes on the back porch. "Suddenly a terrific blast shook the house. Flames leaped out. Splinters flew. Plaster fell. What had happened? Why, the cleaning fluid had exploded. On the bottle of cleaner there was a big warning not to use the fluid near an open flame, but the woman hadn't read the directions."(11)

Reading Rate and Comprehension

Efficiency in reading comprehension is directly related to a pupil's rate of reading. As he progresses from grade to grade, his reading speed becomes a very significant factor in his overall efficiency. Usually, the rapid reader is the efficient reader because impressions are stronger when thought concepts are received in rapid sequence.

It is a mistake to assume, however, that speed per se automatically results in increased reading comprehension. The efficient reader is fluent, and his speed grows out of this fluency. The inefficient reader is not fluent, and his effort to cover the ground more quickly involves hurried reading rather than rapid reading. Hurried reading results in a quick loss of intellectual breath, and comprehension suffers.

Many pupils read slowly because they are inept at phrasing and read one word at a time. Word-by-word reading may be an outgrowth of overanalysis of words or the result of a meager sight vocabulary. If the situation continues for a length of time, the word-by-word pattern crystallizes into a habit and continues to persist even though word-perception difficulties cease to be a problem. It is important, therefore, for the teacher to determine whether the pupil's word-by-word reading pattern is an outgrowth of habituation or whether deficiencies in basic skills are involved.(12) Oral reading tests and word-recognition tests can be employed to make this diagnosis.

Although many silent reading tests include estimates of reading rate, teachers may wish to make informal appraisals of their own. This can be done by asking pupils to read a selection silently while the teacher records the passing time on the blackboard in ten-second intervals. The readers are asked to record the largest number on the board immediately upon completion of the selection. Once this has been done, simple mathematical procedure (dividing the words read by the seconds involved and then multiplying the results by 60) will give a words-per-minute score.

While silent reading is taking place, the teacher should scrutinize each pupil for habits that are known to be detrimental to reading speed. These include finger pointing, head wagging, and lip movements. The latter habit is manifest in many primary-grade pupils because of the instructional emphasis on oral reading. At these early stages, it is not of great concern since the majority of children read no faster silently than they do orally. In the intermediate grades, however, when silent reading speeds begin to exceed oral reading speeds, pupils are admonished if subvocalization is detected. At these grade levels pupils should be able to read two or three times faster silently than orally. Any movement of the vocal mechanism during silent reading can do nothing but impede a pupil's speed.

Flexibility and Reading Speed

Other things being equal, a child's speed of comprehension is dependent on the difficulty of the material read. Good readers are flexible readers who vary and adapt their rates to the nature of the content and the purposes for which they are reading. Poor readers are inept in this regard. A valuable index of efficiency on a silent reading test is the ratio of comprehension items answered correctly to those attempted. It is advisable for a teacher to express the results in fractional form. For example, a glance at the fraction 18/20 would indicate that twenty comprehension items were attempted and eighteen were answered correctly, resulting in an accuracy score of ninety percent. (A score of eighty percent is the usual minimum acceptable.) Such a procedure enables the teacher to categorize a child as a fast-accurate reader, a fast-inaccurate reader, an average-accurate reader, an average-inaccurate reader, a slow-accurate reader, or a slow-inaccurate reader. This information is very important when making a diagnosis.

EXPLORING READING EXPECTANCY OR POTENTIAL

Intelligence Tests

Although scores from group intelligence tests lack the reliability and validity of individually administered intelligence tests, classroom teachers will find the various scores that are available very helpful in their study of reading retardation cases.

Care must be exercised in selecting an intelligence test for a poor reader. Many group intelligence tests are largely verbal and therefore not valid for the retarded reader. These intelligence tests (in reality they are reading tests in disguise) should not be employed with poor readers if one wishes to use the results as a reading-expectancy criterion. Some group intelligence tests, such as the California Test of Mental Maturity, Pintner-Durost Elementary Test, Pintner Intermediate Test, and the Lorge-Thorndike, have nonverbal (quantitative) scores. A quantitative score is often used as an index of a pupil's potential while a verbal (language) score is an indication of how well the pupil is functioning scholastically. Usually, a retarded reader or a child from a bilingual home will score higher on the nonverbal section of an intelligence test.

Listening Comprehension Tests

The level at which a pupil can comprehend material read aloud to him (his auding level) is one of the most valuable indexes of reading potential.(13) Commercial tests based on this premise are available and include the *Brown-Carlsen Listening Comprehension Test* (Harcourt

Brace Jovanovich, Inc.), *Diagnostic Reading Tests,* Section II, Comprehension: Silent and Auditory (The Committee on Diagnostic Reading Tests), *Durrell-Sullivan Reading Capacity Test* (Harcourt Brace Jovanovich, Inc.), STEP tests—listening comprehension section (Educational Testing Service), the listening section of the Spache *Diagnostic Reading Scales* (California Test Bureau), the *Peabody Picture Vocabulary Test* (American Guidance Service, Inc.), and the *Botel Listening Test* (Follett Publishing Company).

IDENTIFYING NONEDUCATIONAL HAZARDS IN LEARNING
SCREENING TESTS IN VISION

Snellen Chart

The Snellen chart is probably the most common screening test* in use today. The chart consists of letters of various sizes arranged in rows with the larger letters at the top and letters in each succeeding row smaller in a measurable amount. Each letter is inscribed in a square whose sides are divided into five equal parts making twenty-five smaller squares. Each smaller square (representing one part of the letter) subtends a visual angle of one degree to the normal eye at the distance marked for that letter or line of letters.

The chart should be well illuminated and the child should stand twenty feet from it. He is then asked to read, without squinting, the lowest line possible, first with both eyes, then with each eye separately. Visual acuity is expressed as a fraction. The numerator is always the distance in feet that he is from the chart and the denominator is the number beside the lowest line that he is able to read. Thus, if the child is twenty feet from the chart and is able to read only the 200 letter with the right eye, his visual acuity is recorded R = 20/200. If he can read to the 30 line with the left eye, his acuity is recorded L = 20/30. Normal visual acuity is indicated when both numerator and denominator are the same, i.e., 20/20.

Stereoscopic Tests

Probably the most popular screening instruments today are those of the Brewster-type stereoscope such as the Telebinocular (part of the Keystone School Visual Survey Service), Ortho-Rater, and Titmus School Vision Tester. These are instruments which use lenses and prisms to obtain parallax, i.e., the different view of an object experienced by

*Also see page 39.

the two retinas by reason of viewing it from two angles. These stereo-scopic instruments allow the viewer to look simultaneously at two photographic pictures taken under a difference of angular view, cor-responding to, or even greater than, the separation of the two eyes. Thus, as in ordinary binocular vision, the two images are fused by the brain and the objects viewed are made to stand out in relief.

Sets of stereoscopic testing cards or slides for these instruments usu-ally comprise a series to measure binocular acuity, monocular acuity, vertical and lateral distance phorias, fusion, depth perception, near phorias, near fusion, and near acuity. Record forms on which to note the findings may be obtained. Individual findings are checked either in or out of the expected columns. Thus, variations from a normal visual pattern can be indicated.

Another screening device employing stereoscopic cards as a part of a battery of tests is the Eames Eye Tests. Although these tests are not as accurate and complete as the Ortho-Rater or Telebinocular, they do detect binocular and other conditions which escape the Snellen chart. The Eames Eye Tests include a Snellen-type acuity test along with a plus lens test; a Coordination Test which employs a simple stereoscope and is designed to detect visual coordination difficulty and heterophoria; and a Function Test designed to reveal defects in binocular vision. The latter test also requires the stereoscope.

When the foregoing instruments are used, it must be remembered that they are screening devices and cannot be considered diagnostic. Care must be exercised with stereoscopic instruments since they all are not manufactured to the same specifications. If the identical stereo-scopic cards are used with two stereoscopes of different make, the results will not be the same. Another factor which must be considered with the use of any stereoscopic device is this: The concept of near-ness of the cards or slides viewed cannot be eliminated in the mind of the individual tested. This may alter the set of the eyes while they are being examined.

Informal Visual Screening Tests

Several informal visual screening tests that require a minimum of equipment may be given by a teacher or reading specialist. These in-clude the cover test, ocular motility test, the near point of convergence test, and the physiological diplopia test.

Cover test

This test may be used to determine the presence of muscular im-balance of the two eyes both at distance and near point. The individual being examined is told to fixate his gaze at a specific target, keeping both eyes open at all times. A card or similar object is then placed before one eye by the examiner. After a period of three to five seconds, the card is shifted quickly from the covered eye to the other eye. Any movement of the eye being uncovered is noted. The card should be shifted from one eye to the other several times to make certain of the presence, or absence, of eye movement of the eye being uncovered.

If movement by an eye is noted when shifting the card from one eye to the other, the presence (but not the degree) of fusion or binocularity may be determined by covering one eye three to five seconds (both eyes being open) and then removing the card. If the eye which turned when covered returns to parallelism when both eyes are uncovered, it indicates that fusion or binocularity is present. The quality of such fusional ability can be determined only by the visual specialist who is able to employ more specific and exacting testing procedures.

Ocular motility test

This test reveals weaknesses in the external muscles of the eyes. The individual being examined is directed to hold his head still and follow with his eyes an object held in the examiner's hand. A jeweled ornament is an excellent target when working with children. A vertically held penlight also can be used. The examiner rotates the target in a circle approximately two feet in diameter about twelve to eighteen inches in front of the child. He then moves the target through the cardinal directions, i.e., right and left, up and down, up to the right and down to the left, and up to the left and down to the right. The examiner watches to see if the child's eyes both follow the target at all times. The examinee is told to report any experience of diplopia (seeing two targets) at any time during the test. Any jerkiness or unsteadiness in following the target should be noted and the test then repeated. If the same jerkiness appears on a repeat test, referral to a visual specialist is recommended.

Near point of convergence test

The same target used for checking motilities can be used for this test. The child being examined is directed to watch the target as it is moved slowly by the examiner toward the tip of the child's nose. Most children are able to follow the target to the tip of the nose. The examiner should watch to see if one eye suddenly diverges as the target is brought close. The distance at which this happens should be noted. If there is any divergence, the subject should be asked whether he is aware of two targets. If he is not, it may be an indication of suspension of vision in the diverging eye. A near-point convergence of four inches from the tip of the nose is generally considered sufficient. The child fails the test if this cannot be done. The examiner should record the distance at which one eye turned away from the target. He also should indicate whether it was the right or the left eye which deviated.

Physiological diplopia test

This is a relatively easy test to administer and it indicates suppression or suspension of vision in one eye. The examiner, facing the subject, holds two targets (i.e., a pen and a pencil, preferably of different colors), one in each hand. One target is held approximately twelve inches from the subject's face and the other twenty-four inches away, both in line with the subject's nose. The individual being examined is directed to hold his fixation on one of the targets and report whether he is aware of one or two images of the target not being fixated. The process is then repeated with fixation being held on the other target. If the individual reports that he is aware of only one image of the nonfixated target (two are expected), it indicates that he is suspending or ignoring the image seen by one eye. When this is discovered, referral to a visual specialist is recommended.

SCREENING TESTS IN HEARING

Audiometer

The most valid test for measuring hearing is the pure tone audiometer.* A pure tone audiometric test yields far more information than any other hearing test. By studying the audiogram (a graphic representation of the measurements of hearing loss) it is possible to determine both the pattern and extent of a hearing loss. In addition, valuable information concerning the etiology of the loss is provided. For testing groups of children, the Western Electric Company's Model 4C and the Verbal Auditory Screen for Children (VASC) can be used.

When audiometric testing is not available, several informal screening tests may be used. These include the whisper test, watch tick test, and the coin click test.

---

*A colleague of one of the authors, Dr. Janet Jeffers, co-director of the hearing clinics at California State College at Los Angeles, recommends the following audiometers for hearing screening: Zenith Screening Audiometer; Ambco Models 601B, 1122, 1122F; Beltone 9D; and Eckstein Brothers #46 and #60. These audiometers range in price from $125.00 (Eckstein #46) to $367.00 (Beltone 9D).

Whisper Test

A series of unrelated words or two-digit numbers are whispered by the examiner with residual breath. A quiet room should be used for testing. The child being tested usually stands at a distance of twenty feet from the examiner, although this distance may be changed if the acoustical properties of the room warrant it. (When this is done, it is necessary to determine the proper distance by noting how far the average person must be in order to hear the whisper.) The child who is being tested stands with his side toward the examiner and responds with one ear occluded, then the other. If the child does poorly, the examiner moves closer. Should the child fail to respond as well as a normal child would at the standardized distance, a hearing loss may be suspected.

Watch Tick Test

Ordinarily a loud ticking watch which the average person can hear at a distance of forty-eight inches is used for this test. When other watches are employed, it is necessary to standardize them on a number of children. Any timepieces other than the watch being used by the examiner should be removed. The child then stands at right angles to the examiner with his finger in the ear not being tested. The youngster also should be required to hold a small card beside his head so he cannot see the watch when he is being tested. The examiner begins by placing the watch close to the child's ear. He withdraws it slowly until the child no longer hears it. He then moves the watch slowly toward the child until it is heard. An average of the two distances is taken. If a child fails to respond as a normal child would at the standardized distance, a hearing loss may be suspected.

Coin Click Test

The coin click test, like the watch tick test, is a test of high frequency. To the extent that it can be standardized for a given room and given coins, the coin click test is a useful supplement to the whisper test.

Some school systems do not provide adequate hearing testing. Instead of employing an audiometer periodically, they rely on the rough screening tests described. Davis(14) feels, however, that these tests will continue to have their place since they are easily given and no expensive equipment or elaborate surroundings are required. He points out that the whisper test checks frequencies in the speech range extending from three hundred to three thousand cycles per second. The coin click and watch tick test reach frequencies above this range. Since hearing loss often begins with high-frequency difficulties, the coin click and watch tick tests prove to be valuable supplementary tests.

There is no doubt that the whisper, watch tick, and coin click tests are better than no tests at all. But a word of warning. There are many hearing losses that may escape detection when these tests are used. It is essential, therefore, that teachers develop a seismographic sensitivity to any manifestations of auditory impairment so intelligent referrals to an otologist can be made.

Another significant aspect of hearing involves auditory discrimination. Deficiencies in auditory discrimination can be detected by reading aloud pairs of words that sound alike and pairs of words that sound different. The child is asked to distinguish between them. Teachers preferring a commercial test may use the Wepman Auditory Discrimination Test (see Appendix C) to measure a child's ability to discriminate between different phonemes of the language.

SUMMARY

Hazards to learning are ever present in constitutional anomalies in addition to the environment of the home and the school. Noneducational hazards to learning frequently considered causal factors in reading disabilities include visual anomalies, auditory defects, speech defects, immaturity, poor health, mixed dominance, neurological impairment, emotional maladjustment, and a meager experiential background.

The role of the teacher in discovering and alleviating these hazards is a challenging one. Discovery involves objective observation and the use of valid tests. Correction or alleviation may be accomplished through the development of a compensating school environment and the cooperation of parents and school specialists available in the problem areas.

A child who reveals no unusual behavior patterns and is eager to improve his scholarship is usually not severely retarded in reading even though he shows deficiencies in oral and silent reading. Diagnosis of his reading problem can be accomplished through observation and informal testing. When the child's difficulties are located, the classroom teacher can provide the correction needed by using self-directed instructional material of appropriate difficulty and content. Systematic recreational reading will provide the added practice needed to insure mastery of the reading skills. All children in a classroom falling in this category can be provided with effective correction in reading by the classroom teacher without increasing her instructional load.

PROBLEMS FOR ORAL AND WRITTEN DISCUSSION

1. What are the advantages and the limitations of observation in studying pupils?
2. What useful information can be obtained about a child through a parent interview?
3. Describe your use of cumulative records.
4. Describe and evaluate the cumulative records used in a particular school.
5. Describe two word lists and indicate their uses.
6. Administer the Dolch word list to an average reader and a retarded reader in a particular grade and interpret the results.
7. Administer the Wide Range Vocabulary Test to an average reader and a retarded reader in a particular grade and interpret the results.
8. Administer a survey test in silent reading to two or more pupils, score the tests and compute grade and age scores. Interpret the results.
9. Administer a diagnostic silent reading test to two or more pupils in the same grade. Score the tests and compute grade and age scores. Interpret the results.
10. Administer an oral reading test to an average reader, record errors and compute grade and age scores.
11. Administer an oral reading test to a retarded reader, record errors and compute grade and age scores.
12. Administer an oral reading test to a pupil and record his performance on a tape recorder. Record the errors and compare your results with two or more teachers listening to the same tape. Repeat until all scores agree on the number and types of errors.
13. Discuss other uses for the tape recorder in the reading program.
14. Using a range of IQ's from 75 to 135, prepare a bar diagram showing the range of M.A.'s at each of the following C.A. levels: 6-0, 8-0, 10-0, 12-0. What significant facts do you observe and what are their implications for teaching?
15. Summarize the following article: "Evaluating Diagnostic Reading Tests" by Priscilla Hayward. See selected readings.
16. Evaluate two or more diagnostic reading tests in terms of their reliabilities.

REFERENCES

1. DELWYN SCHUBERT, *A Dictionary of Terms and Concepts in Reading,* 2nd ed. (Springfield, Ill.: Charles C Thomas, Publisher, 1968).
2. HOMER CARTER and DOROTHY MCGINNIS, *Diagnosis and Treatment of the Disabled Reader* (New York: The Macmillan Co., 1970), p. 78.
3. PAUL WITTY and DAVID KOPEL, *Reading and the Educative Process* (Boston: Ginn and Co., 1939).

4. GUY BOND and MILES TINKER, *Reading Difficulties: Their Diagnosis and Correction* (New York: Appleton-Century-Crofts, 1967), pp. 276-277.
5. ALBERT HARRIS, *How to Increase Reading Ability* (New York: David McKay Co., Inc., 1970), pp. 462-465.
6. EMMETT BETTS, *Foundations of Reading Instruction* (New York: American Book Co., 1957), p. 454.
7. R. STRANG, C. McCULLOUGH, and A. TRAXLER, *The Improvement of Reading* (New York: McGraw-Hill Book Co., Inc., 1961), p. 319.
8. *Gilmore Oral Reading Test. Manual of Directions.* Copyright 1952 by Harcourt, Brace & World, Inc., New York. All rights reserved. Reprinted by permission.
9. WILLIAM KOTTMEYER, *Teacher's Guide for Remedial Reading* (Manchester, Mo.: Webster Publishing Co., 1959).
10. WALTER BARBE, "Measuring Reading Comprehension," *The Clearing House* (February 1958):343.
11. CAROL HOVIOUS, *Flying the Printways* (Boston: D. C. Heath and Co., 1938), p. 355.
12. HELEN ROBINSON and HELEN SMITH, "Rate Problems in the Reading Clinic," *The Reading Teacher* (May 1962):421-426.
13. GEORGE SPACHE and EVELYN SPACHE, *Reading in the Elementary School* (Boston: Allyn and Bacon, Inc., 1969), p. 70.
14. HALLOWELL DAVIS, *Hearing and Deafness* (New York: Murray Co., 1947), p. 126.

SELECTED READINGS

BOND, GUY, and MILES TINKER. *Reading Problems: Their Diagnosis and Correction.* 2nd ed. New York: Appleton-Century-Crofts, 1967, chs. 7-9.

CARTER, HOMER C. J., and DOROTHY J. McGINNIS. *Diagnosis and Treatment of the Disabled Reader.* New York: The Macmillan Co., 1970, chs. 2-9.

HARRIS, ALBERT J. *How to Increase Reading Ability.* 5th ed. New York: David McKay Co., Inc., 1970, chs. 7, 9.

HAYWARD, PRISCILLA. "Evaluating Diagnostic Reading Tests," *The Reading Teacher,* vol. 21, no. 6 (March 1968).

KARLIN, ROBERT. *Teaching Elementary Reading.* New York: Harcourt Brace Jovanovich, 1971, ch. 2.

OTTO, WAYNE, and RICHARD McMENEMY. *Corrective and Remedial Teaching.* Boston: Houghton Mifflin Co., 1966, chs. 3-5.

SCHELL, LEO, and PAUL BURNS. *Remedial Reading.* Boston: Allyn and Bacon, Inc., 1968, chs. 15-25.

SCHUBERT, DELWYN, and THEODORE TORGERSON. *Readings in Reading.* New York: Thomas Y. Crowell Co., 1968, selections 48-55.

STRANG, RUTH. *Diagnostic Teaching of Reading.* 2nd ed. New York: McGraw-Hill Book Co., 1969.

———, CONSTANCE McCULLOUGH, and ARTHUR TRAXLER. *The Improvement of Reading.* 4th ed. New York: McGraw-Hill Book Co., 1967, chs. 4, 5.

WILSON, ROBERT. *Diagnostic and Remedial Reading.* Columbus, O.: Charles E. Merrill, 1967, chs. 2-4.

WITTY, PAUL; ALMA FREELAND, and EDITH GROTBERG. *The Teaching of Reading.* Chicago: D. C. Heath and Co., 1966, pp. 300-312.

6

The Diagnostic Process

THE DIAGNOSTIC STEPS

Locating and studying the types of errors a child makes on an oral reading test helps in the evaluation of a reading difficulty; converting scores on a silent reading test into grade scores provides a measure of a pupil's competence in reading; and determining a pupil's mental age through the use of a nonlanguage test or a grade score from a listening comprehension test provides an index of a child's potential or level of reading expectancy. Accomplishing all these things and arriving at an appropriate corrective program involves a series of systematic diagnostic steps and procedures. A guide to such an analysis follows:

STEP 1. Identify the retarded reader.
STEP 2. Determine the nature of the reading problem.
STEP 3. Determine the pupil's potential.
STEP 4. Determine the severity of the reading problem.
STEP 5. Identify hazards to learning and discover causal factors.
STEP 6. Summarize and record data.
STEP 7. Interpret data and plan an appropriate corrective program for the pupil.

Step 1. Identify the Retarded Reader

Before a teacher can identify pupils who are likely to profit from special help in reading (i.e., pupils whose reading level is below their potential), he must locate all pupils who are experiencing reading difficulty.

One of the simplest ways to locate poor readers in a classroom has been suggested by Dolch.(1) All pupils are told that the teacher wants to find out how hard a new book is. The book is opened to a specified page and each child reads aloud one sentence. Those who cannot read or who have difficulty are quickly brought to the teacher's attention. Since each child reads only one sentence, there is little embarrassment on the part of those pupils who do poorly.

Harris(2) is partial to the Dolch approach but recommends having each child read two or three sentences rather than one. He also suggests administering a short-answer test to the class after pupils have read a short selection silently. By having each pupil close his book and look up as soon as he has finished reading the selection, the slowest readers can be spotted easily.

First-grade students can be given a readiness test and deficiencies can be noted. Their sight vocabulary (an excellent index of reading skill at the first-grade level) can be tested by drawing words from lists at the back of basal readers to which they have been exposed.

Pupils in the second grade and above can be given a silent reading test of the survey type at the beginning of the school year. By converting raw scores into grade scores the teacher can readily discover the poor readers. Those whose grade-placement scores are dubious should be subjected to further testing.

There are a large number of overt signs that reveal the presence of a reading problem. Some of these are—

1. disliking school
2. disliking reading
3. aversion for the library
4. low scholarship
5. behavioral difficulty
6. irregular school attendance
7. emotional disturbance
8. slow, halting reading
9. finger-pointing
10. lip movement
11. inaccurate observation of punctuation
12. inability to understand what is read
13. inability to attack new words
14. limited sight vocabulary.

Step 2. Determine the Nature of the Reading Problem

Often the teacher can determine the general nature of a pupil's reading problem when an overall assessment of reading competence has been made. Later the teacher may want to delve more deeply into the nature of the reading problem. Informal and formal testing procedures are usually amenable to both survey and analytical treatment of data.

For example, the use of an informal reading inventory will quickly enable the teacher to determine a pupil's independent, instructional, and frustration levels. If the teacher wishes to collect more data, she would note things such as enunciation, the pupil's ability to recognize basic sight vocabulary words, phrasing ability, attention to punctuation, fluency, and word-attack skill. If the teacher wishes to include comprehension questions, she can determine whether the pupil can discern main ideas and essential details.

A pupil's performance on an oral reading test will reveal faulty reading habits and his mastery of the skills of word recognition and word analysis. A diagnostic silent reading test will bring to light strengths and weaknesses in comprehension, meaning vocabulary, and study skills. Entering these difficulties on a reading checklist (fig. 1) will provide a useful guide in pinpointing appropriate correction. Converting scores on oral and silent reading tests into grade scores will also prove helpful in highlighting a pupil's general level of competence.

Step 3. Determine the Pupil's Potential

Mental ability as determined by intelligence tests is widely used as a measure of learning capacity. Other things being equal, an intelligent child has more reading potential than the child of limited intelligence.

Intelligence test scores can be expressed in terms of a mental age (MA) and an intelligence quotient (IQ). These scores mean different things, and it is helpful for a teacher to understand the difference. Mental age (MA) refers to mental maturity or the level of a child's mental development. Therefore, a mental age of 10.0 on a given test means that the child can accomplish intellectual tasks on a level of difficulty which the average ten-year-old child can cope with successfully. The MA is a valuable score because it can be compared with other age scores.

The term IQ refers to the rate at which a child develops intellectually. A child with an IQ of 125 is growing 1.25 years mentally for each year of his chronological development; a child with an IQ of 75 advances .75 years mentally for each year of chronological age. Since IQ is equal to MA/CA $\times$ 100, a ten-year-old child with an IQ of 125 has a mental age of 12.5; and a ten-year-old child with an IQ of 75 possesses a mental age of 7.5.

A factor that should be considered, particularly with group tests, is that a poor reader is often completely discouraged because of continued failure and frustration. He develops a defeatist attitude which can easily invalidate intelligence test scores. Many disabled readers with this attitude take tests in a perfunctory manner. Therefore, pupils with intelligence quotients of seventy-five or lower, and those showing a variability of ten or more points on successive administrations, should be given an individual intelligence test by a trained examiner.

READING CHECKLIST

Difficulty present ☒	Difficulty improved ◹	Difficulty corrected ☐

Difficulties	Correction

Instructional Periods

	1	2	3	4	5	6	7	8	9	10
A. FAULTY READING HABITS										
1. Omits words										
2. Inserts words										
3. Substitutes words										
4. Repeats words										
5. Reverses words or word parts										
6. Reads word by word										
7. Vocalizes excessively										
8. Ignores punctuation										
9. Points to words										
10. Expressionless reading										
11. Faulty voice volume or pitch										
12. Poor book-body position										
13. Head movements										
14. Poor enunciation										
B. SIGHT VOCABULARY										
1. Faulty configuration clues										
2. Faulty contextual clues										
3. Faulty phonetic analysis using										
a. initial sounds										
b. initial blends										
c. medial sounds										
d. final sounds										
4. Structural analysis										
a. root words										
b. compound words										
c. syllabication										
d. prefixes										
e. suffixes										
f. endings										
C. MEANING VOCABULARY										
1. Oral vocabulary										
2. General vocabulary										
3. Technical vocabulary										
4. Dictionary skills										
D. COMPREHENSION AND STUDY SKILLS										
1. Reading in thought units (phrasing)										
2. Retelling a story										
3. Following a sequence of events										
4. Following directions										
5. Locating central thoughts of paragraphs										
6. Detecting related details										
7. Locating information										
8. Drawing conclusions										
9. Summarizing										
10. Outlining										
11. Reading maps, charts, tables, graphs										
12. Rate of comprehension										
13. Critical reading										

Figure 1

A number of individual intelligence tests are used by reading specialists and psychologists who work with retarded readers. Two of the most widely used are the Stanford-Binet Intelligence Scale and the Wechsler Intelligence Test for Children (WITC). Another test that is becoming increasingly popular is the Peabody Picture Vocabulary Test (PPVT).

Unlike the Stanford-Binet, the Wechsler Intelligence Test for Children not only yields a verbal score but a performance score as well. This has the advantage of giving disabled readers who are obviously deficient in verbal skill an opportunity to demonstrate their potential. Understandably, poor readers are likely to score higher on the Wechsler than on the Stanford-Binet. Both tests require about forty-five to sixty minutes to give, and it is necessary for the clinician to have special course work in administering and interpreting these tests.

Although more credence can be given to scores obtained from individual intelligence tests than from group tests, caution is still necessary. Bond and Fay report that retarded readers do considerably poorer on the Stanford-Binet than do children of equal ability who have no reading problems.(3)

The Peabody Picture Vocabulary Test is a much shorter and easier test to administer and interpret. In fifteen minutes a teacher can measure the size of a child's oral vocabulary. The resultant IQ score proves to be a good index of the child's listening comprehension or auding skill.

Determining a child's listening or auding level is an index of potential that is considered valuable by many reading specialists. The reader is referred to chapter 5 for a listing of other commercial tests that yield measures of auding skill.

Success in a nonlanguage area, such as arithmetic, is sometimes used as an index of reading potential. Terman has defined intelligence as the ability to deal with abstractions. Thus, there is some basis for believing that the poor reader who handles arithmetic fundamentals successfully has the mental ability needed for successful performance in reading. Sometimes, however, a poor reader with much potential does miserably in arithmetic because habitual frustration growing out of failure in reading results in hatred for school and all subjects associated with it.

Determining a child's reading potential is not a simple matter. Since each criterion has its advantages and disadvantages, its strengths and weaknesses, the conscientious teacher will use a suitable combination of criteria to arrive at individual reading-expectancy levels.

Step 4. Determine the Severity of the Reading Problem

How can one identify severe reading problems and select those pupils who are most likely to benefit from special help in reading? This is an important question which perennially plagues teachers. As Harris states it: "Attempting to serve all usually means giving the right kind of help to none. Lavishing time and energy on the wrong pupils also leads to disappointing results."(4)

The criterion used most universally for determining the severity of a reading problem and for selecting poor readers for special help involves a comparison of reading and mental maturity. For example, if a child possesses a mental age of ten and reads as well as an eight-year-old, a retardation of two years is evidenced. Since reading scores are most often expressed as grade-placement scores, it is helpful to transmit a mental age into a grade-placement score. This can be done by subtracting five from the mental age. (The assumption is that a child is six years of age in the first grade.) Thus a child with a mental age of twelve has the mental level of an average seventh grader. Should he possess a reading grade-placement score of five, it is estimated that he is reading two grades below his mental level or potential reading level. Is this discrepancy sufficient to warrant concern? Harris suggests the following minima in this regard: ". . . six months in the first three grades, nine months for children in grades four and five, or a year for children above the fifth grade."(5)

The use of mental age as a reading expectancy index leads to an awkward situation when very bright or dull students are considered. Many studies show that bright students do not achieve academically on a level commensurate with their mental age. Dull students, on the other hand, overachieve in this regard. To handle such cases, and others as well, Bond and Tinker suggest calculating a reading expectancy score by the following method: Multiply the student's I.Q. by the number of years he has spent in school and then add 1.0.(6) For a student with an I.Q. of 150, halfway through the seventh grade, his reading expectancy score would be $6.5 \times 1.50 + 1.0$, or 10.75. Investigation has shown that calculations based on this formula are far more realistic than those using mental age alone.(6)

Some school systems use a combination of chronological age and mental age in arriving at an expectancy age.(7) Usually this is contingent on the belief that the older student has a greater apperceptive mass and should be expected, therefore, to read on a level above that of a younger one. Harris is of the opinion that the method is too complicated for school use and is of questionable value.(8)

Some reading authorities do not believe that subtracting reading scores from expectancy scores is the best way of arriving at the degree of retardation. They advocate the use of a ratio. To determine a ratio, the reading score is divided by the expectancy score and is then multiplied by 100 so as to eliminate the decimal point. When there is no difference between reading score and expectancy score, the ratio is 100. When the reading score exceeds the expectancy score, the ratio is above 100, indicating overachievement. And when the expectancy score exceeds the reading score, the ratio that results is below 100, indicating underachievement.

Monroe(9) divides reading grade by expectancy grade and arrives at a Reading Index. A sixth-grade pupil who reads as well as a fourth grader (4.0/6.0) would have a Reading Index of approximately sixty-six. According to Monroe, a Reading Index under eighty represents serious retardation in reading.

Johnson and Myklebust(10) prefer age scores to grade scores in arriving at an index. They divide reading age by mental age and refer to the resultant ratio as a Learning Quotient. Any learning quotient below ninety is considered serious.

Another method used to determine the severity or degree of reading retardation is to compare a child's level of listening comprehension with his reading achievement level. For example, scores attained on the Durrell-Sullivan Reading Achievement Test can be compared with the scores of the Durrell-Sullivan Reading Capacity Test. When the reading capacity score is higher than the reading achievement score, the examiner may conclude that the child involved is not measuring up to his potential in reading. (See Appendix C for other listening tests.)

A teacher can develop his own oral comprehension test for determining the severity of a reading problem by utilizing duplicate forms of a suitable reading-comprehension test. One form should be given orally to the pupils while the other is administered as a silent reading test. The poor reader with marked potential will score higher on the form he was given orally: the greater the discrepancy, the greater the promise of reading potential.

When using listening comprehension to judge the severity of a reading problem, the examiner should remember that the retarded reader's opportunity for acquiring a good vocabulary, as well as an understanding of written material, is usually poorer than that of the good reader. The language the underprivileged student may have heard seldom includes the unusual words encountered on vocabulary tests.

What is more, written prose is often more complex structurally than that which is spoken. As a consequence, a poor reader may be bewildered by the unusual language and organization of paragraphs read aloud from a silent reading test.

Step 5. Identify Hazards to Learning and Discover Causal Factors

Both educational and noneducational hazards to learning are usually present in various degrees of severity. While these hazards tend to interfere with learning, their influence upon individuals differs widely, both in form and intensity. If a corrective program of instruction is to succeed, individual hazards to learning must be discovered. Therefore, identifying the specific hazards that are operating as causal factors in retarding and inhibiting an individual's learning becomes a vital part of the diagnostic process.

A corrective program of instruction not only seeks to correct specific individual difficulties in reading; whenever possible, it eliminates or ameliorates causal factors, both primary and contributory. To locate the hazards which act as causal factors, an objective and impartial interpretation of all data is necessary. This involves a careful study and analysis of available information that has been gathered through observation, interviews, cumulative records, formal and informal tests.

Step 6. Summarize and Record Data

Enter all significant and relevant diagnostic data gathered in steps one through five on the Diagnostic Reading Summary, figure 2.

Enter the difficulties in oral and silent reading that were discovered in step 2 on the Reading Checklist, figure 1. (See page 163.)

Step 7. Interpret Data and Plan an Appropriate Corrective Program for the Pupil

The corrective program planned for the pupil must be based on his reading strengths and weaknesses, reading expectancy level, preferred method of learning, causal factors—both educational and noneducational —and the pupil's interests and attitudes.

Enter a descriptive summary of the corrective program on the Diagnostic Reading Summary, figure 2.

DIAGNOSTIC READING SUMMARY

Pupil_____ School_____ Grade_____ Age_____

Teacher_____ Date_____

Attendance_____ Scholarship _____

Onset of Reading Problem _____

Test Results

Oral Reading Test _____ Silent Reading Test _____

Oral Reading Scores: Accuracy_____ Comprehension _____ Rate_____

Grade Equivalents: Accuracy_____ Comprehension_____ Rate_____

Silent Reading Scores: Comprehension _____ Meaning Vocabulary_____ Rate_____

Grade Equivalents: Comprehension_____ Meaning Vocabulary_____ Rate_____

Group Intelligence Test_____

    Date_____ M.A. (Total)_____ Language M.A. _____ Nonlanguage M.A._____

    I.Q. (Total)_____ Language I.Q. _____ Nonlanguage I.Q. _____

Oral Reading Retardation: From Grade_____ From Nonlangauge M.A. _____

                 From Auding Level _____

Silent Reading Retardation: From Grade_____ From Nonlangauge M.A. _____

                 From Auding Level _____

Appropriate Instructional Level_____ Independent Reading Level_____

Potential Reading Level _____

    Educational Hazards to Learning (Enter by No. from pages 4-5)
_____

    Noneducational Hazards to Learning

Health _____

Hearing _____

Vision _____

Personal Adjustment _____

Out of School Environment _____

Hazards to Learning in Need of Correction _____

(continued)

Figure 2

_____

_____

_____

_____

_____

_____

_____

_____

Specific Reading Difficulties

Prevalent Errors from Oral Reading (Informal)_____

_____

Prevalent Errors in Oral Reading Test_____

_____

_____

Difficulties in Silent Reading _____

_____

_____

Faulty Reading Habits _____

_____

Recommended Improvement Program in Reading

Reading Skills to Be Corrected and Mastered:
Word Perception _____

_____

Word Analysis_____

_____

Meaning Vocabulary_____

_____

(continued)

Figure 2 (continued)

Comprehension _____

_____

Study Skills _____

Rate of Comprehension _____

_____

Corrective Material Recommended _____

_____

Difficulty of Material _____ Special Methods Recommended _____

_____

_____

_____

Fields of Interest for Recreational Reading _____

_____

_____

Figure 2 (continued)

SUMMARY

All children who are severely retarded in reading and exhibit behaviorial traits indicating frustration and an aversion for learning reflect problems that are often difficult to diagnose and to correct. It now becomes imperative to determine the child's potential, existing hazards to learning, mental maturity, optimum instructional level, interests, and preferred methods of learning. Causal factors must be discovered and eliminated or ameliorated and the child's self-confidence restored. Screening tests, nonlanguage intelligence tests, listening comprehension tests, oral and silent reading tests, and personality tests are needed. A thorough diagnosis is essential, one involving all seven steps described in this chapter. Records of the diagnosis and correction undertaken should be kept and made a part of the child's longitudinal history.

Utilization of self-directed corrective material described in chapters 7 to 9 can readily be implemented for all retarded readers by the classroom teacher within the framework of her scheduled activities. Recreational reading is a vital supplement to any corrective program. Children with severe psychological and emotional problems may require the services of a school psychologist and a special teacher of reading.

SUMMARY OF THE DIAGNOSTIC PROCESS

Diagnostic Steps	Problems to be Explored	Instruments	Procedures
1. Identify the retarded reader	Low scholarship No interest in school Textbooks too difficult Over-age for grade Behavioral difficulty	Observation Interviews Cumulative records Oral reading Group silent reading tests	Evaluate performance in oral and silent reading

2. Determine the nature of the reading problem	Instructional level
	Independent reading level
	Reading habits
	Reading skills
	  Sight vocabulary
	  Word analysis
	  Meaning vocabulary
	  Comprehension
	  Rate of comprehension
	  Study habits and skills
	Interest in reading
		Observation
		Reading Inventory
		Oral Reading Test
		Diagnostic silent reading test
			Determine highest grade level on an informal reading inventory
			Convert scores on oral and silent reading tests to grade scores and compare with pupil's present grade placement
			Identify and record errors on oral reading tests
			Locate weaknesses on silent reading tests

3. Determine the pupil's potential	Level of mental maturity on nonlanguage intelligence tests. Level of listening comprehension	Nonlanguage group intelligence tests Individual intelligence test Listening comprehension test	Convert scores on intelligence tests and listening comprehension test to grade and age scores
4. Determine the severity of the reading problem	Extent of retardation from grade and potential	Nonlanguage intelligence tests Listening comprehension test Oral and silent reading tests	Apply formulae described on pages 165-166

(continued)

Figure 3

Diagnostic Steps	Problems to be Explored	Instruments	Procedures
5. Identify hazards to learning and discover causal factors	Educational hazards Noneducational hazards	Observation Interviews Behavior Inventories Screening tests in vision and hearing Personality tests	Identify hazards to learning Administer and interpret screening tests Determine preferred method of learning Locate factors that inhibit learning Consult special workers
6. Summarize and record data	Instructional level Independent reading level Reading difficulties Retardation in reading Specific hazards present	Diagnostic Reading Summary page 168 Diagnostic Reading Checklist page 163	Enter data on Reading Summary Enter reading difficulties on Reading Checklist
7. Interpret data	Determine reading difficulties to be corrected Determine causal factors to be corrected Determine learning potential Determine difficulty and nature of corrective material to be used	Diagnostic Reading Summary and Reading Checklist	Enter description of corrective program on the Reading Summary

Figure 3 (continued)

PROBLEMS FOR ORAL AND WRITTEN DISCUSSION

1. Select two or more tests useful in evaluating a pupil's sight vocabulary. Describe and evaluate the tests.
2. Select two or more tests useful in evaluating a pupil's meaning vocabulary. Describe and evaluate the tests.
3. Select two or more tests useful in evaluating a pupil's competence in word analysis. Describe and evaluate the tests.

4. What is the significant difference between immediate recall and delayed recall in a word-recognition test?

5. Compute the language M.A.'s and the nonlanguage M.A.'s for four or more of your retarded readers and compare the results with their appropriate instructional level in reading. Interpret the results.

6. Administer a reading inventory to a retarded reader, an average reader, an accelerated reader in a given grade and determine the instructional level, the independent reading level, and the frustration level for each pupil.

7. Select a retarded reader and apply all tests, procedures, and computations needed to complete the Reading Summary (fig. 2). Interpret the results.

REFERENCES

1. EDWARD W. DOLCH, "How to Diagnose Children's Reading Difficulties by Informal Classroom Techniques," *Reading Teacher* 6 (1953):10-14.

2. ALBERT J. HARRIS, *How to Increase Reading Ability*, 5th ed. (New York: David McKay Co., Inc., 1970), pp. 140-141.

3. GUY L. BOND and LEO C. FAY, "A Comparison of the Performance of Good and Poor Readers on the Individual Items of Stanford-Binet Scale, Forms L and M," *Journal of Educational Research* 43 (1950):475-479.

4. ALBERT J. HARRIS, *How to Increase Reading Ability*, 4th ed. (New York: David McKay Co., Inc., 1961), p. 299.

5. Ibid.

6. GUY L. BOND and MILES A. TINKER, *Reading Difficulties: Their Diagnosis and Correction*, 2nd ed. (New York: Appleton-Century-Crofts, 1967), p. 92.

7. HARRIS, op. cit., p. 300.

8. Ibid., p. 301.

9. MARION MONROE, *Children Who Cannot Read* (Chicago: University of Chicago Press, 1932).

10. DORIS J. JOHNSON and HELMER R. MYKLEBUST, *Learning Disabilities: Educational Principles and Practices* (New York: Grune and Stratton, 1967).

7

The Corrective
Program in Reading

CORRECTIVE INSTRUCTION IN READING

There is one question uppermost in the minds of conscientious teachers everywhere: "How best can I teach boys and girls who are reading far above or below their grade placement?"

This question is particularly pressing because the problem of variability in achievement is always with us. A retardation of twenty-five percent or more and an acceleration of a like amount in reading are prevalent in elementary classrooms everywhere. Third- and fourth-grade teachers encounter a range of talent covering five or more grades. And disconcerting though it may be, the situation becomes worse in this regard as one moves up the educational ladder. Fifth- and sixth-grade teachers are likely to find a still greater range. What is the answer to the chronic problem imposed by extreme heterogeneity in every grade?

Limitations of Group Instruction

With group instruction, the retarded reader is usually confronted with material on a frustration level of difficulty in every subject throughout the school day.

The answer cannot be found in having all children use the same reader, cover the same pages, and answer the same questions. The school that prescribes or encourages a program for all children consisting of the same methods and the same curricular experiences breeds mediocrity. *Such a school is setting the stage for a human drama of failure and discouragement for some of its pupils and boredom and disgust for others. In such a system, scholarship difficulties and behavior problems are sure to flourish.*

Group instruction, the prevailing method used in today's schools, consists of maximum teacher direction and minimum pupil motivation and participation. At its best, group instruction may provide differentiated assignments, individual projects, and special activities. Even then, however, it leaves much to be desired in terms of the systematic and sequential learning experiences required for developing better readers.

It is well to remember that instruction is not an end in itself. Learning is the end product, and instruction is but a means to this end. Learning, the goal of all instruction, involves changes in individuals.

Although learning is an individual experience, it should not be assumed that all instruction must be individualized. Group instruction proves quite effective when all the learners in a class have attained the necessary state of readiness. Children with good listening vocabularies and normal experiences in auding can acquire information and develop concepts just by listening to the teacher. Oral presentation by the teacher, then, proves an effective medium for imparting information. Similarly, when a teacher employs visual aids, all children usually are able to profit. Their learning is limited, of course, by the degree of their native intelligence, experiential background, attitudes, interests, and other conditioning factors.

The story is quite different, however, when a teacher requires all children to read the same material. Proficiency in reading skills is now the all-important factor. Those who are retarded in their reading skills find the text too difficult and suffer confusion and frustration. They fail to profit from this kind of group instruction until they have attained a facility with written language (reading) that is comparable to their facility with spoken language.

The most glaring deficiency of group instruction grows out of its failure to provide adequately for retarded and accelerated readers. It also fails to provide for average readers who have a special handicap or disability.

Group instruction tends to be teacher-directed, employing extrinsic rather than intrinsic methods of motivation. Frequently, the child feels he is working for the teacher. With individualized correction he soon discovers he is working for himself at his own rate to overcome his deficiencies.

Recitation during group instruction is frequently wasteful since each child actually participates for only a fractional part of the class period. Individualized instruction gives each child an opportunity to work independently and to function effectively every moment of the instructional period.

Tutoring has proved effective in clinical settings where a clinician is assigned one child with whom to work. Unfortunately, classroom teachers do not enjoy the luxury of a one-to-one, teacher-pupil ratio. With thirty or forty, or more, pupils in a classroom, it becomes impossible to implement an effective program of tutoring for the retarded readers. Working with a single pupil conceivably could consume a teacher's entire time.

Principles Underlying Corrective Instruction

The following practices and conditions are considered basic to a program of corrective instruction.

1. Learn all you can about the nature of each child and his specific reading problem. As part of the diagnosis, consult his cumulative folder, and catalog all important aspects of his growth. This involves valid measurements of his mental maturity, oral and silent reading levels, and proficiency in various subject matter fields. Other essentials entail awareness of the child's interests, hobbies, attitudes, and personality pattern. Work habits, too, should be scrutinized. General health and physical fitness with particular emphasis on vision and hearing must not be overlooked. Be alert to manifestations of sensory defects. In short, all facets of the child's reading readiness and hazards to learning must be considered. (The reader is referred to chapter 2 for more information pertaining to this section.)

2. Do not assume that an awareness of difficulties and hazards to a child's progress is enough. Appropriate ameliorative or corrective measures must be initiated if anything worthwhile is going to be accomplished. If, for example, a child with a physical defect is encountered, he should be referred to the proper specialist. Thus, a child with a visual problem would be brought to the attention of an optometrist or oculist for fitting of suitable corrective lenses. Only after correction is made can one be confident that this impediment to learning no longer exists.

3. Build a warm relationship with each pupil and recognize that this relationship is basic to his mental health and academic achievement. The child who likes his teacher is more highly motivated to overcome handicaps than the child who is indifferent to his teacher. One way to establish the kind of rapport essential to success is through personal conference. Convince the child by what you do, and tell him you are his friend. Usually, a child who repeatedly has met failure in reading needs a sympathetic and understanding adult who can help him rebuild feelings of adequacy. Be optimistic

about the possibilities of improvement by showing the child you have confidence in his ability to achieve. Help the child understand the nature of his reading problem and provide him with the tools that will enable him to improve.

4. Give the pupil insight into his strengths and weaknesses and indicate the goals toward which he is working. The child who has no idea where he is going is like a ship without a port. He may never reach a destination.

5. Help a pupil capitalize on his strengths rather than on his weaknesses by ascertaining his preferred mode or modes of learning. Some children learn faster when they see words, others when they hear them, and still others when they feel them. It is important, therefore, for a teacher to identify a pupil's preferred mode or modes of learning.

6. Minimize teaching and focus attention on learning. This means reducing the amount of teacher-directed activity—lectures and lengthy explanations. Get the child involved by having him actively engaged in self-directive learning.

7. Recognize that overlearning is an essential part of mastery. However, repetition consisting of isolated drill is to be avoided since it usually is ineffective and at times can have a deadening effect on interest. If repetition is to be effective, it must consist of practice on meaningful material of appropriate difficulty.

8. Acquire and develop corrective instructional materials that allow children to work *independently* in overcoming their weaknesses and consolidating their strengths. Such materials provide simple directions for doing specific exercises and should be accompanied by answers. *Self-directive materials* which permit *individualized corrective instruction* might include reading games, programmed learning materials, workbook exercise files, tape recordings, magic slates, and electric boards. (See chapters 8, 9, and 10 for a more detailed discussion of these and many other self-directive approaches to learning.)

9. Recognize that pupils differ in their rate of learning just as they differ in their maturity and level of achievement. If pupils are to attain personal goals, they must be permitted to progress at their own rate of learning. This can be achieved realistically through the use of self-directed instructional material of appropriate difficulty.

10. To facilitate individualized corrective work, provide each child with a small activity notebook on which his name appears. All such notebooks are kept by the teacher and are made available to pupils during those periods when the group engages in corrective work.

Each notebook lists by date corrective activity which the instructor feels is most appropriate for the child. A sample activity sheet from a notebook might be as follows:

May _____, 19_____

a. In SRA Laboratory 3a, read selection _____ and answer questions _____. Check your answers. If you miss more than three, read the selection again.

b. Get Exercise 28 from the workbook file. Complete it and then check your answers.

c. Work with Harry on card _____, level _____. (Durrell's Word Analysis Practice.) Ask your teacher for help if you get stuck on any of the words.

d. Work with Flash-X level _____, card _____.

e. On Table 2, you'll find many books on your reading level. Find one you like and start reading it.

---

11. Since we know that nothing succeeds like success, one must be sure to use instructional material that is geared to the child's intellectual and educational levels. By beginning at the learner's level of accomplishment (with retarded readers it often is wise to begin slightly below this level), further failure, frustrations, and discouragement can be avoided. When in doubt as to the difficulty level of an ungraded book, it is very helpful to have the child "try it on for size" by having him read several passages orally.

12. Capitalize on the reader's interests by introducing or encouraging pupils to select books and materials through a recreational reading program which coincides with these interests. In this way, reading becomes a vital and worthwhile experience for the child. "Here is something," he says to himself, "that I really want to know about."

13. Implicit in the foregoing conditions is the need for a great variety of reading materials. These materials must vary not only in difficulty but in content and interest appeal as well. Helping the right books come in contact with the right children is foundational to an individualized reading program. In this connection, it is important for a teacher to provide guidance in the choice of books. Some children are prone to choose books that are too difficult. Remember that the ultimate goal of any reading program is to develop in the child a love of reading.

14. Corrective instructional material should be designed to unfold gradually and systematically a logical sequence of skills or concepts to be mastered. It must be of optimum difficulty for the learner. A child should not be introduced to more difficult material until he has thoroughly mastered all that is foundational or prerequisite to it.

15. Evaluate both developmental and corrective instruction at frequent intervals to determine their effectiveness. An inventory of individual reading difficulties prepared by the teacher will serve as a useful guide. If what you are doing isn't paying learning dividends, renovate your approach. Keep in mind that learning and not teacher-dominated instruction is the goal.

16. Help each pupil evolve charts of various types and descriptions as a means of recording achievement in a dramatic way. Such charts, particularly if constructed by the pupil rather than forced on him by the teacher, are valuable incentives to improvement in learning and useful guides for the teacher in planning individual instructional programs.

17. Do not make learning such a serious matter that it ceases to be rewarding. Use games to add spark to repetitive activity and do not overlook the value of humor in the classroom. Humor can do much to add spice to what may be deadening fare. Children who see humor in their errors and problems are less likely to experience frustration. What is more, children who enjoy their classroom and their teacher become satisfied customers who are eager to come back for more.(1)

ADVANTAGES OF INDIVIDUALIZED SELF-DIRECTED CORRECTION

Since reading difficulties of specific pupils differ in number, type, and severity, correction must be individualized. If it is not, the unique array of problems peculiar to each individual cannot be met.

By utilizing *self-directed* material which provides practice in those skills and abilities each child has failed to master, corrective instruction can be *individualized* and made available to all who need it. When the instructional materials are of an appropriate level of difficulty, each pupil can work independently and successfully at his own rate. Consequently, pupils become motivated as they progress. As they become proficient at working independently, they gain skill in evaluating their own performance. Their teacher is relieved of the time-consuming activity of working individually with each child in need of corrective work and is able to direct group and individual projects simultaneously.

Severely retarded readers in the intermediate and upper grades usually are deficient in the basic reading skills of word perception. A reading difficulty at these levels can best be met through *individualized instruction* following a sound diagnosis. When the principles of this approach are understood and appropriate *self-directed* materials employed, reading problems will be minimized. As a result, scholarship problems will be resolved.

Corrective materials in reading tend to fall into two categories: teacher-made and commercial. Teacher-made instructional materials frequently consist of original games, while commercial or published materials encompass games, word lists, workbooks, multilevel materials, devices, and mechanical instruments. Most published materials are teacher-directed. However, in many instances these can be made self-instructive by simplifying directions and by providing answers which make self-evaluation possible.

The teacher should be reminded that an individualized corrective approach to reading is not in addition to but in place of a large portion of the time currently devoted to group instructional practices. The time previously devoted exclusively to teacher-directed group instruction now emphasizes an early diagnosis to discover individual reading difficulties, followed by self-directed corrective instruction. The teacher discovers that while supervising the activities of the normal and accelerated readers, retarded readers are successfully pursuing self-administering corrective material independently.

The teacher begins by acquiring basal readers and supplementary books on several grade levels. These include a good classroom library of books suitable for retarded, average, and superior readers. In addition, the teacher must have an array of workbooks, informal tests, exercises, reading games, and activities which are self-directional in nature. Chapters 8, 9, and 10 contain lists of commercial and teacher-made instructional materials that are, in most instances, self-directive or can be made self-directive.

Assuming a twenty-five percent retardation in reading with a class of thirty, a teacher will have seven or eight pupils in need of remediation. Individualized instruction for these pupils will vary from individual activities to group activities, depending on the skills to be mastered and the materials and techniques used by the teacher. If, for example, the entire group demonstrates a basic sight vocabulary deficiency of service words, a group game such as Look might be employed. On the other hand, if a single child in this group did not know his initial consonant sounds, specific pages from a workbook or specific exercises or games might be assigned individually to help overcome the deficiency.

It is important that the teacher design and acquire materials that are *self-directive*. This will enable her to do developmental work with normal and accelerated readers, while the retarded readers are pursuing individualized self-directive activities independently, without frustration or loss of attention to the tasks at hand. When the normal and accelerated readers are engaged in recreational reading, the teacher is free to extend any needed help to the retarded group.

It is recognized that as a phase of the developmental program, specific reading difficulties arise which require practice on specific skills in which a group is deficient. Group correction directed by the teacher can be effective in such instances if the difficulty of the material employed for corrective work is on an appropriate instructional level.

The Nature of Self-Directed Instructional Materials

Little additional teacher time and effort are needed to make individualized reading materials and exercises self-directive. If a problem does arise, it is likely to center around two areas: (1) simplified directions which will enable pupils to work independently and (2) ways whereby materials can be made self-corrective.

Directions must be simple and specific and must be written on the pupil's independent or free reading level. If directions have a difficulty level that coincides with a pupil's instructional level, he will be unable to understand them without the aid of the teacher.

For example, directions reading "To reinforce your sentence comprehension select the most appropriate words from those offered and insert them in the sentences" are more understandable if they are changed to read: "Read the first sentence. Now look at the words at the bottom of the page. Choose the best word and write it in the blank. Do the same for the other sentences."

Some ways whereby materials can be made self-corrective are as follows:

1. Write answers on the backs of exercises.
2. Write answers upside down in a space somewhat removed from the focal point of attention.
3. Cover answers with a flap which can be folded back.
4. Write answers on a small card which can be inserted in a library card pocket.

5. Write answers on cards which can be filed in an answer box.
6. Write answers on sheets of acetate. These can be placed over exercises for purposes of evaluation.
7. Cut appropriately located holes in sheets of paper or oaktag to form an answer mask. These can be placed over exercises for purposes of evaluation.
8. Cut a picture into parts after pasting it on oaktag. Write answers on the backs of these parts. On another piece of oaktag, write matching problems. As the pupil locates answers, he begins to build a picture. Incorrect answers result in a jumbled picture.
9. Separate questions and answers by a jigsaw cut. If the pieces can be fitted together, the pupil is assured that a correct association has been made.
10. Cut five answer windows in an envelope. On each question card write five answers with only the correct answer positioned so that it will be exposed in an answer window when the card is slipped into the envelope.

Some teachers are concerned about making answers available to their pupils. "They'll cheat," the teachers say.

It is true that some pupils may cheat. However, cheating inhibits learning, and such activity will be minimal if teachers emphasize learning rather than the grading of practice materials. And in spite of dishonesty, pupils who do find the correct answers are bound to make some valid associations so that learning will take place.

OPTIMUM METHOD OF LEARNING

As stated by one of the authors in an earlier publication, when the numerous methods of teaching words are pondered, many teachers are in a quandary.(2) Each specialist (Gates, Monroe, Dolch, Fernald, all renowned in the reading field) advocates a different method. What is the answer? What should be used? Is there a best method?

Basically, there are three methods for teaching words to disabled readers: the visual, the phonic, and the kinesthetic. There is no best method per se. Only when a corrective program is based on individual needs can any method be cited as superior.

For example, Marion Monroe tells of a seven-year-old boy who suffered from a severe reading disability of a neurological origin. No matter how hard the child tried, he was unable to remember words when the usual sight method was employed. As soon as the cause was uncovered, he was taught by tracing large models of words while saying them out loud.(3) This was a kinesthetic approach. And it worked! Soon he was able to recognize words and began to show definite and competent progress.

Bond's research shows that children suffering from hearing losses are at a marked disadvantage in learning to read when a purely phonetic method is employed. On the other hand, he found that the "look and say" method does not penalize the child who has an auditory loss.(4) It is evident that if a child suffers from auditory or visual deficiencies, it is wise to choose a method of instruction that minimizes the handicap as much as possible.

It is also a mistake to assume that just because children are free from discernible sensory impairments they will learn just as easily with one method as another. Any teacher can convince himself of the falsity of this belief by checking the auditory and visual memory spans of a group of children. Not infrequently does one find that students with fine visual memories have much poorer auditory memories or vice versa. For seemingly inexplicable reasons some children have great difficulty in making visual associations but show excellent phonic aptitude. In such cases, Monroe's phonetic approach of blending and forming word elements into whole words is to be recommended.

For the child who is adept at making visual associations but shows ineptitude when phonetic approaches are employed, Gates' method of stressing the general configuration of words as a basis for recognition is appropriate. Since it is not possible to tell which method will work best in an individual case, the teacher must be flexible and versatile. If Harry does not respond favorably to one method, another method must be tried.

In final analysis, if there is a best method, we are forced to term it eclectic. When an individual method is used to the exclusion of others, some children are doomed to failure regardless of how sincere, competent, and enthusiastic the teacher is. Today many teachers use the popular flash method. It is true that most children learn easily and quickly when this method is employed, but still there are needless fatalities. The number of failures could be reduced markedly if the teacher used several avenues of approach so the student could choose the particular method or combination of methods that seem to be best suited to his individual needs.

A simple yet ingenious test developed by Robert E. Mills provides a useful tool in studying this problem. *The Mills Learning Ability Test*(5) introduces groups of words in four ways: visual, phonic, kinesthetic, and combined. It then checks retention after an interval of one day. By means of the test, an examiner can determine the particular approach for which a given child shows the most aptitude. It should be obvious that the test is a valuable tool in a reading diagnosis.

Other tests that are helpful in identifying a pupil's preferred mode of learning are as follows:

The *Wepman Auditory Discrimination Test*(6) involves having a pupil listen to word pairs. He responds by indicating whether each pair is the same or different. The pupil who scores poorly on this test is likely to experience difficulty with phonics.

The *Benton Visual Retention Test*(7) requires a pupil to draw various designs from memory. The pupil who scores poorly on this test is likely to experience difficulty remembering word forms.

The *Illinois Test of Psycholinguistic Abilities* (ITPA)(8) is designed to determine basic weaknesses in the areas of visual and auditory perception, association, and memory. Doing poorly on certain of the nine subtests involved may indicate a pupil's ineptitude for phonics, the kinesthetic approach, or the "look and say" method.

The *Marianne Frostig Development Test of Visual Perception* (DTVP) (9) consists of five subtests. These measure various aspects of visual motor coordination, constancy of form, figure ground relationships, position in space, and spatial relationships. Scoring poorly on these tests would indicate, it is thought, deficiencies that are basic to learning to read.

Robbins Speech Sound Discrimination and Verbal Imagery Type Tests (10) are helpful in determining the specific sensory modality through which a pupil can learn most easily. The tests which are designed for children over four require young children to point to pictures while older ones tell whether the three words they have listened to are alike, and if not, the one that is different.

Screening Tests for Identifying Children with Specific Language Disability(11) comprise a test designed for locating children who have or are likely to develop problems in reading, spelling, and handwriting. Its subtests include measures of visual copying, visual memory, visual discrimination, auditory perception, auditory memory, and auditory-visual association.

SUMMARY

When several pupils in a classroom are retarded in their reading skills, the teacher has to cope with a diversity of individual difficulties. This makes undifferentiated group instruction highly ineffective. Individualized and self-directed corrective material that is selected to provide remediation for known difficulties is needed. These self-instructive materials permit pupils to proceed at their own rate of learning while they are motivated by an awareness of personal goals.

A corrective program of instruction must be based on a thorough diagnosis which serves to uncover individual difficulties to be corrected and causal factors to be eliminated. Materials to be used in the program should be of optimum difficulty. They should provide practice that is systematic and sequential in its development. Preferred modes and methods of learning have to be discovered and pupils must experience immediate success. Recreational reading, an integral part of the corrective program, is needed to reinforce learning and to insure mastery of basic skills.

PROBLEMS FOR ORAL AND WRITTEN DISCUSSION

1. Prepare a corrective program in reading for a pupil of average intelligence who is retarded two years in word analysis and three years in comprehension. Indicate the type of materials you would recommend.
2. Select a teacher-directed workbook in reading and make the necessary revision in the directions for five or more exercises in order to make them self-directed.
3. Select two retarded readers and determine their reading expectancy.
4. What is subvocalization and how does it influence reading?
5. Select five principles of corrective instruction and discuss their implementation in a corrective reading program.
6. Evaluate the place of workbooks as self-corrective material.
7. Procure several workbooks in reading on two or more levels of difficulty. Dissect, combine, and reassemble the workbooks to form a ready file of corrective material.

REFERENCES

1. HAP GILLILAND and HARRIETT MAURITSEN, "Humor in the Classroom," *The Reading Teacher* (May 1971):753-756.
2. DELWYN SCHUBERT, "Whose Brand of Reading Methods Is the Best Buy?" *The Clearing House* (January 1953):266-267.
3. MARION MONROE, *Growing Into Reading* (Chicago: Scott, Foresman and Co., 1951), pp. 63-65.
4. GUY BOND, *The Auditory and Speech Characteristics of Poor Readers,* Teachers College Contributions to Education, No. 657 (New York: Teachers College, Columbia University).
5. The Mills Center, 1512 Broward Blvd., Fort Lauderdale, Fla.
6. Language Research Associates, 950 E. 59th St., Chicago, Ill.
7. The Psychological Corporation, 304 E. 45th St., New York, N. Y. 10017.
8. University of Illinois Press, Urbana, Ill. 61801.
9. Follett Educational Corp., 1010 W. Washington Blvd., Chicago, Ill. 60607.
10. Expression Company, Magnolia, Mass.
11. Educators Publishing Service, 75 Moulten St., Cambridge, Mass. 02138.

SELECTED READINGS

BOND, GUY, and MILES TINKER. *Reading Problems: Their Diagnosis and Correction.* 2nd ed. New York: Appleton-Century-Crofts, 1967, ch. 10.

HARRIS, ALBERT. *How to Increase Reading Ability.* 5th ed. New York: David McKay Co., Inc., 1970, ch. 12.

OTTO, WAYNE, and RICHARD McMENEMY. *Corrective and Remedial Teaching.* Boston: Houghton Mifflin Co., 1966, ch. 3.

SCHUBERT, DELWYN. *Readings in Reading: Practice-Theory-Research.* New York: Thomas Y. Crowell Co., 1968, selections 53, 54, 55, 57.

8

Improving
Word Recognition and
Word Analysis

Pupils in the primary and intermediate grades who are deficient in word-recognition and word-analysis skills are in dire need of help. Teachers need more than basal readers to assist these pupils; they need supplementary instructional material that will provide individualized practice to overcome specific reading difficulties. The following instructional techniques and materials provide a useful approach to the problem.

EMPHASIZING WIDE READING

Practice on common words and an introduction to new words take place most naturally when children engage in easy, pleasurable reading. Individualizing and personalizing a child's reading program requires a knowledge of books and an understanding of the child and his interests. The teacher who is faced with the task of finding the right book for the right child should be guided by the following principles:

1. Utilize the child's present interests. No matter how immature his present interests are, it is essential to begin by introducing materials which are related to them. If the child is given material which he sees as vital and functional, interest becomes spontaneous.
2. Provide reading materials which are on or slightly below the pupil's level of reading ability. Easy material is essential for success. And success generates interest.
3. Acquaint yourself with book lists and bibliographies of children's books. These materials simplify finding the right book for the right child. Two excellent books in this regard are *A Place to Start* and *Good Reading for Poor Readers*.(1) For additional suggestions see Appendix E2.

UTILIZING WORD LISTS

The vocabulary lists described in connection with diagnostic procedures have considerable value in a corrective program for disabled readers. They help answer questions such as "What words are found most frequently in primary books?" "What words should be taught first when working with a disabled reader?" "What fourth-grade words should a pupil know on sight?"

Although compilers of word lists have rendered a great service, certain points should be considered by those who wish to use them.(2)

1. If a word list is based in part or in its entirety on the writing vocabulary of adults, it may not apply to the reading vocabulary of elementary school children.
2. Since a child's reading vocabulary is usually larger than his writing vocabulary, it is not wise to confine children's reading vocabulary to a list based on writing vocabulary.
3. Strict vocabulary control is likely to be debilitating to content. Content area subjects such as social studies and science will suffer if vocabulary control is too stringent. Remedial teachers should be cognizant of the fact that content field reading usually involves a heavier vocabulary burden.
4. Frequency of use, rather than word difficulty, is provided by vocabulary word lists.

When word lists are used for word study with pupils, attempts should be made to provide meaningful contextual settings. It is also advisable to employ a variety of approaches to help sustain interest. When possible, have the child evolve a progress chart that will highlight his vocabulary growth in a dramatic way.

INSTRUCTIONAL MATERIALS FOR CORRECTING DEFICIENCIES IN SIGHT VOCABULARY

When individual pupils or groups of pupils are deficient in word-recognition skill, corrective practice can be individualized by using available *commercial material** such as:

1. *Basic Sight Vocabulary Cards:* These instructional materials are for use with slow readers and include 220 words which constitute more than fifty percent of all words encountered in ordinary reading. (For use with individual children or children working in pairs; $1.50; Garrard.)

*All games are designated by an asterisk.

2. *Durrell's Hand Tachistoscope:* A simple tachistoscope (quick-exposure device) consisting of an oaktag cover, an aperture, a shutter and a series of word lists on strips of oaktag board. (For use with individual children or children working in pairs; $1.30; Harcourt Brace Jovanovich, Inc.)

3. *Christie Word Set:* This set (on 3-by-14-inch cards) contains the twenty new words of highest frequency found in each of the intermediate-grade levels of six current reader series. Designed for use with the *Teacher Syllabascope* ($2.50) which is available from the same publisher. (For use with individual children or an entire class; $1.50; Wordcrafters Guild.)

4. *Educational Flash Words:* These instructional materials involve cards consisting of two sets that help the primary-grade child learn words that are difficult to master through a picture approach. More than 200 sight words are included. (For use with individual children or with a group of children; $1.00 a set; Milton Bradley.)

5. *Educational Password Game:** Based on the popular television show, this game uses basic sight and picture words found in primary and elementary readers. (For use with pairs of children or a group of children; $2.00; Milton Bradley.)

6. *Five First Steps and Pop Words:* These instructional materials involve 150 common sight or pop words printed in large, clear type on four-by-six-inch cards. Consonant and vowel sounds are printed on colored cards and include sixteen easy consonants, four consonant digraphs, the sounds of *y,* and the hard and soft *c* and *g* sounds. (For use with individual children, children working in pairs, or with a group of children under proper direction; $1.80; Kenworthy.)

7. *Flash Words* (Sets I and II): Two sets of flash cards that help the primary-grade child learn words that cannot be mastered through the picture approach. A total of 200 words are involved. (For use with individual children, children working in pairs, or with a group of children under proper direction; $1.00 a set; Milton Bradley.)

8. *Grab:** A sight vocabulary game for remedial or classroom teaching. Three levels are involved: Grab Junior (Sets I and II); Grab Senior (Sets III and IV); Advanced Grab (Sets V and VI). (For use with two to four children, potentially self-directive; two sets on any level, $1.75; Teachers' supplies.)

9. *Group Word Teaching Game:** A bingo-type game designed to teach the 220 basic sight words evolved by Dolch. (For use with two or more children, potentially self-directive; $2.50; Garrard.)

10. *Happy Bears Reading Game:** A game in which children learn common nouns by matching pictures with words under them. Since the pairs of pictures differ, attention is drawn to the word under each picture. (For use with individual children, potentially self-directive; $.75; Garrard.)

11. *Hear** and *Hear & Read** cards come in two boxes. The first box contains one deck each of *Hear* and *Hear & Read* cards emphasizing initial consonant sounds; the second box emphasizes final consonant sounds. *Hear* consists of picture cards which children pair according to sound. Directions for group and independent game activities are included with each set of cards. (For use with individual children, children working in pairs, or with a group of children under proper direction; $5.00 a box; Coast Visual.)

12. *Match** (Sets I and II). A reading game consisting of two sets of cards, each set containing half of the ninety-five commonest nouns evolved by Dolch. (For use with one or two children, potentially self-directive; $1.25 per set; Garrard.)

13. *Matchettes:* A set of ten inlay boards, $8\frac{1}{2}$ by $11\frac{1}{2}$ inches, which provide experiences in identifying and matching illustrations and words. Removable pieces are printed on both sides for dual matching activities. Each board shows six objects and words that are in lower-case manuscript letters. (For use with individual children or children working in pairs; $4.50 per set of ten; Judy.)

14. *New Linguistic Block Series, Set 1W:** These materials consist of thirty plastic blocks involving words. Also included as part of the set is a forty-eight-page Teacher's Instruction Booklet. A workbook for children also can be purchased. (For use with individual children or with a small group of children; $8.70; Scott, Foresman.)

15. *Picture Word Builder:* A training aid in which thirty-six familiar objects on heavy cards are die-cut so only the correct word can be inserted to complete the word and picture matching. (For use with individual children or children working in pairs; $.60; Milton Bradley.)

16. *Picture Word Lotto:** A game that teaches letter and word recognition. Played by matching picture to picture, word to picture, and finally, word to word. (For use with two or more children, potentially self-directive; $1.00; Garrard.)

17. *Picture Words for Beginners:** A matching game which helps primary-grade children add over 100 words to their vocabulary. The child learns to associate pictures with words found in first reading books. (For individual children or with children working in pairs, potentially self-directive; $1.00; Milton Bradley.)

18. *Pictures for Peg Board Classification—Opposites:* This colorful set of 256 pictures and word cards is printed on 4-by-3¼-inch white tag and is for use with a pegboard or can be used as flash cards. (For use with individual children or with a group of children; $4.00 a set; Ideal.)

19. *Popper Words* (Sets I and II): Popper Words, Set I, contains the easier one-half of the 220 Basic Sight Vocabulary evolved by Dolch. Popper Words, Set II, contains the harder one-half of this vocabulary group. (For use with individual children, children working in pairs, or with a group of children under proper direction; $1.25 per set; Garrard.)

20. *Primary Reading Cards* (Beginning and Advanced): These instructional materials consist of two boxes of cards containing words appearing most frequently in primary books. The cards are three by four inches in size and are set in extra large manuscript for easy reading. (For use with individual children, children working in pairs, or with a group of children under proper direction; $1.25 a box; Educational Card.)

21. *Probe:** A provocative game in which each player selects a word of twelve or fewer letters which he keeps secret. (He may use the dictionary in making his selection.) Other players try to guess it, letter by letter. Equipment includes four racks, four decks of letter cards, each of a different color and consisting of ninety-six cards and four letter-card upright holders. The 384 cards in the game provide combinations for thousands of words. (For use with two to four children; $6.00; Parker.)

22. *Read-To-Read Puzzles:* A set of four puzzles that provide drill in matching word forms, associating words with pictures, and building a sight vocabulary of common primer words. (For use with individual children or children working in pairs; $3.50 per set; Ben-G-Products.)

23. *Spuzzle:* These materials involve puzzles which actually spell the objects that are pictured. Four puzzles—two in each set—turn pictures magically into words. (For individual children or with children working in pairs, potentially self-directive; $1.20; McCormick-Mathers.)

24. *Tumble Words:** A vocabulary-building game consisting of lettered cubes and a shaker. The object of the game is to build as many words as possible from the letters appearing on the cubes after they have rolled from the shaker. A point system is described for recording the successes of the players. (For use with two children or a group of children, potentially self-directive; $1.00; Kohner Brothers.)

25. *Wonder Words:** A game using words that have been grouped into levels of difficulty. It is designed to encourage eye movements from left to right and is recommended for remedial programs through grade five. (For use with individual children or a small group of children; $4.60; Dick Blick.)

26. *Word Matching Game:** A game consisting of sixty pairs of cards. It is meant to be played by a child without supervision. Both cards in each pair contain the same word, but only one card has a picture on the back. As the child reads each word, he places it beside the picture to which it corresponds. Then he turns the picture card over and compares the two words. (For use with individual children; $3.48; Open Court.)

27. *Word-Roll:** This game consists of ten colorful cubes, color-keyed to twenty picture cards. Every roll spells a word. After playing with all five sets, the pupil will have been exposed to forty-five new words, fifteen beginning consonants, and fifteen word families. (For use with one to four children; $4.95; McCormick-Mathers.)

When individual pupils or groups of pupils are deficient in word-recognition skill, individualized practice can be provided by using *teacher- or pupil-made materials* such as the following:

1. *Bowling:** Make a bowling-pin tachistoscope (quick-exposure device) from tagboard by doing the following: Color and cut out the form of a bowling pin. At the center of the pin make an opening so words which have been printed on strips of oaktag and slipped behind the structure can be exposed quickly, one at a time. If the child who starts can name ten words, he has made a strike and can try a new strip of words. (For use with two or more children.)

2. *Build-a-Train:** Engines and railway cars are cut from oaktag. Each piece has a word printed or written on it. Children who pronounce the words correctly build a train which becomes longer and longer. The object of the game is to see who can build the longest train. (For use with two or more children.)

3. *Card Method:* Each pupil is equipped with a small pile of cards (3-by-5-inch cards cut in half are fine). When an unknown word is encountered the pupil is instructed to write it on a card. The teacher, too, has cards in readiness at all times so any child in the reading circle who misses a word can be given an immediate written record of it. Several times a week the children are allowed to get together in groups of three for the purpose of quizzing each other on their cards. The chances are good that at least one of the

three children will know a word. When all are uninformed, the teacher or an especially appointed assistant can provide the help needed. (For use with a group of children, potentially self-directive.)

4. *Carpenter:** Draw a picture of a house on a piece of heavy tagboard. Color all but the roof. Paste art corners on the roof, about 1½ inches apart in even rows. On small cards about ½ inch by 1¼ inches print the words for drill. Each card is a shingle. If a child can say the word, he can put it in the art corner and add a shingle to the roof. If he does not know it, it falls to the ground. More than enough cards are given the child so he can have reasonable success in completing the house. (For use with children working in pairs.)

5. *Checkers:** Buy a cheap checkerboard. Cut squares from masking tape that coincide in size with the checkerboard squares and place these on the squares where the checkers are to be placed or moved. Words are then printed on the masking tape (Dolch words frequently are used) right side up and upside down so both players can read any word appearing on the board. The game proceeds like regular checkers, but a child must be able to read the word or words if he is to complete a move. If he fails to call the word correctly, he is told what the word is. He must wait, however, until his next turn before attempting the move again. (For use with two children, potentially self-directive.)

6. *Classification:* Print in color on individual cards two or more words that constitute categories such as *home* and *farm*. Place these in an envelope along with many other cards bearing words such as *kitchen, stove,* and *barn*. The latter must be categorized under the two words printed in color. By numbering the backs of the word cards, the exercise can be made self-corrective. (For use with individual children, potentially self-directive.)

7. *Color Match:* Words pertaining to various colors are printed on pieces of oaktag. Clothespins that have been colored are placed in an accompanying envelope. The child engaged in color-match shows his understanding of the words by attaching the appropriately colored clothespins to the word cards. By coloring the backs of the word cards with the color named, this activity can be made self-corrective. (For use with individual children, potentially self-directive.)

8. *Cookie-pan Magnet Match:* Paste pictures of various objects on the inside surface of a shallow cookie pan. Design matching word cards on the backs of which are glued small pieces of a bar magnet. The pupil engaged in this activity places words in proper position. The

word cards are held in position by the pieces of bar magnet which adhere firmly to the metal of the cookie pan. By numbering the pictures and the backs of the word cards, this activity can be made self-corrective. (For use with individual pupils, potentially self-directive.)

9. *Fishing:** Word cards are cut from tagboard in the shape of fish. A paper clip is slipped over each word card. Fishermen are equipped with a pole (short stick), a fish line (20 inches of store string), and a fishhook (small magnet). Each child gets a turn trying to catch a fish. If he can read the word attracted to the magnet, he may keep the fish involved. If he doesn't know it, he shows the word to the other children for a correct response and then returns it, face down, to the fishpond. (For use with two children or a group of children, potentially self-directive.)

10. *Jallopy Derby:** Make a five-car race track on as large a piece of cardboard as you can find. Divide the track into three-inch spaces and mark a starting line. Let the children make little cars of paper or buy four little cars at a toy store.

On a small piece of tagboard print the words you want the children to learn. A die is tossed for order of beginning. Number One then tosses the die for his first move. He may move as many spaces as the number on the die if he can say the word on the card he draws. If he cannot say the word, he loses his turn and the next child may use the same word or pick a new one. If he decides not to use the missed word, the next player may use it. If no one uses the missed word, it is put at the bottom of the pile. When the game is over, special help is given with the missed words at the bottom of the pile.

Each race is one lap. The winner is the one who first comes out even with the finish line. Should a potential winner throw a six and have only four or five spaces left, he may move just one space for the word he can say. Coming out even with the finish line adds excitement to the game. It gives each other child a chance to become a last-minute winner. (For use with one, two, three, or four children.)

11. *Match-A-Picture:* An ingeniously designed self-corrective exercise can be made by pasting a picture on a piece of oaktag on which two matched and parallel columns of synonyms or antonyms have been written. The left-hand column is numbered from top to bottom so no difficulty can be experienced in arranging it properly at a later time. After this has been done, the oaktag is cut into

individual word cards and the pieces are placed in a stiff manila folder. The pupil who engages in this exercise begins by arranging the left-hand column as numbered. He then arranges in a parallel column the matching pieces. All the pieces involved are put in position inside the folder. When the pupil is ready to check his work, he closes the folder and flips it over. Upon opening the folder a complete picture appears. Any error manifests itself in a jumbled picture. (For use with individual pupils, potentially self-directive.)

12. *Matching:* Print words that designate specific colors (*snow, fire engine, violets,* etc.) on a sheet of oaktag. Place small cards of different colors in an attached envelope. The child matches the colored cards with the words. By using an identification scheme on the backs of the color cards, this activity can be made self-corrective. (For use with individual children, potentially self-directive.)

13. *Old Maid:** Print words on pieces of oaktag the size of playing cards. Complete twenty cards and then make a duplicate set so twenty pairs of words result. Print one Old Maid card or, if you wish, one word alone may be used to designate the Old Maid card. Distribute the cards and begin with the person to the left of the dealer who starts the game by drawing a card from the person at his right. As pairs are formed, the words are called and placed on the table. This continues until all pairs are matched and one person holds the Old Maid. (For use with two to four children, potentially self-directive.)

14. *One Look Game:** The Dolch cards are used with this activity. Pupils work in pairs with one child acting as a helper. The pack of cards is placed before the learner who picks up one card at a time, calls the word and then hands it to the helper. The helper retains those cards called correctly and segregates those called incorrectly. Any marked hesitation constitutes an error. When all cards have been called, the number of words missed is calculated and recorded in chart form. The helper then calls each word for the player who repeats aloud each word he has failed. The entire pack is reshuffled and is made ready for another "one look" trial. (For use with children working in pairs.)

15. *Pairs:*† Pairs is a game similar to rummy and can be played by two to five children. Twenty-five words, each of which appears twice on oaktag playing cards, make a fifty-card deck. The object of the

†A game devised by Edward Fry, Rutgers University.

game is to get as many pairs as possible. When playing the game, five cards are dealt to each player, and the remainder of the deck is placed face down on the table. The player to the right of the dealer begins by asking a fellow player for a specific card that will match one in his hand. If the latter has the card requested, he must give it up. If he does not have it, the asker draws one card from the pile and terminates his play. The player who gets the card for which he asks (should he not know the word, he may solicit help from anyone present), either from another player or from the pile, gets a second turn. As soon as a player has a pair, he places it on the table. The player with the most pairs wins.

16. *Pick-A-Chip:** Divide Dolch's Basic Sight Vocabulary Words into four sections of fifty-five words each. Type or write the words on pieces of masking tape and place these on poker chips of four colors. Deposit the chips in four small boxes of matching colors. A pupil starts the game by choosing a color and then gives a spinner a whirl. He picks as many chips from his color section as the spinner indicates. If he fails to say one of the words, he is told what it is, but he must return the chip to the box and pass the spinner to the next player. The winner is the pupil who has acquired the most chips. (For use with two to four children.)

17. *Picture Checkerboard:** The teacher writes sixteen nouns on the board in numbered order. The children fold a sheet of drawing paper into sixteen squares and number them correspondingly. They then draw pictures of the nouns on the numbered squares. Later, papers can be exchanged and corrected. (For use with individual children or a group of children.)

18. *Picture Dictionary Match:* Paste pictures cut from a ten-cent-store dictionary in a row on a 9-by-12-inch card. Under each picture draw a space box $1\frac{1}{2}$ inches by $\frac{1}{2}$ inch. Prepare small word cards and put these in an envelope which remains attached to the picture card. By numbering the pictures and the backs of the word cards, this activity can be made self-corrective. (For use with individual children, potentially self-directive.)

19. *Picture Riddle Matcho:** Children cut pictures from old magazines and place them in envelopes—five to an envelope. The teacher writes a riddle about one of the pictures and places it in the envelope with the pictures. The child who chooses the envelope selects the pictures which answer the riddle. A marking scheme can be devised to make this activity self-corrective. (For use with individual children, potentially self-directive.)

20. *Ring a Word:** Utilize heavy plywood in constructing a board two by three feet in size. Space five nails on the board and paint numbers from one to five under the nails. Print words on small cards and hang them on the nails. (Easiest cards should be on Number One nail and hardest cards on Number Five nail.) Equip children with a box of mason jar rubber rings. The directions for the game are "Ring a word and score the points if you can say it." (For use with two or more children.)

21. *Shoestring Matcho:* Two rows of mixed synonyms or an antonym and synonym row are written side by side. Shoestrings are attached to the right of the first row by knotting the ends on the reverse side. The child designates the correct answer by slipping the shoestring into the proper hole before words in the second column. A marking scheme can be devised on the reverse side to make this activity self-corrective. (For use with individual children, potentially self-directive.)

22. *Tachistoscope:* Let a child find a picture that interests him. Mount this picture on oaktag and cut two horizontal slits $1\frac{1}{2}$ inches long and $\frac{3}{8}$ of an inch apart. Words to be learned are printed or typed on strips of oaktag about $1\frac{1}{2}$ inches wide. The strips are then inserted in the slits and pulled through so one word is exposed at a time. (For use with children working in pairs.)

23. *Word Basket Ball:** Remove the top and one of the long sides of a packing carton. Use green and white paint to give what remains the appearance of a basketball court. Baskets can be simulated by pasting two small paper bags on the outside ends of the box. If a player can call correctly a word he has drawn from a word pile, he pushes the word card through a slot above his team's basket and his side gets two points. If he calls incorrectly, someone on the other team tries. A referee will determine if the word is said correctly or not. The score can be kept by counting the number of cards in each bag. (For use with two children or two groups of children under proper direction.)

24. *Word Authors:** Words are printed on corners of cards—four cards to a set. A set can consist of four colors, four animals, four synonyms, and the like. Each child is dealt four cards and one child begins the game by calling for a word. If he gets the word, he may continue to call for words. When his opponent indicates that he does not have the card called for, the child draws from the deck of cards that is face down on the table. The child who acquires the most sets wins. (For use with two to four children, potentially self-directive.)

25. *Word File Pictures:* The name of an object is printed at the top of a card, and a picture or drawing is placed below to illustrate it. On the opposite side of the cards just the word is printed. The child tries to read the word and then checks his response by looking at the picture on the front side of the card. (For use with individual children, potentially self-directive.)

26. *Wordo:** The teacher with the help of her children prepares cardboard master cards eight by eleven inches in size. These master cards are blocked off vertically and horizontally into twenty-five small squares. The middle space is marked *free.* Individual words that are troublesome are placed on the twenty-four squares that remain. Each cardboard master card must have the same words but in different positions. The twenty-four words are typed or printed on small cards and placed in an envelope. As individual words are drawn from the envelope and called aloud, the players find the words on their master cards and cover them with a marker of some sort. The marker may be a kernel of corn, a bean, or a small piece of cardboard. The first child to cover a row of words in a straight line, vertically, horizontally or diagonally, calls out "wordo." If he has not erred, he is declared the winner. (For use with two or more children, potentially self-directive.)

UTILIZING CONTEXT CLUES

As stated by Hildreth, "inferring the meaning of a word from what went before, and deliberately reading ahead for clues to meaning is an essential technique for word recognition."(3)

Because of its importance to word recognition, specific training and a variety of methods should be used in teaching pupils to use contextual clues. Some of these are—

1. Show the pupil who fails to use contextual clues how valuable they can be in identifying words.
   a. Read aloud a sentence, omitting the unknown word. Ask the pupil what he thinks the word is.
   b. Provide sample sentences which are designed to show that contextual clues may come before, after, or both before and after a strange word.
   c. Provide samples which show that contextual clues may take the form of a phrase, a sentence, or a paragraph.
   d. Provide sample sentences to show that the context may take the form of an appositive, a definition, or an example.

2. When a pupil encounters a strange word and is stymied by it, suggest that he read on. Too often teachers are prone to encourage an immediate "sound-it-out" approach. It is more judicious to have a pupil skip an unknown word and read the entire sentence. At this point, the pupil might ask himself, for example, "What word starting with *ch* would make sense in this sentence?

When working on contextual clues, teachers should select reading materials on the pupil's instructional level in conformity with his background and interests.

INSTRUCTIONAL MATERIALS FOR CORRECTING DEFICIENCIES IN CONTEXT SKILLS

When individual pupils or groups of pupils are deficient in their use of context clues, corrective practice can be individualized by using teacher-made materials such as the following:

1. Present sentences in which words are missing. The pupils are instructed to read the sentences and decide which words fit the blanks most appropriately. Examples:
   a. They put the _____ in the bank.
      paper, letter, money
   b. The day was bright and _____.
      sunny, dark, cloudy
   c. Bill had to _____ if he should _____ the fort against attack.
      defend, decide
2. Present sentences in which a phonic clue is given to aid the pupil in providing missing words. Pupils are instructed to think of words which fit the blanks most appropriately. Examples:
   a. Betty said she would r_____ the ball on the floor.
   b. The cat dr_____ the milk.
   c. He was going to _____ow his shoe at the barking dog.
3. Present sentences which contain unusual words whose meaning can be arrived at by using contextual clues. Pupils are instructed to read the sentences carefully before deciding on an answer. Examples:
   a. John will *deflate* the tire by opening the valve.
      Deflate means (a) put air in (b) let air out (c) turn over (d) damage
   b. The *edifice* was of brick and covered a city block.
      Edifice means (a) bicycle (b) locomotive (c) building (d) ship
   c. The old trunk was *capacious* enough to hold all John's clothes.
      Capacious means (a) unclean (b) colorful (c) small (d) large

INSTRUCTIONAL MATERIALS FOR CORRECTING
DEFICIENCIES IN DICTIONARY USAGE

Teachers who wish to help pupils use the dictionary effectively must begin by determining which of the major dictionary skills are in need of improvement. (See page 98 for a list of dictionary skills.) After this has been done, a planned sequence of instruction should be initiated.

The following exercises indicate the types of lessons that might be used to assist pupils in becoming more proficient at locating a word in the dictionary.

1. Put these letters in alphabetical order:
   a. *p, m, b, z, o, c, f, d*
   b. *s, n, x, d, c, t, l, h*

2. Fill in the blanks with letters that come before and after the letters listed:
   a. _____ *l* _____
   b. _____ *c* _____
   c. _____ *k* _____
   d. _____ *s* _____
   e. _____ *b* _____
   f. _____ *t* _____
   g. _____ *m* _____
   h. _____ *f* _____

3. Fill in the blanks with the in-between letter.
   a. *n* _____ *p*
   b. *j* _____ *l*
   c. *g* _____ *i*
   d. *s* _____ *u*
   e. *w* _____ *y*
   f. *t* _____ *v*
   g. *p* _____ *r*
   h. *d* _____ *f*

4. Encircle the letter which comes first in the alphabet.
   a. *g-h*
   b. *m-l*
   c. *d-f*
   d. *r-g*
   e. *n-l*
   f. *y-u*
   g. *w-x*
   h. *h-k*

5. Arrange these words in alphabetical order.
   a. people
   b. elephants
   c. zebras
   d. bears
   e. cows
   f. ants

The foregoing exercise should be followed by others which include words to be placed in alphabetical order according to beginning two- and three-letter patterns.

6. The guide words *Joint-Judge* appear at the top of a given page in the dictionary. Encircle the words which could be found on the page.
   a. junk
   b. joist
   c. jigsaw
   d. jot
   e. join
   f. joy
   g. juice
   h. jubilee

After a pupil has located a word for which he has been looking, he must learn to pronounce it correctly. Teachers can help by explaining the various aids to pronunciation which are given by dictionaries. These include accent marks, syllabication, and respelling with diacritical marks or symbols. To profit from the latter, a pupil must learn how to use a pronunciation key.

Pupils need to be taught that the first definition of a word is not always the best one for their purpose. Often they must continue looking until they succeed in locating a definition that helps them understand the unknown word in the particular context involved. Teachers can acquaint pupils with the fact that words may have multiple meanings by having them look up a word such as *run*. An unabridged dictionary lists well over one hundred meanings for *run*. A beginning dictionary lists between thirty and forty.

Scott, Foresman and Company publishes and distributes, free of charge, an enlargement of a dictionary page which is excellent for purposes of group instruction. Other publishers, such as The Macmillan Company and Holt, Rinehart and Winston, issue free pamphlets from time to time which are valuable for dictionary study. Particularly noteworthy are the teachers' manuals accompanying Merriam-Webster's dictionaries for the elementary and secondary school levels.

UTILIZING PHONICS

Most teachers are in a quandary when it comes to phonics.* This is understandable. Research has shown that many experienced teachers lack knowledge in this area.(4) Many have had little or no preparation in the teaching of phonics. In addition, the controversies that have raged and continue to rage over how reading should be taught add to the confusion. If the experts can't agree, what should teachers do? What specific information do teachers need to identify a pupil's weakness or disability in the phonic area? (See Inventory on page 163.)

Opinions regarding phonics and phonic systems are diverse. Most authorities, however, would agree with the following generalizations:

1. *Auditory perception is basic to a phonic program.* Unless a pupil can hear similarities and differences between sounds, he cannot be expected to associate sounds with printed letters. For pupils who lack auditory discrimination, a sequential program in ear training is recommended. It would include auditory perception of initial consonants, blends, rhymes, medial vowels, and syllables.†

2. *Phonics instruction should proceed from simple to complex.* It is unwise for a teacher to spend time on difficult principles that are limited in applicability when simpler elements and generalizations could be employed. For example, a pupil should learn the sounds of initial consonants and digraphs before being introduced to diphthongs.

3. *Periods devoted to phonics should be brief and enjoyable.* There is nothing exciting about phonics. Exposing a child to too much work on sounds at any one time can be deadening. To minimize boredom many teachers employ a game approach to learning phonics.

4. *The phonics program for a given child should be individualized.* A teacher should determine what phonic knowledge a child does and does not possess and then tailor a program to meet these needs. She should not cry phonics and proceed to give a child the entire treatment.

5. *Pupils should be led to discover phonic principles rather than be taught rules.* When, for example, the silent-*e* rule is involved, a teacher should write on the blackboard several words exemplifying the principle. After each word is pronounced and attention is directed to the change from a short to a long vowel because of the final *e*, the children should be asked if they can make up a rule that

---

*For definitions of phonics and related terminology see Appendix A1.

†For particulars, see L. Scott and J. Thompson, *Phonics in Listening, in Speaking, in Reading, in Writing* (Manchester, Mo.: Webster Publishing, 1962), ch. 2.

applies. The child who discovers for himself the silent-*e* generalization is more likely to remember it. More important, he is likely to use it.

6. *To be most effective, phonics should not be used as an isolated word-attack skill.* Phonics proves far more valuable when used in collaboration with other word-attack skills such as contextual and structural analysis.

INSTRUCTIONAL MATERIALS FOR CORRECTING DEFICIENCIES IN INITIAL CONSONANT SOUNDS

When individual pupils or groups of pupils are deficient in initial consonant sounds, corrective practice can be individualized by using available *commercial material* such as—

1. *(The) Alphabet:* Thirty-three ten-by-ten-inch color transparencies for projection purposes. Each transparency carries a letter accompanied by three illustrative words and their pictures. (For use with a group of children; $99.50 a set; Visualcraft.)

2. *Alpha-Square:** A bingo-type game for teaching recognition of uppercase and lowercase letters and initial phonic sounds. The game is teacher-directed. The set includes 36 player cards, 300 markers, and 26 individual alphabet calling cards. (For use with a small group of children; $4.95; American Teaching Aids.)

3. *Amos and His Friends:* This set of materials includes a fifteen-minute tape which allows children to listen to and then sing sounds they hear with "Amos and His Friends." Twenty-six full-color, 8½-by-11-inch picture charts make listening more meaningful. Also included are twenty-four spirit duplicator masters of suitable activity sheets which correlate with the sounds learned. (For use with individual children or a group of children; potentially self-directive; $15.50, on cassettes; Imperial.)

4. *Beginning Consonant Poster Cards:* This instructional material consists of thirty cards, 11¼ by 14 inches in size. The cards are designed for use in practicing consonant sounds. Full-color pictures and picture-words with one or two missing letters appear on the cards. The missing parts are either consonants or consonant blends. Pupils identify the missing parts. The cards are punched for hanging. (For use with any number of children; $3.00; Milton Bradley.)

5. *Build It* (Decks 1 and 3):* Deck 1 involves a phonetic card game that teaches single consonants and short vowels. Deck 3 teaches

*All games are designated by an asterisk.

single consonants, long vowels, and the silent-*e* rule. (For use with any number of children; $3.00; Remedial Education Press.)

6. *Consonant Lotto:** Consonant Lotto consists of eight lotto cards, each of which contains six pictures of familiar objects. Forty-eight picture cover cards have different pictures to be matched by the beginning sound of the word with the pictures on the lotto cards. (For use with a group of children, potentially self-directive; $1.98; Garrard.)

7. *Consonant Pictures for Pegboard:* These materials consist of 179 pictures in color and 29 symbols printed on 3¾-by-4-inch cards for use on pegboard, chalk tray, or as flash cards. (For use with individual children, children working in pairs, or with a group of children under proper direction; $3.25; Ideal.)

8. *Consonant Wall Chart:* This chart is twenty-six by forty inches in size and contains twenty-six consonant sounds with corresponding key-word pictures arranged according to speech pattern. (For use with an entire class; $3.50; Phonovisual.)

9. *Dog House Game:** A phonetic game consisting of eighty-four assorted consonants and consonant blends along with thirty-five phonograms with which to build words. (For use with two or more children; $1.50; Kenworthy.)

10. *Ends 'n Blends:** A game that combines word beginnings with word endings to make word families. It is recommended for remedial programs through grade six. (For use with two to four children; $3.70; Dick Blick.)

11. *Five First Steps and Pop Words:* This instructional material involves 150 common sight or pop words printed in large, clear type on four-by-six-inch cards. Consonant and vowel sounds are printed on colored cards and include sixteen easy consonants, four consonant digraphs, the sounds of *y*, and the hard and soft *c* and *g* sounds. (For use with individual children, children working in pairs, or with a group of children under proper direction; $1.80; Kenworthy.)

12. *Giant Consonant Cards:* Thirty 11¼-by-14-inch cards with color illustrations of familiar objects. Each card shows a consonant or consonant blend with the name of an object illustrated plus additional words containing the consonant or consonant blend. (For use with individual children, children working in pairs, or a group of children, potentially self-directive; $3.00; Milton Bradley.)

13. *Go Fish* (Set I):** This is a rummy-like game designed to teach the sounds of initial consonants. (For use with two to four children, potentially self-directive; $3.00; Remedial Education Press.)

14. *Group Sounding Game:** This game is a complete phonics course beginning with the recognition of initial consonants, blends, and

vowels, and ending with syllabication of three-syllable words. (For use with two or more children, potentially self-directive; $2.50; Garrard.)

15. *Initial and Final Consonant Charts:* These instructional materials involve fifteen charts that are twenty-three by thirty-six inches in size. Each chart supplies a variety of consonant pictures headed by their consonant symbol and a key picture. A manual of directions is included. (For use with individual children or a group of children, potentially self-directive; $8.50; Ideal.)

16. *Magic Cards:* These instructional materials consist of forty exercises printed on six 8½-by-11-inch ply cards. They are designed to stimulate learning of initial and final consonants. A transparent pocket in which the cards are inserted and on which answers are written with crayon is included. The pocket can be wiped clean to make it ready for the next exercise. (For use with individual children or children working in pairs; $2.25; Ideal.)

17. *Magic Road of Sounds:* This instructional material consists of a forty-minute tape containing stories and songs which correlate with thirty-four charts, 8½ by 11 inches in size, depicting basic phonetic sounds. (For use with individual children or a group of children; potentially self-directive; $14.50; Imperial.)

18. *Match-the-Sounds Puzzles* (Instructor): These materials provide practice in visual and auditory discrimination of initial consonants. They consist of eight full-color puzzle cards, 8½ by 11 inches in size, and forty-eight color-coded inset cards. (For use with individual children, potentially self-directive; $6.95 a set; Beckley Cardy.)

19. *New Linguistic Block Series,* Set II:* These materials consist of twenty-one plastic blocks involving letters. Also included as part of the set is a timer and a forty-page Teacher's Instruction Booklet. A workbook also can be purchased. (For use with individual children or a small group of children; $7.35; Scott, Foresman.)

20. *Phonetic Drill Cards:* This instructional material involves twenty-three cards for 345 word combinations. The lettering is one inch high and the cards are 8 by 11¼ inches in size. Consonants and letter combinations for complete words are hinged for the formation of fifteen words on each card. (For use with individual children, children working in pairs, or with a group of children under proper direction; $2.00; Milton Bradley.)

21. *Phonetic Quizmo:* A lotto-type game consisting of thirty-eight Quizmo cards, teacher's word list, direction card, and markers. The game is designed to teach consonant sounds and consonant blends. (For use with two or more children, potentially self-directive; $2.00; Milton Bradley.)

22. *Phonetic Word Analyzer:* A drill device using interchangeable cardboard discs to build words phonetically. Consonants and consonant blends are matched with word endings by turning the discs. (For use with individual children, children working in pairs, or a small group of children; $2.00; Cenco.)

23. *Phonetic Word Drill Cards:* These instructional materials involve three sets of cards. Each set has ten chart cards showing a different word ending on each side. Thus, there are two families of words on each basic chart card, or twenty families per set. Initial·sound cards are suspended by plastic rings from the top of each basic chart card and are in line with the word endings. As each card is flipped, a new word appears and then the chart can be reversed and the operation repeated. With these three sets 864 words can be formed. Sixty common word endings are involved. (For use with individual children, children working in pairs, or with a group of children under proper direction; three sets, $2.75 each; Kenworthy.)

24. *Phonics We Use—Learning Games Kit:** Consonant and consonant digraph games found among the ten games in this kit include *Old Itch, Spin-a-Sound*; *Bingobang*; *Spin Hard, Spin Soft*; *Digraph Whirl*; and *Digraph Hopscotch*. These colorful card and/or board games are adaptable for two or more players. (Complete kit of 10 games, $39.00; Lyons and Carnahan.)

25. *Phono-Word Wheels* (Set A): The fifteen wheels in this set have a simple vocabulary of 120 words selected from commonly used basal series of readers at the primary level. Fifteen initial consonants are used and the lettering involved is large. (For use with individual children, children working in pairs, or with a group of children under proper direction; $3.60; Steck.)

26. *Picture-Phonic Cards:* This set of cards illustrates the sound of every letter of the alphabet and twelve digraphs. (For use with individual children or a small group of children; $2.75 a set; Kenworthy.)

27. *Programmed Reading Kit, I:** Consonant games found among the sixteen games in this kit include *Touch Cards, First-Letter Cards, Dozens, Half Moons, Picture Bingo, Find-the-Letter-Cards 1, First-Letter Bingo, Countries and Cities,* and *Mail Boxes.* In most instances, these games are adaptable for one or more players. (Complete kit of 16 games, $21.00; Scott, Foresman, Elementary-High School Division.)

28. *See and Say Consonant Game:** This game is designed to develop recognition of sounds made by single consonants and consonant combinations. Children learn consonants by looking at the pictures,

saying the name of each object, and listening for the sounds which consonants make. (For use with two or more children, potentially self-directive; $1.00; Milton Bradley.)

29. *Single Consonant Sounds* (Instructor): A set consisting of twenty-four easy-to-see charts and ninety-six flash cards. It gives consonant sounds at the beginning, middle, and end positions of words and includes consonants that have two distinct sounds: *c*, *g*, and *s*. ($4.00; Lakeshore.)

30. *Sound Hunt* (Set I):* A phonics game designed to teach initial consonants and consonant digraphs. The sixty cards in each deck are colored. (For use with two to eight children; potentially self-directive; $1.75; Creative Teaching Press.)

31. *Speech-O:* This is a phonetic game consisting of twenty-five large picture cards, one for each single consonant. Nine pictures on each consonant card are also duplicated singly on small three-by-four-inch cards. The top row of pictures on each large card contains the sound in an initial position, the second row in a medial position, and the bottom row in a final position. (For use with individual children or a small group of children; $3.25; Expression Company.)

32. *Speech-to-Print Phonics:* Although this kit of material was initially designed as a readiness program, it may also be used as supplementary material with any basal series. The kit contains a teacher's manual and specific lessons in relating phonemes to printed forms. It includes consonants and vowels and twenty-one consonant blends. Special response cards are used by pupils so the teacher can detect any children who are experiencing difficulty. (For use with a group of children or an entire class; $21.00; Harcourt Brace Jovanovich, Inc.)

33. *Split Words:* A game consisting of wooden blocks involving consonants, consonant blends, and word endings. The latter are printed in red. A dictionary listing and defining some 500 words that can be built by combining the blocks in various ways is included. (For use with individual children, children working in pairs, or a small group of children, potentially self-directive; $2.50; Teachers' Supplies.)

34. *Tumble Words:* A vocabulary building game consisting of lettered cubes and a shaker. (For use with individual children or a group of children, potentially self-directive; $1.00; Kohner Brothers.)

35. *Visual Phonics Set:* A complete set of thirty-seven full-color transparencies for teaching phonics. There are twenty-one consonant letters, four consonant digraphs, and twelve vowels—one on each

transparency. Each is illustrated with familiar objects whose names utilize corresponding phonetic sounds plus a series of other common words which are part of a child's vocabulary. (For use with any number of children; $109.00; Cenco.)

36. *Webster Word Analysis Charts:* These instructional materials consist of five charts (23 by 35 inches in size) which constitute a permanent, visual guide to consonant sounds, vowel sounds, speech blends, vowel digraphs, prefixes, and the principles of syllabication. (For use with individual children or a group of children, potentially self-directive; $10.00; Webster.)

37. *Webster Word Wheels:* These practice wheels consist of twenty-five beginning blend wheels, twenty prefix wheels, and eighteen suffix wheels. (For use with individual children or children working in pairs; $16.75; Webster.)

38. *What the Letters Say:** This beginning phonics game is designed to teach letter names and letter sounds. (For use with individual children or a group of children, potentially self-directive; $2.50; Garrard.)

39. *Word-Roll:** This game consists of ten colorful cubes, color-keyed to twenty picture cards. Every roll spells a word. After playing with all five sets, the pupil will have learned fifteen beginning consonants, fifteen word families, and forty-five new words. (For use with one to four children; $4.95; McCormick-Mathers.)

When individual pupils or groups of pupils are deficient in initial consonant sounds, individualized practice can be provided by using *teacher- or pupil-made materials* such as the following:

1. *Arrange-O:* Place in an envelope a large picture of an object starting with an initial consonant sound you are teaching. In another envelope, place small pictures of objects, some of which begin with the sound involved. The child arranges the appropriate pictures in a column under the master picture. By using an identification scheme on the back of the pictures, this activity can be made self-corrective. (For use with individual children, potentially self-directive.)

2. *Baseball:** A baseball diamond is drawn on the blackboard or on cardboard. Two groups of children are chosen. The pitcher flashes a letter. If the batter calls a word beginning with the letter, he has made a hit and moves to first base. Should the next batter score

*All games are designated by an asterisk.

a hit also, he moves to first base and the first batter advances to second. Soon the runs begin to come in. Teams change sides just as soon as three outs (wrong answers) have been given. The team with the most runs wins. (For use with groups of children.)

3. *Clothespin Wheel:* Cut out a circular piece of tagboard about twelve inches in diameter. Paste or draw pictures of common objects around the periphery of the oaktag. Equip the child with a box of clothespins on each of which is printed an initial consonant. The child then matches the clothespins with the proper pictures. For example, the *c* clothespin would be placed over the picture of a cat; the *p* clothespin over the picture of a pear. (For use with individual children, potentially self-directive.)

4. *Consonant Fishing:** Consonant cards are cut in the shape of a fish. A paper clip is slipped over each card. Fishermen are equipped with a pole (short stick), a fish line (20 inches of store string), and a fishhook (small magnet). Each child gets a turn trying to catch fish. If he can call a word that begins with the consonant sound on the fish he has caught, he may keep the fish. If he is unable to think of a suitable word, he returns the fish, face down, to the fishpond. (For use with two children or a group of children, potentially self-directive.)

5. *Consonant Lotto:** The teacher with the help of her children prepares cardboard master cards eight by eleven inches in size. These master cards are blocked off vertically and horizontally into twenty-five small squares. The middle space is marked *free.* Individual letters and digraphs are placed on the twenty-four spaces that remain. Each cardboard master card must have the same letters but in different positions. Twenty-four words known by the children on sight that begin with the individual letters or consonant digraphs involved are placed in an envelope. As individual words drawn from the envelope are called, the players find the beginning letter or digraph on their master cards and cover it with a marker. The marker may be a kernel of corn, a bean, or a small piece of cardboard. The first child to cover a row of letters in a straight line, vertically, horizontally, or diagonally, calls out "Lotto." If he has not erred, he is declared the winner. (For use with two children or a group of children, potentially self-directive.)

6. *Matching Letters and Objects:* The teacher pastes a number of small pictures on a sheet of oaktag. (A flannel board, if available, might be used.) The pictures should be of things the children can recognize easily. An envelope containing a number of consonants is clipped to the sheet of oaktag. The child removes the

consonant cards and places them on or below the appropriate pictures. By use of an identification scheme on the backs of the cards, this activity can be made self-corrective. (For use with individual children, potentially self-directive.)

7. *Pockets:* Cut apart some cheap envelopes and mount them on a chart as pockets for three-by-five-inch cards. A consonant is printed on each envelope. The three-by-five-inch cards have pictures or drawings on them which are to be placed in the pockets beginning with the appropriate consonant sound. By using an identification scheme on the backs of the cards, this activity can be made self-corrective. (For use with individual children, potentially self-directive.)

8. *Spin and Call:** Divide a large oaktag circle into eight sections. Place a consonant in each section. Attach a large pointer to the center of the circle so it spins freely. The player spins the pointer and calls a word beginning with the particular consonant to which it points when coming to a stop. If a correct word is called, he scores a point. A record should be kept of the words called so no repetitions take place. (For use with two children or a group of children.)

9. *Taxi:** With the help of children build a little village of letters beside each of which is a small paper house. There can be several streets in Alphabet Village. Tall Street can consist of those letters which extend above the line (*b, d, f, h, k, l* and *t*); Naughty Street can consist of those letters which extend below the line (*j, p,* and *g*); Coward Street of those letters that go together to make a sound (*ch, sh, th,* and *wh*); Vowel Street of the vowels; Main Street of any letters left over.

   One child acts as taxi driver. The other children ask the driver to take them to any word they want. The driver has to "drive" them to the house whose letter starts the word. (For use with a group of children.)

10. *Toss Game:** With the use of alphabet blocks or building blocks on which initial consonants have been painted, children can take turns rolling blocks and giving words beginning with the letters that come up. (For use with two or more children, potentially self-directive.)

11. *Word Authors:** Words are printed on corners of cards—four cards to a set. A set consists of four words beginning with the same consonant. Each child is dealt four cards. One child begins the game by calling for a card beginning with a certain initial consonant sound. If he gets the word, he may continue to call for words.

When his opponent indicates that he does not have the card called, the child draws from the deck of cards that is face down on the table. The child who acquires the most sets wins. (For use with two to four children, potentially self-directive.)

12. *What Am I?:** On individual cards write riddles which give initial sounds as clues. For example, "I am a tree-climbing animal. I have a long tail and like to swing from branches with it. I begin with the *m* sound. What am I?" Each child in the group has a chance at a riddle card. If he guesses the answer he is given the card. The child with the largest number of cards is the winner. By placing the answers on the backs of the cards this activity can be made self-corrective. (For use with a group of children, potentially self-directive.)

INSTRUCTIONAL MATERIALS FOR CORRECTING DEFICIENCIES IN CONSONANT BLENDS

When individual pupils or groups of pupils are deficient in their knowledge of consonant blends, corrective practice can be individualized by using available *commercial material* such as the following:

1. *Blend-o-grams:** A word game designed to teach common blends and word endings by proper matching. (For use with two to four children; $1.25; Teachers' Supplies.)

2. *Amos and His Friends:* These instructional materials consist of twenty-three colorful picture charts, a sound tape, and a set of twenty-three liquid duplicator masters. Children see "Amos" and his friends in situations involving blends, learn a song and poem about each blend, and follow up with an "Amos" coloring sheet for each blend. (For use with individual children or a small group of children; $15.50, on cassettes; Imperial.)

3. *Blends and Digraphs:* Twenty ten-by-ten-inch color transparencies for projection purposes. Each transparency carries several consonant blends accompanied by illustrative words and their pictures. (For use with a group of children; $79.50 a set; Visual Craft.)

4. *Blends and Digraphs Pictures for Pegboard:* This set consists of twenty-six blends consonant cards in full color printed on $3\frac{3}{4}$-by-4-inch white index for use on pegboard, chalk tray, or as flash cards. (For use with individual children or a small group of children; $2.15 a set; Ideal.)

---

*All games are designated by an asterisk.

5. *Build It* (Decks 2 & 4):* Deck 1 involves a phonetic card game that teaches consonant blends and short vowels. Deck 2 teaches consonant blends and long vowels and the silent-*e* rule. (For use with any number of children; $3.00; Remedial Education Press.)

6. *Consonant Blends and Digraphs:* These materials by Hammond consist of twenty-eight multicolored transparencies for use with an overhead projector. (For use with any number of children; $42.00; McGraw-Hill.)

7. *Consonant Pictures for Pegboard:* This set consists of thirty consonant cards in full color printed on $3\frac{3}{4}$-by-4-inch white index for use on pegboard, chalk tray, or as flash cards. (For use with individual children or a small group of children; $3.40 a set; Ideal.)

8. *Dog House:** A phonetic game consisting of thirty-five phonograms along with eighty-four assorted consonants and consonant blends with which to build words. (For use with a group of children; $1.50; Kenworthy.)

9. *Funagrams:** A domino-type game using cardboard strips with consonants and blends on one end and vowel phonograms on the other. The game includes a 6,000-word Phonogram Dictionary. (For use with individual children or a small group of children; $2.50; Listen and Learn.)

10. *Giant Consonant Cards:* Thirty $11\frac{1}{4}$-by-11-inch cards with color illustrations of familiar objects. Each card shows a consonant or consonant blend with the name of an object illustrated, plus additional words that contain the consonant or consonant blend. (For use with individual children, children working in pairs, or a group of children; $3.00; Milton Bradley.)

11. *Go Fish** (Set II): This is a rummy-like game designed to teach the sounds of consonant blends. (For use with two to four children, potentially self-directive; $3.00; Remedial Education Press.)

12. *Group Sounding Game:** This game is a complete phonics course beginning with the recognition of initial consonants, blends, and vowels, and ending with syllabication of three-syllable words. (For use with two or more children, potentially self-directive; $2.98; Garrard.)

13. *Hammond's Phonics Charts:* A set of twenty-eight charts fifteen inches by ten inches in size. These charts cover consonant and vowel sounds, consonant blends and digraphs, vowel blends and principles. In addition to a key word set forth in bold type and visible from a distance, each chart carries an illustration of a key word accompanied by five other words employing the sound. (For

use with individual children or a group of children; $23.80 for all four sets; McGraw-Hill.)

14. *Initial Consonant Blends* (Instructor): A set consisting of twenty-four easy-to-see charts and ninety-six flash cards. It contains twenty-four initial blends and trigraphs that are the easiest to work with in beginning phonics and are heard most readily by children. (For use with individual children or a group of children; $4.00; Lakeshore.)

15. *Magic Cards—Blends and Digraphs:* These instructional materials consist of eight exercises on six $8\frac{1}{2}$-by-11-inch ply cards. They are designed to stimulate the learning of consonant blends and digraphs. The set includes a durable transparent pocket into which the cards are inserted and on which the answers can be marked with wax crayons. The pocket can be wiped clean easily to make it ready for the next exercise. (For use with individual children or a small group of children; $1.10; Ideal.)

16. *Phonetic Quizmo:** A lotto-type game consisting of thirty-eight phonetic Quizmo cards, teacher's word list, direction card, and markers. The game is designed to teach consonant sounds and consonant blends. (For use with two or more children, potentially self-directive; $2.00; Milton Bradley.)

17. *Phonetic Word Drill Cards:* These instructional materials involve three sets of cards. Each set has twin chart cards, showing a different word ending on each side. Thus, there are two families of words on each basic chart card, or twenty families per set. Initial sound cards are suspended by plastic rings from the top of each basic chart card and are in line with the word endings. As each card is flipped, a new word appears and then the chart can be reversed and the operation repeated. With these three sets, 864 words can be formed. Sixty common word endings are involved. (For use with individual children, children working in pairs, or with a group of children under proper direction; three sets, $2.50 each; Kenworthy.)

18. *Phonic Slide Rule:* A plastic-coated device that gives pupils practice with thirty consonant blends, digraphs, short and long vowel sounds. (For use with individual children, children working in pairs, or a small group of children; $1.00; Phonics.)

19. *Phonics We Use—Learning Games Kit:** A consonant blends and symbols game found among the ten games in this kit is titled *Blends Race*. This colorful board and spinner game is adaptable for two or more players. (Complete kit of 10 games, $39.00; Lyons and Carnahan.)

20. *Phono-Word Wheels* (Set B and Set I). The fifteen wheels in set B involve a vocabulary of 110 words and employ six initial consonant blends, four digraphs, and five word endings. Set I involves seventeen wheels, each of which contains a common initial blend. A total of 134 words are included. (For use with individual children, children working in pairs or with a group of children under proper direction; $3.60; Steck.)

21. *Sound and Articulation Game:** This game consists of ninety-six picture cards, each containing a specific consonant blend. Twenty-four blends are represented and four cards of one blend constitute a "book." The game is suitable for children through junior high school level. (For use with two to four children; $2.25; Expression Company.)

22. *Sound Hunt* (Set II):* An exciting phonics game designed to teach consonant blends and trigraphs. The sixty cards in the deck are colored. (For use with two to eight children; potentially self-directive; $1.75; Creative Teaching Press.)

23. *Speech-To-Print Phonics*: Although this kit of material was initially designed as a readiness program, it may also be used as supplementary material with any basal series. The kit contains a teacher's manual and specific lessons in relating phonemes to printed forms. It includes consonants and vowels and twenty-one consonant blends. Special response cards are used by pupils so the teacher can detect any children who are experiencing difficulty. (For use with a group of children or an entire class; $21.00; Harcourt Brace Jovanovich, Inc.)

24. *Split Words:** A game consisting of wooden blocks involving consonants, consonant blends, and word endings. The latter are printed in red. A dictionary listing and defining some 500 words that can be built by combining the blocks in various ways is included. (For use with individual children, children working in pairs, or a small group of children, potentially self-directive; $2.50; Teachers' Supplies.)

25. *Webster Word Wheels*: These practice wheels consist of twenty-five beginning blend wheels, twenty prefix wheels, eighteen suffix wheels, and eight two-letter consonant wheels. The wheels are color-coded and numbered in order of difficulty. The set comes in a colorful cardboard file box. (For use with individual children or children working in pairs; $16.75; Webster.)

26. *Word Blends:* A set of subdivided folding cards that highlight consonant blends and digraphs. A total of 144 words are formed. (For use with individual children, children working in pairs, or a small group of children; $.75; Kenworthy.)

When individual pupils or groups of pupils are deficient in their knowledge of consonant blends, individualized practice can be provided by using *teacher- or pupil-made materials* such as the following:

1. *Authors with Beginnings:** Words are printed on corners of cards— four words to a set. A set consists of four words that begin with the same consonant blend. This can be highlighted by under-lining the first two letters or writing them in red. Each child is dealt four cards and one child begins the game by calling for a word beginning with a given blend. If he gets the word he may continue to call for words. When his opponent indicates that he does not have the blend called for, the child draws from the deck of cards that is face down on the table. The child who ac-quires the most sets wins. (For use with two to four children, po-tentially self-directive.)

2. *Baseball:** A baseball diamond is drawn on the blackboard or on cardboard. Two groups of children are chosen. The pitcher flashes a consonant blend. If the batter calls a word beginning with the blend, he has made a hit and moves to first base. Should the next batter score a hit also, he moves to first base and the previous batter advances to second. Soon the runs begin to come in. Teams change sides just as soon as three outs (wrong answers) have been given. The team with the most "runs" wins. (For use with groups of children.)

3. *Blend Fishing:** Consonant blend cards are cut in the shape of fish. A paper clip is slipped over each card. Fishermen are equipped with a pole (short stick), a fish line (20 inches of store string), and a fishhook (small magnet). Each child gets a turn trying to catch a fish. If he can call a word that begins with the consonant blend sound on the fish he has caught, he may keep the fish. If he is unable to think of a suitable word, he returns the fish, face down, to the fishpond. (For use with two children or a group of children, potentially self-directive.)

4. *Clothespin Wheel:* Cut out a circular piece of tagboard about twelve inches in diameter. Paste or draw pictures of common objects around the periphery of the oaktag. Equip the child with a box of clothes-pins on each of which is printed a consonant blend. He then matches the clothespins with the proper pictures. For example, the *fr* clothespin would be placed over the picture of a frog; the *pl* clothespin over the picture of a plum. (For use with individual children, potentially self-directive.)

---

*All games are designated by an asterisk.

5. *Deezio:** A set of twenty-five cards is constructed. Recommended card size is 2½ by 3 inches. An initial blend is written in two diagonal corners. A word beginning with this initial blend is written in the center of the card. It is necessary to have at least two cards with the same initial blend, but the word in the center should differ. The twenty-fifth card will have no duplicate. This card has a drawing of a funny face and is "Deezio."

   All cards are dealt to the players and each player immediately looks for pairs of cards with the same blends. He places these pairs in front of him, saying the word on each card as he puts it down. If he cannot read the words, another player may tell him, but he must hold the pair until his next turn. Then the player to the left of the person with the most cards begins playing by drawing a card. He draws a card from the player holding the most cards. The drawer attempts to match the card with one in his hand. If he has a pair, he places it in front of him and reads the words. If no match is made, he retains the card in his hand. The playing continues clockwise around the table. The player who matches all his cards first wins. The rest continue to play until one person is left with "Deezio;" he is the "Deezio." (For use with three to five children, potentially self-directive.) This game and the games *Happy Ending* and *Word Flight* were devised by Hildegard Ziegler et al., teachers at the Madison, Wisconsin, public schools.

6. *Finding Partners:** Two types of cards are placed in an envelope—some involve word endings and others consonant blends. The cards are distributed to a group of children. Those children receiving cards with blends move around among the other children to see if they can form a word by combining their cards. When a word has been formed, the child says, "We made —— with our cards." Since there is the possibility that other blends may fit the ending, the teacher asks if anyone else can help make a word. The process continues until all pairing is exhausted. (For use with a group of children.)

7. *Lotto Blends:** With the help of her children, the teacher prepares cardboard master cards eight by eleven inches in size. These master cards are blocked off vertically and horizontally into twenty-five small squares. The middle space is marked *free.* Individual consonant blends are placed on the twenty-four spaces that remain. Each master card must have the same blends on it but in different positions. Twenty-four words known by the children on sight that begin with the consonant blends are placed in an envelope. As individual words are drawn from the envelope and called, the players find the consonant blends on their master cards and cover

them with a marker. The marker may be a kernel of corn, a bean, or a small piece of cardboard. The first child to cover a row of letters in a straight line, vertically, horizontally, or diagonally, calls out "Lotto." If he has not erred, he is declared the winner. (For use with a group of children, potentially self-directive.)

8. *Pockets:* Cut apart some cheap envelopes and mount them on a chart as pockets for three-by-five-inch cards. A consonant blend is printed on each envelope. The cards have pictures or drawings on them which are to be placed in the pockets beginning with the appropriate consonant blend. By using an identification scheme on the backs of the cards, this activity can be made self-corrective. (For use with individual children, potentially self-directive.)

9. *Sound Box:** Choose a cardboard box with subdivisions—one that has been used to package bottles is ideal. By using common pins, label each subdivision with a small card on which a blend has been written. Players draw picture cards from a pile and attempt to place them in the spaces labeled with letters that represent the beginning blend sounds of the words pictured. Points can be given for correct choices. This activity can be made self-corrective by printing the correct letters on the backs of the picture cards. (For use with one or more children, potentially self-directive.)

10. *Spin and Call:** Divide a large oaktag circle into eight sections. Attach a large pointer to the center of the circle so it spins freely. The player spins the pointer and calls a word beginning with the particular consonant blend to which it points when coming to a stop. If a correct word is called, he scores one point. A record should be kept of words called so no repetitions take place. (For use with two children or a group of children.)

11. *What Am I?:** On individual cards write riddles which give initial consonant blends as clues. For example, "I grow in bunches on trees. I am good to eat. I begin with a *gr* sound. What am I?" Each child in the group has a chance at a riddle card. If he guesses the answer he is given the card. The child with the largest number of cards is the winner. By placing the answers on the backs of the cards, this activity can be made self-corrective. (For use with a group of children, potentially self-directive.)

12. *Authors with Blends:** Words are printed on corners of cards—four cards to a set. A set consists of four words beginning with the same consonant blend. Each child is dealt four cards, and one begins the game by calling for a card beginning with a certain consonant blend. If he gets the word, he may continue to call for words. When his opponent indicates that he does not have the card called for, the child draws from the deck of cards that is

face down on the table. The child who acquires the most sets wins. (For use with two to four children, potentially self-directive.)

INSTRUCTIONAL MATERIALS FOR CORRECTING DEFICIENCIES IN VOWEL SOUNDS, LETTER COMBINATIONS, AND PRINCIPLES

When individual pupils or groups of pupils are deficient in their knowledge of vowel sounds, letter combinations, or principles, corrective practice can be individualized by using *commercial material* such as the following:

1. *ABACA:** A word-building card game consisting of 108 cards, two decks. Six different games are involved. They include vowel-consonant combinations and vowel and consonant blends. (For use with two to five students; $4.95; McCormick Mathers.)

2. *Bulletin Board of Basic Phonics:* A set of thirty-five six-by-nine-inch cards with large type and colored pictures introducing difficult consonants, vowel digraphs, and vowel sounds. In addition to a key word, six additional words employing the sound appear on each card. At the bottom of the card a key-word sentence is provided. (For use with individual children or a group of children; $2.75 per set; Educational Aids.)

3. *End-in-E Game:** This game is designed to show how words change as *e* is added. There are fifteen word cards, each with a flap that turns in to add the letter *e*, changing the word. For example, *at* with an *e* added is *ate*. There is a story to be used with the cards that adds fun to the learning. The letters on the cards involved are quite large. (For use with individual children, children working in pairs or with a group of children under proper direction; $1.00; Ideal.)

4. *Giant Vowel Poster Cards:* This instructional material consists of thirty cards, 11¼ by 14 inches in size. The cards are designed for practicing vowel sounds. Full-color pictures of familiar objects are accompanied by the names of the objects. Additional words are printed in large type. Vowels and vowel combinations are printed in red. The matching letter or letters also appear in red in each word. The cards are punched for hanging. (For use with any number of children; $3.00; Milton Bradley.)

5. *Group-size Vowel Cards:* These instructional materials consist of two cards each for all short and long vowels, digraphs, diphthongs, and

*All games are designated by an asterisk.

other vowel combinations with consonants. Four phonetic rules are covered. (For use with individual children, children working in pairs, or with a group of children under proper direction; $2.50; Garrard.)

6. *Group Sounding Game:** This game is a complete phonics course beginning with the recognition of initial consonants, blends, and vowels, and ending with syllabication of three-syllable words. (For use with two or more children, potentially self-directive; $2.98; Garrard.)

7. *Hammond's Phonics Charts:* A set of twenty-eight charts fifteen by ten inches in size. These charts cover consonant and vowel sounds, consonant blends and digraphs, vowel blends, and principles. In addition to a key word set forth in bold type and visible from a distance, each chart carries an illustration of a key word accompanied by five other words employing the sound. (For use with individual children or a group of children; $23.80 for all four sets; McGraw-Hill.)

8. *Junior Phonic Rummy:** This game employs 110 most frequently occurring short vowel words from the most widely used first-grade basic reading books. A key picture is provided for each of the short vowel sounds. (For use with two or more children, potentially self-directive; $1.50; Kenworthy.)

9. *Magic Cards—Vowels:* These instructional materials consist of twenty-four exercises on six $8\frac{1}{2}$-by-11-inch ply cards. Exercises can be reworked again and again because of a transparent plastic pocket into which cards are inserted and on which answers are marked with any wax crayon. The pocket is then wiped clean to make it ready for the next exercise. (For use with individual children or a group of children; $1.60; Ideal.)

10. *Magic Vowel:* A set of cards which carry silent-*e* words on one side and the same words without the silent *e* on the other side. (For use with individual children, children working in pairs, or a group of children; $1.50 a set; Educational Aids.)

11. *Match the Vowel:** A two-deck matching game designed to teach vowels and vowel combinations: digraphs and diphthongs. (For use with individual children, children working in pairs, or a group of children; $1.50; Educational Aids.)

12. *Phonetic Word Wheel:* The Phonetic Word Wheel is a device that gives a child varied practice in recognition of vowels, consonants, and phonetic blends. Countless variations of this game are possible depending on the needs of the pupils. (For use with individual children or children working in pairs; $1.00; Milton Bradley.)

13. *Phonic Rummy** (four sets): These games are designed to teach short vowels and vowel principles. Each set contains two packs of sixty cards presenting words suitable for the grades on each set. (For use with two to four children, potentially self-directive; $1.50 per set; Kenworthy.)

14. *Phonics We Use—Learning Game Kit:** Vowel games found among the ten games in this kit include *Vowel Dominoes* and *Full House.* These colorful games are adaptable for two or more players. (Complete kit of 10 games, $39.00; Lyons and Carnahan.)

15. *Programmed Reading Kit, I:** Vowel games found among the sixteen games in this kit include *Green Dozens, Half-Moons, Port-Holes,* and *Pattern Bingo.* In most instances, these games are adaptable for one or more players. (Complete kit of 16 games, $21.00; Scott, Foresman, Elementary High School Division.)

16. *Quiet Pal Game:** A game that builds words with silent letters in them. The word card has a flap that turns over to cover the end letter. The word is changed instantly to make a new word—one with a silent letter, as *ran* to *rain* with its silent *i.* The set includes fifteen story cards. (For use with individual children, children working in pairs, or with a group of children under proper direction; $.80; Ideal.)

17. *Sight and Sound of Phonics:* Set four consists of twenty colorful transparencies devoted to vowels and vowel diphthongs. Other transparencies (40 in all) are devoted to consonants, consonant blends, and digraphs. (For use with any number of children; $84.50, including carrying and storage case; Educational Electronics, Inc.)

18. *Short Shorts:** This game teaches first steps in phonetic analysis using one-syllable words with short vowel sounds. (For use with two to five children; $3.00; Remedial Education Press.)

19. *Short Vowel Drill:* This drill involves categorizing pictures of objects containing a short vowel sound. Each vowel is represented by a number of picture words. (For use with individual children or children working in pairs; $2.00; Remedial Educational Center.)

20. *Short Vowel Game:** This is a rummy-like game designed to teach the sounds of the short vowels. (For use with an individual child or children working in pairs; $.50; Beckley-Cardy Co.)

21. *Vowel Charts:* This set of vowel charts is in brilliant color showing vowel pictures, symbols, and rules. Each set contains ten twenty-three-by-thirty-six-inch charts (nine vowel charts and one key chart) with metal eyelets to prevent tearing and a complete manual of directions. (For use with individual children or a group of children, potentially self-directive; $6.00; Ideal.)

22. *Vowel Dominoes:*° This game teaches the short vowel sounds through a version of dominoes. (For use with two to four children, potentially self-directive; $3.00; Remedial Education Center.)

23. *Vowel Flipstrips:* Two complete sets of key-word pictures printed in two colors with their corresponding letter symbols in the form of 3⅜-inch-by-6¼-inch strips are involved. One set of strips may be folded so pictures and their related sounds are back to back; the second set may be cut in two, backed with flannel, and used on a flannel board. (For use with individual children, children working in pairs, or a small group of children; $1.95; Cenco.)

24. *Vowel-Links Poster Cards:* This instructional material consists of thirty cards, 11½ by 14 inches in size. The cards are designed for practicing vowel sounds. On each card is a full-color illustration and a picture-word with one or two missing letters. The missing part is either a single or double vowel. The pupil must identify the missing part to pronounce the word correctly. (For use with individual children or a group of children; $3.00; Milton Bradley.)

25. *Vowel Lotto:*° Vowel Lotto is a game that gives practice in hearing and learning short vowels, long vowels, vowel digraphs, and diphthongs. Children match cover card pictures with those on the lotto cards having the same vowel sound. (For use with two or more children, potentially self-directive; $1.98; Garrard.)

26. *Vowel Pictures for Pegboard:* These instructional materials include 102 picture cards, 228 word cards, and 21 vowel symbols cards 4 by 3¾ inches in size. These cards can be used on pegboard, chalk tray, or as flash cards. For use with individual children or a group of children; $4.50; Ideal.)

27. *Vowel Wall Chart:* This chart is twenty-six by forty inches in size and contains seventeen fundamental vowel sounds with corresponding key-word pictures. (For use with an entire class; $3.50; Phonovisual.)

28. *Vowels and Vowel Digraphs* (Instructor): A set consisting of twenty-four easy-to-see charts and ninety-six flash cards. It contains long and short sounds of the five vowels with three sounds of *y*, two sounds of *oo*, and the nine most frequent remaining digraphs: *ai, au, ay, ea* (long), *ea* (short), *e, ee, ie, oa,* and *ou.* (For use with individual children or a small group of children; $4.00; Lakeshore.)

29. *Vowels and Vowel Variations:* These materials by Hammond consist of two sets of thirty-eight multicolored transparencies for use with an overhead projector. (For use with any number of children; $42.00; McGraw-Hill.)

When individual pupils or groups of pupils are deficient in their knowledge of vowel sounds, letter combinations, and principles, individualized practice can be provided by using *teacher- or pupil-made materials* such as the following:

1. *Ask Me:** Prepare about forty to fifty word cards on each of which is a word containing a vowel sound. Some cards should have duplicate vowel sounds, although the words themselves should differ. Four cards are dealt to each player, and the remainder are put in a pile on the table. The player to the left of the dealer reads one of his words. Other players holding cards with a similar vowel sound give their cards to the caller. The latter places any sets he acquires on the table. If the caller does not call his word correctly, he discards it but must draw another word from the pile. After drawing he waits until his next turn before calling for another card. The winner is the player with the fewest cards. (For use with two to four children, potentially self-directive.)

2. *Baseball:** A baseball diamond is drawn on the blackboard or on cardboard. Two groups of children are chosen. The pitcher flashes a word. If the batter can designate the short vowel sound in the word, he has made a hit and moves to first base. Should the next batter score a hit also, he moves to first base and the first batter advances to second. Soon the runs begin to come in. Teams change sides just as soon as three outs (wrong answers) have been given. The team with the most "runs" wins. (For use with groups of children.)

3. *Matching Vowels and Objects:* The teacher pastes a number of small pictures on a sheet of oaktag. The pictures should be of things the children can recognize easily. An envelope containing a number of vowels (several of each kind) is clipped to the sheet of oaktag. The child removes the vowel cards and places them on or below the pictures whose names contain the vowel sounds. (For use with individual children.)

4. *Pockets:* Cut apart some cheap envelopes and mount them on a chart as pockets for three-by-five-inch cards. A vowel is printed on each envelope. The cards have pictures or drawings on them which are to be placed in the pockets having the appropriate vowel sounds. By using an identification scheme on the backs of the cards, this activity can be made self-corrective. (For use with individual children, potentially self-directive.)

*All games are designated by an asterisk.

5. *Shoe-box Match:* Paste pictures or drawings of objects beginning with a short vowel sound on the front of shoe boxes. Players engaging in this activity attempt to sort small picture cards containing short vowel sounds. These are placed in the appropriate shoe boxes. The activity can be made self-corrective by numbering, correspondingly, the boxes and the backs of the small picture cards. (For use with individual children, potentially self-directive.)

6. *Spin and Call:** Divide a large oaktag circle into eight sections. Place a vowel in each section. Attach a larger pointer to the center of the circle so it spins freely. The player spins the pointer and calls a word containing the short vowel to which it points when coming to a stop. If a correct word is called, he scores one point. A record should be kept of words called so no repetitions take place. (For use with two children or a group of children.)

7. *Win-a-Row:** Cut cards 7½ inches square. Rule five or more cards into 1½-inch squares so there are twenty-five squares on the cards. Write or print selected words in the squares. Write the same word in a different position on all the cards so no two cards are identical; however, each row must have one word with each of the short vowel sounds. Twenty-five different words with the short vowel sounds will be written on a number of small cards. These will be numbered 1, 2, 3, 4, and 5. Numbers will represent rows on the playing card. Small paper circles can be made to be used as counters or markers to cover the words. The game is played very much like Bingo. The caller reads a row number and a word from the small cards. The players cover a word in the designated row which has the same vowel sound as the word read. The child who first covers five words vertically, diagonally, or horizontally reads his winning row. If he has not erred, he is declared the winner and may be the caller for the next game. (For use with more than two children, potentially self-directive.)

SUPPLEMENTARY INSTRUCTIONAL ACTIVITIES FOR CORRECTING DEFICIENCIES IN VOWEL SOUNDS, LETTER COMBINATIONS, AND PRINCIPLES

When individual pupils or groups of pupils are deficient in their knowledge of vowel sounds, letter combinations or principles, provide individualized practice by employing activities such as the following:†

† All these activities can be made self-directive by furnishing simple directions and accompanying answer keys.

1. The child is given a list of words. He underlines all the words that have the same vowel sound as that appearing in the first word.
2. The child is given a list of words containing long and short vowel sounds. He classifies the words into long and short vowels.
3. The child is given a list of words containing vowel blends or diphthongs. He classifies the words according to their vowel blends.
4. The child is given a list of words that have vowel combinations missing. He chooses that vowel combination from several given which will complete each word.
5. A series of pictures of objects are given to the child. He names each picture and tells whether the vowel in the name is long or short.
6. A list of words is given to the child. He checks the words in the list that have the same vowel sound.
7. The rules governing vowel sounds are given to the child along with a list of words. The child indicates the rule that governs the vowel sound of the words by writing the number of the rule before or after each word.
8. The child is given a list of words containing both the long and the short sounds of a given vowel. He checks the words that contain the long sound of the given vowel.
9. The child is given a list of words containing different long and short vowels. He draws a line under each word that contains a long vowel.
10. Lists of words containing long and short vowels are given to the child. He underlines each word that contains a short vowel.

INSTRUCTIONAL MATERIALS FOR CORRECTING DEFICIENCIES IN STRUCTURAL ANALYSIS

When individual pupils or groups of pupils are deficient in their knowledge of structural analysis, corrective practice can be individualized by using available *commercial material* such as the following:

1. *Affixo:** This is a word-building game using roots, prefixes, and suffixes. (For use with two to five players; $3.00; Remedial Education Press.)
2. *Grab** (Set IV): A sight vocabulary game consisting of fifteen polysyllabic words which are subdivided into individual syllables. (For use with two to four children, potentially self-directive; two sets on any level, $2.00; Teachers' Supplies.)

---

*All games are designated by an asterisk.

3. *Phonetic Word Drill Cards:* These instructional materials involve three sets of cards. Each set has ten chart cards, showing a different word ending on each side. Thus there are two families of words on each basic chart card, or twenty families per set. Suspended by plastic rings from the top of each basic chart card and in line with the word endings are initial sound cards. As each card is flipped, a new word appears and then the chart can be reversed and the operation repeated, showing an entirely different family of words. With these three sets, 864 words can be formed. These cover sixty common word endings. (For use with individual children, children working in pairs, or with a group of children under proper direction; three sets, $2.75 each; Kenworthy.)

4. *Phono Word Wheels* (Sets II and III): Set II has seventeen wheels designed to give practice on the most common prefixes. Set III has seventeen wheels designed to give practice on the most common suffixes. Both sets involve a vocabulary of 136 words which are drawn from commonly used basal readers in grades five through seven. (For use with individual children, children working in pairs, or with a group of children under proper direction; $3.60; Steck.)

5. *Programmed Reading Kit, II:** Structural analysis games found among the seventeen games in this kit include *Lazy E Exercises* and *Long-Word Jigsaws.* Both games are adaptable for one or more players. (Complete kit of 17 games, $21.00; Scott, Foresman Elementary High School Division.)

6. *Student Word Set:* This set contains 300 words drawn from the syllabication materials of Dr. William Kottmeyer. The cards are designed for use with the Student Syllabascope ($1.50) which is available from the same publisher. (For use with individual children; $2.00; Wordcrafters Guild.)

7. *Syllable Game:** The Syllable Game contains three decks of cards. The words in the first two decks are of two syllables and the player learns by sight the syllables in these words. The third deck has words up to four syllables in length. (For use with one student or two students playing solitaire, potentially self-directive; $2.50; Garrard.)

8. *Teacher Syllabication Set:* This set of 150 words (on 3-by-14-inch cards) has been prepared for the teacher who is introducing the concepts of syllable division. The cards are designed for use with the *Teacher Syllabascope* ($2.50) which is available from the same publisher. (For use with individual children or an entire class; $2.70; Wordcrafters Guild.)

9. *Third Syllable Game:** A set of cards that provides practice in attacking polysyllabic words one syllable at a time. (For use with individual children, children working in pairs, or a group of children, potentially self-directive; $1.50; Educational Aids.)

10. *Word Prefixes:* A set of subdivided, folding cards which highlight twenty-three prefixes that blend to form 216 words. The meaning of each prefix is given, and the words being shown are keyed on back of each card. (For use with individual children, children working in pairs, or a group of children; $.75; Kenworthy.)

11. *Word Suffixes:* A set of subdivided, folding cards that highlight twenty-four word endings. A total of 144 words are formed. The meaning of each suffix is given and words being shown are keyed in small type. (For use with individual children, children working in pairs, or a small group of children; $.75; Kenworthy.)

12. *Webster Word Analysis Charts:* These instructional materials consist of five charts (34 by 35 inches in size) which constitute a permanent, visual guide to consonant sounds, vowel sounds, speech blends, vowel digraphs, prefixes, and the principles of syllabication. (Potentially self-directive; $10.00; Webster.)

13. *Webster Word Wheels:* These practice wheels consist of twenty-five beginning blend wheels, twenty prefix wheels, eighteen suffix wheels, and eight two-letter consonant wheels. The wheels are color-coded and numbered in order of difficulty. The set comes in a colorful cardboard file box. (For use with individual children or children working in pairs; $15.75; Webster.)

When individual pupils or groups of pupils are deficient in their knowledge of structural analysis, individualized practice can be provided by using *teacher- or pupil-made materials* such as the following:

1. *Authors with Endings:** Words are printed on corners of cards—four cards to a set. A set consists of four words that have the same ending. This can be highlighted by underlining the endings in red. Each child is dealt four cards and one child begins the game by calling for a word with a given ending. If he gets the word, he may continue to call for words. When his opponent indicates that he does not have the ending called for, the child draws from the deck of cards that is face down on the table. The child who acquires the most sets wins. (For use with two to four children, potentially self-directive.)

2. *Baseball:** Two groups of children are chosen. The pitcher flashes a word. If the batter can tell the number of syllables in the word,

*All games are designated by an asterisk.

he has made a hit and moves to first base. Should the next batter also score a hit, he moves to first base and the previous batter advances to second. Soon the runs begin to come in. Teams change sides just as soon as three outs (wrong answers) have been given. The team with the most "runs" wins. (For use with groups of children.)

3. *Happy Ending:*[*] This is a structural analysis game consisting of 108 playing cards divided into eleven units of eight cards, two units of four cards, and one unit of twelve cards. The first unit (12 cards) is labeled *Perfect Fit*. The second unit (4 cards) is labeled *Wait*, and four cards are labeled *Surprise*. The remaining eleven units make up the rest of the deck, and each of these units will have eight different words with the same ending. The ending is printed in color.

The cards are shuffled, and eleven cards are dealt to each player. The remaining cards are put into a pack in the center of the table. The top card is turned up next to the deck and starts the discard pile.

Anyone having a *Surprise* card in his hand places it on the table face up in front of him and immediately draws another card from the pack. The player to the left of the dealer begins playing. He will draw the card turned up or draw from the top of the deck. If he draws the turned up card, he must be able to use it immediately either in a triangle or on a triangle. (A triangle is three or more cards with the same ending put down face up in front of the player.) A player may add to any triangle that he or she has on the table. A triangle of three cards may have one *Perfect Fit* in it. *It is important that each card played on the table is read.* If a player cannot read the triangle or an individual card, his partner can attempt to read them. If neither can read the card or cards, a monitor may tell the player, but he must keep it or them in his hand until his next turn.

A player terminates his play by putting a card on the discard pile and reading it. If a player needs assistance in reading this card, he discards it. The playing continues clockwise around the table. One person in the partnership keeps the cards in front of him, and his partner plays on them or adds to the "lay down." As the playing continues, the player who wants the top card of the discard pile for playing on a triangle or in a triangle must take all the cards in the pile and read and play the top one immediately.

Perfect Fit can be called any card and can help to make three or more of a kind. A *Wait* card on a discarded pile *Stops* the discard pile for the next player who then must draw from the unused pack.

A *Happy Ending* is made when seven cards with the same ending have been played. This may include the *Perfect Fits;* however, only three *Perfect Fits* can be used in one *Happy Ending.*

The game is over when a player has a *Happy Ending* and is rid of all the cards in his hands. The player will try to get as many *Happy Endings* as he can.

Scoring is as follows: A *Happy Ending* counts 100; going out counts 50; *Surprises* count 50; *Perfect Fits* count 10; every other card counts five. The score of all the cards left in the hands of the other players when a player goes out is subtracted from his score on the table. The remaining score for each couple is added and tallied. The couple who first attains a score of 1,000 is declared winner. (For use with two sets of partners.)

4. *Word Flight:** This is a structural analysis game consisting of fifty-two playing cards on each of which is a two-, three-, or four-syllable word. The difficulty of the game can be increased by having many multiple-syllable words.

The playing board is constructed by placing a mimeographed map of the United States on tagboard. A flight route should be drawn between major cities. Miniature airplanes of different colors should be made for use by each player.

To begin the playing, the deck of cards is placed in the center of the table near the playing board. Each player draws his first card from the center deck. The player who draws a word with the least number of syllables is the first to play. If he has a one-syllable word, he may travel to the first city on the route. If he has a two-syllable word, he travels to the second city, and so forth. Each player in turn draws a card, says the word on the card, tells how many syllables are in the word, and moves his airplane along the flight route. If he cannot say the word or determine the number of syllables in it, someone tells him, but he cannot move his airplane. The player who reaches the home field first wins the game. (For use with two to four children, potentially self-directive.)

SUPPLEMENTARY INSTRUCTIONAL ACTIVITIES FOR CORRECTING DEFICIENCIES IN STRUCTURAL ANALYSIS

When individual pupils or groups of pupils are deficient in their knowledge of structural analysis, corrective practice can be individualized by employing activities such as the following:†

---

†Many of these activities can be made self-directive by furnishing simple directions and accompanying answer keys.

1. Syllabication
   a. The child is given a list of common words. He divides the words into syllables.
   b. The child is given a list of words. He underlines words ending in a certain syllable such as *-ight* and *-ing*.
   c. The child is given a series of pictures. He names each object pictured and writes the number of syllables in the name under the picture.
   d. A list of words is given to the child. He indicates the number of syllables in each word.
   e. The child is given the rules governing syllabication together with a list of words. He divides the words into syllables and indicates which rule he used.
2. Suffixes
   a. A list of words containing suffixes is given to the child. He identifies the root word in each word.
   b. The child is given a list of words containing suffixes. He uses the root word in a sentence.
   c. The child is given a list of unknown words. He separates the suffix from the word and pronounces both suffix and root word.
   d. The child is given a list of words with definitions after each word. He adds one of a given group of suffixes to the words so the newly formed word complies with the definition after the word.
   e. The child is given a list of words. He makes new words by adding a given suffix to the words on the list.
3. Prefixes
   a. The child is given a list of words. He writes a given prefix before the words and gives the meaning of the new words.
   b. A series of sentences with one word missing in each is given to the child. He fills in the words using the correct prefixes.
   c. A group of prefixes and a list of words with definitions are given to the child. He adds one of the prefixes from the group to each word so it corresponds to the definition written after each word.
   d. A list of words with prefixes is given to the child. He writes the words without the prefix and indicates how the meaning has been changed.
   e. The child is given a list of unknown words with a known prefix. He finds the meaning of the new word.
   f. The child is given a list of words with prefixes. He underlines the prefixes.
   g. The child is given a list of words containing common prefixes. He underlines the root word.

4. Common Compound Words
   a. A list of compound words is given to the child. He draws a line between the two words making up each compound word.
   b. Two columns of words are given to the child. He makes compound words by matching the words in one column with the words in the other column.
   c. The child is given a list of compound words. He writes the two short words that make up the compound beside each word.
   d. The child is given two lists of words. He combines words from the two lists to form single compound words.
5. Endings of Words
   a. A series of phrases are given to the child. If a phrase refers to more than one, the child adds the plural to the subject of the phrases.
   b. The child is given a group of pictures. The child names the objects in the pictures and gives the plural of the name if there is more than one object involved.
   c. The child is given a list of singular words. He forms the plurals of each word in the list.
   d. The child is given a list of words. He forms new words by adding endings to the words.

USING WORKBOOKS

In an effort to help pupils build their word-recognition and word-analysis skills, teachers should capitalize on the vast supply of practice material available in the form of workbooks.* Some of these workbooks are designed to accompany basal series; others are supplemental skill-type workbooks. Both types can be used to advantage. Following is a representative sample of workbooks that are suitable.

A World of Words by I. F. FORST, G. GOLDBERG, and A. L. BOCK, Philadelphia: Winston. This workbook has as its principal objective the building of vocabulary for junior high students. Its method is essentially the successful direct method used to teach foreign language.

Building Words by E. SAVAGE, Chicago: Beckley-Cardy Co. A first-grade workbook which provides ear and eye training in beginning, middle, and ending sounds of words with emphasis on vowel sounds. Suggestions are given for the teacher.

Building Word Power by D. D. DURRELL and H. B. SULLIVAN, New York: World Book. This workbook is accompanied by a teacher's manual and is devoted to exercises in auditory and visual discrimination on the primary level.

*See pages 236-240 for a more detailed discussion of workbooks and their proper use.

Building Reading Skills by L. ARMSTRONG and R. HARGRAVE, Wichita: McCormick-Mathers. These six workbooks are for elementary-grade children and are designed to build essential reading skills. Practice material is included to train children in phonetic and structural analysis, sight vocabulary development, word meaning, phrase perception, paragraph comprehension, and the like. These workbooks can be used with any series of readers.

Eye and Ear Fun by C. STONE, Manchester, Mo.: Webster Publishing. A series of four books which can be used in connection with any basic series of readers. The workbooks are designed to provide a carefully organized course for developing fluency, accuracy, and independence in word recognition.

Fun with Words and Pictures by G. L. GARSON, Chicago: Follett Publishing Co. A series of workbooks for the primary grades. Considerable space is devoted to coloring and pasting.

Functional Phonetic Books by A. D. CORDTS, Westchester: Benefic Press. A series of three phonics workbooks that employ whole-word approach (words appear contextually, in sentences) that is compatible with the look-say method of teaching reading. A teacher's manual also is available.

Happy Times with Sounds by L. M. THOMPSON, Boston: Allyn and Bacon, Inc. A series of three workbooks which give training in sounding for the primary grades. A teacher's handbook accompanies the series.

Iroquois Phonics Program by W. K. EATON and B. F. FAMES, Syracuse: Iroquois. These three workbooks with accompanying manuals stress letter phonics, combinations, and syllabication. Advanced sections include contextual reading.

Learning the Letters by M. A. STANGER and E. K. DONOHUE, New York: Oxford University Press. A series of six workbooks for the primary grades which stress the sounds of consonants and vowels.

Learning for Letter Sounds by P. McKEE and L. M. HARRISON, Boston: Houghton Mifflin Co. A first-grade workbook for teaching initial consonant sounds.

Macmillan Reading Spectrum by M. W. SULLIVAN, Palo Alto, Calif.: Behavioral Research Laboratories. A self-checking series of workbooks that include letters and short regular words.

Primary Seatwork by J. McDADE, Chicago: Plymouth Press. Seatwork material designed to teach reading by the nonoral method.

Puzzle Pages by F. SHELTON and L. TATE, Wichita: McCormick-Mathers. These simple workbooks for primer and first-grade work involve pasting and cutting of words and sentences in connection with pictures.

Phonic Fun by G. N. EDWARDS et al., Chicago: Beckley-Cardy Co. Two workbooks for grades one and two presenting phonic elements (initial sounds, vowels, and endings) with word frequencies as contained in basic readers.

Phonics by S. HERR, Los Angeles: Educational Research Associates. A series of three phonic workbooks for the elementary grades designed to give a thorough understanding of basic phonic principles through the use of extensive materials. Liberal use is made of pictures and illustrations.

Phonics Skilltexts by M. McCRORY and P. WATTS, Columbus, Ohio: Charles E. Merrill Books, Inc. A series of four workbooks (A, B, C, D) for the elementary grades that give training in word-recognition skills through visual, auditory, and kinesthetic activities.

Phonics We Use, 1966 edition, by MARY MEIGHAN et al., Chicago: Lyons and Carnahan. A series of six workbooks which can be used in connection with any basic series of readers.

Phonogram Books by P. B. RADNER, Maplewood, N. J.: Hammond Incorporated. A series of four six-by-eight-inch workbooks that teach simple phonograms, vowel digraphs, and medial phonograms, initial digraphs, and terminal digraphs, respectively. Words employed are drawn from the speaking vocabulary of the beginner.

Programmed Reading by SULLIVAN ASSOCIATES, C. D. BUCHANAN, Program Director, New York: McGraw-Hill. This series is very much like the *Macmillan Reading Spectrum.*

Reading with Phonics by JULIE HAY and CHARLES WINGO, Philadelphia, Penn.: Lippincott Co. A hard-cover book for the pupil, accompanied by three workbooks and a teacher's manual. Training involves isolated words, many of which are of the nonsense variety. Red ink is used to highlight phonic elements.

Remedial Reading Drills by T. G. HEGGE, S. A. KIRK, and W. A. KIRK, Ann Arbor: George Wahr. A booklet for primary or intermediate grades containing isolated words in list form. Teaching centers around letter-by-letter sounding with kinesthetic reinforcement.

Time for Phonics by LOUISE B. SCOTT and VIRGINIA A. PAVELKO, Manchester, Mo.: Webster. A series of workbooks for primary children that teach phonics via picture and context cues.

Words Are Important by H. C. HARDWICKE, Maplewood, N. J.: C. S. Hammond & Company. A series of meaning vocabulary workbooks for junior and senior high school. Graded words are based on frequency categories of *Thorndike and Lorge Teacher's Word Book of 30,000 Words.*

EMPLOYING READING GAMES

In seeking material that will strengthen individual weaknesses, many teachers turn to reading games since they are or can be made self-directive. Although teachers have experienced varying degrees of success with reading games, they are in general agreement that the play technique does arouse interest and provides needed motivation. Recent articles appearing in the *Saturday Review of Literature*(5) and the *Los Angeles Times*(6) attest to the appeal of games at all age levels.

Reading games have advantages as effective instrumental devices, but they also have their limitations. Most reading games are designed to provide extra practice in word recognition, word analysis, and word meaning, but the material is limited to practice on words in isolation. Unless the games are supplemented by recreational reading and developmental instruction on meaningful content, their effectiveness in most cases will be of doubtful value. Especially valuable in this regard are the Dolch *Basic Vocabulary Series,* published by Garrard Publishing Company, which are written almost entirely with the Dolch 220 basic sight words and 95 commonest nouns. Unfortunately, too many teachers use games as mere busy work with no follow-up to determine their effectiveness. These teachers fail to evaluate and reevaluate reading games by asking, "When and for whom is this game valuable and useful?

Care must be taken that the reading game employed is not too juvenile and that it provides meaningful practice in terms of the individual's reading difficulty. Often, too, meaningful practice can be assured only if the teacher or an able child provides some surveillance during the playing of the game. Certainly there is no need to continue a game for an individual or group when progress in the skill the game purports to develop comes to a halt. Once children fail to enjoy a game they fail to profit from it, and it should be withdrawn.

Reading games provide self-competition when the results are recorded by the pupil. Keeping a record of the number of successes per unit of playing time proves motivation for the child. It also enables the teacher to evaluate pupil progress and determine the effectiveness of the game for the learner.

In short, when reading games are selected carefully on the basis of appropriate content, difficulty, and pupil interest, and when the results are charted by the pupil and evaluated by the teacher, they serve as a useful individualized and self-directed instructional activity.

The reader will find that many of the instructional aids presented in this chapter take the form of games. As indicated on page 188, all games are designated by an asterisk.

MAKING READING GAMES

Some school districts known to the writers have enlisted the help of parents in developing self-directive games for classroom teachers.

Teachers and interested parents meet in a room which provides ample table surface for working. All materials needed for the construction of games are made available. These might include—

Crayons and colored pencils; felt pens in a variety of colors	Brads
	Staplers
Paints	Cards of various sizes
Paper of several types, sizes, and colors	Paper clips
	Library card pockets
Oaktag	Envelopes of varying sizes
Scissors	Scotch tape
Paper cutters	Masking tape
Sheets of acetate	Glue, paste

Parents are shown the half-hour sound filmstrip *Teaching Reading Through Games.** The filmstrip enables them to see in color a great variety of teacher-made games while they are being described by a recorded voice. Booklets of *Reading Games that Teach*† are also made available. Help is given by the teachers present.

PROBLEMS FOR ORAL AND WRITTEN DISCUSSION

1. Why are the skills of word analysis important in reading?
2. What are the advantages and limitations of reading games?
3. Use an appropriate reading game with a group of pupils. Provide an objective method of recording results. Evaluate its effectiveness.
4. Construct an original reading game and have it evaluated by your colleagues.
5. Select three or more items from the list of corrective material appearing in this chapter. Describe the nature and functions of these materials; revise the directions for these materials in order to make them more self-directive.
6. Organize a self-corrective program in reading for a pupil who is deficient in word recognition or word analysis, indicating the pupil's grade placement, instructional level, intelligence, degree of retardation, reading expectancy, and nature of his difficulties in reading. Select the corrective material to be used, indicating type and difficulty.

REFERENCES

1. *A Place to Start: A Graded Bibliography for Children with Reading Difficulties* (Syracuse: Syracuse University Press); GEORGE SPACHE, *Good Reading for Poor Readers,* revised 1970 (Champaign, Ill.: Garrard Publishing Co.).
2. For a more extensive treatment see JOHN DeBOER and MARTHA DALLMAN, *The Teaching of Reading* (New York: Holt, Rinehart and Winston, Inc., 1964), pp. 105-106.
3. GERTRUDE HILDRETH, *Teaching Reading* (New York: Henry Holt and Co., Inc., 1959), p. 155.
4. DELWYN SCHUBERT, "Teachers and Word Analysis Skills," *Journal of Developmental Reading* (Summer 1959):62-64.

*Available through BFA Educational Media, 2211 Michigan Ave., Santa Monica, California 90404.

†*Reading Games that Teach* consists of the following: Book I: *Readiness*; Book II: *Phonics*; Book III: *Word Recognition*; Book IV: *Word Attack Skills*; and Book V: *Comprehension*. The step-by-step format and illustrations make the games easy to understand and use in the classroom. The follow-up form on the back of every page enables teachers to record for future reference their own ideas and reactions. Available through Creative Teaching Press, Inc., 514 Hermosa Vista Ave., Monterey Park, Calif. 91754. Cost: $1.95 each.

5. GARRY SHIRTS, "Games Students Play," *Saturday Review*, May 16, 1970, 81-82.
6. "A Popularity Explosion in Adult Games," *Los Angeles Times*, December 19, 1970.

SELECTED READINGS

BOND, GUY, and MILES TINKER. *Reading Problems: Their Diagnosis and Correction.* 2nd ed. New York: Appleton-Century-Crofts, 1967, ch. 12.

BURMEISTER, LOU. "Phonics in a Word Attack Program—Place and Content," *Proceedings of the International Reading Association*, 1970.

CARTER, HOMER, and DOROTHY McGINNIS. *Diagnosis and Treatment of the Disabled Reader.* New York: The Macmillan Co., 1970, ch. 12.

DURKIN, DOLORES. "Phonics Materials: A Big Seller." *The Reading Teacher* (April 1967):610-614.

GRAY, WILLIAM. *On Their Own in Reading.* 2nd ed. Chicago: Scott, Foresman and Co., 1960.

HARRIS, ALBERT. *How to Increase Reading Ability.* 5th ed. New York: David McKay Co., Inc., 1970, chs. 13-14.

JONES, LINDA. "Games, Games, Games—and Reading Class." *The Reading Teacher* (October 1971):41-46.

KARLIN, ROBERT. *Teaching Elementary Reading.* New York: Harcourt Brace Jovanovich, Inc., 1971, ch. 5.

SLOBODIAN, JUNE, and HERBERT HAFFNER. "Using Games for Reading Improvement." *Reading Improvement* (Fall 1971): 52-54.

SPACHE, GEORGE. *Toward Better Reading.* Champaign, Ill.: Garrard Publishing Co., 1963, ch. 13.

————. *Reading in the Elementary School.* 2nd ed. Boston: Allyn and Bacon, Inc., 1969, ch. 12.

WILSON, ROBERT. *Diagnostic and Remedial Reading.* Columbus, O.: Charles E. Merrill Publishing Co., 1967, ch. 7.

9

Improving
Comprehension and
the Study Skills

CORRECTING AND IMPROVING COMPREHENSION DIFFICULTIES

This chapter is devoted to specific games, techniques, and materials
that are of value in helping children overcome deficiencies in reading
comprehension if properly used.* The teacher who wishes to help pupils
whose comprehension problems stem from limited sight and meaning
vocabularies is referred to chapter 8.

Workbooks

Workbooks which are widely used in developmental and corrective
reading programs are of two types: those that accompany basal readers
and those that are independent of any series of readers. The former are
designed for group instruction directed by the teacher. Their content
usually is divided into units paralleling the basal reader and is designed
to provide additional practice on those reading skills developed in the
basal reader.

The content of independent workbooks does not parallel basal readers. Some independent workbooks emphasize a single group of skills
such as word analysis or comprehension. Usually their difficulty is not
expressed in grade levels, and many of them provide simple directions

---

*For information regarding a fifteen-minute color and sound filmstrip that is rele-
vant to the contents of this chapter, write to International Educational Films, 11320
Weddington St., North Hollywood, Calif. 91601. The filmstrip, *Developing Effective Reading-Study Skills*, is designed for use with junior and senior high school
students and adult groups. It is authored by Delwyn G. Schubert and Leslie W.
Nelson.

written for the pupils. Because of this, the teacher is able to utilize books on several levels of difficulty in meeting class needs.

Independent workbooks are of particular value in meeting the needs of pupils above the third grade who are retarded one to three years in their reading skills. For these pupils, the regular basal reader and the accompanying workbooks are too difficult. In such cases, the teacher can turn to an independent series of workbooks for the purpose of selecting those of optimum difficulty for specific pupils. Such workbooks should have simple directions that have been written for the pupils so they can pursue the materials independently at their own rate.

An example of a particularly popular independent workbook series is the *Readers Digest Reading Skill Builders.** This series contains short and highly motivating selections that have great appeal and are ideally suited to developmental and remedial work. Booklets are now available on each grade level from one to eight. A variety of exercises for developing comprehension, rate, and vocabulary are included. Audio Lesson Units on cassettes are available for levels 2, 4, and 6.

Pupils who are retarded in any reading skills should be assigned only the skills or units they have not mastered. If the workbook does not provide enough practice, a second book should be provided in which the desired units are indicated. Answer sheets on which responses are to be written should be furnished so the books are not consumed by one pupil but can be used over and over by many children.

Another method of providing flexibility with effectiveness in the use of workbooks is to secure two copies of two or three series of independent workbooks. Cut the pages apart and mount them on tagboard. Assemble and classify the material by units or skills according to the level of difficulty and then provide a file in which the pupil can readily locate the exercises he needs. Mounting paper of various colors can be employed to designate levels of difficulty, if desired. By combining materials from two or three workbooks, an adequate supply of self-directed practice material on several levels of difficulty is assured. Having the pupils write their responses on separate answer sheets insures continued use of the workbook exercises.

When evolving an answer file, it is best to write the answers to single exercises on small cards. Exercises and cards must be marked to correspond. Letters or numbers can be used for this purpose.

Following is a representative list of workbooks that contains material suitable for developing pupils' comprehension and study skills.

---

*Available through Reader's Digest Services, Inc., Educational Division, Pleasantville, New York 10570. See page 282 for a more complete description.

Be a Better Reader by NILA B. SMITH, Englewood Cliffs, N. J.: Prentice-Hall, 1968. Workbooks for grades four through twelve that contain exercises to develop phonics, use and meaning of prefixes and suffixes, syllabication, rapid and critical reading, location of information, and vocabulary development. Special study skills in the content fields are emphasized.

Better Reading by J. C. GAINSBURG and S. I. SPECTOR, New York: Globe Book Company, Inc., 1962. A recently revised and modernized text for corrective work on the high school level. Exercises are provided on skimming, main ideas, outlining, and other reading areas.

Cowboy Sam Workbooks by E. W. CHANDLER, Chicago: Beckley-Cardy Co. A series of four workbooks which parallel the *Cowboy Sam Readers*. The workbooks range from primer to third-grade level and provide checks for reading vocabulary, understanding, following directions, and so forth. Space is provided for coloring.

Developing Reading Efficiency by LYLE L. MILLER, Minneapolis: Burgess Publishing Co., 1965. A workbook for the junior high school. Exercises are devoted to word recognition, phrase and sentence reading, and timed reading of more lengthy selections.

Developmental Reading Text-Workbook Series by W. H. BURTON et al., Indianapolis: The Bobbs-Merrill Co., Inc., 1961. This series provides a complete developmental program in reading. Each workbook is organized into units with each unit consisting of a story followed by exercises in comprehension and word-analysis skills. The series can be used in conjunction with or supplementary to basal reading materials to reinforce learning. It also can be used independently of basal reading materials, as in programs emphasizing individualized or independent reading.

Diagnostic Reading Workbooks by R. F. GREENWOOD and J. V. WILLIAM, Columbus, O.: Harrison. This series of workbooks is designed to give elementary children practice in four important skills. These include (1) ability to comprehend facts, (2) ability to do independent things and to evaluate, (3) development of vocabulary and word mastery, (4) ability to find the main ideas in a selection. Grade level is indicated by stars on the cover and the title page.

Diagnostic Tests and Exercises in Reading by L. J. BRUECKNER and W. D. LEWIS, Philadelphia: Winston Co., 1935. A workbook for retarded readers having fourth-grade reading ability. It contains tests and exercises in word recognition, vocabulary, phrasing, central thoughts, related details, and rate.

Mastery of Reading by M. BAILEY and U. LEAVELL, New York: American Book Company. These three workbooks are for junior high school students and can be used independently of the three texts they parallel. Each chapter provides students with drills and exercises centered around a single reading skill.

Mother Hubbard's Seatwork Cupboard by D. E. KIBBE, Eau Claire, Wis.: E. M. Hale and Company. Two workbooks are involved. The first workbook is for first-grade children and concentrates on ninety-three words. Word-picture matching, coloring, and pasting are the predominant activities. The second workbook introduces sentence and paragraph reading.

My Work Book in Reading by E. M. ALDREDGE and J. F. McKEE, Chicago: Beckley-Cardy Co. These workbooks in reading for the primary grades contain a variety of reading and numbers materials. Considerable space is devoted to coloring and pasting.

Practice Readers by C. R. Stone and C. C. Graver, Manchester, Mo.: Webster Publishing, 1961. A series of four workbooks consisting of short selections followed by exercises pertaining to direct details, implied details, meaning of the whole, correctness of a statement in relation to the selection, understanding the meaning of reference words, and perception of the truth or falseness of a statement.

Practice Exercises in Reading by A. I. Gates and C. C. Peardon, Bureau of Publication, Teachers College, Columbia University, 1963. A series of four workbooks which train students in the four types of reading corresponding to the types of ability measured by the Gates Silent Reading Tests. These involve (1) reading to appreciate the general significance of a selection, (2) reading to predict the outcome of given events, (3) reading to understand precise directions, (4) reading to note details. These widely used booklets are provided for grades two to six.

Reading Comprehension by Adrian B. Sanford et al., New York: Macmillan, 1964. Six programmed workbooks comprise this series. Difficulty levels vary from grades three to eight.

Reading Essential Series by U. W. Leavell et al., Austin, Texas: Steck-Vaughn Company, 1953. This series of workbooks which cover grades one through eight can be used to fit different reading levels in the various grades. Exercises include the development of phonetic skills, structural analysis, dictionary skills, and comprehension skills. The selections have high interest appeal and are carefully graded.

Reading for Meaning by W. S. Guiler and J. H. Coleman, Philadelphia: J. B. Lippincott Co., 1935. A series of nine workbooks designed to improve the following basic reading skills: (1) word meanings, (2) total meaning, (3) central thought, (4) detailed meanings, (5) organization, (6) summarization.

Reading Skilltext by E. M. Johnson, Columbus, O.: Charles E. Merrill Books, Inc., 1956. A series of six workbooks that consist of illustrated stories followed by questions pertaining to comprehension, word meanings, and word-attack skills.

Reading Workbooks by A. L. McDonald, Austin, Texas: Steck-Vaughn Company. Three workbooks for grades one and two which provide readiness material and purposeful activities to develop reading skills.

Specific Skills Series by Richard A. Boning, Rockville Centre, N. Y.: Barnell Loft, Ltd., 1962. These workbooks are available on levels one through six for each of the following: *Using the Context, Getting the Facts, Following Directions, Locating the Answer, and Working with Sounds.*

SRA Better Reading Books by E. A. Simpson, Chicago: Science Research Associates, 1962. A series of four workbooks for grades five to six, seven to eight, nine to ten, and eleven to twelve, respectively. The workbooks consist of timed reading selections followed by multiple-choice questions.

Standard Test Lessons in Reading by W. A. McCall and L. M. Crabbs, Bureau of Publications, Teachers College, Columbia University, 1961. These widely used workbooks cover grades two to twelve. Five workbooks are involved, each of which contains short selections followed by questions and grade scores.

Step Up Your Reading Power by Jim Olson, St. Louis: Webster Division, McGraw-Hill, 1966. Five workbooks comprise this series. The workbooks are designed for use with remedial students on the secondary level. Each selection is followed by six fact questions and two thought questions.

Think and Do by W. S. GRAY, A. S. ARTLEY, and M. MONROE, Chicago: Scott, Foresman and Co. A series of workbooks designed to accompany the Scott, Foresman basic readers. These workbooks cover grades one to eight and can be used independently of the series by pupils who need carefully planned practice.

Your Reading Guide by N. F. RYAN, Chicago: Lyons & Carnahan, 1956. Two workbooks for junior high level that pertain to reading and study skills.

Corrective Practice for Pupils Deficient in Word Meaning Vocabulary

To acquire a large meaning vocabulary, one must read widely and must possess a curiosity about new words.* Helpful, too, is a system whereby new words can be recorded and reviewed until mastered.

A number of years ago the reading specialist Luella Cole evolved a vocabulary-building system for children that was completely individualized and self-directive. It is ideally suited for corrective work. She described it as follows:

There is only one really efficient way of individualizing training in word study, and that is to have each pupil keep track of the words he does not know. The procedures involved are simple. The teacher first supplies each child with twenty-five or thirty slips of paper. If she can obtain 3″ by 5″ library cards and cut them in half, these small cards are better than paper slips because they can be handled more easily. She then instructs the pupils to copy each unknown word out of the books they read, writing one word on each card. The cards should be in readiness whenever the pupil is reading anything, no matter what the subject matter of the book may be. Since almost all the words thus recorded will be within a child's understanding as soon as they are pronounced, the teacher should let the pupils get together from time to time in groups of three, in which each one shows the others the words he does not know. Most of the words that have been collected by all three will be recognized by one child or another. Any remaining words may be looked up in the dictionary if the children are old enough or handed to the teacher for her to explain. After the words are identified, each pupil goes through his own cards, saying each word he can remember over to himself. The cards containing those words he can now identify he puts in one pile; the words he cannot remember he puts in another. (1)

Cole suggests that the children continue quizzing each other until the pile of unknown words has disappeared. When pupils accumulate twenty to thirty cards, the reading period should be used for the drill described. Cards are to be kept and reviewed two or three times before they are discarded.

Facile use of the dictionary is a real asset to meaning vocabulary development. The various subskills involved in efficient dictionary usage

*Some of the materials and techniques described in chapter 8 in connection with developing sight vocabulary can also be used for meaning vocabulary development.

should be cataloged, and pupils in the upper grades who show weaknesses should be given proper corrective instruction. (See page 98 and pages 200-201 for a discussion of dictionary skills.)

Teachers are often in a quandary regarding which words pupils should learn. In making a decision as to the importance of specific words, the teacher should consult the following:

COLE, LUELLA. *The Teachers Handbook of Technical Vocabulary.* New York: Holt, Rinehart & Winston, Inc., 1938.

HERBER, HAROLD. *Success with Words.* New York: Scholastic Book Service, 1964.

THORNDIKE, EDWARD, and IRVING LORGE. *The Teachers Word Book of 30,000 Words.* New York: Bureau of Publications, Teachers College, Columbia University, 1944.

The book by Thorndike and Lorge deals with general vocabulary, while the other two contain listings of words in various subject matter fields.

One of the most fascinating approaches to vocabulary enrichment involves a study of etymology, the origin or development of words. Pupils of all ages are intrigued by it. Since we have begged, borrowed, and stolen words, without compunction, from everyone—the Spanish, French, American Indians, and others—there is no dearth of words from which to choose.

Every teacher ought to have a book in his professional library such as Wilfred Funk's *Word Origins and Their Romantic Stories.** It's an open sesame to many hours of enjoyment and personal enrichment. In addition, it proves a valuable source of instructional material for stimulating the vocabulary development of readers of all ages.

Since a large number of words in the English language start with prefixes, a knowledge of them is helpful when unfamiliar words are encountered. Some of the most common prefixes are as follows:

ab (from)	*dis* (apart)	*ob, op, ov* (against)
ad, a, ap, at (to)	*en* (in)	*pre* (before)
be (by)	*ex, e* (out of)	*pro* (in front of)
com, con, col (with)	*in, en, im, em* (into)	*re* (back, again)
de (from)	*in* (not)	*sub* (under)
		un (not) (2)

Suffixes are more difficult for children to learn than prefixes. Fortunately, suffixes are less valuable as clues than prefixes since they are less consistent in their meanings. Some of the more common suffixes are *ment, tion, able, ous, ly, er, ful, less, ness, ing, age, ed, ance*.

*New York: Grosset & Dunlap, Inc., 1950.

Many words in the English language mean approximately the same thing. Children learn that such words are called synonyms. Words that are opposite in meaning are antonyms. Pupils enjoy and benefit from exercises dealing with synonyms and antonyms. An excellent source of synonyms and antonyms can be found in Fernald's *English Synonyms, Antonyms, and Prepositions.** This book is far superior to other books of its kind because it not only lists synonyms and antonyms but employs them in sentences. In this way, fine differentiations between words are readily discernible. The words presented vary greatly in difficulty; therefore, teachers at all grade levels find it valuable for instructional purposes.

Scott, Foresman Company has published two student thesauri which, at the time of this writing, are unique. *In Other Words I . . . A Beginning Thesaurus* (priced at $2.55) offers children over 1,000 substitute words for 100 they use and overuse. Pupils who read at third-grade level or above and who can use alphabetical order and interpret related sentences can use the book independently. *In Other Words II . . . A Junior Thesaurus* (priced at $3.06) gives pupils reading at fifth-grade level or above the means whereby they can add 3,000 words to their working vocabularies. Three-hundred commonly used entry words are involved.

Additional kinds of corrective practice for pupils who are deficient in their meaning vocabulary can be individualized by using materials and techniques such as the following:

1. *Add On:* Lists of three words belonging to a category are followed by blank spaces. Pupils are encouraged to think of other words that fit the same classification. Examples:

   a. small, minute, little, _____, _____.
   b. coat, hat, shoes, _____, _____.
   c. dog, cat, horse, _____, _____.

   Probable answers can appear on the back of the exercise. (For use with individual pupils, potentially self-directive.)

2. *Classifying Words:* Present lists of words which pupils must classify under three or more headings. Examples:

	Vegetables	*Fruits*	*Meats*
a. carrots			
b. apples			
c. pork			
d. celery			
e. oranges			
f. lamb			

*New York: Funk & Wagnalls, 1954.

Correct answers can appear on the back of the exercise. (For use with individual pupils, potentially self-directive.)

3. *Cross It Out:* Lists of words which belong to a specific classification are presented along with one word which is completely foreign to the group. Pupils are told to cross out the word which does not belong with the others. Examples:

   a. run, jump, walk, sleep, crawl
   b. cold, hot, windy, chilly, torrid
   c. milk, turpentine, cocoa, coffee, tea

   Correct answers can appear on the back of the exercise. (For use with individual pupils, potentially self-directive.)

4. *Label Me:* On a piece of tagboard paste a large picture of any scene relating to the unit being taught. Provide small word cards and put these in an accompanying envelope. Pupils are directed to place the word cards on or near the proper items in the picture. Correct answers in the form of pictures can appear on the back of the individual word cards. (For use with individual pupils, potentially self-directive.)

5. *Matching:* Prepare parallel columns of synonyms or antonyms and direct pupils to match the two. Examples:

   a. strong _____   a. gigantic
   b. large _____   b. powerful
   c. fast _____   c. rapid

   Correct answers can appear on the back of the exercise. (For use with individual pupils, potentially self-directive.)

6. *Picture Dictionaries:* Pupils are instructed to build a dictionary of words they have encountered in their reading. Old books, magazines, workbooks, and newspapers can be furnished to provide pictures for illustrating the words. Pictures can also be drawn by the children for illustrative purposes. A shoe box that has been painted with tempera colors is fine for housing the materials. Dividers can be cut from tagboard and labeled with letters of the alphabet. (For use with individual children, potentially self-directive.)

7. *Prefixes, Suffixes, and Word Stems:* Devise exercises consisting of three prefixes, suffixes, or word stems for which examples of usage are given. Pupils will think of additional words. Examples:

   a. *pre* (before): preheat, preschool, _____, _____.
   b. *re* (again, back): repay, refill, _____, _____.
   c. *un* (not): unhappy, unhurt, _____, _____.

Probable answers may appear on the back of the exercise. (For use with individual pupils, potentially self-directive.)

8. *Puzzle Words:* Furnish pupils with space blanks designed to accommodate words which are defined. The definitions should be in mixed order. Examples:

   a. The wife of an American Indian
      (squaw)
   b. A raccoon
      (coon)
   c. A weapon for shooting arrows
      (bow)

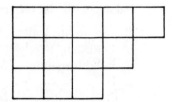

Correct answers can appear on the back of the exercise. (For use with individual pupils, potentially self-directive.)

9. *Riddles:* Riddles can be used to stimulate dictionary usage and interest in new words. Example:

   a. There are many of us in Norway. We are frequently long and narrow. Steep, rocky banks come right down to the water of which we are made. We are called _____.

Correct answers can appear on the back of the exercise. (For use with individual pupils, potentially self-directive.)

10. *See, Hear, or Smell?* List words which fall in one of these sensory categories. Pupils are expected to classify the words. Examples:

    a. tulips
    b. clocks
    c. sunsets

Correct answers can appear on the back of the exercise. (For use with individual pupils, potentially self-directive.)

11. *Seeing Relationships:* Lists of sample words having a certain relationship to each other are followed by several words in parentheses. The pupils must find and underline two words in the parentheses that have the same relationship as the sample words. Examples:

    a. baker, bread (sailor, tailor, mason, teacher, clothes)
    b. cup, coffee (bookcase, table, store, dresser, books)
    c. dog, barks (cat, snake, horse, lion, roars)

Correct answers can appear on the back of the exercise. (For use with individual pupils, potentially self-directive.)

12. *Stick Me:* Paste pictures of objects on a suitably sized square of corkboard. Type words on small squares of oaktag and penetrate

each with a common pin. When a pupil who engages in this activity finds a picture which matches a given word card, he labels it by pushing the pin through the picture into the corkboard beneath. (For use with individual children or children working in pairs.)

13. *Think of the Word:* Sentences containing word groups for which an individual word can be substituted are presented. The pupil writes the word needed. He consults the dictionary if necessary. Examples:

   a. The man was *being very careful* because the ice underfoot was thin. (cautious)
   b. The general was afraid the enemy would *gain a victory over* them. (defeat)
   c. The tiger was *going about slowly and secretly for something to eat or steal.* (prowling)

   Correct answers can appear on the back of the exercise. (For use with individual pupils, potentially self-directive.)

14. *Which Is It?* Sentences are prepared with two inserted words in parentheses. The pupil chooses the one he considers correct. Examples:

   a. The man was (right, write) about the distance.
   b. The boy (road, rode) the horse home.
   c. The (pail, pale) was filled with water.

   Correct answers can appear on the back of the exercise. (For use with individual pupils, potentially self-directive.)

15. *Yes or No:* Numbered lists of words are followed by statements relating to the words. Pupils answer each statement "yes" or "no." Examples:

   a. onion (This is something that makes your eyes water.)
   b. cucumber (Your father drives this to work.)
   c. bathe (You do this in a bathtub.)

   Correct answers can appear on the back of the exercise. (For use with individual pupils, potentially self-directive.)

Corrective Practice for Pupils Deficient in Sentence Comprehension

Pupils who experience sentence comprehension difficulties and an inability to group words into thought units may profit from use of the Dolch Phrase Cards (Garrard Publishing Co.). Helpful, too, is the tachistoscope presentation of phrases using the Keystone Overhead Projector and Flashmeter (Keystone View Co.) or the Tachist-O-Flasher with accompanying phrase filmstrips (*Learning Through Seeing*).

Reading aloud several sentences in which words are incorrectly grouped dramatizes the need for proper phrasing in an entertaining manner. The following paragraph provides an example:

(For my) (breakfast I have) (jungle fruit, rice) (and coffee when) (I eat fresh) (fish from a) (stream or eggs) (from a little jungle) (town, things) (are not so) (very bad.)

Other kinds of corrective practice for pupils who are deficient in their ability to comprehend sentences can be individualized by using materials and techniques such as the following:

1. *Jumbled Sentences:* Disarrange sentences. Direct pupils to put the parts in proper order. Examples:

   a. in an accident / Jane thought / were injured / that the boys.
   b. is true / you read / don't believe / that everything.

   Correctly arranged sentences can appear on the back of the exercise. (For use with individual pupils, potentially self-directive.)

2. *Missing Words:* Numbered sentences containing missing words are prepared. Pupils demonstrate comprehension of the sentences by choosing correct missing words. Examples:

   a. Many people have _____ for family pets.
   b. Children learn many interesting things in _____.
   c. _____ are those times during the year when people should relax and enjoy themselves.
      (1) dogs
      (2) vacations
      (3) schools

   Correct answers can appear on the back of the exercise. (For use with individual pupils, potentially self-directive.)

3. *Omit Two:* Mount a picture on an individual card together with three sentences that tell something about the picture. Print two extra sentences that do not relate to the picture. Pupils are instructed to find the two irrelevant sentences. Correct answers can appear on the back of the exercise. (For use with individual pupils, potentially self-directive.)

4. *Pictures and Sentences:* Two or three pictures are mounted on individual cards together with fifteen or twenty sentences which have

been printed on separate cards. Pupils are instructed to read each sentence and match it with the picture to which it refers. A marking scheme can be devised on the reverse side of the cards to make this activity self-corrective. (For use with individual pupils, potentially self-directive.)

5. *Punctuate Me:* Type paragraphs in which all periods and capital letters have been omitted. Pupils are directed to designate the beginnings and endings of sentences by employing proper punctuation and capitalization. The correctly written paragraphs can appear on the back of the exercise. (For use with individual pupils, potentially self-directive.)

6. *Sentence Detective:* Give directions which refer pupils to a picture appearing in a story previously read. Ask them to find all sentences on the page or pages that give more information than what is found in the picture. Correct sentences can appear on the back of the exercise. (For use with individual pupils, potentially self-directive.)

7. *Sentence Match:* Four sentences are prepared. Two of the four say approximately the same thing. Pupils are directed to find the synonymous sentences. Examples:

   a. The man went on and on until he became very tired.
   b. The man wandered about until he found what he was looking for.
   c. The man entered the wilderness looking for a place to build a cabin.
   d. The man continued walking for a great distance until he was exhausted.

   Correct answers can appear on the back of the exercise. (For use with individual pupils, potentially self-directive.)

8. *Split Sentences:* Pupils are given two envelopes. One envelope contains cards with sentence beginnings and the other contains cards with sentence endings. Pupils are directed to match suitable parts to form sentences. Examples:

   a. Jack and Jill went up the hill   1. lighter and warmer.
   b. I ran and ran until I was   2. all out of breath.
   c. As the sun began to rise it became   3. to fetch a pail of water.

   Correct answers can appear on the back of the exercise. (For use with individual pupils, potentially self-directive.)

9. *True or False:* True and false statements that are related or unrelated to the reading lesson can be used to help develop sentence

comprehension. Since many such statements are humorous, children enjoy these exercises immensely. Examples:

a. A 12-year-old boy can run 100 miles an hour.
b. This sentence has more than seven words in it.
c. A wild tiger would make a fine house pet.

Correct answers can appear on back of the exercise. (For use with individual pupils, potentially self-directive.)

10. *When, What, Where?* Sentences which tell when, what, or where are prepared. Pupils read each sentence and categorize it according to these designations. Examples:

a. The Jones family spent their summer in the country.
b. A slender piece of metal that is driven into two blocks of wood can hold them together.
c. He said the world would come to an end last week.

Correct answers can appear on the back of the exercise. (For use with individual pupils, potentially self-directive.)

11. *Where's the Joker?* Sentences pertaining to a given subject are presented together with a sentence that does not belong. Pupils are directed to find the foreign sentence. Examples:

a. The car is a Ford. b. The body is red and the wheels are black. c. The sky became dark and cloudy. d. The top speed is 100 miles an hour.

Correct answers can appear on the back of the exercise. (For use with individual pupils, potentially self-directive.)

Corrective Practice Material for Deficiencies in Following Directions

When individual pupils or groups of pupils are deficient in their ability to follow directions, corrective practice can be individualized by using materials and techniques such as the following:

1. *Can You Eat Me?* Pupils are given a list of simple words with the directions, "Find things you can eat." Examples:

a. orange   c. door   e. butter
b. window   d. crayon   f. cookie

Correct answers can appear on the back of the exercise. (For use with individual pupils, potentially self-directive.)

2. *Do This:* Pupils are given a list of simple words with directions, "Draw a circle around all words you can make pictures of." Examples:

a. go   c. squirrel   e. see
b. dog   d. chicken   f. with

Correct answers can appear on the back of the exercise. (For use with individual pupils, potentially self-directive.)

3. *Following Directions:* Provide pupils with a number of statements such as the following:

a. If the fifth letter in the alphabet is E, write that letter in this space ___.
b. Draw a circle around all words in this sentence that have four letters.
c. If March comes after June write your last name backwards in this space _____.

Correct answers for most of the directions can appear on the back of the exercise. (For use with individual pupils, potentially self-directive.)

4. *Read and Do:* Pupils are given a number of directions to carry out:

a. Draw a house.
b. Put three windows in the house.
c. Put two panes of glass in each window.
d. Draw a chimney on the right-hand side of the roof.
e. Color the chimney brown.
f. Color the house red.
g. Draw a circle on the bottom right-hand side of your paper.
h. Now draw a square around the circle.

(For use with individual pupils, potentially self-directive.)

5. *What's Cooking?* Provide girls with directions for preparing different foods (French toast, pancakes, pies, etc.) and require them to identify the particular dish or food involved. Correct answers can appear on the back of the exercise. (For use with individual pupils, potentially self-directive.)

6. *What's Wrong?* Provide boys with directions for making or assembling model airplanes, mixing paint, repairing flat tires, and so forth; provide girls with various cooking recipes. Reverse some of the directions. Pupils are expected to indicate what is wrong. Correct answers can appear on the back of the exercise. (For use with individual pupils, potentially self-directive.)

Corrective Practice Material for Deficiencies in Locating Central Thoughts

When individual pupils or groups of pupils are deficient in their ability to find central thoughts of paragraphs, corrective practice can be individualized by using materials and techniques as those following:

1. *Best Central Thought:* Select short paragraphs and have them followed by several statements. Pupils are directed to read each paragraph and then choose the particular statement they feel is the most adequate expression of the central thought. Correct answers can appear on the back of the exercise. (For use with individual pupils, potentially self-directive.)

2. *Composing Topic Sentences:* Furnish pupils with paragraphs consisting of details (the key sentences must be removed) and direct them to write their own key sentences. Later they compare their efforts with the original key sentences found on the back of the exercise. (For use with individual pupils, potentially self-directive.)

3. *Decapitated Headings:* Cut headings from three or four short articles. Place the headings in one envelope and the articles in another. Pupils are directed to match the headings with the proper articles. A marking scheme appearing on the back of the headings and articles can be used to make the exercises self-corrective. (For use with individual pupils, potentially self-directive.)

   A more difficult version of exercises using the decapitated-heading technique involves having pupils compose their own headings. Later they compare their efforts with those of the journalists who wrote the articles.

4. *Find the Paragraph:* Designate a story or articles in a book to which pupils have access. Provide a series of key sentences. Pupils are instructed to find the paragraph from which each was taken. Key paragraphs can appear on the back of the exercise. (For use with individual pupils, potentially self-directive.)

5. *What's the Number?* Number the sentences in paragraphs and direct pupils to find the number of the key sentence. Correct answers can appear on the back of the exercise. (For use with individual pupils, potentially self-directive.)

Corrective Practice Material for Deficiencies in Detecting and Remembering Details

When individual pupils or groups of pupils are deficient in their ability to read for details, corrective practice can be individualized by using materials and techniques such as the following:

1. *Answering Questions:* Provide pupils with paragraphs followed by questions (true-false or multiple-choice) which are designed to test understanding of the details in each paragraph. Correct answers can appear on the back of each exercise. (For use with individual pupils, potentially self-directive.)

2. *Finding Irrelevant Details:* Provide pupils with paragraphs in which the sentences have been numbered. One of the sentences carries an irrelevant detail. Pupils are directed to read each paragraph carefully and detect the irrelevant sentence. Correct answers can appear on the back of the exercise. (For use with individual pupils, potentially self-directive.)

3. *Finding Nonsense Phrases:* Provide pupils with a series of paragraphs in each of which a nonsensical phrase has been inserted. Pupils are directed to read each paragraph carefully and detect the absurd phrase. Correct answers can appear on the back of the exercise. (For use with individual pupils, potentially self-directive.)

4. *Skeletal Outlines:* Provide pupils with an outline of a selection which presents main ideas but no details. Pupils are instructed to read the selection and complete the outline. The complete outline can appear on the back of the exercise. (For use with individual pupils, potentially self-directive.)

5. *Which Paragraph Is Best?* Mount a detailed picture on a piece of cardboard. In an accompanying envelope, provide pupils with three-by-five-inch cards on which individual paragraphs about the picture have been typed and numbered. Pupils are directed to find the paragraph which gives the most accurate details about the picture. Correct answers can appear on the back of the exercise. (For use with individual pupils, potentially self-directive.)

6. *Writing Details:* Provide pupils with a main idea and direct them to compose a paragraph by adding related details. (For use with individual pupils.)

Corrective Practice Material for Deficiencies in Following a Sequence of Events

When individual pupils or groups of pupils are deficient in their ability to follow a sequence of events, corrective practice can be individualized by using materials and techniques such as the following:

1. *Drawing Endings:* Mount a series of pictures that tell a sequential story on cardboard. Omit the last picture and place it in an accompanying envelope. Pupils are directed to draw the last picture. After the drawing, pupils may compare their efforts with the picture in

the envelope. (For use with individual children, potentially self-directive.)

2. *How Does It End?* Present unfinished stories which stop at a critical point. Pupils are directed to make up suitable endings. The story ending can appear on the back of the exercise. (For use with individual pupils, potentially self-directive.)

3. *Paragraph Shuffle:* Prepare stories in which the numbered paragraphs are out of order. Pupils are directed to rearrange the paragraphs so the sequence is proper. Correct answers can appear on the back of the exercise. (For use with individual pupils, potentially self-directive.)

4. *Sentence Shuffle:* Prepare short stories in which the numbered sentences are out of order. Pupils are directed to rearrange the sentences so the sequence is proper. Example:

   a. The strange man walked to the door and rapped.
   b. The man was invited into the house.
   c. The dog barked when he heard the sound.
   d. The lady of the house went to the door and opened it.

Correct answers can appear on the back of the exercise. (For use with individual pupils, potentially self-directive.)

Corrective Practice for Pupils Deficient in Critical Reading Ability

Teachers will find the following suggestions helpful in working with pupils who do not critically evaluate the material they read:

1. *Encourage students to talk back to the book.* Have them evaluate statements in the light of their previous knowledge and beliefs. The good reader its always on his guard. He asks himself questions such as "Does that make good sense?" "Is that possible?"

2. *Encourage pupils to check copyright dates.* Indicate the rapid advance that has taken place in many fields during the last few years. What may have been true a few years ago does not always hold today. The following serve as examples:

   a. "The top speed for all fighter craft does not exceed 500 miles per hour." Copyright 1941.
   b. "The population of the United States totals 130,000,000." Copyright 1947.

3. *Give pupils training in distinguishing between statements of fact and opinion.* Show that opinions are merely beliefs which cannot be

supported by objective evidence and that facts, on the contrary, are capable of being proved through objective evidence. Use statements such as the four listed:

a. Men make better legislators than women. (Opinion)
b. The majority of legislators are men. (Fact)
c. California oranges are better than Florida oranges. (Opinion)
d. Oranges contain vitamin C. (Fact)

4. *Have pupils compare several sources of information.* Select from a given field different authorities who contradict each other, or bring to class two newspapers or magazines of opposed political complexions and compare them. Strike up a discussion as to why discrepancies exist. Exercises such as these will indicate to pupils that a critical reader does not accept as final the viewpoint of any one author.

5. *Have pupils investigate an author's competence and possible prejudice.* Students should learn to look at the title page or book cover for information pertaining to an author's background and experience. Checking the appropriate *Who's Who* and sampling the opinions of other authorities are also helpful in determining the reliability of an author. Frequently, the preface is of value in giving a clue as to an author's purpose in writing. Bringing to class for study a number of advertisements or political speeches is an excellent way to train students to recognize prejudiced writings.

6. *Encourage students to test statements for possible exceptions.* Many authors make dogmatic and sweeping statements which do not hold under all circumstances. The following are suggestive of suitable drill:

a. An apple a day keeps the doctor away.
b. You can't teach an old dog new tricks.
c. He who hesitates is lost.

7. *Train students to identify and be on the alert for various advertising and propaganda devices that are commonly used to influence people.* Students should be made aware of the needs to which writers of this kind appeal. Some of the most common are (a) the social need: the desire to be accepted by the group by doing what it does; (b) the ego need: the desire to feel important; (c) the physical need: comfort, food, rest; (d) the desire for social and economic security; (e) the desire for excitement. Paragraphs like the following might be used to sensitize students to how advertisers capitalize on these needs:

Rideway is the car of tomorrow. It's faster, it's smoother, and more economical than any car manufactured. Sales are mounting by leaps and bounds. People from all walks of life are choosing this upper-class car. Be smart. Stay out in front. Buy the beautiful and economical adventure car of the future. Rideway.

8. Have students be alert to words which evoke emotional reactions. The semanticist, Hayakawa, has labeled words such as *communism* and *totalitarianism* as growl words; others such as *freedom* and *statesman* are categorized as purr words. Students can be asked to underline all emotionally loaded words in a selection.

Corrective Practice for Pupils Deficient in the Ability to Remember What They Have Read

A pupil's ability to remember what he has read has little value unless understanding accompanies it. On the other hand, understanding what one has read is of questionable value if nothing can be retained.

Usually, as pupils improve in their ability to sustain attention and become more adept at spotting main ideas and related details, retention is enhanced. For the pupil who is chronically inattentive to the meaning of what he reads, the following procedure is suggested.

Start with a short sentence and direct the pupil to read it to himself. When he finishes, cover the sentence with a small card or close the book and ask, "What did it say?" If the pupil is unable to respond satisfactorily, allow him to reread the sentence and then query him again. Continue this on various occasions until he is able to tell, after a single reading, what a short sentence says. At this point, move on to more complex sentences.

The foregoing method is effective for the following reason. When a pupil realizes that as inevitably as death and taxes he has to tell you what he has read, he begins to pay closer attention. Greater concentration spells better retention.

Corrective Practice for Pupils Who Have Difficulty in Concentrating

Concentration difficulties are often associated with emotional disturbances. The teacher, therefore, should do what she can to uncover any causes of emotional disturbances. If the services of a school psychologist are available, his help should be enlisted.

Practical suggestions which a teacher can give to pupils who have difficulty concentrating are as follows:

1. *Assume a questioning attitude.* Instruct pupils to immediately turn all headings into questions so they are seeking something when reading takes place. The words *how, what, when, where,* and *why* are helpful in this regard. For example, the section heading "Causes of Tooth Decay" should become "What are the causes of tooth decay?" By assuming a questioning attitude children become active readers rather than passive readers. Active readers have little trouble concentrating.

2. *Reduce distracting influences.* Pupils would not think of playing tennis while trying to memorize a poem. Yet at home they frequently read while listening to the radio. No wonder concentration is difficult!

   For maximum concentration at home, pupils should study by themselves, away from the family and all distracting influences. Pictures, banners, and souvenirs should be removed from view. If possible, their desks should face a blank wall. Blank walls offer books little competition.

   When studying in a library, pupils should seat themselves in a place where they will not be disturbed. Sitting near friends who will tempt them to visit is not recommended. It is also advisable for pupils to sit with their backs toward the library entrance. This will discourage their looking up to check on the identity of newcomers.

3. *Sit in a straight-backed chair.* Soft chairs and reclining davenports are not conducive to maximum concentration. Through the years of conditioning they have become associated with rest and relaxation. The slight muscular tension that accompanies sitting up in a straight chair keeps students alert and makes concentration easier.

4. *Work rapidly.* The auto racer driving to win has to attain a maximum speed and hold it. The greater his speed the greater his need to concentrate on steering. To divert any part of his full attention from the task at hand would be to lose the race. Similarly, readers who force themselves to work as fast as they can to accomplish their purpose have no time for mind wandering.

5. *Adopt a study schedule.* Pupils should plan and adhere to a schedule which will require them to study the same subject in the same place at the same time each day. It is easier to get down to business and concentrate on those things which have become routine and habitual.

6. *Provide proper lighting.* Reading makes heavy demands on the eyes. Frequently, improper lighting in the home causes visual fatigue which quickly hinders concentration. To reduce eyestrain, pupils

should read under lights that are sufficiently strong. Desk lamps should be equipped with a minimum wattage of 75 and floor lamps should have 150 watts. In addition to having direct lighting on the book a pupil is reading, the entire room should be dimly lighted. This reduces extreme contrasts which the eyes cannot tolerate. Glare should be guarded against by covering shiny surfaces or shifting lamps slightly to avoid reflections. Finally, students should be told not to read on and on without respite. Occasionally, they should rest their eyes by closing them or by looking at a distant object across the room or through a window.

A method of study that can aid concentration and boost retention tremendously was evolved by Francis Robinson.(3) It is particularly effective with content field material and can be introduced most profitably as early as the fourth-grade level. (See page 100 for a simplified version of this valuable method of study.)

Mechanical Devices for Improving Rate of Comprehension

Manufacturers wish to convince us that mechanical devices have great value in helping pupils overcome reading difficulties. Magazines have popularized mechanical gadgets and often give the impression that they constitute a panacea for ills. Much of this, of course, is an outgrowth of a tremendous emphasis on "speed reading."

Controlled readers, tachistoscopes, and pacers of many types are found in schools throughout the country. How valuable are these machines?

Spache, in his discussion of the machine approach to reading rate, indicates the following concerns:

1. Does a pupil's accomplishment achieved while using machines transfer to the act of book reading?
2. What dangers to vision does the machine approach pose?
3. What are the effects of after-image on recall following tachistoscopic presentation?
4. Do machines that expose material in a constant fixed span introduce an element of artificiality that should be given consideration?(4)

In his review of research relevant to the use of mechanical devices in the teaching of reading, Karlin concludes:

From some of these studies it appears that gains in rate of reading can be achieved through the use of a mechanical device. To what extent credit may be given to such a device for such achievement is unknown. Few, if any, of these studies were sufficiently tight to minimize the influences of extraneous variables upon the outcomes.

A second conclusion may be reached: In eleven of the twelve investigations which measured natural reading against machine reading, the groups that received training in the former either equaled or surpassed the machine groups in rate of reading. From these data it can be said that outcomes in speed of reading similar to those achieved through the use of special instruments may be expected from suitable reading instruction which does not include these same instruments. (5)

Although studies of the future may prove to the contrary, available data seem to indicate that unless money is plentiful, a school would be wiser to invest in good books and efficient teachers than in machines.

A description of some of the mechanical devices available for improving rate of comprehension follows.

Tachistoscopes

1. *Adjustable Lens Barrel Tachistoscope:* This model retains all the features of the standard Lens-Type Tachistoscope and is attachable to any projector with lens barrel size 1 7/8 inches to 2 1/2 inches O.D. Placement onto the projector lens barrel is easy and quick. The shutter is activated remotely from a hand switch and from the included power supply. Exposure times are 1/125, 1/60, 1/30, 1/8, 1/4, 1/2, and 1 second. (Lafayette Instrument Company; $190.00.)

2. *All-Purpose Electric Tachistoscope:* The All-Purpose Electric Tachistoscope is a more advanced version of the standard All-Purpose Tachistoscope. This unit is to be controlled remotely by a hand switch and included power source. Shutter speeds are 1/125, 1/60, 1/30, 1/15, 1/4, 1/2, and 1 second. (Lafayette Instrument Company; $194.00.)

3. *All-Purpose Tachistoscope:* A tachistoscope that can be used for presentation to an entire classroom or for individual training. It is usable with any make projector. Exposure times of the shutter are 1/125, 1/60, 1/30, 1/15, 1/8, 1/4, 1/2, and 1 second. (Lafayette Instrument Company; $98.00, carrying case, $11.00.)

4. *Attachable Lens Barrel Tachistoscope:* This tachistoscope is adaptable to any projector having a lens barrel size of 1 7/8 inches to 2 1/2 inches O.D., and it is mounted directly to the lens barrel of the projector. It slides on easily and is tightened securely by means of three thumbscrews. Shutter exposure times are 1/125,

1/60, 1/30, 1/8, 1/4, 1/2, and 1 second. (Lafayette Instrument Company; $94.00, carrying case, $8.00.)

5. *Automatic Projection Tachistoscope:* All operations of this projection tachistoscope are completely automatic. Slides can be presented automatically at five-, eight-, and fifteen-second intervals as the shutter is triggered automatically when the slide changes. Shutter exposure times are 1/125, 1/60, 1/30, 1/8, 1/4, 1/2, and 1 second. Forward and reversing of slides, focusing of lens, or changing of slides may be accomplished by remote control. Switching is also provided on the remote control to skip slides or to repeat slides. (Lafayette Instrument Company; $345.00.)

6. *AVR Flash Tachment:* A tachistoscope usable with both slide and filmstrip projectors. Speeds of exposure vary from approximately 1/25 to 1/100 of a second. (Audio-Visual Research; $5.95.)

7. *Cenco Tachistoscopic Attachment:* A device designed to convert the Projection Reader into a tachistoscope. Adjustable exposure times range from 1/100 to 1/4 of a second. (Cenco; $65.00.)

8. *Craig Reader:* A combination tachistoscope and controlled reader using filmstrips mounted on plastic. One to three individuals can use the device simultaneously. (Craig Research, Incorporated; $249.50.)

9. *Electronic T-Matic 150:* A tachistoscopic filmstrip projector designed for use at both far point and near point. Interval of exposure ranges from 1/100 to four seconds. (Psychotechnics, Incorporated. $99.50; Remedial Filmstrips, $60.00.)

10. *Electro-Tach:* A tachistoscope for individual use. It employs an electronic flash unit and has shutter speeds of 1/100, 1/50, 1/25, 1/10, and 1 second. Five hundred targets accompany purchase of the machine. (Lafayette; $98.00.)

11. *E-S-T 10 Eye Span Trainer:* A simple hand-operated tachistoscope made of vinyl plastic requiring no electric power. It has variable shutter speeds of 1/25, 1/50, or 1/100 of a second. Available slides are classed as No. 3—elementary and junior high; No. 1—senior high and college; and No. 2—advanced. (Audio-Visual Research; $6.50 with No. 1 or No. 3 slides; $8.95 with No. 2 or No. 3 slides; No. 1, No. 2, or No. 3 slides or blank slides, $1.50 per set.)

12. *Flash-Meter:* A tachistoscopic attachment for the Keystone Overhead Projector which permits varying the interval of exposure from "time" to 1/100 of a second. (Keystone View Company; $144.00.)

13. *Flash-X:* A hand-tachistoscope for individual training using 4 3/4-inch discs. (Educational Development Laboratories; $8.20.)

14. *Perceptoscope:* A combination tachistoscope and controlled reader employing two filmstrips, one of which takes the place of a shutter. (Perceptual Development Laboratories; $1,595.00.)

15. *Phrase-Flasher:* A hand-operated tachistoscopic device which trains students to read in meaningful phrases. Included are cards containing over 1,200 lines of varying widths, beginning with simple words and digits, and culminating in complete paragraphs. (The Reading Laboratory, Inc.; $18.50.)

16. *Protach:* An electronic version of the Tachist-O-Flasher with variable speed control. Designed for use with all projectors. (Learning Through Seeing; $99.50.)

17. *Rheem-T-Scope:* A light, portable, tachistoscope which employs circular reels with forty-two exposures per reel. The interval of exposure varies from 1/10 to 1/100 of a second. (Rheem Califone; $135.00.)

18. *Speed-i-o-Scope:* A tachistoscopic attachment for slide or filmstrip projectors having a front lens diameter of 2 1/16 inches. It permits varying the interval of exposure from "time" to 1/100 of a second. (Society for Visual Education; $97.65.)

19. *Standard Film Strip or Slide Tachistoscope:* Standard Tachistoscope utilizes a Viewlex Projector. This particular projector projects either slides or filmstrips. The standard shutter is attached to the lens barrel. The exposure durations are 1/125, 1/60, 1/30, 1/8, 1/4, 1/2, and 1 second. (Lafayette Instrument Company; $179.00.)

20. *Tachist-O-Flasher:* A tachistoscope that projects single frame filmstrips for individual or group training. (Learning Through Seeing; $14.50.)

21. *Tach-X:* A tachistoscope using filmstrips which permits varying the interval of exposure from 1 1/2 seconds to 1/100 of a second. (Educational Development Laboratories; $210.)

22. *Viewtach:* A simply operated four-speed tachistoscopic device for individual or small group use. (Learning Through Seeing; $59.50.)

Visualizer: A hand-held tachistoscope requiring no electric power. Three speed-settings are available: 1/25, 1/50, or 1/100 of a second. The machine is specifically designed for presentation of units of the Better Reading Program. (Better Reading Program, Inc.; $24.95 for Visualizer and sample material.)

23. VS-1 *Tachistoscope:* A tachistoscope adaptable to any projector which has a lens barrel diameter between 1 7/8 inches to 2 1/2 inches O.D. Shutter speeds are 1/125, 1/60, 1/30, 1/15, 1/4, 1/2, and 1 second. (Lafayette Instrument Company; $94.00.)

Controlled readers and pacers

1. AVR *Reading Rateometer:* An inexpensive device designed for individual use. It consists of an electrically driven plastic bar which descends over the page at a speed determined by the user. (Audio-Visual Research; $39.95.)

2. *Cenco Reading Pacer:* A nonelectric, student-operated reading device especially designed for use with sets of lesson rolls available on four levels—Child, Pre-High-School, Adult, and Pre-College. (Cenco; $40.00; each set of roles, $30.00.)

3. *Controlled Reader:* A machine designed for group work (individual pupils can use it, however.) It employs a filmstrip projector which exposes printed material on a screen at varying rates of speed as determined by the operator. The material can be exposed one line at a time in a left-to-right manner by employing a moving slot. (Educational Developmental Laboratories, Inc.; $290; a smaller model, the Controlled Reader Junior, is available for $220.)

4. *Prep Pacer:* A pacing device which impels a student to higher reading speeds by lowering a disk over any printed page. Speeds ranging from 80 to 3,000 words per minute are possible. It operates on 110 volts and has a built-in calculator. (The Reading Laboratory, Inc.; $49.50.)

5. *Shadowscope Reading Pacer:* A device designed for individual use. It employs an inch-wide beam of light to pace the user's reading speed. The horizontal beam gradually descends over the page at a speed controlled by the user. (Psychotechnics, Inc.; $94.00; case, $27.50.)

6. SRA *Reading Accelerator, Model III:* A device designed for individual use. It is constructed of metal and employs a mechanically operated shutter which descends over the page of a book at a speed determined by the user. (Science Research Associates; $68.95.)

7. SRA *Reading Accelerator, Model IV:* A lightweight plastic version of the foregoing device. It weighs one and a half pounds. (Science Research Associates; $48.95.)

8. SRA *Reading Accelerator, Model V:* A lightweight plastic device weighing nineteen ounces. Reading exposure speeds range from 16 to 2,200 words per minute. (Science Research Associates; $22.95.)

9. *Tachomatic 500:* A device designed for group work (individuals or small groups can use it, too). It is specifically designed for the presentation of Tachomatic film essays, in single line, two or three fixations per line, at rates from 100 to 1,200 words per minute. (Psychotechnics, Inc.; $325.)

10. *TT-50 Reading Pacer:* A spring-operated device designed for individual use. An adjustable aluminum reading wing descends over the page at a speed determined by the user. This can range between 80 to 3,000 words per minute. (Teaching Technology Corporation; $44.50.)

11. TTC *Pacer:* A device requiring no electricity or batteries. It is powered by a lifetime governor control spring. Adjustable to speeds from 80 to 3,600 words per minute. (Milliron; $44.50.)

Corrective Practice Materials for Improving Rate of Comprehension

When individual pupils or groups of pupils are deficient in rate of comprehension, corrective practices can be individualized by using *teacher-made material* such as follows:

1. Magazine articles that are fairly easy and interesting for the grade being taught are ideally suited for practice in improving rate of comprehension. It is suggested that expository articles, 500 to 1,000 words in length, be mounted on cardboard. On the back of the cardboard, ten questions pertaining to the article should appear. A library-card pocket can be used to conceal a slip of paper on which the answers to the questions are written. A file of similar articles should be evolved so pupils can be given periodic practice in improving their comprehension rate. Each pupil is encouraged to keep his own progress chart and to enter into vigorous competition with himself. (See page 150 for information on giving informal speed tests.)

2. Provide pupils with three-by-five-inch cards. Show them how to expose a line of print very briefly by means of a quick pull-push movement with the fingers. Encourage pupils to practice in this manner so they broaden their recognition span. (For use with individual pupils, potentially self-directive.)

3. Provide pupils with paragraphs in which they are instructed to underline key words. The selection with key words underlined can appear on the back of the exercise. (For use with individual pupils, potentially self-directive.)

4. Provide pupils with selections in which they are instructed to insert vertical lines between words to highlight the phrasing. The selection with lines inserted to show proper phrasing can appear on the back of the exercise. (For use with individual pupils, potentially self-directive.)

5. Provide a variety of easy and interesting reading materials and encourage pupils to do a large amount of pleasurable reading. When pupils read interesting materials, they become eager to learn what is going to happen. This results in a natural increase in reading rate.

Corrective Practice Material for Improving Deficiencies in Locating Information

When individual pupils or groups of pupils are deficient in their ability to locate information, corrective practice can be individualized by using materials and techniques such as the following:

1. Provide pupils with a pack of cards on each of which a topic appears. Pupils are directed to place the cards in alphabetical order. Numbers can be written on the backs of the cards to indicate correct sequence. (For use with individual pupils, potentially self-directive.)
2. Provide pupils with a list of words and instruct them to place these in alphabetical order. The correct sequence can appear on the back of the exercise. (For use with individual pupils, potentially self-directive.)
3. Remove a page from the table of contents of a discarded book and mount it on cardboard. Follow the selection by specific questions such as "How many topics are listed?" "On what page would you first find information about __?" "What kind of book do you think this was?" Correct answers can appear on the back of the exercise. (For use with individual pupils, potentially self-directive.)
4. The index of the want ads from a daily paper can be cut out and mounted on a piece of cardboard. Pupils are asked questions such as "In what section would you look if you wished to buy a violin?" "Where would you look if you were interested in used furniture?" Correct answer can appear on the back of the exercise. (For use with individual pupils, potentially self-directive.)
5. The index of the features from the Sunday paper can be cut out and mounted on a piece of cardboard. Pupils are asked questions such as "On what page would you find an article about space travel?" "If you wish to go to the movies, where would you find the theaters listed?" Correct answers can appear on the back of the exercise. (For use with individual pupils, potentially self-directive.)
6. Provide pupils with a series of questions based on an indexed book to which they have access. Pupils are directed to indicate the key word in the question which appears in the index, for example, "How much *iron ore* is mined yearly in the United States?" Correct answers

can appear on the back of the exercise. (For use with individual pupils, potentially self-directive.)

7. Ask pupils which of four numbered words or phrases, if looked up in an index, would *not* be likely to lead to the answer of a given question; for example, "What water routes in America are considered important? 1. rivers 2. lakes 3. canals 4. rainstorms." Correct answers can appear on the back of the exercise. (For use with individual pupils, potentially self-directive.)

8. Provide pupils with a question and instruct them to think of headings under which the information might be found if an index were consulted. Possible correct answers can appear on the back of the exercise. (For use with individual pupils, potentially self-directive.)

9. Provide pupils with a list of reference books to which they have had access. Follow this by a series of questions. Pupils are instructed to indicate which reference books would be consulted to answer the questions involved. Correct answers can appear on the back of the exercise. (For use with individual pupils, potentially self-directive.)

Corrective Practice Material for Improving Deficiencies in Reading Maps, Charts, Tables, and Graphs

When individual pupils or groups of pupils are deficient in their ability to read maps, charts, tables, and graphs, corrective practice can be individualized by using materials and techniques such as the following:

1. Provide pupils with exercises consisting of mounted maps, charts, tables, and graphs that have been taken from discarded books or magazines. Write a series of questions which pertain to the interpretation and use of each. For example, a bar graph pertaining to the annual oil production of Texas, California, Louisiana, Oklahoma, and Kansas might be followed by true-and-false statements such as "Oklahoma produces more oil than California." "The state that produces the most oil is Texas." A map of Sweden might be followed by questions such as "What is the name of the river passing through Goteburg?" "What city is located farthest south in Sweden?" Correct answers to questions can appear on the back of the exercises. (For use with individual pupils, potentially self-directive.)

2. Provide pupils with data of various kinds. Direct them to prepare their own charts, graphs, and tables to represent these data. Correct

representations can appear on the back of the exercises. (For use with individual pupils, potentially self-directive.)

Corrective Practice Material for Improving Deficiencies in Outlining Skill

When individual pupils or groups of pupils are deficient in their ability to outline,* corrective practice can be individualized by using the following materials and techniques:

1. Provide pupils with paragraphs followed by a simplified outline of the main ideas and related details. Follow this by comparable paragraphs and a skeletal outline. Pupils are instructed to complete the skeletal outline. The correct outline can appear on the back of the exercise. (For use with individual pupils, potentially self-directive.)

2. List main ideas and related details in sequential order but do not indicate any degree of subordination. Pupils are directed to show subordination by numbering, lettering, and indenting properly. The correct form can appear on the back of the exercise. (For use with individual pupils, potentially self-directive.)

3. Provide pupils with a number of main ideas and related details in mixed order. Pupils are directed to straighten out the sequence and show subordination by numbering, lettering, and indenting properly. The correct outline can appear on the back of the exercise. (For use with individual pupils, potentially self-directive.)

4. Provide pupils with a number of paragraphs. Pupils are directed to discern the main ideas and related details and put them into proper outline form. The correct outline can appear on the back of the exercise. (For use with individual pupils, potentially self-directive.)

Corrective Practice Material for Improving Deficiencies in Summarizing

When individual pupils or groups of pupils are deficient in their ability to summarize what they have read, corrective practice can be individualized by using the following materials and techniques:

1. Refer pupils to a story in a book to which they have access. Place pictures which depict the story in an envelope together with some

---

*Since outlining skill is dependent on the ability to detect main ideas and related details, exercises designed to develop these subskills should be reviewed.

which are unrelated to the story. Instruct pupils to find the pictures that depict the story and to place these in proper sequence. A numbering scheme on the backs of the proper pictures can make this exercise self-corrective. (For use with individual pupils, potentially self-directive.)

2. Refer pupils to a story in a book to which they have access. Pupils are instructed to read the selection and then draw a series of pictures which tell the story. (For use with individual pupils, potentially self-directive.)

3. Provide pupils with a selection, consisting of several paragraphs, which is followed by a summary. Pupils are instructed to read the selection and then evaluate the summary in light of the following questions.

   a. Does the summary include all main ideas?
      (1) List any omitted.
   b. Does the summary include all related details?
      (1) List any omitted.
   c. Does the summary include any unnecessary details?
      (1) List these.
   d. Does the summary keep ideas in proper order?
   e. Does the summary use complete sentences?

   Correct answers can appear on the back of the exercise. (For use with individual pupils, potentially self-directive.)

4. Provide pupils with a selection, consisting of several paragraphs, which is followed by several summaries. Pupils are instructed to read the selection and then decide which summary is best. The correct answer can appear on the back of the exercise. (For use with individual pupils, potentially self-directive.)

PROBLEMS FOR ORAL AND WRITTEN DISCUSSION

1. Select five principles of corrective instruction from the following list and discuss how they could be implemented in a school reading program.

   a. Correction must be based on a diagnosis of reading difficulties.
   b. A variety of materials should be provided.
   c. Materials used should be self-directive.
   d. Materials must be of optimum difficulty.
   e. Materials must be ample for each type of difficulty.
   f. Materials must sustain the child's interest.
   g. Materials must not carry a grade level and should have an appealing format.

h. The teacher should be enthusiastic and reassuring.
i. The teacher should be alert to manifestations of sensory defects.
j. The teacher should be acquainted with the child's home environment.
k. The teacher's relationship with the child should be wholesome.
l. Hazards to the child's learning should be ameliorated whenever possible.
m. The teacher must employ a variety of techniques.
n. The child should be made aware of his reading difficulties.
o. The child should be made aware of his progress and keep a record of it.
p. The child should progress at his own rate.
q. The program must not interfere with other enjoyable school activities.
r. The program must foster a child's self-confidence.
s. Recreational reading under supervision must become an integral part of the program.
t. The program should engender in the child a love of reading.

2. Evaluate the place of workbooks as self-corrective materials.
3. Obtain a workbook in reading. Set up criteria for its evaluation and apply the criteria.
4. Procure several workbooks in reading on two or more levels of difficulty. Dissect, combine, and assemble the workbooks to form a ready file of corrective reading material as described in this chapter.
5. Obtain a completed cumulative record for a pupil with a reading problem and record all pertinent data on the Diagnostic Reading Summary appearing in chapter 6. What additional data are needed in order to provide a more complete diagnosis?
6. Select a pupil with a reading problem. Apply and consult all available and appropriate diagnostic techniques needed to analyze his problem. Utilize the Reading Checklist and the Reading Summary (see chapter 6).
7. Organize a self-corrective program in reading for a pupil who is deficient in reading comprehension, indicating the pupil's grade placement, instructional level, intelligence, degree of retardation, reading expectancy, and specific difficulties to be corrected. Select the corrective material to be used, indicating type and difficulty.

REFERENCES

1. LUELLA COLE, *The Improvement of Reading*, copyright 1938 by Holt, Rinehart and Winston, Inc., copyright 1966 by Luella Cole, pp. 142-143.
2. RUSSELL STAUFFER, "A Study of Prefixes in the Thorndike List to Establish a List of Prefixes That Should Be Taught in the Elementary School," *Journal of Educational Research* (1942):453-458.
3. FRANCIS ROBINSON, *Effective Study* (New York: Harper and Row, Publishers, 1946), p. 28.

4. GEORGE SPACHE, *Toward Better Reading* (Champaign, Ill.: Garrard Publishing Co., 1962), pp. 260-264.
5. ROBERT KARLIN, "Machines and Reading: A Review of Research," *Clearing House* (February 1958):352.

SELECTED READINGS

BOND, GUY, and MILES TINKER. *Reading Problems: Their Diagnosis and Correction.* 2nd ed. New York: Appleton-Century-Crofts, 1967, chs. 11, 16.

CARTER, HOMER, and DOROTHY McGINNIS. *Diagnosis and Treatment of the Disabled Reader.* New York: The Macmillan Co., 1970, ch. 13.

DECHANT, EMERALD. *Improving the Teaching of Reading.* Englewood Cliffs, N. J.: Prentice-Hall, Inc., 1964, ch. 13.

HARRIS, ALBERT. *How to Increase Reading Ability.* 5th ed. New York: David McKay Co., Inc., 1970, chs. 15, 16.

KARLIN, ROBERT. *Teaching Elementary Reading.* New York: Harcourt Brace Jovanovich, Inc., 1971, ch. 6.

SCHUBERT, DELWYN. *Readings in Reading: Practice-Theory-Research.* New York: Thomas Y. Crowell Co., 1968, selections 31, 32.

SPACHE, GEORGE. *Toward Better Reading.* Champaign, Ill.: Garrard Publishing Co., 1963, chs. 4, 14, 15.

———. *Reading in the Elementary School.* 2nd ed. Boston: Allyn and Bacon, Inc., 1969, ch. 14.

10

Multilevel
Materials and Devices

Chapters 8 and 9 were devoted to descriptions of materials, methods, and devices* that were designed rather specifically to meet individual deficiencies in word perception, word analysis, comprehension, and study skills. The content of this chapter is devoted to descriptions of commercial and teacher-made materials and devices applicable to several kinds of reading and/or study skills on various levels of difficulty. These materials are designed for use with individuals or groups.

MAGIC SLATES

Some heavy cardboard and a sheet of acetate can be turned into a magic slate. After the acetate is placed over the cardboard, the sides are taped, leaving the top and bottom open. With a magic slate of the proper size (9 inches by 12 inches is recommended) individual exercises can be slipped between the cardboard and the sheet of acetate and marked with crayon. Crayon marks will rub off very easily with a dry cloth or cleansing tissue. With five or six magic slates on hand, it isn't difficult to keep a sizable number of children working independently with a variety of materials of an individualized nature.

Many teachers provide children with answer files so they can carry on independently with a minimum amount of supervision. There is, however, an ingenious way of making an acetate-covered exercise of alternate choice items immediately self-corrective. To do this, the teacher should encircle the correct answers on the surface of a second sheet

*Machines and other devices for improving rate of comprehension appear in chapter 9, pages 256-261.

of transparent acetate which is hinged to the one on which the pupil will record his responses. The acetate sheet carrying the answers is then folded under the cardboard. When a pupil completes the exercise, he swings the hinged sheet of acetate over the one on which he has written his answers. If the superimposed key does not coincide with his answers, the pupil knows he has erred.

STUDY-SCOPE

The Study-Scope* uses basic principles of programmed instruction and provides students with a method of self-instruction. It employs two plastic cylinders that fit together like a telescope. The outside one is opaque, with a question window and an answer window which is revealed when the pupil twists the Scope a quarter turn. The information, which has been printed commercially or by the teacher or student on a sheet, is inserted into the clear inner cylinder.

The Study-Scope Classroom Laboratory for Reading contains 588 programs that cover all the basic reading skills taught in grades 1, 2, and 3.

Study-Scope Laboratories are designed to enable the teacher to individualize instruction in the primary grades. It is also excellent for remedial use at the intermediate level and is invaluable at any elementary grade level as a means of diagnosing reading problems and providing for review work. (For use with individual pupils; potentially self-directive; Study-Scope Reading Laboratory, including 15 Study Scopes and Teacher's Manual, $99.50.)

THE ELECTRIC BOARD

A relatively inexpensive and versatile teaching device which intrigues pupils of all ages is the electric board. It is entirely self-instructive and can be used to teach many things. Through its use pupils can learn to match synonyms, antonyms, and blends, as well as questions and answers of all sorts.

In constructing an electric board the first item needed is a wooden board. Pegboard is highly recommended because of the ready-made holes. The board may be of any desired dimensions, but twenty-four by thirty inches seems to be an optimum size.

In addition to the board, the following materials are needed: stove bolts (about $\frac{1}{2}$ inch in length), small pegboard hooks, No. 25 copper wire, a radio battery (about $4\frac{1}{2}$ volts), a flashlight bulb, some three-

*Available through Benefic Press, 10300 W. Roosevelt Rd., Westchester, Ill. 60153.

by-five-inch cards. The entire set of equipment needed should not cost more than $5.00.

Two-thirds of the board (from left to right) can be devoted to spaced stove bolts that are placed so sufficient room remains directly under each for a hook on which will hang a three-by-five-inch card. Questions for which an answer must be found are written on these cards.

The answer column is set up at the right of the board. It consists of a series of bolts placed in a single, vertical row. Sufficient space between the bolts or to the right of the bolts is provided for small hooks on which answer cards will hang.

On the reverse side of the board, pieces of insulated wire are used to connect a bolt at the left of the board with one of the bolts in the answer column to the right. The battery is fastened to the base of the board on the back. A small hole is made in the board for inserting the bulb.

One of the battery terminals is now connected with one of the lamp-socket terminals. On the other battery terminal, a piece of free wire is connected. This wire should be long enough to reach completely around the board to the bolts in the answer column at the right. Another free wire is connected to the remaining lamp-socket terminal. This wire should be long enough to reach the remaining bolts (questions are under these) on the front of the board.

When the ends of both of the free wires are in contact with two bolts that have been connected behind the board, the light goes on. The pupil knows he has made a correct association.

TEACHER-MADE FILED MATERIAL

Teachers can evolve their own files of material by cutting up old copies of children's magazines or newspapers. Typewritten copies of children's own stories can be kept in notebooks for easy, interesting reading. Sometimes, too, copies of discarded readers can be obtained, dissected, and accompanied by comprehension, vocabulary, and word-attack exercises of a self-directive nature. Workbooks of different types can be cut up and incorporated into a valuable file of self-corrective exercises.

Stiff-paper folders of different colors can be used to house separate numbers of *My Weekly Reader*. Upper grades can be provided with articles drawn from back issues of *Scholastic Scope* magazine and the *Reader's Digest*. These can be mounted in stiff-paper covers and placed in a subject file.

Children can be encouraged to assist in the cutting, pasting, and mounting of materials. They can make attractive illustrated covers for certain stories and can classify them under headings like "Rocket Travel," "Airplanes," "The Wild West."

COMMERCIALLY-MADE FILED MATERIAL

Files of commercially-made material such as the SRA Reading Laboratories and the EDL Study Skills-Library* have self-directive exercises accompanying them which pertain to practically all areas of reading improvement and study skills. These are extremely valuable in any program that stresses individualization. Following is a description of these materials.

SRA Reading Laboratory 1A (Grade 1)

These self-corrective materials are written on seven carefully graded reading levels—1.2, 1.4, 1.7, 2.0, 2.3, 2.6, and 3.0—and are designed to accommodate the range of individual differences found in first-grade classrooms. Skills provided for include basic sight vocabulary, word attack, vocabulary development, reading comprehension, and listening comprehension. A color scheme is employed to designate grade levels. Additional materials for the individual pupil, class, and teacher are included also. Replacement materials can be purchased. (Price of kit, $69.95; student book, $.81.)

SRA Reading Laboratory 1B (Grade 2)

These self-corrective materials are written on eight carefully graded reading levels—1.4, 1.7, 2.0, 2.3, 2.6, 3.0, 3.5, and 4.0—and are designed to accommodate the range of individual differences found in second-grade classrooms. Skills provided for include basic sight vocabulary, word attack, vocabulary development, reading comprehension, and listening comprehension. A color scheme is employed to designate difficulty levels. Additional materials for the individual pupil, class, and teacher are included also. Replacement materials can be purchased. (Price of kit, $69.95; student book, $.81.)

SRA Reading Laboratory 1C (Grade 3)

These self-corrective materials are written on ten carefully graded reading levels varying from 1.4 to 5.0. They are designed to accommodate the range of individual differences found in third-grade classrooms. Skills provided for include basic sight vocabulary, word attack,

---

*Available through Science Research Associates, Inc., and Coast Visual Education Co., Inc., respectively. See Appendix G for complete addresses.

vocabulary development, reading comprehension, and listening comprehension. A color scheme is employed to designate difficulty levels. Additional materials for the individual pupil, class, and teacher are included also. Replacement materials can be purchased. (Price of kit, $69.95; student book, $.81.)

SRA Reading Laboratory 1—Word Games (Grades 1-6)

This box contains the phonics portion of the reading laboratory program. It is a separate laboratory designed to supplement laboratories 1a, 1b, and 1c in grades 1, 2, and 3. It can also be used successfully in grades 4, 5, and 6. It consists of forty-four, color-coded, word-building games that help students develop their reading vocabulary to match their listening vocabulary. (Price of kit, $106.95; student book, $.21.)

SRA Reading Laboratory Series (Grades 4-6)

Each laboratory kit contains Power Builders with key cards; Rate Builders with key booklets; a Teacher's Handbook containing Listening Skill Builders; a Student Record Book; and colored pencils with which students chart their progress.

Power Builders are illustrated, four-page reading selections. These are accompanied by exercises designed to help students develop vocabulary, comprehension, and language skills. Fifteen Power Builders are provided at each of the ten reading levels.

Rate Builders are short, timed reading selections designed to develop reading speed and concentration. Each selection is followed by comprehension questions. Fifteen Rate Builders are provided at each of the ten reading levels.

Listening Skill Builders are selections that are read to the students to develop their ability to understand, retain, and analyze what they hear. The Listening Skill Builders are included in the Teacher's Handbook. After hearing each selection, the students test their comprehension by answering questions in the Student Record Book.

Description	Price
Reading Laboratory 2A for grade 4 (reading levels 2.0, 2.5, 3.0, 3.5, 4.0, 4.5, 5.0, 5.5., 6.0, 7.0)	$74.95
Reading Laboratory 2B for grade 5 (reading levels 2.5, 3.0, 3.5, 4.0, 4.5, 5.0, 5.5, 6.0, 7.0, 8.0)	74.95
Reading Laboratory 2C for grade 6 (reading levels 3.0, 3.5, 4.0, 4.5, 5.0, 5.5, 6.0, 7.0, 8.0, 9.0)	74.95
Student Record Books for Labs 2A, 2B, and 2C	.58

SRA Reading Laboratory Series
(Grades 7-12)

Each laboratory kit contains Power Builders with key cards; one Teacher's Handbook with Listening Skill Builder selections for 3A, 3B, and 4A, plus Listening-Notetaking Skill Builder selections for 3B and 4A; Rate Builders for improving reading speed; and a Student Record Book.

Power Builders are four-page reading selections that are designed to help students develop vocabulary, comprehension, and word-attack skills. From fifteen to twenty are provided at each reading level. Subject matter varies, including biography, social studies, natural science, adventure, and everyday life. The booklets also include comprehension checks and exercises for developing vocabulary and skill in phonic and structural analysis of words. Key Cards are used by students to check responses.

Listening Skill Builders for 3A, 3B, and 4A are included in the Teacher's Handbook and are designed to develop students' ability to sift, understand, and retain what they hear. The teacher reads selections, and students answer comprehension questions in their record books.

Listening-Notetaking Skill Builders are for 3B and 4A. Students listen carefully as the teacher reads the lesson from the Teacher's Handbook, then organize and record their thoughts on paper and compare their notes with models provided.

Rate Builders are designed to develop speed and concentration. Each card includes a short reading selection followed by comprehension questions to be answered in the Student Record Book. The teacher limits reading and answering time to three minutes. Students check their responses with the Rate Builder Key Booklet.

The Student Record Book contains material on Reading Laboratory procedures, reading and study skills, and listening skills. Students use it to record all comprehension responses and to chart their daily progress. One is recommended for each student.

Description	Price
Reading Laboratory 3A for grades 7-9. (reading levels 3.0, 3.5, 4.0, 5.0, 6.0, 7.0, 8.0, 9.0, 10.0, 11.0)	$74.95
Reading Laboratory 3B for grades 8-10. (reading levels 5.0, 5.5, 6.0, 7.0, 8.0, 9.0, 10.0, 11.0, 12.0)	74.95
Reading Laboratory 4A for grades 9-12 (reading levels 8.0, 9.0, 10.0, 11.0, 12.0, 13.0, 14.0)	74.95
Student Record Books for Labs 3A, 3B, and 4A	.58

SRA Dimensions Series

Each dimensions kit focuses on a different interest area. The reading selections explore the major theme, presenting a wide range of information, viewpoints, and writing styles. The stories, selected for their high interest level, are designed to make students want to read.

Countries and Cultures explores the world, presenting stories about life as others live it. The 120 selections include stories about the fire-walking natives of the South Seas, the flea markets of Europe, going to school in Ghana, security measures at Monte Carlo, life on an Israeli kibbutz, and other exciting vignettes. Each selection is followed by comprehension questions and questions that require critical thinking.

We Are Black, a program about black people for all students, contains 120 four-page reading selections about famous and unknown, contemporary and historical, American and non-American black people. The kit is designed to give today's student an opportunity to enjoy and improve his reading with stories about people he should know, people whose stories have been neglected in traditional textbooks.

We Are Black is appropriate for use in all grades from elementary through high school. The selections vary in length from 300 to 900 words. Each selection is accompanied by a Skill Card. The student answers the Skill Card questions in his own Student Book.

Manpower and Natural Resources is for use in high school developmental reading, guidance, vocational, and technical courses, and all types of adult retraining programs. It is designed to enrich basic reading or special training programs with a wealth of reading material (300 selections) from popular books and magazines. Topics fall into three broad categories: (1) conservation and the skills involved; (2) related facts of natural history, geology, botany, zoology, weather, conservation, and mineralogy; (3) occupational skills such as those of the welder, carpenter, telephone repairman, soil scientist, and electrician. Comprehension questions follow each selection, and Key Booklets are used to check answers.

An American Album includes varied reading selections that constitute an anecdotal history of America's growth from Columbus's discovery to President Kennedy's assassination. It contains 300 four-page reading selections divided into six reading levels with fifty stories at each level. A comprehension check is provided at the end of each story. The wealth of subject matter can give the child insight into the origins and development of the American people and their institutions.

Description	Price
Countries and Cultures Kit (reading levels 4.5-9.5)	$52.50
Student Book	.33
We Are Black Kit (reading levels 2.0-6.0)	
Student Book	.36
Manpower and Natural Resources Kit	74.25
An American Album	74.25

SRA Reading for Understanding (Grades 3-12 and College)

This individualized reading program is designed to develop the student's ability to grasp the full meaning of what he reads by teaching him to analyze ideas and reach logical conclusions. It is available in three editions, each accommodating a number of grade levels.

Exercises consist of a card bearing ten short, provocative paragraphs in areas such as education, politics, history, art, science, business, sports, agriculture, and philosophy. The student reads the selection and chooses the best of four suggested conclusions, implied in the selection but not stated directly. Correct conclusions are provided in the Answer Key booklets.

Each of the three units in the series includes 400 lesson cards arranged in progressive levels of difficulty. A simple Placement Test indicates the level at which each student should begin. The student progresses to more difficult levels as he demonstrates proficiency.

Each student works independently, recording his responses in his Student Record Book, checking his own work with answer keys provided, and charting his progress.

Description	Price
Reading for Understanding—General Edition (Grades 5 through College)	$44.55
Reading for Understanding—Junior Edition (Grades 3 through 8)	44.55
Reading for Understanding—Senior Edition (Grades 8 through 12)	44.55
Student Record Book for any of the foregoing programs	.33

SRA Pilot Library Series (Grades 4-9)

The Pilot Library Series is designed to bridge the gap between reading training and independent reading with short excerpts from noted literature. Each Pilot Library set contains seventy-two selections from full-length books to whet the young reader's appetite and lead him to the original books. The selections, called Pilot Books, are excerpts of twenty-four or thirty-two pages carefully selected for their interest appeal and reading level.

Pilot Library Books are keyed to Power Builder selections in a particular Reading Laboratory kit so that a student who finds a selection interesting can go to the Pilot Library Books for further reading on the same topic and at his individual reading level. A short bibliography at the end of the Pilot Library Book leads him to other books of similar content and difficulty. Key Booklets permit him to check his own comprehension exercises, contained in the Student Record Book.

Description	Price
Pilot Library Set 2A for grade 4 (reading levels 2.0, 2.3, 2.6, 3.0, 3.5, 4.0, 4.5, 5.0, 5.5, 6.0, 6.5, 7.0)	$69.50
Pilot Library Set 2B for grade 5 (reading levels 3.0, 3.5, 4.0, 4.5, 5.0, 6.0, 6.5, 7.0, 7.5, 8.0)	69.50
Pilot Library Set 2C for grades 6-7 (reading levels 4.0, 4.3, 4.6, 5.0, 5.5, 6.0, 6.5, 7.0, 7.5, 8.0, 8.5, 9.0)	69.50
Pilot Library Set 3B for grades 8-9 (reading levels 5.0, 5.5, 6.0, 7.0, 8.0, 9.0, 10.0, 11.0, 12.0)	69.50
Student Record Books for Pilot Library Sets 2A, 2B, 2C, and 3B	.59

EDL Study-Skills Library

The Study-Skills Library* consists of a series of kits containing graded and sequential exercises for grade levels three through nine. On each grade level, there are three kits: one each in the areas of science, social studies, and reference skills. A total of twenty-one kits are available.

The major study skills developed include interpretation (detecting author's purpose, drawing conclusions, making comparisons, making inferences, visualizing); evaluation (judging relevancy, noting significance, recognizing validity, verifying accuracy); organization (finding main ideas, selecting details to support main ideas, outlining, classifying, determining sequential order); and reference (using alphabetical order, using parts of a book, using reference material, using library facilities).

A Study Skills Library kit represents one reading level in science, social studies, or reference skills. Ten text-related lessons with answer keys are contained in each kit, along with 70 worksheets per selection, or a total of 700 worksheets in a box.

These self-corrective and self-directive materials can be used with individual pupils or a group of pupils.

*Available through Coast Visual Education Co., Inc., 5610 Hollywood Blvd., Hollywood, Calif. 90028.

Description	Level	Price
C Science	3	$15.00
D Science	4	15.00
E Science	5	15.00
F Science	6	15.00
G Science	7	15.00
H Science	8	15.00
I Science	9	15.00
CC Social Studies	3	15.00
DD Social Studies	4	15.00
EE Social Studies	5	15.00
FF Social Studies	6	15.00
GG Social Studies	7	15.00
HH Social Studies	8	15.00
II Social Studies	9	15.00
CCC Reference	3	15.00
DDD Reference	4	15.00
EEE Reference	5	15.00
FFF Reference	6	15.00
GGG Reference	7	15.00
HHH Reference	8	15.00
III Reference	9	15.00
Orientation Kit C	3	6.00
Orientation Kit D-J	4-9	6.00
Study Skills Record (packets of 35)	—	1.50
Study Skills Library Teacher's Guide	—	1.00

The Literature Samplers

The junior edition (reading levels 2-9 for grades 4 and up) consists of a boxed kit of 120 word-for-word excerpts from a wide variety of popular books for children. Stories are grouped in six high-interest areas: Tales of Courage and Daring, Fun for All, Sports, People, Animals, and Mystery.

The secondary edition (reading levels 5-11 for grades 7 and up) consists of a boxed kit of 144 word-for-word excerpts from a wide variety of books especially liked by teen-agers. Interest areas represented are Adventure, Mystery, Humor, Success, Sports, Rebellion, Science and Science Fiction, Animals, People, and Teen-Age World.

On both levels, a *how* and *why* question card follows each selection and is accompanied by a discussion card which informs the pupil which answer is best and why it is best. (For use with individual pupils or a group of pupils; The Junior Edition, including 120 book previews, 120 discussions, 30 pupil logs, and a teacher's guide, $52.50;

The Secondary Edition, including 144 book previews, 144 discussions, 1 pupil log, and a teacher's guide, $54.50.)*

Building Word Power

These self-corrective materials are designed to help students identify the meaning of unknown words through context clues, establish the meaning of a whole word if the base word is known through structural analysis, and assist students in developing their comprehension skills by learning to find the main idea or central thought of a paragraph. The kit is designed for use by any student reading on or above the fifth-grade level. (For use with individual pupils or an entire classroom, potentially self-directive; $40.00.)†

Word-Analysis Practice

These materials consist of three sets of thirty cards each for intermediate grade levels. Level A cards contain 720 words and can be used with pupils of low fourth-grade reading ability. Levels B and C cards contain 1,200 words each and can be used respectively with average pupils of fourth- to low fifth- and average fifth- to low sixth-grade reading ability.

The pupils are required to read words and decide under which of three suggested categories the words are to be classed. Pupils then write each word on paper under its proper classification. To accomplish this, the individual pupil, according to the author, must first read and recognize each word. If the word is not in his reading vocabulary, his first attack is phonetic. Since he knows the word must fit one of the category headings, he has a meaning clue he can apply to verify or reject the result of his phonetic analysis. He therefore gets practice in combining phonetic analysis with context clues. (For use with individual pupils, potentially self-directive; three sets, $1.80 each.)‡

Mission: Read

Mission: Read§ consists of four attractively packaged kits that are multiethnic in approach and content. The stories involve tales of ad-

*Learning Research Associates, Inc., 1501 Broadway, New York, N. Y. 10036.
†Charles E. Merrill Books, Inc., 1300 Alum Creek Drive, Columbus, O. 43216.
‡By Donald Durrell et al., comes in three 7-by-10-inch envelopes and is published by Harcourt Brace Jovanovich, Inc.
§Available through Random House/Singer, School Division, Westminster, Md. 21157.

venture, realism, fantasy, mystery, and humor that are written to appeal to elementary school readers both emotionally and intellectually. The twenty different stories in each kit are organized into four units of five stories each. Each of these four units focuses upon a central subject, theme, character, or idea. Each story is only four pages in length, allowing the child a sense of confidence and accomplishment as he successfully completes one story and moves on to the next. The reading level remains the same within a single kit, while the skills developed through the Skill Exercise Sheets increase in difficulty. Each selection, numbered and color-coded according to group, includes comprehension questions for discussion.

Each of the four kits contains materials for up to twenty students. These involve twenty copies of twenty original stories; twenty copies of twenty different Skill Exercises for developing word-attack, comprehension, and vocabulary skills; a set of answer keys; and a comprehensive Teacher's Guide that contains individual lesson plans for each story, answers for all exercises and questions, scope and sequence charts of reading skills, and a detailed statement of the purpose and philosophy of the program.

Description	Price
Launch	$74.25
Challenge	74.25
Search	74.25
Reach	74.25

Reading Skill File

Administered as both a testing and teaching aid, the 180 timed reading exercises and 107 supplementary exercises included in the Skill File* provide the student with an opportunity to measure his progress in practical prose and to develop his skills in the language arts.

The timed readings, containing vocabulary and comprehension questions, are divided into nine levels of difficulty (equivalent to the fifth through thirteenth grades) and five subject categories: Literature, American and World History, Natural and Social Science, Art and Music and Humor, Sport and Adventure. The Skill File is designed to teach critical reading skills, greater comprehension, increased reading speed, and effective study habits. The supplementary exercises contribute to the development of the student's reading skills through the use of

*Available through The Reading Laboratory, Inc., 55 Day Street, South Norwalk, Conn. 06854, at a cost of $99.50.

prefatory material, sentence jumble, sentence correction, sentence completion and inference, correlated readings, direction reading and visualizing, and visual aids.

The Skill File is accompanied by an Administrator's Guide, a Cal-Q-Rator, and a sample Student Manual. The Administrator's Guide provides a step-by-step presentation of all materials, theories, and techniques of the program, plus detailed lesson plans, complete instructions, and suggested schedules for its administration.

Addison-Wesley Reading Development Kits

This three-kit program* teaches essential word-attack and comprehension skills from early reading level through grade ten. It is designed for the disabled reader in his teens or adult years. Within five subject matter areas—health, law, safety, science, and the world of words—topics of concern to the student (drug abuse, mail fraud, looking for a job, income tax, etc.) are presented.

To build student confidence in their abilities to "go it alone," the authors have carefully constructed each lesson to follow a carefully plotted sequence. Each lesson has three distinct but interrelated and interdependent parts: (1) Getting Ready—vocabulary building exercises, presentation of the new word-attack and/or comprehension skills to be mastered in the lesson; (2) Reading the Selection—a short (350-500 words) selection of high interest in which the student practices the skills presented in Getting Ready; (3) Follow-Up—questions to test comprehension and recall, checks on skill mastery, and open-end questions and activities to extend student interests and experiences.

Description	Price
Kit A: (Early Reading Level) is a learning laboratory designed to aid the disabled reader, older children, and may be used in junior and senior high school or in adult education courses.	$48.00
Kit B: (Reading Level 4-6) contains materials at grade level of approximately 4-6 and may be used in reading improvement program at the junior or senior high school level.	48.00
Kit C: (Reading Level 7-10) is designed for adolescents and adults reading at grade levels 7 through 10 plus and provides secondary school and college reading instructors with a program that provides reading class materials and meets individual interests as well.	67.50

*Available through Addison-Wesley Publishing Co., Inc., Sand Hill Road, Menlo Park, Calif. 94025.

Reading Attainment System

The *Reading Attainment System** consists of two kits. Kit 1 covers reading levels three and four; kit 2 covers reading levels five and six. Each kit contains 120 individual Reading Selections arranged in six color-keyed groups. The reading level gradually increases from group to group, allowing the student to move forward at his own pace.

Each kit has 120 Skill Cards, one for each Reading Selection, color-and-content-matched. These cards contain glossaries of difficult words used in the corresponding Reading Selection, word-attack exercises, and vocabulary-building aids. Also included in each kit are thirty Reader Record Books. Answer keys for the Reading Selections and Skills Cards are included so that students can monitor their own progress. The instructor is provided with a sixty-page guide containing full information on methods of administration, suggested student activities, and a bibliography.

Description	Price
Reading Attainment System 1	$ 99.50
Reading Attainment System 2	99.50
Reading Attainment Systems Combined	189.00
Additional student record books in packages of 30	10.00

Reading Skills Lab

These boxed materials consist of workbooks developed for use in regular classroom situations to serve either basal or individualized reading programs. Each box of the Reading Skills Lab† workbooks contains ten each of three ninety-six-page, consumable workbooks. The books have perforated pages (7″ by 9½″) and are printed in two attractive colors. Also included are two Pupil's Answer Books and one Teacher's Edition for each workbook. The pages are perforated so that they can be removed and given to a number of students at the same time. They are designated "Level 1, Level 2, or Level 3" so that pupils of any grade can use whichever level they need.

In addition to the workbooks, there are sets of diagnostic tests available. These can be administered at the beginning of the school year to help pinpoint each child's strengths and weaknesses.

*Available through Grolier Educational Corp., 845 Third Avenue, New York, N. Y. 10022.
†Available through Houghton Mifflin Co., Department M, 110 Tremont Street, Boston, Mass. 02107.

The three workbooks on Level 1 (fourth grade) include "Unlocking Strange Words," "Overcoming Meaning Difficulties," and "Reading for Different Purposes." Workbooks on Level 2 (fifth grade) include "Overcoming Meaning Difficulties," "Reading for Different Purposes," and "Using Reference Aids." Workbooks on Level 3 (sixth grade) include "Studying Informative Materials," "Using Reference Aids," and "Reading Critically."

Description	Price
Level 1 (Grade 4)	
Box A. Diagnostic Tests	$10.50
Box B. Workbooks	27.00
Level 2 (Grade 5)	
Box A. Diagnostic Tests	10.50
Box B. Workbooks	24.75
Level 3 (Grade 6)	
Box A. Diagnostic Tests	10.50
Box B. Workbooks	24.75

MULTILEVEL BOOKS AND WORKBOOKS

A few of the many multilevel books and workbooks are described here. See chapter 9 for descriptions of additional workbooks.

Specific Skill Series

This series* consists of forty-two workbooks with work sheets for thirty-eight of them. The latter permits optional self-correction. A complete breakdown of the series is as follows:

> Getting the Main Idea, Levels 1 to 6 (Books A, B, C, D, E, F)
> Using the Context, Levels 1 to 6 (Books A, B, C, D, E, F)
> Working with Sounds, Levels 1 to 6 (Books A, B, C, D, E, F)
> Following Directions, Levels 1 to 6 (Books A, B, C, D, E, F)
> Locating the Answer, Levels 1 to 6 (Books A, B, C, D, E, F)
> Getting the Facts, Levels 1 to 6 (Books A, B, C, D, E, F)
> Drawing Conclusions, Levels 1 to 6 (Books A, B, C, D, E, F)
>
> (Each workbook is $.89; each Answer Key is $.10; Work sheets, available for books C through F, are $1.50 per 100.)

Reading Skill Builders

The Reading Skill Builders† are attractive supplementary readers containing articles and stories from *The Reader's Digest* adapted to

*Available through Barnell Loft, Ltd., 111 S. Centre Ave., Rockville Center, N. Y. 11571.

†Available through Reader's Digest Services, Inc., Pleasantville, N. Y. 10570.

eight different reading levels, 1 through 8. These work-type readers combine inviting reading matter with exercises that promote specific reading skills. The reading level of each book is indicated by the number of winged horses on the cover. With the exception of the books at reading level 1, "Parts" at the same reading level may be used interchangeably.

ORIGINAL SERIES

Level 1 (middle months) ....Two Books, Parts A and B	66¢ each.
Level 1 (second semester) .....Two Books, Parts One and Two	66¢ each.
Level 2 ....Three Books, Parts One, Two, Three 90¢ each.
Level 3 ....Three Books, Parts One, Two, Three 90¢ each.
Level 4 ....Three Books, Parts One, Two, Three 90¢ each.
Level 5 ....Three Books, Parts One, Two, Three 90¢ each.
Level 6 ....Three Books, Parts One, Two, Three 90¢ each.
Level 7 ....Two Books, Books One and Two	90¢ each.
Level 8 ....Two Books, Books Three and Four 90¢ each.

NEW SERIES

Level 1 (middle months) ....Two Books, Parts One and Two	66¢ each.
Level 1 plus (second semester) Two Books, Parts One and Two	66¢ each.
Level 2 ....Three Books, Parts One, Two, Three 90¢ each.
Level 3 ....Three Books, Parts One, Two, Three 90¢ each.
Level 4 ....Two Books, Parts One and Two	90¢ each.
Level 5 ....Two Books, Parts One and Two	90¢ each.
Level 6 ....Two Books, Parts One and Two	90¢ each.

Audio lessons are available for the New Series at levels two, four, and six. Music and other sound effects are used to dramatize the selections. (Level 2 Cassettes, $17.85; Level 4 Cassettes, $23.80; Level 6 Cassettes, $11.90.)

SRA Kaleidoscope of Skills: Reading (Grades 5, 6, and 7)

Kaleidoscope is a self-study program* designed for average students. It is especially useful in summer sessions and can be used as a supplement to regular classroom learning under a teacher's direction or as a self-study program at home. The student's book includes a section entitled "To the Parent," which describes the program and suggests ways in which parents can help the student.

*Available through Science Research Associates, Inc., 259 East Erie Street, Chicago, Ill., 60611.

The reading program includes a series of four books for each grade level and a Teacher's Handbook.

Description	Price
Set of 4 books for students entering grade 5	$5.70
Set of 4 books for students entering grade 6	5.70
Set of 4 books for students entering grade 7	5.70
Teacher's Handbook, each	.33

McCall-Crabbs Standard Test Lessons in Reading

These popular booklets* have a combined grade range of two through twelve. Each of the five booklets involved contains seventy-eight lessons that are designed to develop rate of speed and power of comprehension. Multiple-choice-type questions follow each selection, and answer keys which are provided make the exercises self-corrective. Booklets, grade levels, and prices are as follows:

Description	Price
Lesson Booklet A (grade 3)	60¢
Lesson Booklet B (grade 4)	60¢
Lesson Booklet C (grade 5)	60¢
Lesson Booklet D (grade 6)	60¢
Lesson Booklet E (grade 7)	60¢

Each order includes a Manual and Answer Key.
Additional Manuals and Keys are provided free with orders of 25 additional booklets.

Gates-Peardon Reading Exercises

These widely used booklets† total thirteen in number and are designed to strengthen and build reading skills in the elementary grades. They are ideally suited for developmental and remedial use. The booklets contain short selections and employ three types of questions: (1) getting the main idea, (2) following directions, and (3) reading for details. Introductory, Levels A and B (Grade 2), and Preparatory, Levels A and B (grade 3), have the three types of questions following each selection. The Elementary (grade 4), Intermediate (grade 5), and Advanced (grade 6) levels have separate booklets for the main idea, following directions, and reading for details.

*Available through Teachers College Press, 1234 Amsterdam Ave., New York, N.Y. 10027.
†Ibid.

Description	Price
Introductory Level A	55¢
Introductory Level B	55¢
Preparatory A	55¢
Preparatory B	55¢
Elementary SA (What Is Story About?)	60¢
Elementary RD (Can You Remember Details?)	60¢
Elementary FD (Can You Follow Directions?)	60¢
Intermediate SA	60¢
Intermediate RD	60¢
Intermediate FD	60¢
Advanced SA	60¢
Advanced RD	60¢
Advanced FD	60¢
Gates-Peardon Manual	25¢

SRA's New Rochester Occupational Reading Series (Grades 9-12 and Adult)

This series* provides reading instruction and information about the world of work. The material is mature in content but is scaled as low as second-grade reading level. The series emphasizes, in story form, the attitudes and skills that lead to success on the job and in society.

The hard-bound text *The Job Ahead* is printed at three reading levels, but the program is designed so that all three levels can be used in a single class without obvious grouping. The three levels look almost exactly alike, with subject matter, sequence, and illustrations the same. Reading difficulty is varied in terms of story length, vocabulary, and the complexity of sentences and paragraphs.

Description	Price
Level 1 (grade 2 reading level)	
The Job Ahead	$4.50
Exercise Book (set of 5 books)	3.60
Teacher's Guide	1.29
Level 2 (grades 3 and 4 reading levels)	
The Job Ahead	4.50
Exercise Book (set of 5 books)	3.36
Teacher's Guide	1.29
Level 3 (grades 4 and 5 reading levels)	
The Job Ahead	4.50
Exercise Book (set of 5 books)	3.36
Teacher's Guide	1.29

*Available through Science Research Associates, Inc., 259 East Erie Street, Chicago, Ill., 60611.

EDL Word Clues

The EDL Word Clues series* is a multilevel program designed to help students develop and refine their vocabulary and to teach students a technique for unlocking the meaning of words through a study of context. The program consists of seven books for reading levels seven through thirteen. Placement tests are available so that each student may be assigned a book on an appropriate level.

Each Word Clues book consists of thirty lessons of 10 words each with a total of 300 words per level. The words involved are taken from the EDL Core Vocabulary and are those judged to be of the highest frequency of usage at each level.

A programmed format allows each student to work at his own pace. Since context determines meaning, all words are presented in contextual settings, and each lesson is developed around a theme or center of interest which is introduced in the first frame of the lesson. Each of the ten words in the lesson is then developed in three frames, each appearing on a separate page.

Frame A introduces the new word. The student looks at the word, says it to himself, and then reads the sentence or sentences in which it is used. He is then asked to write down what he thinks the word means so that he becomes aware of the extent of his knowledge of the word's meaning. In frame B, clues to the word's meaning are given in the context. The student reads carefully to discover the meaning and then completes a multiple-choice exercise. At the left of the C frame, the student learns whether his choice was right or wrong. Then he studies the dictionary entry, with special attention to multiple meanings. Next, he applies his accumulated word knowledge in a usage exercise. He turns the page to check his answer and continues with the next word.

At some point following the lesson, the ten words are exposed tachistoscopically for word-recognition training. (Flash-X Sets 27-33 correlate with Word Clues Books G-M. A number of the Tach-X Sets also correlate with the Word Clues Books.) The student checks his retention of each word's central meaning with a multiple-choice word-meaning exercise.

Description	Level	Price
Word Clues Book G	7	$2.20
Word Clues Book H	8	2.20
Word Clues Book I	9	2.20

(Continued)

*Available through Coast Visual Education Co., Inc., 6510 Hollywood Blvd., Hollywood, Calif. 90028.

Description	Level	Price
Word Clues Book J	10	$2.20
Word Clues Book K	11	2.20
Word Clues Book L	12	2.20
Word Clues Book M	13	2.20
Word Clues Teacher's Guide	—	1.00
Word Clue Test, Form A	—	.25
Word Clue Test, Form B	—	.25
Manual of Directions (included with orders of 25 or more tests)	—	.50
Word Clue Specimen Set (includes one copy of each Word Clue Test form, an answer sheet, and Manual of Directions)	—	.65
Word Clue Appraisal, Form AA	—	.25
Word Clue Appraisal, Form BB	—	.25
Word Clue Answer Sheets (Packet of 100)	—	2.00
Scoring Stencils Form A, each	—	.20
Scoring Stencils Form B, each	—	.20
Scoring Stencils Form AA, each	—	.20
Scoring Stencils Form BB, each	—	.20

Lessons for Self-Instruction in Basic Skills (Reading)

These programmed lessons* consist of sixteen books with difficulty levels ranging from third through ninth grades. Although designed primarily for intensive review, the materials are useful in strengthening the reading skills of weaker students. A complete breakdown of the series is as follows:

Following Directions	Each of these categories has four books
Reference Skills	with the following difficulty levels: A-B
Reading Interpretations I	(3rd- to 4th-grade level); C-D (5th- to
Reading Interpretations II	6th-grade level); E-F (7th- to 8th-grade level); G (9th-grade level and above).

(For use with individual students working alone or in a group, potentially self-directive; each booklet, $1.10.)

Developmental Reading Series

Unique among basal readers is Bond's *Developmental Reading Series*† for grades one through eight. Each reader has a "Classmate" edition

*Available through California Test Bureau, Monterey, Calif.
†*The Developmental Reading Series* by Guy L. Bond is published by Lyons & Carnahan, Chicago, Ill.

which presents the identical stories with the same page numbering and illustrations. The latter, however, is a simplified version and has a difficulty level about one grade below the regular reader. This permits a teacher to differentiate her instruction more effectively when working with two groups of pupils who vary in reading ability. (For use with individual pupils or a group of pupils; readers 1 to 8, Classmate—Simplified edition—$2.56 to $4.28, each.)

FILMSTRIPS, DISCS, AND SLIDES

EDL Controlled Reader Program

Controlled reading refers to a form of training in which reading materials are projected in a left-to-right manner at a predetermined rate in order to develop a wide range of visual-functional and interpretive skills. The teacher can stop and start projection of picture games, vocabulary, or oral reading. By using automatic speeds, she can project silent reading stories at 60 to 1,000 words per minute. A moving slot is designed to encourage left-to-right perception and improve visual motility and coordination.

Two types of controlled readers are available.* The Controlled Reader Sr. is used in group training and the Controlled Reader Jr. is used by an individual or teams of two or three. The program employed with these controlled readers consists of 1,200 filmstrips organized into fifty sets.

The readiness filmstrips (Set 4c) are used in the very beginning stages of learning to read, or with nonreaders in the primary grades. These full-color picture filmstrips are used, informally, in game and play activities for periods of time in keeping with the attention spans of younger children—usually five minutes. The preprimer filmstrips (Set 4a) are used in the stage of reading in which children are first introduced to the printed word. The set contains small and capital letters strips, letter discrimination strips, picture and letter association strips, word discrimination strips, preprimer section strips, and a word review strip.

The motility training series (Set CR-MT) are designed to help students develop ocular motility or visual facility; precision in fixating and coordinating visually; and better left-to-right directional attack. Numbers, letters, or symbols are projected in a left-to-right manner at rates ranging from 15 to 120 lines per minute.

*Available through Coast Visual Education Co., Inc., 5610 Hollywood Blvd., Hollywood, Calif. 90028.

Accelerated discrimination training (Set CR-AD) is designed to develop accurate visual discrimination, stronger visual memory, and more precise ocular control. Each filmstrip contains five training exercises. During each exercise, lines of letters from 5 to 25 are projected in a left-to-right manner. The rate of projection may be varied from fifteen to ninety lines per minute. As students follow the material, they count the number of times a designated letter appears in a given exercise consisting of several lines.

The primary-grade material (Sets A, B, C) consists of factual and fictional selections dealing with animals, monsters, space exploration, mystery, and fantasy. Story lengths are planned to provide five minutes of reading time: first-grade story lengths range from 320 to 400 words; second-grade stories from 500 to 600 words; and third-grade stories from 625 to 675 words. Filmstrips are printed with an average of 4 words per line. A Study Guide accompanies each set of these primary filmstrips. With the Guide a lesson can be either a directed or independent reading activity. The Guide provides a preview activity, a word study section, and a page of comprehension questions. Each filmstrip set is also accompanied by a booklet of lesson plans which provides the teacher with questions for establishing a common background of experiences, vocabulary study activities, purpose-setting directions, discussion and review questions.

The intermediate-grade material (Sets D, DD, E, EE, F, and FF) consists of fictional classics, history, foreign lands and peoples, exploration, and true adventure stories of high interest appeal. Average selection length for grade four is 500 words; for grade five, 865 words; and for grade six, 925 words. Selections provide approximately five minutes of reading time. On the average, six new words are introduced with each selection. Films are printed with an average of five words per line. A Study Guide is provided for student use.

The junior high school materials (Sets GH, HG, IJ, and JI) range from tales of action and adventure, through inspirational essays, to selections that are informative in nature, dealing with biography, applied science, history, inventions, and nature. Films in the series are graduated in difficulty with readability controlled to be suitable for individuals reading at levels seven through ten. Average selection lengths for grades seven and eight are 1,250 words and for grades nine and ten, 1,400 words. Selections provide approximately five minutes of reading time, and about 8 new words are introduced with each new selection. Films contain an average of 6 words per line. A Study Guide is provided for student use.

The high school and college materials (Sets KL, LK, and MN) include autobiographical sketches, reports of contemporary events, and historical pieces taken from such sources as *Saturday Review, American Heritage, Newsweek, New York Times,* and *Science Digest.* Selections are graduated in difficulty, with readability controlled to be suitable for individuals reading at levels eleven through fourteen. Average selection length for levels eleven and twelve is 1,500 words, and for levels thirteen and fourteen, 1,700 words. Selections provide approximately six minutes of reading time and introduce an average of 8 new words. Films are printed with an average of 6 words per line in Sets KL and LK and with an average of 7 words per line in Set MN. A Study Guide is provided for student use.

Description	Level	Price
Controlled Reader Sr. with masking device, 3-wire cord, adapter, Teacher's Guide, demo strip and case	—	$290.00
Controlled Reader Jr. with masking device, 3-wire cord, adapter, Teacher's Guide, demo strip and case	—	220.00
Set 4c, 25 filmstrips in color with Teacher's Manual	readiness	115.00
Set 4d, 25 B&W filmstrips with Teacher's Manual	preprimer	87.50
Set CR-MT, 15 filmstrips with Instructor's Guide	motility-training	52.50
Set CR-AD, 10 filmstrips with Instructor's Guide	accelerated discrimination	35.00
Set A, Lessons 1-25, 25 B&W filmstrips with Study Guide and Lesson Plans	1	87.50
Set A, Lessons 26-50, 25 B&W filmstrips with Study Guide and Lesson Plans	1	87.50
Set B, Lessons 1-25, 25 B&W filmstrips with Study Guide and Lesson Plans	2	87.50
Set B, Lessons 25-50, 25 B&W filmstrips with Study Guide and Lesson Plans	2	87.50
Set C, Lessons 1-25, 25 B&W filmstrips with Study Guide and Lesson Plans	3	87.50
Set C, Lessons 25-50, 25 B&W filmstrips with Study Guide and Lesson Plans	3	87.50
Set D, 25 B&W filmstrips with Study Guide D	4	87.50
Set DD, 25 B&W filmstrips with Study Guide DD	4	87.50
Set E, 25 B&W filmstrips with Study Guide E	5	87.50

(Continued)

Description	Level	Price
Set EE, 25 B&W filmstrips with Study Guide EE	5	$87.50
Set F, 25 B&W filmstrips with Study Guide F	6	87.50
Set FF, 25 B&W filmstrips with Study Guide FF	6	87.50
Set GH, 25 B&W filmstrips with Study Guide GH	7-8	87.50
Set HG, 25 B&W filmstrips with Study Guide HG	7-8	87.50
Set IJ, 25 B&W filmstrips with Study Guide IJ	9-10	87.50
Set JI, 25 B&W filmstrips with Study Guide JI	9-10	87.50
Set KL, 25 B&W filmstrips with Study Guide KL	11-12	87.50
Set LK, 25 B&W filmstrips with Study Guide LK	11-12	87.50
Set MN, 25 B&W filmstrips with Study Guide MN	13-14	87.50

Project Life/General Electric Program

The Project Life System* consists of programmed instruction filmstrips that are used in connection with a device called a "Student Response Program Master." This device is about the size of a small radio and has a number of keys which the student presses to select his choice of answers to the questions presented to him. If the student selects the correct key, a light is turned on to so indicate, and he is able to advance to the next frame in the filmstrip. It will operate most remote-controllable filmstrip or slide projectors.

Description	Price
Student Response Program Master	$198.50
Connector Cord (projector used must be specified)	5.25
Mounted SRPM Rear Projector Screen	10.50
Perceptual Training Series	
Set 1 Introductory and Supplementary Units (9 Filmstrips)	40.50
Set 2 Visual Properties Unit (7 Filmstrips)	31.50
Set 3 Additions-Omissions and Figure-Ground Units (8 Filmstrips)	36.00
Set 4 Position-in-Space and Spatial Relationships Units (6 Filmstrips)	27.00

(Continued)

*Available through General Electric Company, P.O. Box 43, Schenectady, New York 12301.

Description	Price
Programmed Language Series (First-Year Level)	
Set 1 Self (8 Filmstrips)	$ 36.00
Set 2 Animals (8 Filmstrips)	36.00
Set 3 Foods (6 Filmstrips)	27.00
Set 4 Playthings (9 Filmstrips)	40.50
Set 5 Activities (5 Filmstrips)	22.50
Set 6 Self (8 Filmstrips)	36.00
Set 7 Clothing (5 Filmstrips)	22.50
Set 8 Shelter (6 Filmstrips)	27.00
Programmed Language Series (Second-Year Level)	
Set 9 School (8 Filmstrips)	36.00
Set 10 Self (6 Filmstrips)	27.00
Set 11 Self (7 Filmstrips)	31.50
Set 12 Community (8 Filmstrips)	36.00
Set 13 Foods (9 Filmstrips)	40.50
Set 14 Home (6 Filmstrips)	27.00
Set 15 Home (7 Filmstrips)	31.50
Set 16 Clothing (8 Filmstrips)	36.00
Thinking Activity Series	
Set 1 Level I (9 Filmstrips)	40.50
Set 2 Level I (8 Filmstrips)	36.00
Set 3 Level II (8 Filmstrips)	36.00
Set 4 Level II (9 Filmstrips)	40.50

Tachist-O-Filmstrips

These filmstrips* are organized into four kits: elementary, junior high, senior high, and college-adult. They are designed to help increase attention span, speed of perception, speed of recognition, and accuracy of recognition. A more detailed listing of these filmstrips is as follows:

ELEMENTARY LTS PROGRAM

Phonics Practice I	Instant Word Phrases I
Phonics Practice II	Instant Word Phrases II
Instant Words I	Reading Mastery C
Instant Words II	Seeing Skills B
Prefix Mastery	Teacher's Manual
Suffix Mastery	Tachist-O-Flasher

JUNIOR HIGH LTS PROGRAM

Word Mastery B	Reading Mastery C
Prefix Mastery	Reading Mastery D
Suffix Mastery	Seeing Skills G
Instant Word Phrases I	Number Recognition C
Instant Word Phrases II	Teacher's Manual
Phrase Mastery B	Tachist-O-Flasher

*Available through Learning Through Seeing, Inc., Box 368, Sunland, Calif. 91040.

SENIOR HIGH LTS PROGRAM

Word Mastery C
Prefix Mastery
Suffix Mastery
Instant Word Phrases I
Instant Word Phrases II
Phrase Mastery B

Phrase Mastery C
Reading Mastery D
Reading Development A
Seeing Skills G
Teacher's Manual
Tachist-O-Flasher

COLLEGE-ADULT LTS PROGRAM

Building Blocks of
    Vocabulary
Word Mastery F
Instant Word Phrases II
Phrase Mastery B
Phrase Mastery C

Reading Development A
Reading Development B
Seeing Skills C
Number Recognition F
Teacher's Manual
Tachist-O-Flasher

(For use with individual pupils or a group of pupils; $359.50 a kit)

Cenco Filmstrip Program

The filmstrip materials in this series* are used in connection with a mechanical device called the Projection Reader/Tachistoscope. This machine combines a Projection Reader and a Tachistoscope in a single unit. It eliminates the need to remove film from the projector in order to both present story material on a line-by-line basis and introduce new vocabulary tachistoscopically without cutting or removing the filmstrip from the projector.

On a readiness level, full-color picture filmstrips assist in developing the powers of concentration, retention, logical reasoning, both visual and auditory discrimination, and left-to-right directional movement. On the preprimer level, filmstrips are provided for three types of experiences in beginning reading: (1) experiences with the correct perception and identification of letter forms; (2) experiences with word forms to promote rapid and accurate identification of such forms by their general configurations; and (3) experiences involving the reinforcement of the basic sight vocabulary in a broader associative area by means of paragraph context and story continuity.

Description	Price
Projection Reader/Tachistoscope	$350.00
Projection Reader Jr./Tachistoscope	305.00
Tachistoscopic Series—Grades 2, 3 (23 Filmstrips)	28.00
Tachistoscopic Series—Grades 4, 5, 6 (24 Filmstrips)	42.00
Readiness, 25 Filmstrips (color)	100.00

(Continued)

*Available through Cenco Educational Aids, 2600 S. Kostner Ave., Chicago, Ill. 60623.

Description	Price
Teacher's Guide	$ .75
Preprimer, 25 Filmstrips (B & W)	75.00
Teacher's Guide	.75

Psychotechnics Reading Programs

The filmstrip materials in the various series* are used in connection with a mechanical device called the Tachomatic 500 Projector. This machine has fully automatic controls and offers a speed range from 100 to 1,200 words per minute. A flip of a switch holds an image on the screen indefinitely. With use of the filmstrips, two and three fixations per line, or an entire line, can be presented. Students progress from word-by-word to phrase-by-phrase reading.

DEVELOPMENTAL READING SERIES

This series is based on Lyons & Carnahan's Developmental Reading Series. Each set includes a copy of the reader (or readers) used with the set, a copy of each Teacher's Edition of the reader, and a Teacher's Manual.

Description	Price
"Happy Times" (Grade 1—40 films)	$125.00
"Down Our Way" and "Just for Fun" (Grade 2—20 films)	75.00
"Stories from Everywhere" and "Once Upon a Lifetime" (Grade 3—20 films)	75.00
"Meeting New Friends" (Grade 4—20 films)	75.00
"Days of Adventure" (Grade 5—20 films)	75.00
"Stories to Remember" (Grade 6—20 films)	75.00

PURDUE TRAINING FILMSTRIPS

This filmstrip series is a reproduction of the Purdue Reading Films. The set includes an Instructor's Book with comprehension texts and vocabulary.

Description	Price
"Purdue Training Filmstrips" (Grades 6-8—20 filmstrips)	65.00

OPTIMUM READING ACHIEVEMENT SERIES

This series consists of three sets of filmstrips designed for use with Optimum Reading Achievement texts. Each text contains 20 essays together with corresponding vocabulary and comprehension checks.

Description	Price
ORA Level 1 (Grades 7-8—20 filmstrips)	65.00
ORA Level 2 (Grades 9-10—20 filmstrips)	65.00
ORA Level 3 (Grades 11-adult—20 filmstrips)	65.00

*Available through Photo & Sound Company, 870 Monterey Pass Road, Monterey Park, Calif. 91754.

Comprehension Skills

*Comprehension Skills** is a teacher-oriented reading program designed to help students read and think simultaneously. The thirty filmstrips which may be shown on any standard filmstrip projector are used by the teacher to present the lesson material. Lessons 1 to 10, at the 4th reader level, introduce phrase meaning. Lessons 11 to 20, at the 5th reader level, progress to sentence meaning. Lessons 21 to 30, covering the more advanced reading/thinking skills for the 6th reader level, present paragraph and story meaning. Using a building-block approach, *Comprehension Skills* helps stimulate creative thinking by training students to recognize similar and opposite meanings, isolate irrelevant information, establish cause and effect, make inferences, interpret and transfer facts, and draw valid conclusions.

Because of its multilevel format, *Comprehension Skills* can be easily integrated into the established curriculum and may be started at any time during the school year. The lessons are suitable for use with individuals, small groups, or an entire class.

Description	Price
Level 4 (10 Filmstrips)	$ 49.50
Level 5 (10 Filmstrips)	49.50
Level 6 (10 Filmstrips)	49.50
Level 4, 5, 6 (30 Filmstrips)	129.50

Context Vocabulary

Context Vocabulary† is a teacher-oriented reading program that can help improve comprehension and promote transition to good silent reading skills through vocabulary development. The approach is to train students to determine word meaning by using the clues found in context. Once this skill is acquired, it is no longer always necessary to look up every word in a dictionary.

The program is for use in the 4th, 5th, and 6th reader levels. It is designed as supplementary material in the established reading curriculum. It can be started at any time during the school year and is easily integrated into the on-going reading program. *Context Vocabulary* can be used as enrichment material as well as a developmental and re-

*Available through Teaching Technology Corporation, Box 3817, 6837 Hayvenhurst Ave., Van Nuys, Calif. 91407.
†Available through Teaching Technology Corporation, Box 3817, 6837 Hayvenhurst Ave., Van Nuys, Calif. 91407.

medial teaching aid. Because of its multilevel format, the program can be used even in a class that reflects a wide range of ability.

Rather than teaching specific vocabulary lists, the program encourages the student to pinpoint the meaning of any word by using the total idea expressed in the reading matter. The main objective is to make reading and thinking a simultaneous process.

Lessons 1 to 10, for the 4th reader level, present familiar words in a variety of simple contexts in order to emphasize how the most common words can change in meaning according to their setting. Some of the words include fair, hand, plane, bank, set, and base. Lessons 11 to 20, at 5th reader level, introduce more difficult vocabulary in contextual setting purposely constructed to clarify their meaning. In lessons 21 to 30, for use at the sixth-grade level, the new words appear in more complex, but precise, settings. Here the task is to analyze the context to grasp the total idea and determine the exact meaning of any given word.

Description	Price
Level 4 (10 Filmstrips)	$ 49.50
Level 5 (10 Filmstrips)	49.50
Level 6 (10 Filmstrips)	49.50
Level 4, 5, 6 (30 Filmstrips)	129.50

Readwell Essays

*Readwell Essays** are sound filmstrips designed to help build the reading skills of weak readers in the fifth and sixth grades and in all grades above the sixth, including the adult level. The essays are narrated as the student group or the individual student reads them silently on the screen. After a first reading, comprehension questions are introduced. The questions, like the essay, are projected onto the screen and narrated simultaneously for the student. The student may use earphones (this is considered most effective) or may listen as the recorded voice is heard via a phonograph.

Description	Price
Series 1: 20 Reading Units (20 color filmstrips; 10 recordings, 12″ microgroove)	$180.00
Series 2: 20 Reading Units (20 color filmstrips; 10 recordings, 12″ microgroove)	180.00
Series 1 & 2: 40 Reading Units	350.00

*Available through Herbert M. Elkins Company, 10031 Commerce Ave., Tujunga, Calif. 91042.

Califone Perceptamatic Reading Series

The materials in this series* are used in connection with a mechanical device called the Rheem T-Scope. The Rheem T-Scope is a light, portable tachistoscope which employs circular reels with forty-two exposures per reel. The interval of exposure varies from 1/10 to 1/100 of a second. The materials themselves are designed to correlate with existing reading programs in today's schools. Each of the eight reading levels includes three steps to improve reading skills: Step 1 (Digit Reels) to sharpen visual perception and eliminate transpositions and reversals; Step 2 (Vocabulary Reels) to reinforce grade-level vocabulary skills; Step 3 (Phrase Reels) to improve phrase perception.

Description	Price
Rheem T-Scope	$135.00
Reading Level 1 (first grade)	35.25
Reading Level 2 (second grade)	35.25
Reading Level 3 (third grade)	35.25
Reading Level 4 (fourth grade)	35.25
Reading Level 5 (fifth grade)	35.25
Reading Level 6 (sixth grade)	35.25
Reading Level 7 (seventh grade)	35.25
Reading Level 8 (eighth grade)	35.25

EDL Flash-X

The EDL Flash-X† is a small hand-tachistoscope employing 4 3/4-inch discs. The drill materials available are ideal for students who need extra practice in seeing skills and/or reinforcement. Individual or team practice in the classroom supported by home practice can help a student "keep up with his classmates." Because a student can also prepare his own materials, he can extend this training into areas of study where he needs special help.

Each set contains twelve discs with 40 exposures each, or a total of 480 exposures. Materials range from readiness levels through high school and college.

Description	Level	Price
EDL Flash-X Tachistoscope, all metal, with manual.	—	$8.20
Flash-X Instruction Manual	—	.10
Teacher's Guide	—	1.00

(Continued)

*Available through Rheem Califone, 5922 Bowcroft St., Los Angeles, Calif. 90016.
†Available through Coast Visual Education Co., Inc., 610 Hollywood Blvd., Hollywood, Calif. 90028.

Description	Level	Price
Set X-1, 12 discs, 480 exposures with activity card. (This set is designed for beginning readers and contains picture nouns, categories, reasoning, beginning sounds, and rhyming sounds.)	1	$ 3.60
Set X-2, 12 discs, 480 exposures with activity card. (This set contains pictures and letters, small letters, capital letters, letter discrimination, single numbers, double numbers and number discrimination.)	2	3.60
Set X-3, 12 discs, 480 exposures with activity card. (This set contains discs with 3 to 8 digits and is designed to teach the student to pay careful attention.)	2-12	3.60
Set X-4, 12 discs, 480 exposures with activity card. (This set contains discs 2 to 7 scrambled letters and is designed to teach the student to pay close attention to order.)	2-12	3.60
Set X-9, 12 discs, 480 exposures with activity card. This set is designed for the advanced student and offers special exercises with nine numbers and seven letters.)	C-A	3.60
Set X-V1, 2 boxes of 13 discs each, 1,000 exposures, with activity card. (This set contains words taken from the 1968 revision of the EDL Core Vocabulary.)	1	7.80
Set X-V2, 2 boxes of 13 discs each, 1,000 exposures, with activity card. (This set contains words taken from the 1968 revision of the EDL Core Vocabulary.)	2	7.80
Set X-V3, 2 boxes of 13 discs each, 1,000 exposures, with activity card. (This set contains words taken from the 1968 revision of the EDL Core Vocabulary.)	3	7.80
Spelling Set X-12, 8 discs, 320 exposures with activity card. (This set, as well as sets X-13 through X-19, contains words taken from the EDL Core Vocabulary. The words are those that were rated as most difficult on the Iowa Spelling Scale.)	2	3.60
Spelling Set X-13, 8 discs, 320 exposures, with activity card.	3	3.60
Spelling Set X-14, 16 discs, 640 exposures, with activity card.	4	3.60
Spelling Set X-15, 16 discs, 640 exposures, with activity card.	5	3.60
Spelling Set X-16, 16 discs, 640 exposures, with activity card.	6	3.60

(Continued)

Description	Level	Price
Spelling Set X-17, 16 discs, 640 exposures, with activity card.	7	$ 3.60
Spelling Set X-18, 16 discs, 640 exposures, with activity card.	8	3.60
Spelling Set X-19, 16 discs, 640 exposures, with activity card.	9	3.60
Set X-27, 12 discs, 480 exposures, with activity card. (This set, as well as sets X-28 through X-33, contains 300 high frequency words taken from the EDL Core Vocabulary.)	7	3.60
Set X-28, 12 discs, 480 exposures, with activity card.	8	3.60
Set X-29, 12 discs, 480 exposures, with activity card.	9	3.60
Set X-30, 12 discs, 480 exposures, with activity card.	10	3.60
Set X-31, 12 discs, 480 exposures, with activity card.	11	3.60
Set X-32, 12 discs, 480 exposures, with activity card.	12	3.60
Set X-33, 12 discs, 480 exposures, with activity card.	13	3.60
Set X-0, 12 discs, 380 exposures, with activity card.	—	3.60

Craig Reader Programs

The *Craig Reader** is a fully-automated individual reading training instrument, resembling a miniature TV set. It is engineered for laboratory-type training in reading skills and comprehension. Variable speed control features permit the student to set his own pace in laboratory-applied serial tachistoscopic, expanded-line and perceptual training techniques. A light bar projects 35 mm slide-textual matter in programmed sequences from 100 to over 1,600 words per minute. A variety of Craig Reader Programs range from elementary grades through college level.

Description	Price
Craig Reader	$249.50
Reading Program A (Adv. high school, college, and adult)	59.50
Reading Program A-1 (Adv. high school, college, and adult)	59.50
Reading Program B (8th-, 9th-, & 10th-grade vocabulary)	89.50
Reading Program C (4th-grade vocabulary)	39.50
Reading Program C-1 (5th-grade vocabulary)	39.00

(Continued)

*Available through A. F. Milliron Co., Inc., 1198 So. La Brea, Los Angeles, Calif. 90019.

Description	Price
Reading Program C-2 (6th-grade vocabulary)	$ 36.50
Reading Program C-3 (7th-grade vocabulary)	42.50
Reading Program C-4 (8th-grade vocabulary)	36.50
Reading Program C-5 (9th-grade vocabulary)	49.50
Reading Program Perception I (1½- and 2nd-grade level)	24.50
Reading Program Perception II (2nd- and 2½-grade level)	23.00
Reading Program Perception III (2½- and 3rd-grade level)	24.50
Reading Program Perception IV (3rd- and 3½-grade level)	19.00
Reading Program Reading Skills I (4th-grade level)	49.50

COMMERCIALLY-MADE TAPE RECORDINGS

EDL Listen and Read Programs

The EDL *Listen and Read* programs* are available on four levels: intermediate, junior high school, senior high school, and college. Each lesson begins with an introductory sketch, dialogue, or sequence of sound effects designed to capture students' interest and attention. The narrator introduces the students to the skill or concept being dealt with and then guides them through listening and workbook exercises in which they gain practice in various phases of the skill or concept. The student workbook provides both visual reinforcement for the ideas being introduced and exercises in which the student applies what is learned at each step of the lesson. Each lesson lasts from twenty-five to thirty minutes, including response time. Cassettes have replaced tapes, althought the latter still are available. With the use of a connecting jack box for nine headsets, a number of students can work independently.

EDL listen and read D (fourth-grade level listening and reading skills)

1. Visualizing
2. Identifying Main Ideas
3. Using Details
4. Recognizing Sequence
5. Comparing
6. Recognizing Cause and Effect
7. Using Maps and Graphs
8. Using PQR (Preview, Question, Read)
9. Outlining
10. Summarizing
11. Interpreting Figurative Language
12. Making Inferences
13. Interpreting Character
14. Predicting Outcomes
15. Interpreting Poetry

*Available through Coast Visual Education Co., Inc., 5610 Hollywood Blvd., Hollywood, Calif. 90028.

EDL listen and read GHI album 1 (seventh- and eighth-grade reading and study skills)

1. Listening and Reading
2. Meeting New Words, Part 1
3. Meeting New Words, Part 2
4. Using Context Clues
5. Using Your Senses, Part 1
6. Using Your Senses, Part 2
7. Recognizing the Power of Words
8. Recognizing the Power of Words (continued)
9. Unlocking Sentence Meaning, Part 1
10. Unlocking Sentence Meaning, Part 2
11. Noticing Signs and Signals in Reading
12. Recognizing Main Ideas in Paragraphs
13. Understanding Paragraphs That Tell a Story
14. Understanding Paragraphs That Describe
15. Understanding Paragraphs That Explain

EDL listen and read GHI album 2 (eighth- and ninth-grade reading and study skills)

1. Checking Your Study Habits
2. Making Remembering Easier
3. Using the Dictionary
4. Using Maps
5. Using Graphs
6. Reading Illustrations and Cartoons
7. Reading a Textbook, Part 1
8. Reading a Textbook, Part 2
9. Reading a Textbook, Part 3
10. Using Library References
11. Note-taking
12. Summarizing
13. Shifting Gears in Reading
14. Skimming and Scanning
15. Taking Examinations

EDL listen and read JKL (tenth-, eleventh-, and twelfth-grade literature reading skills)

1. What Is Literature?
2. Following Sequence
3. Summarizing
4. Outlining
5. Words and Our Senses
6. Figurative Language in Prose
7. Making Inferences
8. Understanding Persuasion
9. Finding Viewpoints in Essays
10. Understanding the Autobiography
11. Biography—The Story of People
12. The Magic of Storytelling
13. Understanding the Novel
14. The Play's the Thing
15. The Sound of Poetry

Description	Level	Price
Set LR-D, 15 Cassettes	4	$107.50
LR-D Lesson Book	4	1.35
Listening Programs Teacher's Guide	—	1.00
Set LR-GHI Album 1, 15 Cassettes	7, 8, 9	107.50
Set LR-GHI Album 2, 15 Cassettes	7, 8, 9	107.50
LR-GHI Album 1, Lesson Book	7, 8, 9	1.35

(Continued)

Description	Level	Price
LR-GHI Album 2, Lesson Book	7, 8, 9	$ 1.35
Listening Programs Teacher's Guide	—	1.00
Set LR-JKL, 15 Cassettes	10, 11, 12	107.50
LR-JKL Lesson Book	10, 11, 12	1.35
Listening Programs Teacher's Guide	—	1.00
Set LR-MN, 36 Cassettes	College	215.00
LR-MN Lesson Book	College	2.50
Listening Programs Teacher's Guide	—	1.00

Listen and Think Program

The *Listen and Think* series* develops listening comprehension and its competent thinking skills. Each program provides a sequence of fifteen lessons that move the student from analytical skills (recognizing and organizing information, to interpretive skills (inferring, predicting, visualizing), to appreciative skills, to critical skills. Each lesson takes one skill or aspect of a skill and develops it thoroughly. Each tape starts with an attention-getting situation demonstrating the specific skill. The skill is introduced. Then the student alternates between listening to the taped material and responding in his lesson book to taped instruction. Compressed speech is used during the latter portion of the tapes, challenging the student's attention, improving his concentration and thus his retention. Within the developmental organization of the series, programs AR (Auditory Readiness) for level 1, and B for level 2, develop listening and thinking skills that precede and facilitate reading, such as recognition of concepts of space and time, cause and effect, alike-different, and serial order.

Programs C through F (levels 3-6) develop and reinforce the listening and thinking skills most needed at these levels. The skills treated at levels C through F are—

Identifying Main Ideas
Recognizing Sequence
Summarizing
Comparing
Recognizing Cause and Effect
Predicting Outcomes
Using Our Senses
Visualizing

Understanding Character
Understanding Setting
Recognizing Foreshadowing
Sharing Feelings
Enjoying Humor
Recognizing Speaker's Purpose
Fact and Opinion
Drawing Conclusions

Programs G, H, and I (levels 7-9) use works of acknowledged literary merit to develop the listening, thinking, and comprehension skill

*Available through Coast Visual Education Co., Inc., 5610 Hollywood Blvd., Hollywood, Calif. 90028.

needed for effective response to literature. The skills introduced at levels G, H, and I are—

Understanding Character	Understanding Theme
Understanding Setting	Understanding Conflict
Recognizing Foreshadowing and Climax	Understanding Qualities of Literature

Each *Listen and Think* set contains fifteen recordings. Each tape contains thirteen minutes of playing time. Teacher's handbooks ($1.00 each) are available for levels AR through F. Individual lesson books (85 each) are provided for each level (1-9). They contain introductory material, exercises, and activity pages to be used during recorded lessons. A chart in the back of each lesson book permits the student to record his own progress.

Description	Level	Tape Price	Cassette Price
Auditory Readiness Tapes (15)	K-1	$97.50	$107.50
B Tapes (15)	2	97.50	107.50
C Tapes (15)	3	97.50	107.50
D Tapes (15)	4	97.50	107.50
E Tapes (15)	5	97.50	107.50
F Tapes (15)	6	97.50	107.50
G Tapes (15)	7	97.50	107.50
H Tapes (15)	8	97.50	107.50
I Tapes (15)	9	97.50	107.50

(For use with individual students or a group of students, potentially self-directive; headsets (1-5) $38.00; headsets (6 up) $30.00; Jack Box for up to 9 headsets $14.50.)

Gateway to Good Reading

This supplemental reading readiness program* consists of forty tapes, each accompanied by thirty response booklets. The program seeks to develop eye-motor coordination, spatial relationships, and listening and speaking vocabularies. The child listens, follows directions, identifies, selects, discriminates, and learns. Throughout each tape, which is paced to match the young child's attention span, the listener is actively involved in the learning process.

The program can be used in the early school years, or as remedial work at a later level, with children of all social, economic, and cul-

---

*Available through Coast Visual Education Co., Inc., 5610 Hollywood Blvd., Hollywood, Calif. 90028.

tural backgrounds. It is also useful in classes for the mentally retarded at the primary and intermediate levels.

(For use with individual students, small groups, or in total class situations; potentially self-directive; *Auditory Discrimination* consists of a set of 20 tapes, 30 booklets for each tape, and 3 teacher's manuals. The tapes are devoted to the development of auditory recognition and discrimination, comprehension, and directional skills, $159.00; on cassettes, $179.00; *Visual Perception* consists of a set of 20 tapes, 30 pupil booklets for each tape, and 3 teacher's manuals. The tapes are devoted to the development of the visual and perceptual skills in four main perception areas—position in space, constancy of shape, eye-motor co-ordination, and figure-ground relationships, $159.00; on cassettes, $179.00. Complete program of both auditory and visual perception, $299.00; on cassettes, $399.00.)

St. Louis Program

The *St. Louis Program** consists of twenty-eight tapes and accompanying pupil response booklets. It was written to help disadvantaged primary children become aware of standard speech sounds and to help correct substandard patterns. Portions of the program, however, are recommended for use by children of all ability levels as an introduction to the sounds of consonants and vowels. These portions (also available as separate units) may be used in prereading programs, thereby making the program valuable for either speech improvement or reading readiness, or both.

On the twenty-eight tapes of the *St. Louis Program*, each approximately fifteen minutes long, children are introduced to sounds of consonants, vowels, and digraphs through stories, rhymes, and songs. The listener hears the correct sound, imitates it, discriminates between correct and incorrect versions, then records responses by marking illustration in his individual booklet. Throughout the program sounds of the letters are given alone and in words. Thirty-five booklets accompany each of the tapes. A convenient, indexed storage box for pupil materials is provided with the program. The teacher's manual contains word lists and enrichment games (often to be read to the group), provides follow-up material for additional ten-minute sessions for each lesson, and makes suggestions for using the program.

(For use with individual pupils or small groups of pupils; Complete program of 28 tapes, 35 booklets for each, and 3 teacher's manuals, $224.00; on cassettes, $252.00.)

*Available through Coast Visual Education Co., Inc., 6510 Hollywood Blvd., Hollywood, Calif. 90028.

Primary Reading Program

The forty prerecorded tapes and thirty booklets of the Imperial Primary Reading Program* make it possible for pupils to carry on independently. Each tape acts as the pupil's talking companion and guide for the wide range of reading activities provided. The materials are well suited for individuals or small groups of pupils with special needs. Reading categories covered by the tapes and booklets include the following:

Readiness
    Developing proper attitude
    Following direction and left-to-right progression
    Associating meaning with recognition and categorizing of words and
        phrases
    Opposites
Study Skills
    Punctuation
    Locating information by choosing proper references
    Skimming, grasping relevant facts
    Locating the main idea
    Using table of contents and index
    Dictionary skills
    Using pictures, graphs, and maps
Comprehension Skills
    Fourteen lessons at the preprimer, primer, first-grade, second-grade
        and third-grade levels of comprehension
Word-attack Skills
    Initial consonants
    Word discrimination
    Final and medial consonants
    Consonant blends
    Long and short vowels
    Digraphs and diphthongs
    Closed and open syllables
    Prefixes and suffixes
    Context clues and discrimination of word meanings
    Accents

(For use with individual students or a group of students, potentially self-directive; set of 40 tapes and 30 pupil booklets for each tape, and 3 teacher's manuals, $299.00; on cassettes, $339.00.)

*Available through Coast Visual Education Co., Inc., 5610 Hollywood Blvd., Hollywood, Calif. 90028.

Junior High School Aural Reading Laboratory

This program* consists of forty tapes that are self-directing and self-evaluating. Each tape is accompanied by six identical story cards. This makes it possible for six students to use the program at one time.

Students listen to the tape while reading and working with the story cards. They write their answers in the pupil response book which contains space for all forty lessons. A special section in the back of the pupil response book is provided for charting progress in both comprehension and effective reading rate.

All the lessons are directed at building the student's vocabulary and increasing his comprehension and speed. The final portion of each lesson is devoted to a specific word-attack skill, in which the student is provided with many interesting discovery exercises. Stories on the cards are chosen for their interest to junior high students, for their level of difficulty, and for their scholastic value.

The teacher's manual contains a brief description of each lesson, what the lesson is intended to accomplish, all questions and answers on the tape, and suggestions pertaining to the further development of the specific word-attack skill taught.

(For use with individual students or a small group of students, potentially self-directive; Complete program of 240 story cards, 40 tapes, 30 pupil response books, and 3 teacher's manuals, $299.00; on cassettes, $339.00.)

SRA Listening Skills Program (Grades 1-6)

This program† consists of a series of recordings designed to develop and strengthen children's listening abilities. The recordings are available on tape cassettes, open-reel tapes, and 33 1/3 rpm discs.

In the primary program, each lesson consists of recorded stories and listening activities requiring responses to directions and questions. Material is carefully selected and sequenced to generate high interest, to provide progressive development of skills, and to allow for diversified responses.

Lesson topics covered in the primary program include awareness of pitch and volume and the language for describing them; following directions; developing sentence patterns; the concept that sound implies

*Available through Coast Visual Education Co., Inc., 5610 Hollywood Blvd., Hollywood, Calif. 90028.

†Available through Science Research Associates, Inc., 259 East Erie Street, Chicago, Ill., 60611.

action; awareness of fantasy; use of context to develop vocabulary; and others.

At the intermediate level, a recorded pretest is used to evaluate each student's listening ability and to determine which lessons he should listen to. Each lesson contains motivational material, instruction in a given skill, sample listening passages, a quiz on the content of the passages or on points in the instruction, and an opportunity for children to check their answers to the quiz. A recorded post-test evaluates the student's achievement at the conclusion of the program.

Skills covered at the intermediate level include auditory discrimination; instant recall; following directions; remembering sequence; listening for main ideas and remembering sequence; listening for main ideas and details; listening for cause and effect; visualizing and listening for mood; inferring information; and distinguishing fact from opinion. These skills are sequenced according to difficulty.

Description	Price
Listening Skills Program 1A for Grade 1 in Cassette Format	$108.90
Listening Skills Program 1B for Grade 2 in Cassette Format	108.90
Listening Skills Program 1C for Grade 3 in Cassette Format	108.90
Listening Skills Program 2A for Grade 4 in Cassette Format	108.90
Listening Skills Program 2B for Grade 5 in Cassette Format	108.90
Listening Skills Program 2C for Grade 6 in Cassette Format	108.90

Ginn Word Enrichment Program

This seven-level program* is designed to teach successful application of word-analysis skills, build vocabulary, and extend word meaning. The sequence of introduction, reinforcement, and review of each skill reflects modern trends in linguistics research and learning theory. Diagnostic mastery tests measure student gain at each level. Although GWEP is largely teacher-directed, self-evaluation is an important feature of the program. GWEP is designed for use in the primary grades with any basal series and is equally suitable for remedial work on the intermediate level.

Description	Price
Level 1—Look and Listen	$ 1.56
Teachers' Edition	2.92
Cassette for Level 1	180.00
Level 2—Consonant Sounds and Symbols	1.56
Teachers' Edition	2.92
Cassette for Level 2	140.00
	(continued)

*Available through Ginn and Company, 125 Second Ave., Waltham, Mass. 02154.

Description	Price
Level 3—Vowels and Variants	$ 1.56
Teachers' Edition	2.92
Cassette for Level 3	150.00
Level 4—More Vowels and Variants	1.56
Teachers' Edition	2.92
Level 5—Sounds and Syllables	1.56
Teachers' Edition	2.92
Level 6—More Sounds and Syllables	1.56
Teachers' Edition	2.92

Califone Audio Reader Program

The Califone Audio Reader Program* is multileveled and is designed to stimulate vocabulary growth, oral reading skill, and comprehension. Each contains twenty prerecorded tape lessons, twelve student story cards for each lesson, a teacher's manual, and an answer key for quizzes. Each tape reel has one lesson recorded in both directions, thereby eliminating the need to rewind.

Description	Price
First-grade reading kit (red)	$150.00
Second-grade reading kit (orange)	150.00
Third-grade reading kit (yellow)	150.00
Fourth-grade reading kit (green)	150.00
Fifth-grade reading kit (blue)	150.00
Sixth-grade reading kit (purple)	150.00

MULTIMODAL SYSTEMS

Borg-Warner System 80

System 80† consists of a boxlike device (16 inches wide, 14 inches high, and 14 inches deep) that provides simultaneous visual and auditory stimulation. Its TV-like screen measures eight by four inches. This audiovisual unit utilizes twelve-inch vinyl records and a filmstrip encased in transparent plastic.

Computer-type markings on the filmstrip units make it possible for the instrument to move forward when a correct answer is given or repeat if an incorrect answer is given. A child responds to a recorded voice by pressing one of five selection buttons.

*Available through Rheem Califone, 5922 Bowcroft St., Los Angeles, Calif. 90016.
†Available through Coast Visual Education Co., Inc., 5610 Hollywood Blvd., Hollywood, Calif. 90028.

Each kit contains an average of twelve lessons with every fourth lesson serving as a review. In the review lesson, a branching technique is used. This means that a different contextual setting is presented if the pupil answers incorrectly. (For use with individual students, completely self-directive; each audio visual unit, $495.00; kits, $125.00 each.)

Learning Letter Names and Sounds
   Kindergarten (2 kits)
   First grade (2 kits)
Reading Words in Context
   Kindergarten (1 kit)
   First grade (3 kits)
   Second grade (3 kits)
   Third grade (2 kits)
Developing Spelling Skills
   First grade (2 kits)
   Second grade (2 kits)
   Third grade (3 kits)

Aud-X Mark 3

The EDL Aud-X* provides motivating reading instruction for primary pupils and older students with limited reading ability. Aud-X instruction has unique features. It provides sight-sound synchronization or simultaneous visual and aural presentation of words. The use of aural context for sight-word presentation makes it possible to provide high-interest story content while building sight vocabulary. Student-controlled pacing allows the student to respond at his own pace and to control the rate at which the lesson progresses.

The Mark 3 Aud-X consists of a cassette player and a projector. The cassette audio unit has fast forward and rewind functions as well as operator-controlled program start, stop, and advance buttons. The projector has a 2-inch lens and 150-watt lamp. It can be operated easily by a first grader. The HOLD switch allows the teacher to hold the program for additional comment when necessary. EDL's color-coding system correlates filmstrip cartridge with matching cassette; it eases selection of the desired lesson and offers a no-fuss replacement at a lesson's conclusion. Self-threading filmstrip cartridges are rewound automatically. Cassettes are easily loaded, also, and can be rewound at the touch of a button. Each recorded lesson has a playing time of approximately thirteen minutes.

*Available through Coast Visual Education Co., Inc., 5610 Hollywood Blvd., Hollywood, Calif. 90028.

The Aud-X is used with an eighteen-by-twenty-inch table top projection screen and the special Aud-X table. Headsets with a connecting jack box allow up to nine students to participate in small-group Aud-X instruction.

Description	Price
Aud-X Mark 3 projector and cassette audio unit	$530.00
Table Top Projection Screen	10.95
Headsets (1-5)	38.00
Headsets (6 up)	30.00
Jack Box for up to 9 headsets	14.50

Aud-X programs for the *Listen Look Learn System* provide instruction in a wide range of readiness, listening, word-attack, and comprehension skills for the first three levels of reading instruction. These programs can be used to supplement and reinforce other beginning reading programs, adding multimodal and self-instructional dimensions. They can also serve as a component of remedial reading programs at the elementary level.

The *Listen Look Learn System* consists of six ensembles. Ensemble 1 serves the readiness level. It contains twenty-nine lessons, accompanied by introductory readiness work sheets and a workbook. These Aud-X lessons help children learn to look, to listen, to follow directions, and to understand the function of letters and words and the relationship between letters and sounds. Ensembles 2 through 6 provide continuing skill development for reading levels 1 through 3. In these ensembles, Aud-X lessons introduce new words, comprehension skills, and word-attack skills through the story mode, the words mode, and the word-study mode. With each cassette/filmstrip set there is a workbook which provides writing, word building, and sentence completion activities to reinforce learning and provide feedback on student progress.

Description	Level	Price
Listen Look Learn Ensemble 1		
Mark 3 Cassette/Filmstrip Set	K-1	$217.50
Aud-X Introductory Readiness Work Sheets	K-1	5.00
Aud-X Readiness Book R-3	K-1	1.00
Listen Look Learn Ensemble 2		
Mark 3 Cassette/Filmstrip Set	1	382.50
Aud-X Word Introduction Book	1	1.50
Aud-X Reading Sheets (40 copies of 38 sheets)	1	32.00
Listen Look Learn Ensemble 3		
Mark 3 Cassette/Filmstrip Set	1-2	300.00
Aud-X Word Introduction Book	1-2	1.15

(Continued)

Description	Level	Price
Listen Look Learn Ensemble 4		
Mark 3 Cassette/Filmstrip Set	2	$225.00
Aud-X Word & Skill Introduction Book	2	1.00
Listen Look Learn Ensemble 5		
Mark 3 Cassette/Filmstrip Set	2-3	225.00
Aud-X Word & Skill Introduction Book	2-3	1.00
Listen Look Learn Ensemble 6		
Mark 3 Cassette/Filmstrip Set	3	225.00
Aud-X Word & Skill Introduction Book	3	1.00

Aud-X programs for the *Learning 100 System* serve older students who are nonreaders or who are reading at levels 1-3. Undereducated adults, school-alienated students, and dropouts are motivated by the adult-oriented content of these materials. Each ensemble consists of a number of paired story and word study lessons. Story lessons introduce new vocabulary in aural context and build skill in story comprehension. Word study lessons call attention to graphic, phonic, and structural characteristics of words and teach word-attack skills. Workbook activities throughout each lesson reinforce learning and provide feedback on student progress. For each Aud-X set there is a GO book which provides a story and activities correlated with each pair of Aud-X lessons.

Description	Level	Price
Learning 100 Ensemble 1		
Mark 3 Cassette/Filmstrip Set	Beg.	$157.00
Aud-X Study Guide	Beg.	1.85
GO volume and GO answer key	Beg.	
Learning 100 Ensemble 2		
Mark 3 Cassette/Filmstrip Set	1	450.00
Aud-X Study Guide	1	1.85
GO volume	1	2.25
GO answer key	1	1.00
Learning 100 Ensemble 3		
Mark 3 Cassette/Filmstrip Set	2	450.00
Aud-X Study Guide	2	1.85
GO volume	2	2.00
GO answer key	2	1.00
Learning 100 Ensemble 4		
Mark 3 Cassette/Filmstrip Set	3	450.00
Aud-X Study Guide	3	1.85
GO volume	3	2.00
GO answer key	3	1.00
Learning 100 Ensemble 5		
Mark 3 Cassette/Filmstrip Set	4-5-6	225.00
Aud-X Word Attack Review Study Guide	4-5-6	.85

Hoffman Audiovisual Instructional System

The Hoffman Audiovisual Instructional System* is centered around the Mark IV Projector, an instrument which presents a simultaneous visual and audio signal. Its sound system and viewing screen are in one unit.

Study units consist of forty-minute lessons that are organized in ten-minute modules. Materials covering the primary and intermediate grades are available. These are presented on four filmstrips and two records which are packaged in colorful albums. (Primary study units consist of two filmstrips and one record in an album.) Each achievement unit consists of ten study units which are packaged in a durable file box. Workbooks accompany each achievement unit. Questions that are presented audiovisually are printed in the answer book. By using headphones, students can work independently or in a small group.

Description	Unit Price
Hoffman Mark IV Projector	$389.00
Headset with air cushions	6.95
Jackbox	24.48
Listening center	67.95
Speaker	16.33

Primary Achievement units (60 Study Units)

Program	Unit Price	Work Sheets	Unit Price
100-0	$ 99.00	100-00-WS through 100-09-WS	$ .35
101-0	99.00	101-00-WS through 101-09-WS	.35
102-0	99.00	102-00-WS through 102-09-WS	.35
103-0	99.00	103-00-WS through 103-09-WS	.35
104-0	99.00	104-00-WS through 104-09-WS	.35
105-0	99.00	105-00-WS through 105-09-WS	.35

3rd Level Achievement Units (30 Study Units)

Program		Answer Books	
100-3	$125.00	100-3-AB	$ .35
101-3	125.00	101-3-AB	.35
102-3	125.00	102-3-AB	.35

4th Level Achievement Units (30 Study Units)

Program		Answer Books	
100-4	$125.00	100-4-AB	$ .35
101-4	125.00	101-4-AB	.35
102-4	125.00	102-4-AB	.35

(Continued)

*Available through Hoffman Information Systems, 5623 Peck Road, Arcadia, Calif. 91006.

Description	Unit Price	Description	Unit Price

5th Level Achievement Units (30 Study Units)

Program		*Answer Books*	
100-5	$125.00	100-5-AB	$ .35
101-5	125.00	101-5-AB	.35
102-5	125.00	102-5-AB	.35

6th Level Achievement Units (30 Study Units)

Program		*Answer Books*	
100-6	$125.00	100-6-AB	$ .35
101-6	125.00	101-6-AB	.35
102-6	125.00	102-6-AB	.35

Language Master

The Language Master* is an instructional device that provides simultaneous auditory and visual stimulation. It is based on the principle of the tape recorder in that the cards employed with the device have lengths of magnetic tape adhered parallel to their bottom edges. This feature allows the Language Master unit to function as a dual-channel audio recorder and playback device with the following functions: The positioning of a concealed switch enables the instructor to record words, phrases, and sentences on the master track. After such recordings have been completed and the switch returned to its normal position, the master track cannot be accidentally erased by the learner. The student may listen to the master-track recording as a model when he views the material in printed form. He may then record his own version on the student track. At this time, the student listens to his responses and checks them with master-track recording. The student can re-record his own efforts until he is satisfied that he has approximated the model recording. A detailed listing of the basic equipment and accessory cards follows:

Language Master, $250.00

Headphones, $28.00

Multiphone Panel (when used with headphones, allows six students to simultaneously listen to sound tracks, $26.00)

Interconnecting Cable (required for each multiphone panel to be used, $2.00)

Dual Headphone Adapter (when used with headphones, teacher and student may listen to sound track, $3.75)

*Available through Bell & Howell Co., 7100 McCormick Road, Chicago, Ill. 60645.

Language Master Prerecorded Card Sets, $35.00 each
  Vocabulary Builder Program
    Set I   Basic
    Set II   Intermediate
    Set III   Advanced
  Word-Picture Program
    Set I   Nouns: Everyday Things
    Set II   Verbs: Action Words
    Set III   Basic Concepts
  Language Stimulation Program
    Set I   Phrases
    Set II   Sentences
    Set III   Language Reinforcement and Auditory Retention Span
  English Development Program
    Set I   Practical Vocabulary and Expressions
    Set II   Everyday Expressions
  The Sounds of English Program
    Set I   Basic English Phonetics
  The Phonics Program
    Set I   Sound Blending and Beginning Phonetic Skills
    Set II   Consonant Blends and Irregular Phonetic Elements
    Set III   Word-Building and Word Analysis Technique

EFI Audio Flashcard System

This self-learning system* employs cards which are used in conjunction with a three-push-button machine. The lesson cards employ color in depicting situations or objects. When used with the Model 101 Machine, they remain stationary and provide six seconds audio and another six seconds for recording. Children can read descriptions and simultaneously hear the correct sounds. Also, they can record and compare their responses with the programmed lesson. The system is powered by AC or rechargeable batteries and has a built-in loudspeaker and microphone. A headset may be used if desired. Available card sets include the following:

Description	Price
Reading Readiness Program	
Set 1—Familiar Sounds	$36.00
Set 2—Animal Sounds	21.00
Set 3—Rhymes and Rhyming Words	51.00
Set 4—Missing Parts	50.00
Set 5—Information	61.00
Set 6—Directional-Structural Words	72.00

(Continued)

*The EFI Model 101 Audio Flashcard Reader is available through Electronic Futures, Inc., 57 Dodge Ave., North Haven, Conn., at a cost of $270.00.

Description	Price
Set 7—Likenesses and Differences I: Circles, Squares, and Triangles	$52.00
Set 8—Likenesses and Differences II: Colors, Shapes, and Sizes	78.00
Set 9—Likenesses and Differences III: Internal Detail	59.00
Set 10—Likenesses and Differences IV: Letter, 2 Letters, and 3 Letters	82.00
Phonics Program	
Set 1—Capital Letters	59.00
Set 2—Small Letters	45.00
Set 3—Initial Consonants, and Simple Phonograms	64.00
Set 4—Digraphs, Blends, and Phonograms	73.00
Set 5—Initial Consonants, Digraphs, Blends, and Phonograms	55.00
Phonics 1 Teacher's Manual	3.95
Phonics 1 Diagnostic Chart Pad	6.50
Blank Cards per 100	15.00

RX Reading Program

The RX Reading Program* is a self-instructional and multisensory program that incorporates the senses of touch, hearing, and sight. It is considered ideal for kindergarten, grades one, two, three, four, non-graded classes, special-education classes, and remedial classes from grades two through eight.

The program is self-correctional and is designed for use as either a teacher-directed activity or as a completely self-correctional teaching device. Its purpose is to provide actual teaching and/or reinforcement necessary for children to learn the skills of letter recognition, common nouns and pictures, basic sight words, and phonetic word analysis.

The complete RX Reading Program includes an Audio Tract Instructional Center with tape cassette module, an RX Carrousel Storage System, 160 single concept lessons (including eight skill cards and two checkstrips per lesson), eighty instructional tapes (160 lessons), four headsets, Teacher's Manual and Diagnostic Tests, Prescription Forms, a wall Progress Chart, and Record Sheets for thirty students.

PROGRAMMED LEARNING

The terms *teaching machine* and *programmed learning* are used interchangeably by many people. Actually, they are not the same. The program is the important thing. The machine merely acts as a vehicle for presenting the program.

---

*The complete RX Reading Program is available through Psychotechnics, Inc., 1900 Pickwick Avenue, Glenview, Ill. 60025, at a cost of $769.00.

A learning program consists of a carefully ordered and organized sequence of material to which a student responds. His response takes the form of filling in a space, selecting one of a number of multiple-choice answers, indicating agreement or disagreement, and so forth. Immediately after a student has made a choice or answered a question, he is permitted to see the correct answer so he knows whether an error was made.

At the present time, programs are available on many grade levels and with a variety of subjects. Spelling, geography, arithmetic, algebra, biology, psychology, political science, logic, engineering, foreign languages, and reading are among the areas covered.

Some of the specific principles that characterize successful programs are as follows:

1. *Logical Sequence of Small Steps:* Subject matter is broken down into information fragments and is presented one step at a time so it can be easily understood. The sequence is orderly, and the difficulty increment narrow. This permits steady student progress uncomplicated by undue frustration.

2. *Immediate Feedback:* Since nothing succeeds like success, it is important that the program provides an immediate appraisal of each response. The theory of reinforcement emphasizes that a student profits from the consequences of his responses. Since a student is constantly appraised for how well he is doing, there is little danger he will go far astray.

3. *Self-pacing:* The student engaged in programmed learning activity can work at his own rate. He is not held back by other students who do not comprehend readily or who lack the drive to persist. On the other hand, the student is not discouraged by others capable of working at a more rapid rate than he. The programmed learning process is completely individualized.

4. *Teacher Evaluation:* The teacher can easily evaluate a student's progress by checking the nature of the responses made to the items involved. Thus the kind of special help a student needs is easy to pinpoint.

Some available programmed materials which do not require teaching machines are the following:

1. American Guidance Service, Inc., Circle Pines, Minnesota
   Peabody Rebus Reading Program
   (readiness and beginning reading instruction)

2. Ann Arbor Publishers, 711 North University, Ann Arbor, Michigan
   Michigan Successive Discrimination Language Program
   (auditory, visual, and space discrimination, letters, words, phrases, paragraphs, manuscript writing, phonemic analysis, spelling, oral composition, and comprehension)

3. Appleton-Century-Crofts, 440 Park Ave. South, New York, N. Y.
   Programmed Vocabulary
   (word power and general reading ability)

4. Behavioral Research Laboratories, Box 577, Palo Alto, Calif.
   Reading
   (basic alphabetic, phonic, and structural skills)

5. California Test Bureau, Monterey, Calif.
   Lessons for Self-Instruction in Basic Skills
   (vocabulary, following directions, reference skills, interpretation; grades three to nine)

6. Center for Programmed Instruction, 365 West End Ave., New York
   Phonetic Analysis and *Structural Analysis*
   (primary grades and remedial work)

7. Charles E. Merrill Books, Inc., 1300 Alum Creek Drive, Columbus, O.
   Building Word Power
   (meaning vocabulary and comprehension; fifth grade and above)
   McGraw-Hill Book Co., 330 West 42nd St., New York

8. Coronet Instructional Films, 65 East South Water St., Chicago, Ill.
   How to Improve Your Vocabulary
   (developmental reading skills for seventh-grade reading level)
   David Discovers the Dictionary
   (programmed text for fourth grade)
   Maps: How We Read Them
   (programmed text for the sixth grade)

9. Croft Educational Services, New London, Conn.
   Part I
   (alphabet, vowels, consonants, blends, digraphs and endings)
   Part II
   (vowel digraphs, diphthongs, prefixes, suffixes, syllabication)

10. EDL, Huntington, N. Y.
    Word Clues Series
    (for grades seven through twelve)

11. Educators Publishing Service, 301 Vassar St., Cambridge, Mass.
    Programmed Phonics
    (remedial phonics; grades four through six)

12. Ginn & Company, Boston, Mass.
    By Myself
    (letter and word recognition, following directions, reading for meaning, phonic and structural elements; primary)

13. Honor Products Co., 20 Moulton St., Cambridge, Mass.
    Word Clues: Be a Word Detective
    (context clues program for intermediate grades)

14. Imperial Productions, Kankakee, Ill.
    Imperial Primary Reading Program
    (primary reading program materials on tape)

15. Inrad, Lubbock, Tex.
    Your Personal Tutor in: Spelling
    (phonics and structural analysis and spelling; sixth-grade level)
16. Institute of Educational Research, 2226 Wisconsin Ave., N. W., Washington, D. C.
    Basal Progressive Choice Reading Program
    (letter forms, sounds, words; primary grades)
17. Learning, Inc., Tempe, Ariz.
    Using the Dictionary
    (a program for elementary grades)
18. The Macmillan Company, 60 5th Ave., New York
    How to Use the Dictionary
    (intermediate grades)
    Spectrum of Skills
    (vocabulary, word attack skills and comprehension; intermediate grades)
19. Institute of Educational Research, 2226 Wisconsin Ave., N.W., Washington, D. C.
    Programmed Reading
    (letter sounds, words; 14 programs for grade one)
20. Science Research Associates, Chicago, Ill.
    A Programed Course in Vocabulary Development
    (for eighth grade and beyond)
    Lift-Off to Reading
    (phonics, comprehension; grades one to six)
    Words
    (vocabulary; grades seven to eight)
    Reading in High Gear
    (basic reading skills; for culturally deprived and nonreaders; grades seven to twelve)
21. TMI-Grolier, N. Y.
    Modern English Series: Spelling
    (phonics, word structure, and spelling; third grade and above)
    Modern English Series: Remedial Reading
    (beginning readers who show deficiencies)

The following are among the programmed materials requiring suitable teaching machines:

1. Cenco Center, 2600 S. Kostner Ave., Chicago, Ill.
   Vocabulary Building I and *Vocabulary Building II*
   (elementary and secondary)
2. General Education, 96 Mt. Auburn St., Cambridge, Mass.
   Studentutor Library of Matching Exercises
   (readiness; primary level)
3. Publishers' Co., 1106 Connecticut Ave., N.W., Washington, D. C.
   Reading: Word Recognition
   (primary level)
4. Honor Products, 20 Moulton St., Cambridge, Mass.
   Word Clues: Be a Word Detective
   (context clues; intermediate grades)

Fun with Words
(homonyms; intermediate grades)
5. Learning Inc., 1317 West 8th St., Tempe, Ariz.
   Synonyms, Antonyms, Homonyms
   (intermediate grades)
6. E-Z Sort Systems, 45 Second St., San Francisco, Calif.
   Beginning Sight Vocabulary
   (primary grades)
   Beginning Spelling
   (primary grades)

11

Reading
Improvement
Program in Action

Elementary school teachers and administrators usually are aware of the large number of pupils who fail to reach expected goals in reading every year but may not always avail themselves of appropriate corrective measures. The extensive retardation in reading found in most schools is the millstone that prevents raising the level of teacher and pupil efficiency and the basis for much of the criticism directed at the schools by the public. In order to resolve the reading problem the school must become acquainted with underlying causes or learning deficiencies and accept responsibility for their improvement and correction. The school must show concern for individual learning problems and provide a school environment that compensates for an underprivileged or unwholesome out-of-school life. When reading difficulties are permitted to accumulate and become more severe each year, when reading problems are tolerated but not diagnosed and corrected, and when pupils handicapped in reading are struggling with instructional material on the frustration level of difficulty, problems in reading will continue to flourish.

The learning process is unique. Each pupil and the methods best suited to him differ widely. There is no best method of teaching all pupils to read effectively. The question to be resolved is not whether phonics or look-and-say is the most effective method of teaching word perception. It is not whether systematic instruction using basal readers is superior to wide reading and incidental learning. The problem before the teacher is this: What combination and emphasis on phonics, look-and-say, systematic developmental instruction, individualized correction, and recreational reading will best meet the needs of the individual and teach him to become an efficient reader?(1)

The authors maintain that a complete mastery of the basic reading skills of word recognition and word analysis at each grade level is an essential prerequisite to independence in reading. While a mastery of the mechanics of reading is but a means to the end, it is vital to the attainment of competence in reading comprehension. Pupils in the third grade who have not attained the status of an independent reader need appropriate corrective instruction. The authors emphasize the importance of doing this before pupils enter the fourth grade where the emphasis is on content and independent reading habits are essential. By the same token, disabled readers already in the middle and upper grades should first be studied for deficiencies in the basic skills of word recognition and word analysis. If these deficiencies exist, they must be met before improvement of comprehension skills is undertaken. The basic reading skills are foundational to all high-level reading.

Considerable space and emphasis are given to the need for individualized correction of reading difficulties through the use of self-directed material. The instructional material described in this volume is designed to correct reading difficulties and improve the reading status of all pupils on the elementary school level. Because the material is largely self-directive, it enables the teacher to meet individual needs with relative ease.

Independent readers above the primary grades may experience difficulty in their reading because of deficiencies in meaning vocabulary, comprehension, and study skills associated with textbooks in the content fields. Teachers must become aware of these difficulties as soon as they arise. The self-directive aids described in chapters 8, 9, and 10 are valuable in helping these pupils.

The authors feel that recreational reading has great value for improving the reading status of normal and accelerated readers. If books are properly selected and evaluated, it proves a valuable supplement to individualized practice for retarded readers as well. However, a recreational reading program which does not include recognition of hazards to learning, an awareness of individual reading levels, specific reading difficulties, and individual interests is largely ineffective with retarded readers.

In summary, the essentials of reading improvement as set forth by the authors and reflecting their philosophy and experiences are as follows:

1. Child study which discovers individual hazards to learning and adjustment. Such a child study program will provide a better understanding of children and will facilitate planning a wholesome and more effective school environment.

2. Functional and systematic evaluation that is designed to discover individual reading levels, specific reading difficulties, and reading potentials. This program would employ intelligence tests, listening tests, silent reading tests, oral reading tests, teacher observation, interviews, and cumulative records.
3. A developmental instructional program in reading which (a) provides both group and individual balance, (b) provides instructional material on multilevels of difficulty, (c) provides systematic and sequential instruction in the reading skills, (d) avoids frustration levels of difficulty, (e) prevents an accumulation of reading difficulties, (f) promotes total mastery of reading skills, (g) has independent reading status as a goal for all pupils at the end of the primary grades.
4. A diagnostic and corrective program which uncovers and analyzes reading difficulties and utilizes self-directed instructional material designed to eliminate individual reading difficulties.
5. A wide reading program designed to provide all pupils with additional practice and stimulation. Such a program would use specially adapted books and materials for retarded readers. Included, too, would be supplementary readers and materials on many levels of difficulty that would interest and appeal to average and accelerated readers.

IN-SERVICE READING PROGRAMS

Many teachers enter service with minimal professional training in reading and are unable to cope with the problems they face in their classrooms. Other teachers received their training and teaching credentials so long ago that they feel the necessity of familiarizing themselves with more modern approaches to reading instruction. It is evident, therefore, that the principle of individual differences is as applicable to teachers as it is to the children they teach. Any in-service training program must take cognizance of this by being broad enough to meet the needs of the neophyte teacher as well as those of the veteran staff member who has had years of experience. The program must begin where each teacher is and move toward the goal of maximum teaching effectiveness for all. Such a program is most effective if centered around specific problems which both new and experienced teachers encounter. To be a genuine success, planning should grow out of a cooperative effort of both administration and staff. Teachers tend to reject an in-service training program imposed from above.

IN-SERVICE TRAINING PRACTICES

Preschool and postschool workshops, orientation weeks, teacher institutes, and teachers' meetings are scheduled by many schools as part of an in-service training program. Criscuolo(2) describes a number of other approaches to in-service reading programs. With most programs, consultants in reading from nearby colleges and universities may be used for these purposes, although on occasions individuals with little professional training in reading attempt to provide leadership. In any event, these one-shot attempts seldom provide any lasting benefits since more than momentary teacher enthusiasm is needed to sustain a program throughout the year.

More permanent benefits are achieved when school districts employ consultants who make classroom visits and carry out on-the-spot demonstrations of effective techniques and approaches for the teachers. Often such consultants give additional assistance to counselors, nurses, administrators, and parents.

Some schools have experienced success by initiating an intraschool visitation plan whereby new teachers are given opportunities to observe experienced teachers at work with children. Informal, small group discussions according to grade level may continue throughout the year. These may be led by experienced teachers. The groups devote attention to the causes of reading retardation, classroom grouping techniques, methods that are helpful in overcoming specific weaknesses and problems, interpreting test scores, utilizing school records, and so forth.

Teachers should be encouraged to take advantage of extension courses, summer courses, and extended workshops in the reading area. Alert administrators should hold conferences with teachers and bring to their attention specific courses which will be of benefit to them and will strengthen the staff as a whole. Teachers availing themselves of prescribed opportunities for professional growth should be given opportunities to share their learnings with other interested teachers.

Larger districts can encourage teachers to contribute practical ideas for the publication of an inexpensive bulletin which might bear the title "It Worked for Me" or "Here's How I Did It."

Material centers which house the latest devices and materials can be organized for teacher use. A section of the school library or a shelf in the teacher's room may be set aside for books and magazines which constitute an up-to-date professional library in reading. Copies of reading and language arts bulletins which have been purchased with school funds may also be displayed. Teachers are invited to check out such materials for study away from school.

Some school districts encourage teachers to carry out individual and group research projects and experiments. These projects are not only of benefit to teachers who participate in them directly but benefit all teachers in the district with whom the results can be shared.

A few city school systems have developed reading clinics which are used as training centers for teachers who, after a semester's work in the clinic, go back into their classrooms bristling with new insights and competencies. Such a plan has been employed in the St. Louis schools for a number of years. A group of select teachers are trained in the clinic under close supervision. After a full year in the clinic, the teachers are returned to the classroom. Dr. Kottmeyer states, "Although the efficiency of the clinic program is no doubt curtailed, the values of the in-service training for many teachers justify the policy."(3)

PROFESSIONAL LIBRARY

Teachers can build a library of professional books in reading which will enable them to keep abreast of current trends. (See Appendix E1 for a listing of recommended books.) Although teachers have access to public, university, and college libraries, they are not absolved of the responsibility of accumulating a personal library of authoritative books that deal with a process as important to learning as reading. Indeed, one would be suspicious of a medical doctor or lawyer who practiced his profession without the fingertip accessibility of literature relating to his work.(4) As a matter of fact, functional books and manuals should be kept on the teacher's desk for ready reference.

Teachers should join professional organizations such as the International Reading Association and subscribe to professional magazines which devote space to studies and articles in the area of reading. Periodicals particularly valuable in this respect are as follows:

Childhood Education. Association for Childhood Education International, 3615 Wisconsin Avenue, N. W., Washington, D. C. 20016.
Class: Reading. CCM Information Corporation, 909 Third Avenue, New York, N. Y. 10022.
Education. University of Wisconsin, P. O. Box 5504, Milwaukee, Wis. 53211.
Elementary English. National Council of Teachers of English, 508 South Sixth Street, Champaign, Ill. 61820.
Elementary School Journal. The University of Chicago Press, University of Chicago, 5835 Kimbark Avenue, Chicago, Ill. 60637.
English Journal. National Council of Teachers of English, 508 South Sixth Street, Champaign, Ill. 61820.
Grade Teacher. CCM Professional Magazines, Inc., 22 West Putnam Avenue, Greenwich, Conn. 06830.
The Instructor. The Instructor Publications Inc., Dansville, N. Y. 14437.
Journal of Education. Boston University School of Education, Boston, Mass.

Journal of Educational Psychology. The American Psychological Association, 1200 Seventeenth Street, N. W., Washington, D. C. 20036.

Journal of Educational Research. Dembar Educational Research Services, Inc., Box 1605, Madison, Wis. 53701.

Journal of Reading. IRA, 6 Tyre Avenue, Newark, Del. 19711.

Journal of Reading Specialists. College Reading Association, Reading Clinic, Lehigh University, Bethlehem, Penn. 18015.

Parents' Magazine. Parents' Magazine Enterprises, Inc., 52 Vanderbilt Avenue, New York, N. Y. 10017.

Reading Improvement. Academic Press, P.O. Box 125, Oshkosh, Wis. 54901.

Reading in High School. Box 75, College Station, Pullman, Wash. 99163.

Reading Newsreport. 11 West 42nd Street, New York, N. Y. 10036.

Reading Research Quarterly. IRA, 6 Tyre Avenue, Newark, Del. 19711.

The Reading Teacher. International Reading Association, Six Tyre Avenue, Newark, Del. 19711.

Review of Educational Research. American Educational Research Association, N. E. A., 1201 Sixteenth Street, N. W., Washington, D. C.

School and Society. Society for the Advancement of Education, Inc., 1860 Broadway, New York, N. Y. 10023.

Teachers can keep a file of advertising materials which lists the names and addresses of companies, along with the latest teaching aids available in the reading field. Another file can be devoted to free and inexpensive materials (booklets, charts, posters, filmstrips, etc.) which innumerable industrial, governmental, and business firms will send to any teacher who makes a request. Hundreds of such sources are to be found in the booklet titled *Catalog of Free Teaching Materials.** This booklet will prove invaluable to teachers at all grade levels.

Teachers should not overlook but should exploit to the fullest all available school resources. For example, manuals accompanying basal and supplementary readers furnished by the school should be studied carefully to glean all value from them. Certainly, too, the counsel of any available reading consultants, psychologists, and other specialists should be sought in an effort to implement an instructional program in reading that is geared to individual needs.

SUGGESTIONS FOR INITIATING A READING IMPROVEMENT PROGRAM

When an objective assessment of the school's present reading program is undertaken, consideration should be given to the presence of any of the following vulnerable factors:

1. Failing to discover or alleviate individual hazards to learning.
2. Failing to be concerned with the reading difficulties of pupils who receive low scores on a silent reading test.

*Available through Gordon Salisbury, Post Office Box 1075, Ventura, Calif., at a cost of $2.50. Mailing charges, $.15.

3. Using instructional material on a single level of difficulty in each grade.
4. Permitting reading difficulties to accumulate and assigning new material on the frustration level of difficulty.
5. Exposing pupils to fourth-grade materials before they have become independent readers.
6. Failing to use oral reading for diagnostic purposes.
7. Failing to utilize a systematic and diagnostic approach to discover reading difficulties.
8. Failing to utilize self-directed instructional material for corrective reading.
9. Failing to provide systematic practice in reading through a program of recreational reading.

The efficiency of a reading program can be measured best by its success in teaching all pupils to read in terms of their potential. The school must therefore be concerned with reducing all retardation in reading. While retardation from grade placement is a rough measure of reading success, it must be remembered that pupils of below average intelligence may be reading at their potential even though they score below grade in their reading. Pupils of above average intelligence who are reading at grade level are usually retarded in terms of their potential. In evaluating the efficiency of the current reading program it is important to determine the following:

1. Percent of pupils in the primary grades who are retarded more than six months in oral and silent reading.
2. Percent of pupils in the intermediate grades who are retarded more than nine months in silent reading.
3. Percent of pupils in the upper grades who are retarded more than a year in silent reading.
4. Percent of pupils above the primary grades who have not attained independent reading habits.
5. Percent of pupils not participating in recreational reading.

In seeking to improve the current reading program, the following areas of instruction should be evaluated for balance and completeness:

1. A developmental program in reading that

   a. provides instruction for every pupil on his instructional level;
   b. seeks mastery of the reading skills for every pupil at each grade level;
   c. emphasizes prevention by correcting reading problems when they first appear;

d. develops independent reading habits for every pupil in the primary grades;

e. promotes wide reading for all pupils throughout the calendar year;

f. utilizes cumulative records in order to maintain a complete longitudinal progress record in reading for each pupil;

g. provides a special instructional program for the culturally disadvantaged.

What evolves from a school's efforts to initiate and maintain a reading improvement program will vary from school to school. These differences will, in large measure, determine the emphasis the improvement program should take; however, factors such as the following must not be overlooked.

1. An enthusiastic and conscientious principal who has a sympathetic understanding of the reading problem and who wishes to see something done about it. Such a principal will assume responsibility for the following:

   a. Obtaining the kinds of materials needed to implement the program. (For example, commercially-made materials such as reading laboratories, workbooks, and other self-directive materials.) In addition, teachers may request special materials that are needed to build their own files of learning aids.

   b. Supporting and encouraging an in-service training program in reading. Use may be made of teachers' meetings, workshops, institutes, preschool conferences, postschool conferences, and extension classes which could be given at the school by a neighboring college or university.

   c. Acquiring the trained personnel needed to carry out an efficient program in reading. Personnel needed would include remedial teachers, speech therapists, school psychologists, and a reading consultant. When hiring a reading specialist, care should be taken that he has the personal qualifications for the job as well as the training.

2. Education means involvement. Therefore, all teachers must work together in developing the program. Librarians, counselors, and school nurses also should share responsibility. If this is done, each individual will feel that the program's success is dependent on him. Another advantage stemming from group participation is that the principles, aims, and purposes around which the program is built will be better understood by all.

3. Periodic evaluations of the improvement program should be made. And when modifications seem necessary, they should be introduced without hesitation. As the program develops, parents need to be informed of the progress taking place.
4. Study many programs and choose the best features from each in light of the needs of your own school. Seldom does the reading program of one school apply to another in all respects.
5. Particular attention should be given to developing a program that is coordinated at all levels. This means that intermediate grade and junior high teachers should understand what primary teachers are seeking to accomplish. By the same token, primary teachers should be interested in knowing how best they can prepare children for the grades lying ahead.

INVENTORY OF INSTRUCTIONAL PRACTICES IN READING

When the school staff is ready to initiate an improvement program in reading, the problem of its organization and implementation is of immediate concern. One useful approach to the problem is to undertake a survey or evaluation of the present reading program in terms of pupil achievement. It is also important to ascertain if the prevailing practices are wholesome and efficient. The following *Inventory of Instructional Practices in Reading* suggests an overall evaluation which may be applied to the entire school or to a particular grade. This *Inventory* may serve as a guide to a committee that is organized to evaluate the reading program.

1. Child Study
   a. Evaluate the activities of the school involving home visitation and parent conferences during the year. Indicate the reasons for the visits and the conferences and the results obtained.
   b. List the names of the children in each grade who have been identified as having impaired health, hearing, and vision, and indicate the corrective steps taken by the parents and the school.
   c. List the names of the children in each grade who are socially and emotionally maladjusted, indicating the nature of the maladjustment in each case. What corrective measures have been taken by the school?
   d. How are cumulative records used and kept up to date?
2. Reading Readiness in the First Grade
   a. List the reading readiness tests and the intelligence test used, indicating date each test was administered.

b. List the names of the children receiving low ratings on each of these tests.
c. What part did teacher judgment play in determining children's reading readiness?
d. What part did visual maturity play in the reading readiness program?
e. Evaluate the materials used and the types of experiences provided in the reading readiness program. What was the length of this period?
f. List the names of the children retained in the reading readiness program for a longer period, indicating the length of the second period.
g. Evaluate the reading readiness materials used.

3. Reading in the First Grade
a. When and how was phonics introduced?
b. What percent of the children in the first grade mastered the first-grade reader?
c. What percent mastered only the preprimers and primers?
d. What percent mastered only the preprimers?
e. Identify the children with an inadequate mastery of a first-grade sight vocabulary.

4. Oral Reading (grades 1 to 4)
a. What percent of time devoted to instruction in reading is spent on oral reading in class? Oral reading to the teacher?
b. How do the instructional activities in oral reading for retarded readers differ from the activities for nonretarded readers?
c. Evaluate the purposes, frequency, and extent of pupil-teacher oral reading.
d. Evaluate the nature and frequency of audience reading.

5. Analysis of Reading Difficulties (grades 1 to 8)
a. Check the methods and materials listed below which were used to identify individual reading problems.

__Observation	__Oral reading to the teacher
__Oral reading in class	__Word recognition tests
__Silent reading test	__Standardized oral reading test
__Interview	__Other

b. Check the reading difficulties such as those listed below which are most prevalent.

__Word recognition	__Comprehension
__Word analysis	__Study skills
__Faulty reading habits	__Rate of comprehension

6. Word Recognition
   a. What materials and techniques were used to develop skill in word recognition?
   b. What sight vocabulary were pupils expected to master?
   c. How was mastery in word recognition evaluated?
   d. What level of mastery in word recognition did the nonretarded readers attain?
   e. What level of mastery in word recognition did the retarded readers attain?
   f. What level of mastery in word recognition is required of retarded readers before more difficult reading material is undertaken?

7. Word Attack
   a. What elements of phonetic and structural analysis are emphasized with retarded readers?
   b. Check the instructional materials and procedures listed below which are used to develop word-attack skill.
   —Oral reading in class
   —Oral reading to the teacher
   —Developmental exercises in word analysis
   —Phonics workbooks
   —Word analysis games
   —Others

8. Meaning Vocabulary (grades 4 to 8)
   a. What percent of the children in the grade are retarded in meaning vocabulary as measured by a meaning vocabulary test?
   b. Describe the materials and procedures used to develop a more effective meaning vocabulary.

9. Comprehension (grades 4 to 8)
   a. What percent of the children in the grade are retarded six or more months in reading comprehension?
   b. What materials and procedures are used to help retarded readers improve their comprehension?

10. Recreational Reading
    a. How and by whom are books for recreational reading selected?
    b. What records are kept of the recreational reading done by the pupils?
    c. How are retarded readers motivated to engage in recreational reading?
    d. How extensive is the recreational reading done by retarded readers?

     e. How many books adapted for retarded readers are there in the room or library?

     f. What provision is made to extend the recreational reading program during the summer vacation?

11. Correction

     a. Is the corrective work in reading individualized? If so, describe the materials and procedures used.

12. Summary

     a. List the names of the children in each grade who are retarded in silent reading and indicate the amount of retardation for each. (See page 326 for detailed standards.)

     b. List the names of the children in each grade who are retarded in oral reading and indicate the amount of retardation for each. (See page 326 for detailed standards.)

     c. Identify the children in each grade who have failed to reach their full reading potential.

     d. Identify the children in each grade who have attained their full reading potential.

     e. Identify the children in the fourth grade who find the text too difficult.

     f. List the instructional practices found to be most helpful in preventing retardation in reading.

     g. List the instructional practices found to be most helpful in correcting difficulties in reading.

PROBLEMS FOR ORAL AND WRITTEN DISCUSSION

1. Examine the teacher's manual accompanying a series of basic readers for a specific grade:

     a. Summarize the suggestions given for the diagnosis and correction of difficulties in word analysis and word recognition.

     b. Summarize the suggestions given for the diagnosis and correction of difficulties in comprehension.

2. Determine the reading status of a class in the intermediate or upper grades in terms of oral and silent reading skills:

     a. Indicate specific tests utilized.

     b. Identify the pupils who are retarded in oral reading.

     c. Identify the pupils who are retarded in silent reading.

     d. Indicate the amount of retardation for each pupil.

     e. Make a list of each pupil's reading difficulties in need of correction.

3. Select and organize a program of self-directed corrective material in reading for a specific grade.

4. Describe and evaluate the in-service program in reading provided by a school system of your choice or as reported in a magazine.

5. Obtain the aid of a teacher in-service. Summarize her reading program by using the Inventory of Instructional Practices appearing in this chapter.

REFERENCES

1. ALBERT J. HARRIS, *Effective Teaching of Reading* (New York: David McKay Co., Inc., 1962), p. 166.
2. NICHOLAS P. CRISCUOLO, "Approaches to In-Service Reading Programs, *The Reading Teacher* (February 1971).
3. WILLIAM KOTTMEYER, *Teacher's Guide for Remedial Reading* (Manchester, Mo.: Webster Publishing, 1959), p. 243.
4. DELWYN G. SCHUBERT, "Do Teachers Read About Reading?" *California Journal of Educational Research* (March, 1960).

Appendixes

APPENDIX A
ELEMENTS AND PRINCIPLES OF PHONICS

A fluent reader will have mastered the skills of phonics along with underlying principles. Appendix A provides an outline of elements and principles involved in this area for ready reference.* These are drawn from manuals accompanying widely used basal reader series.

Elements and Principles of Phonics

Consonants

I. A consonant is a letter which is produced by stopping or interrupting the breath by a speech organ. Those consonants that are produced with no vocal-cord vibration are called voiceless consonants. Examples are *p, t, s.* Consonants that involve vocal-cord vibration in their production are known as voiced consonants. Examples are *g, l,*

Any material appearing in these appendixes may be reproduced by teachers for their own use.

*For more definitive information about this subject see William S. Gray, *On Their Own in Reading* and Albert J. Harris, *How to Increase Reading Ability.* Also, T. Clymer, "The Utility of Phonic Generalizations in the Primary Grades," *The Reading Teacher* (January 1963); C. Winkley, "Which Accent Generalizations Are Worth Teaching?" *The Reading Teacher* (December 1966); M. H. Bailey, "The Utility of Phonic Generalizations in Grades One Through Six," *The Reading Teacher* (February 1967); R. Emans, "The Usefulness of Phonic Generalizations Above the Primary Grades," *The Reading Teacher* (February 1967); L. E. Burmeister, "Usefulness of Phonic Generalizations," *The Reading Teacher* (January 1968); L. E. Burmeister, "Phonics in a Word Attack Program—Place and Content," *Proceedings of the International Reading Association, 1970;* and L. E. Burmeister, "Final Vowel-consonant-e," *The Reading Teacher* (February 1971).

m. When consonants are sounded in isolation, teachers should do their best to minimize the *uh* sound which inescapably must be added to some of them.

A. Some consonants represent several sounds.

1. Most often *c* sounds like *k: cone, candy, cup.* Once children generalize this principle, the following rhyme can be employed.

> When *c* comes before *o, u,* and *a*
> It sounds exactly like a *k.*

    a. When the letter *c* precedes the vowels *i, e,* or *y,* usually it has the sound of *s.* Examples are *cent, cigar, cyclone.* Once children generalize this principle, the following rhyme can be employed.

> When *c* comes before an *i, y,* or *e,*
> It makes a hissing sound for me.

2. Most often *g* has a hard sound: *go, game, gun.*

    a. When the letter *g* precedes the vowels *i, e,* or *y,* usually it has the sound of the letter *j.* Examples: *gist, gem, gym.* (Exceptions to this rule are fairly prevalent.)

3. When *y* begins a word, it acts as a consonant. Examples are *yes, yard, yoke.*

    a. When *y* ends a one-syllable word, it sounds like a long *i.* Examples: *by, cry, sly.*

4. The letter *x* usually has the sound of *ks.* Examples: *box, tax, six.*

    a. When *x* begins a word it never has the *ks* sound. Examples: *X-ray, xylophone.*

5. The letter *s* usually has the sound of *s* when it follows a voiceless sound. Examples: *boats* (*t* is voiceless), *rips* (*p* is voiceless).

    a. The letter *s* usually has the sound of *z* when it follows a voiced sound. Examples are *cars* (*r* is voiced), *hums* (*m* is voiced).

B. Consonant blends are combinations of two or three letters which when pronounced give credence to each letter. The first letter blends into the second: *grapes, stick, black.* Blends also may appear in terminal positions. Examples: *first, chasm, clasp.*

C. Consonant digraphs are two-letter sounds. Examples: *chicken, shoe, thumb, that, wing, phone, where, rough.* (It is important for the child to learn that each letter loses its individual sound when the letters are working together to make a new sound.)

D. When two consonants appear together, one of them may be silent.

1. When *b* follows *m*, the *b* usually is silent: *lamb, comb.*

2. When *t* follows *b*, the *b* usually is silent: *doubt, debt.*

3. When a vowel follows *gh*, the *h* is usually silent: *ghost, ghastly.*

4. When a vowel precedes *gh*, the *gh* usually is silent: *taught, light, weigh.*

5. When *d, m,* or *k* follow *l*, the *l* is usually silent: *would, talk, palm.*

6. When *s* follows *p*, the *p* usually is silent: *psalm, psychic.*

7. When *r* follows *w*, the *w* usually is silent: *wrench, write.*

8. When *ch* follows *t*, the *t* usually is silent: *witch, watch.*

Vowels

I. A vowel is a sound which is produced with little or no narrowing or obstructing of the speech organs. Phonetically, single vowels are the most inconsistent letters in the English alphabet. Each vowel—*a, e, i, o, u* (sometimes *y* and *w*)—has a number of sounds. Fortunately, however, these sounds seem to fall roughly into two broad categories. These are the long and short sounds. Examples of the long and short vowel sounds are *ate, at; even, elephant; iron, ink; old, ox; unicorn, uncle.*

A. As stated previously, when *y* begins a word, it acts like a consonant, but when *y* ends a one-syllable word, it has a long *i* sound.

1. When *y* ends a two-syllable word, it may sound like a short *i* or a long *e*. A difference of opinion exists among lexicographers. Actually, the sound of the *y* in these instances seems to be somewhere between a short *i* and a long *e*. Examples: *slowly, lovely.*

B. In words like *crow, blow,* and *know,* the *w* acts as a vowel so the *o* says its name.

C. Vowel diphthongs involve a slurring of two vowels; that is, one vowel glides or slides into the other. Examples are b*oy*, *oil*; c*ow*, h*ou*se. (It should be noted that the double vowel rule does not apply to diphthongs.)

D. Following are principles that aid in determining vowel sounds:

1. When a word has one vowel and that vowel is at the end of the word, usually it has a long sound. Examples: *go, me.*

2. When a word has one vowel and that vowel is *not* at the end of the word, usually it has the short vowel sound. Examples: *at, in, cut, hot, bet.*

3. When there are two vowels together in a word, usually the first says its name and the second one is silent. Examples: *boat, feet, seal.* When children generalize this principle, it can be turned into the following rhyme.

> When two vowels go walking
> The first one does the talking

4. When there are two vowels in a word, one of which is a final *e*, the first vowel says its name and the *e* is silent. Examples: *fine, home, tune.* Children like to call this principle the "Magic E Rule."

5. If a single vowel in a word is followed by an *r* the sound of the vowel usually is controlled by the sound of *r*. Examples: *bird, hurt, work, hard.*
   a. When *r* follows *e, i,* or *u,* only the *r* sound is heard: *her, fur, sir.*
   b. When *r* follows *a* or *o,* the vowel and the *r* are pronounced. The *a* has an *ah* sound and the *o* sounds like *aw: far, car, order, north.*

6. When the only vowel in a word is an *a,* followed by *l* or *w,* the *a* usually has neither the long nor short vowel sound.

Principles That Aid in Understanding Accent

1. When two-syllable words end in a consonant followed by *y,* the first syllable is accented. Examples: *lovely, slowly.*

2. When the first syllable of a word is *de, re, be, ex,* or *in,* the accent involves the last syllable. Examples: *depress, return, beware, expect, inspect.*

3. When the final syllable of a word ends in *le,* the syllable preceding it usually is accented. Examples: *table, little.*

4. When endings form syllables, they usually are unaccented. Examples: *foxes, tallest, tested.*

5. When a word ends in a suffix, the accent usually falls on the root word. Examples: *sneeze, sneezing; fool, foolish.*

6. When words end in *ity, ic, ical, ian, ial,* and *ious,* the primary accent usually involves the syllable preceding the suffix. Examples: *publicity, artistic, typical, musician, official, religious.*

7. When words end in *ate,* the primary accent usually falls on the third syllable from the end. Examples: *intermediate, depreciate.*

Generalizations That Apply in Attacking Compound, Inflected, or Derived Forms

1. Root words, prefixes, and suffixes are meaning units in words.
2. Doubling the final consonant, changing a final *y* to *i* or dropping a final *e* before an ending or suffix usually does not change the sound of the root word.
3. When an ending or a suffix is preceded by a single vowel letter followed by a single consonant, the root word usually ends in *e.*
4. When an ending or a suffix is preceded by the letter *i,* the root word usually ends in *e.*
5. Inflectional variants can be formed by adding an ending or suffix without changing the root word. Examples: *hunting, talked, foxes, shorter.*
6. When root words end in a single consonant, the consonant is usually doubled before an ending is added. Examples: *hitting, running.*
7. When root words end in *e,* the *e* usually is dropped before adding an ending that begins with a vowel. Examples: *wiping, strangest.*
8. When root words end in *y,* the *y* usually is changed to *i* before an ending or suffix is added. Examples: *fried, replied.*
9. When root words end in *f,* the *f* usually is changed to *v* before an ending is added. Examples: *wharves, calves.*

Principles That Aid in Determining Syllables in Words

1. When the first vowel in a word is followed by a double consonant, the word is divided between the consonants. Examples: *rabbit, chipmunk.* (This is not true, however, when the digraphs *sh, ch, th, wh,* and *ph* are involved.)
2. When the first vowel in a word is followed by a single consonant, that consonant usually begins the second syllable. Examples: *above, pupil.*
3. When a word ends in *le,* the consonant preceding the *le* begins the last syllable. Examples: *circle, able.*
4. When the ending *ed* is preceded by *d* or *t,* it usually forms a separate syllable. Examples: *padded, fitted.*
5. When the various endings *less, ment, cion,* and *sion* appear, they usually form separate syllables. Examples: *careless, government, suspicion, decision.*

APPENDIX A1
WORD ANALYSIS GLOSSARY

ACCENT: The stress given a certain syllable of a word to make it stand out over the other syllables of the word.

ACCENT, PRIMARY: The syllable receiving the main emphasis in the pronunciation of a given word.

ACCENT, SECONDARY: A stress weaker than the primary accent and one falling upon a different syllable of a given word.

AFFIX: That which is added to a root of a word; a suffix or prefix.

ANALYSIS, PHONETIC: A method of analyzing a printed word to determine its pronunciation through the use of consonant and vowel sounds, blends, syllables, etc.

ANALYSIS, STRUCTURAL: A method of analyzing a printed word to determine its pronunciation by identifying meaningful parts—roots, inflectional endings, syllables, prefixes, and suffixes—which in turn may be blended into the sound of the word.

ANALYSIS, WORD: Analyzing an unfamiliar printed word for clues to its sound and/or meaning. Synonym: word attack.

ANTONYM: A word which is directly opposite in meaning to another word, for example, *small* is the antonym of *large*.

BLEND: The fusion of two or more letter sounds in a word without the identity of either sound being lost. A blend may consist of two or more consonant letters (*st, bl, st*) or one or more consonants and a vowel (*bi* as in *big*).

BLEND, CONSONANT: See definition of blend.

BLEND, FINAL: The fusion of two or more letter sounds at the end of a word with each sound maintaining its identity.

BLENDING, SOUND: The fusion of two or more letter sounds without losing the identity of either sound, for example, *t* and *r* in *train*.

BREVE: A curved mark placed over a vowel to indicate the short sound, for example, *bĭg*.

CLUE, CONFIGURATION: A clue to word analysis based on the general shape or pattern of a printed word.

CLUE, CONTEXT: Utilizing surrounding words, phrases, or sentences as an approach to word recognition and meaning.

CLUE, PICTURE: A picture related to a unit in reading that provides a useful clue to its meaning.

CONSONANT: A letter representing a speech sound characterized by a closure or very strongly modified narrowing of the mouth or throat, for instance, *b, t, s.*

From D. Schubert, A *Dictionary of Terms and Concepts in Reading,* 2d ed. (Springfield, Ill.: Charles C Thomas, Publisher, 1968).

CONSONANT, FINAL: A consonant which appears at the end of a word.

CONSONANT, INITIAL: A consonant appearing as the first letter of a word.

CONSONANT, MEDIAL: A consonant appearing inside a word.

CONSONANT, VOICED: A consonant sound which when produced is accompanied by vocal-cord vibration, for instance, *b, d, g.*

CONSONANT, VOICELESS: A consonant sound which when produced is not accompanied by vocal-cord vibration, for instance, *f, h, s.*

DERIVATIVE: A word composed of a root plus a prefix and/or suffix, for example, *unhappy, happiness, unhappiness.* Synonym-derived form.

DIACRITICAL MARK: A symbol placed over a letter to indicate the pronunciation.

DIGRAPH, CONSONANT: Two consonants which lose their individual identity and go together to represent a single sound, for example, *ch* as in *chicken.*

DIGRAPH, VOWEL: Two vowels that together make one sound, for example, *oa* in *boat.*

DIPHTHONG: A union of two vowels to make a gliding sound, as *oy* in *boy* or *ow* in *owl.*

GRAPHEME: A letter of the alphabet; the sum of all written letters and letter combinations that represent one phoneme.

HETERONYM: A word spelled the same as another but having a different pronunciation and meaning, for example, *lead* (to conduct) and *lead* (a metal).

HOMOGRAPH: One of two or more words identical in spelling but different in derivation and meaning, as *bow* (a tie) and *bow* (to bend).

HOMONYM: A word having the same pronunciation as another but differing from it in origin, meaning, and often, in spelling, for example, *bare* and *bear.*

HOMOPHONE: Words that are spelled differently but pronounced alike, for instance, *to, too, two.*

INFLECTED FORM: A word to which an inflectional ending has been added, for example, *s* may be added to the root word *fight.*

INFLECTIONAL ENDING: Designating or pertaining to an affix used in inflection, for example, John'*s*, sing*s*, play*ed*, long*er.*

MORPHEME: The smallest meaningful unit in the structure of words (a root word, a prefix, a suffix, or an inflectional ending), for instance, *rainy* consists of two morphemes, the root *rain* and the suffix *y.*

PHONEME: A speech sound or group of variants of one speech sound.

PHONETICS: The science of speech sounds, including their pronunciation, the action of the larynx, tongue, and lips in sound production and the symbolization of sounds.

PHONICS: The study of sound-letter relationships in reading and spelling and the use of this knowledge in recognizing and pronouncing words.

PHONOGRAM: A letter or group of letters representing a speech sound.

PREFIX: A letter, syllable, or group of syllables placed at the beginning of a word to modify or qualify its meaning.

ROOT, WORD: The basic form from which words are developed by the addition of prefixes, suffixes, and inflectional endings.

SCHWA: A term borrowed from Hebrew phonetics, designating an indistinct vowel, one represented by the letters, *a, e, i, o,* and *u* in unaccented syllables, for example, *April, problems*; represented in phonetic script by an inverted *e*.

SIGHT WORD: A word recognized because of its shape or configuration rather than by the blending of parts into the whole.

SUFFIX: A letter or syllable added at the end of a word or root to modify its meaning, such as the *ment* in *agreement*.

SYLLABICATION: Synonym of syllabification.

SYLLABIFICATION: The act of forming or separating words into syllables.

SYLLABLE: A unit of pronunciation consisting of a vowel sound alone or with one or more consonant sounds and pronounced with one impulse of the voice.

SYLLABLE, CLOSED: A syllable ending with a consonant, for example: *set.*

SYLLABLE, OPEN: A syllable ending in a vowel, for example, *we.*

SYNONYM: A word that expresses the same idea as another word but usually differs from it in some shade of meaning.

TRIGRAPH, CONSONANT: A combination of three consonants, for example, *str.*

VOWEL: A single, open vocal sound in which there is no audible friction or stoppage.

WORD, COMPOUND: A word composed of two or more elements, themselves usually words: *housetop, bluebird.*

WORD, MONOSYLLABIC: A one-syllable word.

WORD, POLYSYLLABIC: A word having two or more syllables.

WORD-ATTACK SKILLS: Synonym of word analysis.

APPENDIX B
KINESTHETIC METHOD IN READING

Pupils vary widely in their response to and acceptance of different instructional methods. The pupil who has been in school several years but is a nonreader should be exposed to new and novel instructional methods and materials. The kinesthetic method involving the visual, auditory, and motor senses is frequently a most effective way of teaching the nonreader. Teachers seeking to employ the kinesthetic method should consult the original source by Fernald. (See Appendix E1 for title and publisher.) A summary of this method follows.

The Kinesthetic Method

Explain to the child that we have a new way of learning words and that many bright people who have had the same difficulty as we have learned easily by this method. Let *him* select any *words he wants to learn. Teach* him the words in this manner:

1. Teacher writes the word in manuscript with crayon.
2. Child traces the word with his finger and says each part of the word as he traces it.
3. Child writes the word without looking at the copy and then compares his effort with the copy.
4. If he has made an error, he continues to trace the copy until he can write it correctly.

After the child has learned several words in this manner and has discovered that he can learn, he begins to write stories about any subject he chooses. The following procedure is used:

1. The child asks the teacher to write any word which he needs in his story.
2. He learns the word by tracing it and saying the parts as he does so.
3. He writes the word first on scrap paper and then in his story.
3. He files the word.
5. Teacher types the story.
6. The child reads the story to the teacher or to the group.

Cautions to the teacher:

1. Be sure the child always writes the word in the story without looking at the copy.
2. Be sure the child's finger actually touches the paper as he traces the word.
3. The word should always be written as a unit and should never be patched up by erasing or substituting.
4. Emphasize success. Call attention to the new words he has learned.

Reading Readiness: Group

Name of Test	Grade Level	Description	Number of Forms	Working Time Minutes	Publisher
American School Reading Readiness Test	1	Vocabulary, discrimination of letter forms, recognition of words, discrimination of geometric forms, following directions, memory for geometric shapes	1	45	Bobbs-Merrill Company
Binson-Beck Reading Readiness Test	Kg-1	Picture vocabulary, visual discrimination, following directions, memory for story, motor control	1	40	Acorn Publishing Co., Inc.
Gates-MacGinitie Reading Readiness Test	Kg-1	Listening comprehension, auditory discrimination, visual discrimination, following directions, letter recognition, visual-motor coordination, auditory blending	1	Untimed	Teachers College, Columbia University
Harrison-Stroud Reading Readiness Profiles	Kg-1	Using symbols, visual discrimination, using the context, auditory discrimination, naming letters	1	76	Houghton Mifflin Company
Lee-Clark Readiness Test	K-1	Discrimination of letter forms and word forms	1	20	California Test Bureau
Metropolitan Readiness Tests	K-1	Linguistic maturity, perceptual abilities, muscular coordination and motor skills, number and letter knowledge, ability to follow directions, and attention span	2	60	Harcourt Brace Jovanovich, Inc.

Test	Grade/Level	Purpose	Forms	Time (min.)	Publisher
Murphy-Durrell Diagnostic Reading Readiness Test	1	Auditory perception, visual perception, rate of learning	1	72	Harcourt Brace Jovanovich, Inc.
Reading Readiness Test. (M. J. Van Wagenen)	1	Information, perception of relations, vocabulary, memory span, word discrimination, word learning	2	30	U.S. Educational Test Bureau

Oral Reading: Individual

Test	Grade/Level	Purpose	Forms	Time (min.)	Publisher
Diagnostic Reading Tests, Lower Level, Section IV, Oral Reading. Frances Triggs et al.	4-6	Accuracy and comprehension of oral reading	2	20	Committee on Diagnostic Reading Tests
Gilmore Oral Reading Test	1-8	Accuracy, comprehension, and rate of oral reading	4	20	Harcourt Brace Jovanovich, Inc.
Gray's Oral Reading Paragraphs	1-12	Accuracy of oral reading	4	Untimed	The Psychological Corporation
Leavell Analytical Oral Reading Test	1-8	Accuracy and comprehension	2	20	U.S. Educational Test Bureau

Word Recognition and Word Analysis

Test	Grade/Level	Purpose	Forms	Time (min.)	Publisher
California Phonics Survey	7-Adult	Word Analysis	2	40	California Test Bureau
Diagnostic Reading Test of Word Analysis. Ross, Chall (Individual)	2-6	Word Analysis	1	5	Essay Press

Name of Test	Grade Level	Description	Number of Forms	Working Time Minutes	Publisher
Doren Diagnostic Reading Test	3-8	Eleven word-recognition skills	1	Untimed	American Guidance Service
Diagnostic Silent Reading Test. Bond et al.	3-8	Word recognition, auding	2	45	Lyons & Carnahan
Flash-X Sight Vocabulary	1-2	Word recognition	1	Untimed	Bausch & Lomb
McCullough Word Analysis Test	4-8	Word Analysis	1	Untimed	Teachers College, Columbia University
Phonics Knowledge Survey	1-6	Word analysis, phonics	1	30	Teachers College, Columbia University
Wide Range Vocabulary	3-Adult	Word recognition	2	Untimed	Psych Corporation
Gates-McKillop Reading Diagnostic Tests	1-6	Word recognition, word analysis	2	60-90	Bureau of Publications, Teachers College, Columbia

Silent Reading (Diagnostic)

Name of Test	Grade Level	Description	Number of Forms	Working Time Minutes	Publisher
Learning Methods Test. Mills	Kg-3	Learning proficiency visual-auditory, kinesthetic	1	80	Mills Center, Fort Lauderdale, Fla.
New Development Reading Tests. Bond et al. (Group)	1-2	Word recognition, comprehension	2	40	Lyons & Carnahan
Diagnostic Battery Sec II. Triggs	7-12	Five comprehension skills	4	Untimed	Committee on Diagnostic Reading Tests

Test	Grade	Areas Measured	Forms	Time	Publisher
Iowa Silent Reading Elem.	4-8	Eight comprehension skills	4	49	Harcourt Brace Jovanovich, Inc.
Stroud-Hieronymous Primary Reading Profile	1-2	Word recognition, word analysis, comprehension	1	six tests 6-18	Houghton Mifflin Company
Test of Study Skills	4-9	References, graphs, tables, maps	2	60	Steck-Vaughn

Silent Reading (Survey): Group

Test	Grade	Areas Measured	Forms	Time	Publisher
California Reading Tests Elementary Junior High	4-6 7-9	Meaning vocabulary comprehension	2	20 to 50 Minutes	California Test Bureau
The Developmental Reading Tests (Bond, Clymer, Hoyt) 3 parts	3-6	Word recognition, comprehension, study skills	1	Two 45-Minute Periods	Lyons & Carnahan
Iowa Every-Pupil Test of Basic Skills Test B Work-Study Skills Elementary Advanced	3-5 5-9	Reading maps, graphs, charts and tables; use of references, index, and dictionary	4	Two 45-Minute Periods	Houghton Mifflin Company
Garvey Primary Reading Test	1-3	Recognition of form, sight vocabulary, and comprehension	2	40	California Test Bureau
Gates-MacGinitie Reading Tests Primary Survey D Survey E	1-3 4-6 7-9	Vocabulary, comprehension Vocabulary, comprehension, speed Vocabulary, comprehension, speed	2 3 3	47 45 45	Teachers College, Columbia University
Ingraham-Clark Diagnostic Reading Tests Primary Intermediate	1-3 4-8	Meaning vocabulary, comprehension, speed and accuracy of reading	2	40	California Test Bureau

Name of Test	Grade Level	Description	Number of Forms	Working Time Minutes	Publisher
Iowa Every-Pupil Tests of Basic Skills in Silent Reading Comprehension		Meaning vocabulary, comprehension; noting details, organization, total meaning			Houghton Mifflin Company
Elementary	3-5		4	46	
Advanced	5-9		4	68	
Iowa Silent Reading Test Elementary	4-8	Rate of reading, meaning vocabulary, comprehension, work-study skills	4	49	Harcourt Brace Jovanovich, Inc.
Nelson Silent Reading Test	3-9	Meaning vocabulary, comprehension; general significance, details, prediction of outcomes	3	30	Houghton Mifflin Company
Sangren-Woody Silent Reading Test	4-8	Word meaning, rate, fact material, total meaning, central thought, following directions, organization	2	27	Harcourt Brace Jovanovich, Inc.
Traxler Silent Reading Test	7-10	Rate, story comprehension, word meaning, paragraph comprehension	4	46	Bobbs-Merrill Company
(Additional tests contained in test batteries)					

Listening Tests (Oral and Silent)

Brown-Carlsen Listening Comprehension Test	9-12	Comprehension of spoken language	2	50	Harcourt Brace Jovanovich, Inc.
Botel Reading Inventory (Group-Ind.)	1-12	Word recognition, word analysis, auding	1	Untimed	Follett Publishing Co.

Test	Grade	Description	No.	Min.	Publisher
Diagnostic Reading Scales. Spache (Individual)	1-8	Vocabulary, comprehension word analysis, auding	1	60	California Test Bureau
Durrell Reading Listening Series	1-9	Comprehension of spoken language	2	65	Harcourt Brace Jovanovich, Inc.
Peabody Picture Vocabulary Test	Kg-12	Auding	2	15	American Guidance Service
Step Listening Tests	4-9	Comprehension of spoken language	4	35	Cooperative Test Division
Test of Auditory Discrimination (Individual)	Kg-13	Auditory discrimination	1	15	American Guidance Service, Inc.
Wepman Auditory Discrimination Test (Individual)	1-6	Auditory discrimination	2	10	Language Research Associates

Group Intelligence Tests

Test	Grade	Description	No.	Min.	Publisher
California Test of Mental Maturity		Language and nonlanguage tests of memory, spatial relationships, logical reasoning and vocabulary			California Test Bureau
Preprimary Series	K-1		1	90	
Primary Series	1-3		1	90	
Elementary Series	4-8		1	90	
Intermediate Series	7-10		1	90	
California Short-Form Test of Mental Maturity		Language test of numerical quantity, inference, and vocabulary; nonlanguage tests of sensing right and left, manipulation of areas and similarities			California Test Bureau
Preprimary Series	K-1		1	45	
Primary Series	1-3		1	45	
Elementary Series	4-8		1	45	
Intermediate Series	7-10		1	45	

Name of Test	Grade Level	Description	Number of Forms	Working Time Minutes	Publisher
Chicago Non-Verbal Examination	1-12	Designed to measure the intelligence of deaf and foreign-born children and children who are handicapped in the language area	1	25	The Psychological Corporation
Davis-Eells Test of General Intelligence or Problem Solving Ability		Ability to solve problems common to all urban cultural groups			Harcourt Brace Jovanovich, Inc.
Grade	1		1	60	
Grade	2		1	90	
Elementary	3-6		1	120	
Goodenough Intelligence Test	K-1	Based on spontaneous drawings of the children	1		Harcourt Brace Jovanovich, Inc.
Henmon-Nelson Tests of Mental Ability (self-marking)	3-8	Vocabulary, number completion, analogies	3	30	The Psychological Corporation
Kuhlmann-Anderson Intelligence Tests	K-8	Separate booklet for each grade	1	30	Educational Test Bureau
Otis Quick-Scoring Test of Mental Ability		Revision of the Otis Self-Administering Intelligence Test			Harcourt Brace Jovanovich, Inc.
Alpha Test	1-4		2	25	
Beta Test	4-9		2	30	
Pintner General Ability Tests—Verbal Series Primary	K-2	Seven tests composed entirely of pictures	3	25	Harcourt Brace Jovanovich, Inc.
Elementary	2-4	Scale 1, picture content; Scale 2, reading content	2	45	

Test	Grade	Purpose			Publisher
Intermediate	4-9	Verbal content; reasoning, vocabulary, logical selection, etc.	2	45	Harcourt Brace Jovanovich, Inc.
Pintner General Ability Tests—Non-language Series	4-9	Mental functions independent of word knowledge and facility	2	50	Science Research Associates
SRA Primary Mental Abilities, Ages 5-7	K-2	Verbal meaning, quantitative, space, perceptual, speed, motor	1	35	
Ages 7-11	2-6	Verbal meaning, space, reasoning, perception, numbers	1	35	
Ages 11-17	6-12	Verbal meaning, space, reasoning, number, word fluency	1	26	

Screening Tests—Vision

Test	Purpose			Publisher
Eames Eye Test	Near-point visual skills	1	5-10	Harcourt Brace Jovanovich, Inc.
Keystone Telebinocular	Far- and near-point visual skills	1	10-15	Keystone View Company
Massachusetts Vision Test	Far-point acuity, eye muscle balance at distance and near	1	5-10	American Optical Company
Orthorater	Far- and near-point visual skills	1	10-15	Keystone View Company
Pola-Mirror Test	Near-point binocularity, suppression	1	1	College Bookstore, 950 W. Jefferson Blvd., Los Angeles, Calif. 90007
Reduced Snellen	Near-point acuity	1	2-4	Bausch & Lomb Optical Company
Snellen Chart	Far-point acuity	1	2-4	American Optical Company
Worth 4-Dot Test	Binocularity, near-point fusion, suppression	1	1-3	House of Vision

What Do Diagnostic Reading Tests Diagnose? Skills Included in Six Analytical Reading Measures*

DEVELOPMENTAL READING TESTS

	Botel Reading Inventory	Silent Reading Diagnostic Tests	Durrell Analysis of Reading Difficulty	Gilmore Oral Reading Test	Diagnostic Reading Scale	Gates-McKillop Reading Diagnostic Tests
Silent Reading Comprehension			X		X	
Oral Reading Comprehension			X	X	X	
Oral Reading Accuracy			X	X	X	X
Oral Reading Rate			X	X	X	
Listening Comprehension			X		X	
Word Recognition (oral)	X		X		X	X
Word Recognition (silent)		X				
Word Recognition in context (silent)	X					
Phrase Reading (oral)						X
Recognition of phonetic word elements (oral)	X				X	X
Recognition of phonetic word parts (silent and listening)		X	X			
Root Words (silent)		X				

*T. Trela, "What Do Diagnostic Reading Tests Diagnose? Skills Included in Six Analytical Reading Measures," *Elementary English Journal* 43 (April 1966): 370-372. Used by permission of author and the National Council of Teachers of English.

Rhyming Words (listening or silent)				X	X
Word Opposites (listening and/or silent)					X
Word Blending (silent)				X	
Word Blending (oral)	X	X			
Saying Syllables	X	X			
Number and accent syllables (listening)					X
Syllabication (silent)				X	X
Identifying Letter Sounds (listening)			X	X	X
Identifying Beginning Word Sounds (listening)	X		X	X	
Identifying Word Endings (listening)	X		X		
Saying Letter Sounds	X	X			
Identifying consonant blends and/or digraphs (listening)					X
Saying consonant blends and/or digraphs	X	X	X		
Identifying long and short vowels (oral)	X	X			
Identifying long and short vowels (listening)	X				X
Naming capital and lowercase letters (oral)	X		X		
Spelling (listening)			X		
Spelling (oral)					
Reversible Words (silent)	X			X	
Visual memory of words (silent)			X		

APPENDIX D
LETTER TO PARENTS OF DISABLED READERS

Dear_____:

A parent can do a great deal to help his child with his reading. Here is a list of some practical suggestions:

1. Have your child receive an annual physical examination which gives particular attention to his vision, hearing, and general health. *Make sure the vision specialist to whom you go is interested in how well your child's eyes function at reading distance.* If you have a child about to enter first grade, a before-school visual examination is good insurance.

2. Should the teacher or nurse observe symptoms of problems that require referral to another medical specialist (neurologist, psychiatrist, endocrinologist, etc.) do your best to cooperate. The specialist may report that nothing is wrong, but it is unwise to take a chance when your child's welfare is at stake.

3. Make sure your child gets enough sleep and a hot breakfast in the morning. A youngster who is tired finds it difficult to remain alert in school; a child who is hungry finds concentration a chore.

4. Provide a healthy home atmosphere. A child is more likely to do poorly in reading when parents are inconsistent in their discipline, when they reject the child or are overly solicitous or when they subject him to unfavorable comparisons with other children. As parents, it is important to build your child's confidence and feelings of self-worth. Give him plenty of love and accept him as an individual. Above all, do not resort to threats and bribes.

5. Enrich your child's language experiences by providing him with a rich background. Since reading involves bringing meaning to printed symbols, taking him on picnics, trips, and excursions, and explaining the "what," "how" and "why" of situations or happenings proves invaluable.

6. Provide a comfortable and inviting atmosphere for reading at home. Set aside a period for reading to and with your child. If he wishes to share with you something he has read, take the time to listen. And that means giving your undivided attention. More is needed than an "uh-huh."

7. Set a good example. Actions speak louder than words. If you wish your child to develop a love of reading, you have to do a lot of reading yourself. Soon he will begin thinking, "Gee, Dad and Mom like to read. Reading must be fun. I want to do it, too."

8. Help your child develop the library habit. Take him to the neighborhood library and get to know the librarian. Perhaps she can show him around before she gives him his own library card.

9. Provide a place for whatever books your child acquires. Perhaps you can give him a special shelf in the family bookcase. Even a drawer in a dresser or the kitchen cupboard is better than no place at all. Having a place for his books and other reading material will help your child develop pride in his library and an interest in reading.

10. Help your child evolve a television-viewing schedule that will not interfere with his reading and school work. Allowing him to choose with your help a select number of programs he wishes to view each week is a good democratic approach. In any event, an hour of television viewing daily should be sufficient. This means, of course, curtailing your own viewing of television on school nights. A child can't concentrate on books when others are watching television.

11. Don't negate what is being done by the school. Get to know your child's teacher and find out what you can do to help. She may provide you with a list of books that have high interest appeal and are not too difficult. She also may recommend some reading game activities that are ideally suited to your child's needs. Many good books and reading games are available for purchase. They make fine birthday or Christmas gifts. But if your child has a severe reading problem, neither should be purchased without professional guidance.

12. Acquaint yourself with books that will help you understand the school's reading program and how to assist your child. Some recommendations follow:

ARTLEY, A. STERL. *Your Child Learns to Read.* Chicago: Scott, Foresman and Co., 1953.
CASEY, SALLY L. *Ways You Can Help Your Child with Reading.* Evanston, Ill.: Row, Peterson and Co., 1950.
GOLDENSON, ROBERT M. *Helping Your Child to Reading Better.* New York: Thomas Y. Crowell Co., 1957.
LARRICK, NANCY. *A Parent's Guide to Children's Reading.* 3rd ed., revised and enlarged. Garden City, N.Y.: Doubleday and Company, Inc., 1969.

13. If the school your child attends has no remedial specialist, avail yourself of a college or university reading clinic should one be in the community. Reading clinics often have a team of specialists who can diagnose your child's reading problem and provide him

with proper instruction. Sometimes, too, remedial reading specialists are available outside the school; but choosing a good one isn't a simple matter. Reading specialists vary greatly in their background. If possible, select one who has had experience and training in a college or university reading clinic. And most important, make sure the individual is the kind of person who is capable of establishing a good relationship with your child. Whether your child likes or hates his reading lesson is dependent on whether he likes his teacher.

14. Tutoring your own child is not recommended. As a parent you are emotionally involved, and it is almost impossible to sustain the patience that is needed in a learning situation. Although there is no danger in furnishing your child with a word when he is stymied, it would be hazardous to attempt formal reading instruction involving phonics. Most parents not only lack the patience needed to teach word-attack skills but the knowledge as well.

APPENDIX E
BIBLIOGRAPHY OF PROFESSIONAL BOOKS
AND OTHER MATERIALS IN READING

As an aid to teachers and administrators in selecting useful books for their personal library and for the school library as well, Appendix E has been prepared. Teachers as professional workers cannot afford to neglect their professional library if they are to maintain professional status. Appendix E1 will help them in selecting worthwhile professional books and materials. Appendix E2 gives a list of sources of books adapted for retarded readers. Appendix E3 lists books of high interest and low vocabulary. An ample supply of these books is essential in every grade if retarded readers are to be provided with books for recreational reading that are of appropriate difficulty and interest.

APPENDIX E1

Selected Professional Books and Pamphlets

ALLEN, ROACH VAN, and DORIS LEE. *Learning to Read Through Experience.* New York: Appleton-Century-Crofts, 1963.

ANDERSON, IRVING H., and WALTER F. DEARBORN. *The Psychology of Teaching Reading.* New York: The Ronald Press, 1952.

ARBUTHNOT, MAY. *Children and Books.* Chicago: Scott, Foresman and Co., 1947.

ARTLEY, STERL. *Your Child Learns to Read*. Chicago: Scott, Foresman and Co., 1953.

AUSTIN, MARY C., and others. *The Torch Lighters: Tomorrow's Teachers of Reading*. Cambridge: Harvard University Press, 1961.

BARBE, WALTER. *Personalized Reading Instruction*. Englewood Cliffs, N. J.: Prentice-Hall, Inc., 1961.

BARBE, WALTER B. *Teaching Reading: Selected Materials*. New York: Oxford University Press, 1965.

BETTS, EMMETT. *Foundations of Reading Instruction*. New York: American Book Company, 1946.

————. *The Prevention and Correction of Reading Difficulties*. Evanston, Ill.: Row, Peterson and Co., 1936.

BLOOMER, RICHARD. *Swirl Games to Teach Reading*. Dansville, N. Y.: F. A. Owen Co., 1961.

BOND, GUY, and MILES TINKER. *Reading Difficulties, Their Diagnosis and Correction*. 2nd ed. New York: Appleton-Century-Crofts, 1967.

BOTEL, MORTON. *How to Teach Reading*. Chicago: Follett Publishing Co., 1962.

BRUECKNER, LEO, and GUY BOND. *The Diagnosis and Treatment of Learning Difficulties*. New York: Appleton-Century-Crofts, 1955.

CARTER, HOMER, and DOROTHY McGINNIS. *Diagnosis and Treatment of the Disabled Reader*. New York: The Macmillan Co., 1970.

COHN, JACK, and STELLA COHN. *Teaching the Retarded Reader*. New York: The Odyssey Press, Inc., 1967.

COLE, LUELLA. *The Improvement of Reading*. New York: Holt, Rinehart and Winston, Inc., 1938.

CORDTS, ANNA D. *Phonics for the Reading Teacher*. New York: Holt, Rinehart and Winston, Inc., 1965.

CUTTS, WARREN G. *Modern Reading Instruction*. Washington: Center for Applied Research in Education, 1964.

DARROW, HELEN, and VIRGIL HOWES. *Approaches to Individualized Reading*. New York: Appleton-Century-Crofts, 1960.

DAWSON, MILDRED, and HENRY BAMMAN. *Fundamentals of Basic Reading Instruction*. New York: David McKay Co., Inc., 1959.

DEBOER, JOHN, and MARTHA DALLMANN. *The Teaching of Reading*. 3rd ed. Holt, Rinehart and Winston, Inc., 1970.

DECHANT, EMERALD V. *Improving the Teaching of Reading*. Englewood Cliffs, N. J.: Prentice-Hall, Inc., 1964.

DECHANT, EMERALD V. *Diagnosis and Remediation of Reading Disability*. West Nyack, N. Y.: Parker Publishing Co., Inc., 1968.

DURKIN, DOLORES. *Phonics and the Teaching of Reading*. New York: Bureau of Publications, Teachers College, Columbia University, 1962.

DURRELL, DONALD D. *Improving Reading Instruction*. New York: Harcourt Brace Jovanovich, Inc., 1956.

DURROW, HELEN, and VIRGIL HOWES. *Approaches to Individualized Reading*. New York: Appleton-Century-Crofts, 1960.

FERNALD, GRACE. *Remedial Techniques in Basic School Subjects*. New York: McGraw-Hill Book Co., 1943.

FRIES, CHARLES C. *Linguistic and Reading*. New York: Holt, Rinehart and Winston, Inc., 1963.

GANS, ROMA. *Common Sense in Teaching Reading.* Indianapolis: Bobbs-Merrill, Co., Inc., 1963.

——. *Fact and Fiction About Phonics.* Indianapolis: Bobbs-Merrill Co., Inc., 1964.

GATES, ARTHUR. *The Improvement of Reading.* New York: The Macmillan Co., 1947.

GETMAN, G. N., and ELMER R. KANE. *The Physiology of Readiness.* Minneapolis, Minn.: P.A.S.S., Inc., 1964.

GILLILAND, HAP. *Materials for Remedial Reading and Their Use.* Billings: Eastern Montana College, 1965.

GRAY, LILLIAN. *Teaching Children to Read.* 3rd ed. New York: The Ronald Press Company, 1963.

GRAY, WILLIAM, et al. *Developing Children's Word-Perception Power.* Chicago: Scott, Foresman & Company, 1954.

——. *On Their Own in Reading.* Rev. ed. New York: Scott, Foresman and Co., 1960.

HARRIS, ALBERT. *Casebook on Reading Disability.* New York: David McKay Co., Inc., 1970.

——. *Effective Teaching of Reading.* New York: David McKay Co., Inc., 1962.

——. *How to Increase Reading Ability.* 5th ed. New York: David McKay Co., Inc., 1970.

HEGG, THORLEIF. *Remedial Reading Drills.* Ann Arbor, Mich.: George Wahr, 1953.

HEILMAN, ARTHUR W. *Phonics in Proper Perspective.* Indianapolis: Bobbs-Merrill Co., Inc., 1964.

——. *Principles and Practices of Teaching Reading.* Columbus, O.: Charles E. Merrill Books, Inc., 1961.

HILDRETH, GERTRUDE. *Teaching Reading.* New York: Henry Holt and Co., 1958.

KARLIN, ROBERT. *Teaching Elementary Reading.* New York: Harcourt Brace Jovanovich, Inc., 1971.

KEPHART, NEWELL. *The Slow Learner in the Classroom.* Indianapolis: Bobbs-Merrill Co., Inc., 1960.

KOTTMEYER, WILLIAM. *Teacher's Guide for Remedial Reading.* Manchester, Mo.: Webster Publishing, 1959.

Learning to Read: A Report of a Conference of Reading Experts. Princeton: Educational Testing Service, 1962.

LEFEVRE, CARL. *Linguistics and the Teaching of Reading.* New York: McGraw-Hill Book Co., 1964.

MARKSHEFFEL, NED D. *Better Reading in the Secondary School.* New York: The Ronald Press Co., 1966.

MIEL, ALICE. *Individualized Reading Practices.* New York: Bureau of Publications, Teachers College, Columbia University, 1958.

MCKEE, PAUL, and WILLIAM DURR. *A Program of Instruction for the Elementary School.* Boston: Houghton Mifflin Co., 1966.

MCKIM, MARGARET. *Guiding Growth in Reading in the Modern Elementary School.* New York: The Macmillan Co., 1955.

MONROE, MARION, and BERTIE BACKUS. *Remedial Reading.* Boston: Houghton Mifflin Co., 1937.

——. *Growing into Reading.* Chicago: Scott, Foresman and Co., 1951.

ORTON, SAMUEL. *Reading, Writing and Speech Problems in Children.* New York: W. W. Norton and Co., Inc., 1937.

OTTO, WAYNE, and RICHARD McMENEMY. *Corrective and Remedial Teaching.* Boston: Houghton Mifflin Company, 1966.

REEVES, RUTH. *The Teaching of Reading in Our Schools.* New York: The Macmillan Co., 1966.

ROBINSON, HELEN. *Why Pupils Fail in Reading.* Chicago: University of Chicago Press, 1946.

RUSSELL, DAVID. *Children Learn to Read.* Rev. ed. Boston: Ginn and Co., 1961.

———, et al. *Reading Aids Through the Grades.* New York: Bureau of Publications, Teachers College, Columbia University, 1956.

SCHELL, LEO, and P. BURNS. *Remedial Reading.* Boston: Allyn and Bacon, Inc., 1968.

SCHUBERT, DELWYN G., *A Dictionary of Terms and Concepts in Reading,* Springfield, Ill.: Charles C Thomas, Publisher, 1968.

———. *Reading Games That Teach.* Monterey Park, Calif.: Creative Teaching Press, Inc., 1965.

SCHUBERT, DELWYN G., ed. *Readings in Reading: Practice – Theory – Research.* New York: Thomas Y. Crowell Company, 1968.

SCOTT, LOUISE, and JAMES THOMPSON. *Phonics in Listening, in Speaking, in Reading, in Writing.* Manchester, Mo.: Webster Publishing, 1962.

SMITH, DONALD, and M. CARRIGAN. *The Nature of Reading Disability.* New York: Harcourt Brace Jovanovich, Inc., 1959.

SMITH, NILA B. *American Reading Instruction.* Newark, Del.: International Reading Association, 1965.

SPACHE, GEORGE. *Good Reading for Poor Readers.* Rev. ed. Champaign, Ill.: Garrard Publishing Co., 1970.

———. *Reading in the Elementary School.* 2nd ed. Boston: Allyn and Bacon, Inc., 1969.

———. *Toward Better Reading.* Champaign, Ill.: Garrard Publishing Co., 1963.

STAUFFFER, RUSSELL. *Individualized Reading Instruction.* University of Delaware, School of Education, 1957.

STRANG, RUTH. *Diagnostic Teaching of Reading.* 2nd ed. New York: McGraw-Hill Book Co., 1969.

———, and DOROTHY BRACKEN. *Making Better Readers.* Boston: D. C. Heath and Co., 1957.

———, CONSTANCE McCULLOUGH, and ARTHUR TRAXLER. *The Improvement of Reading.* 3rd ed. New York: McGraw-Hill Book Co., 1961.

WILSON, ROBERT M. *Diagnostic and Remedial Reading.* Columbus, O.: Charles E. Merrill Books, Inc., 1967.

WITTY, PAUL, and DAVID KOPEL. *Reading and the Educative Process.* Boston: Ginn and Co., 1939.

WITTY, PAUL, A. FREELAND, and E. GROTBERG. *The Teaching of Reading.* Lexington, Mass.: D. C. Heath and Co., 1968.

ZINTZ, MILES V. *Corrective Reading.* 2nd ed. Dubuque, Ia.: Wm. C. Brown Co. Publishers, 1972.

———. *The Reading Process.* Dubuque, Ia.: Wm. C. Brown Co. Publishers, 1970.

Selected Publications of the National Society for the Study of Education*

Twentieth Yearbook, 1921, Part II—*Report of the Society's Committee on Silent Reading*, M. A. Burgess et al.

Twenty-fourth Yearbook, 1925, Part I—*Report of the National Committee on Reading*, W. S. Gray, chairman.

Twenty-fourth Yearbook, 1925, Part II—*Adapting the Schools to Individual Differences*. Report of the Society's Committee, Carleton W. Washburne, chairman.

Thirty-sixth Yearbook, 1937, Part I—*The Teaching of Reading*. Prepared by the Society's Committee, W. S. Gray, chairman.

Forty-third Yearbook, 1944, Part II—*Teaching Language in the Elementary School*. Prepared by the Society's Committee, M. R. Trabue, chairman.

Forty-eighth Yearbook, 1949, Part II—*Reading in the Elementary School*. Prepared by the Society's Committee, Arthur I. Gates, chairman.

Sixtieth Yearbook, 1961, Part I—*Development in and through Reading*. Prepared by the Society's Committee, Paul A. Witty, chairman.

Sixty-first Yearbook, 1962, Part I—*Individualizing Instruction*. Prepared by the Society's Committee, Fred T. Tyler, chairman.

Sixty-sixth Yearbook, 1967, Part I—*The Educationally Retarded and Disadvantaged*. Prepared by the Society's Committee, Paul A. Witty, editor.

Sixty-sixth Yearbook, 1967, Part II—*Programmed Instruction*. Prepared by the Society's Committee, Phil C. Lange, editor.

Sixty-seventh Yearbook, 1968, Part II—*Innovations and Change in Reading Instruction*. Prepared by the Society's Committee, Helen M. Robinson, editor.

Sixty-ninth Yearbook, 1970, Part II—*Linguistics in School Programs*. Prepared by the Society's Committee, Albert H. Marchwardt, editor.

International Reading Association Conference Proceedings†

Better Readers for Our Times, W. S. Gray and Nancy Larrick, editors, 1956.

Reading in Action, Nancy Larrick, editor, 1957.

Reading for Effective Living, J. Allen Figural, editor, 1958.

Reading in a Changing Society, J. Allen Figural, editor, 1959.

New Frontiers in Reading, J. Allen Figural, editor, 1960.

Changing Concepts of Reading Instruction, J. Allen Figural, editor, 1961.

Challenge and Experiment in Reading, J. Allen Figural, editor, 1962.

Reading as an Intellectual Activity, J. Allen Figural, editor, 1963.

Improvement of Reading Through Classroom Practice, J. Allen Figural, editor, 1964.

Reading and Inquiry, J. Allen Figural, editor, 1965.

Vistas in Reading, J. Allen Figural, editor, 1966.

Forging Ahead in Reading, J. Allen Figural, editor, 1967.

Part I, *Forging Ahead in Reading*, J. Allen Figural, editor, 1968.

*Published by Scholastic Magazines, 33 W. 42nd St., New York 36, N. Y. (The official organ of the International Reading Association is *The Reading Teacher*, 5454 South Shore Drive, Chicago 15, Ill.)

†Published by the University of Chicago Press, 5750 Ellis Ave., Chicago 37, Ill.

Part II, *Ivory, Apes, and Peacocks: The Literature Point of View,* Sam Deaton Sebesta, editor, 1968.

Part I, *Reading and Realism,* J. Allen Figural, editor, 1969.

Part II, *Current Issues in Reading,* Nila Banton Smith, editor, 1969.

Part III, *Reading Disability and Perception,* George D. Spache, editor, 1969.

Selected Publications of the International Reading Association*

Case Studies in Reading compiled by Thaddeus Trela and George Becker. Annotated Bibliography. 1971, 16 pp. Members, $ .50; Nonmembers, $ .75.

Combining Research Results and Good Practice edited by Mildred A. Dawson. Selected convention papers. 1966, 154 pp. Members, $1.50; Nonmembers, $1.75.

Conducting Inservice Programs in Reading compiled by Gus P. Plessas. Annotated Bibliography. 1965, 46 pp. Members, $1.75; Nonmembers, $2.00.

Critical Reading: A Broader View compiled by William Eller and Judith G. Wolf. Annotated Bibliography. 1969, 15 pp. Members, $ .50; Nonmembers, $ .75.

Corrective Reading in the Elementary Classroom edited by Marjorie S. Johnson and Roy A. Kress. Perspectives 7. 1967, 142 pp. Members, $3.00; Nonmembers, $3.50.

Corrective Reading in the High School Classroom edited by H. Alan Robinson and Sidney J. Rauch. Perspectives 6. 1966, 135 pp. Members, $3.00; Nonmembers, $3.50.

Correcting Reading Problems in the Classroom, Book Four. 1969, 72 pp. Members, $1.50; Nonmembers, $2.00.

Current Issues in Reading edited by Nila Banton Smith. Selected convention papers. 1968, 487 pp. Members, $3.00; Nonmembers, $3.50.

Developing Comprehension/Including Critical Reading compiled by Mildred A. Dawson. Selected IRA reprints. 1968, 263 pp. Members, $3.00; Nonmembers, $3.50.

Developing Study Skills in Secondary Schools edited by Harold L. Herber. Perspectives 4. 1965, 169 pp. Members, $3.00; Nonmembers, $3.50.

Diagnostic Viewpoints in Reading edited by Robert Leibert. Selected convention papers. 1971, 134 pp. Members, $3.00; Nonmembers, $4.00.

Establishing Central Reading Clinics: The Administrator's Role, Book Two. 1969, 55 pp. Members, $1.50; Nonmembers, $2.00.

Evaluating Reading and Study Skills in the Secondary Classroom by Ruth G. Viox. Reading Aids Series. 1968, 56 pp. Members, $1.75; Nonmembers, $2.00.

First Grade Reading Studies: Findings of Individual Investigations (reprinted from *The Reading Teacher*), edited by Russell G. Stauffer. 1967, 165 pp. Members, $3.00; Nonmembers, $3.50.

Fusing Reading Skills and Content edited by H. Alan Robinson and Ellen Lamar Thomas. Selected convention papers. 1969, 225 pp. Members, $3.75; Nonmembers, $6.50.

*Published by The International Reading Association, Six Tyre Avenue, Newark, Delaware 19711.

Guidance and the Teaching of Reading by Ruth Strang. Reading Aids Series. 1969, 39 pp. Members, $1.75; Nonmembers, $2.00.

How to Read a Book by Eileen E. Sargent, Helen Huus, and Oliver Andresen. Reading Aids Series. 1970, 44 pp. Members, $1.75; Nonmembers, $2.00.

Individualized Reading compiled by Harry Sartain. Annotated Bibliography. Revised 1970, 19 pp. Members, $ .50; Nonmembers, $ .75.

Informal Reading Inventories by Marjorie S. Johnson and Roy A. Kress. Reading Aids Series. 1965, 44 pp. Members, $1.75; Nonmembers, $2.00.

Language, Reading, and the Communication Process edited by Carl Braun. Selected convention papers. 1971, 172 pp. Members, $3.50; Nonmembers, $4.50.

Providing Clinical Services in Reading compiled by Roy A. Kress and Marjorie S. Johnson. Annotated Bibliography. 1966, 9 pp. Members, $ .50; Nonmembers, $ .75.

Reading and the Kindergarten compiled by Dolores Durkin. Annotated Bibliography. Revised 1969, 8 pp. Members, $ .50; Nonmembers, $ .75.

Reading Diagnosis and Remediation by Ruth Strang. Eric/Crier + IRA Reading Review Series. 1968, 190 pp. Members, $3.00; Nonmembers, $3.50.

Reading Difficulties: Diagnosis, Correction, and Remediation edited by William K. Durr. Selected convention papers. 1970, 276 pp. Members, $3.75; Nonmembers, $6.50.

Reading Disability and Perception edited by George D. Spache. Selected convention papers. 1968, 151 pp. Members, $3.00; Nonmembers, $3.50.

Reading for Children Without—Our Disadvantaged Youth compiled by Gertrude Whipple and Millard H. Black. Reading Aids Series. 1966, 53 pp. Members, $1.75; Nonmembers, $2.00.

Reading for the Disadvantaged: Problems of Linguistically Different Learners edited by Thomas D. Horn. Recommendations for teachers, preschool through high school. 1970, 267 pp. Members, $4.05; Nonmembers, $4.50.

Reading Goals for the Disadvantaged edited by J. Allen Figurel. Selected convention papers. 1969, 339 pp. Members, $3.70; Nonmembers, $6.50.

Reading Methods and Teacher Improvement edited by Nila Banton Smith. Selected convention papers. 1971, 196 pp. Members, $3.75; Nonmembers, $4.75.

Reading Problems and the Environment: The Principal's Role, Book One. 1969, 48 pp. Members, $1.50; Nonmembers, $2.00.

Reading Research: Methodology, Summaries, and Application compiled by Leo Fay. Eric/Crier + IRA Reading Research Profiles Bibliography. 1971, 76 pp. Members, $1.00; Nonmembers, $1.50.

Sources of Good Books for Poor Readers compiled by George S. Spache. Annotated Bibliography. Revised 1969, 12 pp. Members, $ .50; Nonmembers, $ .75.

Speed Reading compiled by Allen Berger. Annotated Bibliography. Revised 1970, 44 pp. Members, $ .50; Nonmembers, $ .75.

Teaching Critical Reading at the Primary Level by Russell G. Stauffer and Ronald Cramer. Reading Aids Series. 1968, 50 pp. Members, $1.75; Nonmembers, $2.00.

Teaching Word Recognition Skills compiled by Mildred A. Dawson. Selected IRA reprints. 1970, 296 pp. Members, $3.00; Nonmembers, $4.00.

Treating Reading Disabilities: The Specialist's Role, Book Three. 1969, 80 pp. Members, $1.50; Nonmembers, $2.00.

Trends and Practices in Secondary School Reading by A. Sterl Artley. Eric/Crier + IRA Reading Review Series. 1968, 131 pp. Members, $3.00; Nonmembers, $3.50.

Upgrading Elementary Reading Programs by Gertrude Whipple. Discusses materials, facilities, and resources; basic instruction; and reading in content fields. 1966, 19 pp. Members, $1.00; Nonmembers, $1.25.

Visual Perception and Its Relation to Reading compiled by Magdalen D. Vernon. Annotated Bibliography. Revised 1969, 144 pp. Members, $ .50; Nonmembers, $ .75.

Supplementary Educational Monographs*

Vol. I	*Recent Trends in Reading,* William S. Gray, editor, 1939.
Vol. II	*Reading and Pupil Development,* William S. Gray, editor, 1940.
Vol. III	*Adjusting Reading Programs to Individuals,* William S. Gray, editor, 1941.
Vol. IV	*Cooperative Efforts in Schools to Improve Reading,* William S. Gray, editor, 1942.
Vol. VI	*Reading in Relation to Experience and Language,* William S. Gray, editor, 1944.
Vol. VII	*The Appraisal of Current Practices in Reading,* William S. Gray, editor, 1945.
Vol. VIII	*Improving Reading in the Content Fields,* William S. Gray, editor, 1946.
Vol. IX	*Promoting Personal and Social Development Through Reading,* William S. Gray, editor, 1947.
Vol. X	*Basic Instruction in Reading in Elementary and High Schools,* William S. Gray, editor, 1948.
Vol. XI	*Classroom Techniques in Improving Reading.* William S. Gray, editor, 1949.
Vol. XII	*Keeping Reading Abreast of the Times,* William S. Gray, editor, 1950.
Vol. XIII	*Promoting Growth Toward Maturity in Interpreting What Is Read,* William S. Gray, editor, 1951.
Vol. XIV	*Improving Reading in All Curriculum Areas,* Helen Robinson, editor, 1952.
Vol. XV	*Corrective Reading in Classroom and Clinic,* Helen Robinson, editor, 1953.
Vol. XVI	*Promoting Maximal Reading Growth Among Able Learners,* Helen Robinson, editor, 1954.

*The Supplementary Educational Monographs which have been published since 1939 include the Proceedings of the Annual Conference on Reading held each year at the University of Chicago as well as other reports pertaining to the subject of reading. These monographs are published by the University of Chicago Press, 5750 Ellis Ave., Chicago, Illinois 60600.

Vol. XVII	*Oral Aspects of Reading,* Helen Robinson, editor, 1955.
Vol. XVIII	*Developing Permanent Interest in Reading,* Helen Robinson, editor, 1956.
Vol. XIX	*Materials for Reading,* Helen Robinson, editor, 1957.
Vol. XX	*Visual Perceptual Abilities and Early Reading Progress,* Helen Robinson, editor, 1958.
Vol. XXI	*Reading Instruction in Various Patterns of Grouping,* Helen Robinson, editor, 1959.
Vol. XXII	*Sequential Development of Reading Abilities,* Helen Robinson, editor, 1960.
Vol. XXIII	*Controversial Issues in Reading and Promising Solutions,* Helen Robinson, editor, 1961.
Vol. XXIV	*The Underachiever in Reading,* Helen Robinson. Helen Robinson, editor, 1962.
Vol. XXV	*Reading and the Language Arts,* Helen Robinson. Helen Robinson, editor, 1963.
Vol. XXVI	*Meeting Individual Differences in Reading,* Helen Robinson, editor, 1964.
Vol. XXVII	*Recent Developments in Reading,* Helen Robinson, editor, 1965.
Vol. XXVIII	*Reading: Seventy-Five Years of Progress,* Helen Robinson, editor, 1966.
Vol. XXIX	*Clinical Studies in Reading III,* Helen Robinson, editor, 1967.

APPENDIX E2

Publications Which Contain Bibliographies of Books for Retarded Readers

BLAIR, GLENN. *Diagnostic and Remedial Teaching.* Rev. ed. New York: The Macmillan Co., 1956, pp. 180-198.

BOTEL, MORTON. *How to Teach Reading.* Chicago: Follett Publishing Co., 1962, pp. 117-120.

CARLSEN, G. ROBERT. *Books and the Teen-Age Reader: A Guide for Teachers, Librarians, and Parents.* New York: Harper and Row, Publishers, 1967.

CARPENTER, HELEN. *Gateways to American History: An Annotated Graded List of Books for Slow Learners in Junior High School.* New York: H. W. Wilson Co., 1942.

CARTER, HOMER, and DOROTHY MCGINNIS. *Learning to Read.* New York: McGraw-Hill Book Co., 1953, pp. 115-118.

DAWSON, MILDRED, and HENRY BAMMAN. *Fundamentals of Basic Reading Instruction.* 2nd ed. New York: Longmans, Green and Co., 1963.

DECHANT, EMERALD. *Diagnosis and Remediation of Reading Disability.* West Nyack, N. Y.: Parker Publishing Co., Inc., 1968, pp. 174-175.

DELLA-PIANA, GABRIEL. *Reading Diagnosis and Prescription.* New York: Holt. Rinehart and Winston, Inc., 1968, Appendix E.

DUNN, ANITA, and MABEL JACKMAN. *Fare for the Reluctant Reader.* 3rd ed. Albany: Capital Area School Development Association, State University of New York at Albany, 1964.

EAKIN, MARY. *Good Books for Children*. 3rd ed. Chicago: University of Chicago Press, 1966.

———. *Library Materials for Remedial Reading, Bibliography*. No. 4, Instructional Materials Bulletin, May, 1959, Cedar Falls, Ia.: Iowa State Teachers College Library.

FRY, EDWARD, and WARREN JOHNSON. "Books for Remedial Reading," *Elementary English* 35 (1958):373-379.

GUILFOILE, ELIZABETH. *Adventuring with Books*. Rev. ed. Champaign, Ill.: National Council of Teachers of English, 1966.

HARRIS, ALBERT J. *How to Increase Reading Ability*. 5th ed. New York: David McKay Co., Inc., 1970, Appendix B.

HART, J. A. *Books for the Retarded Reader: A Teacher's Guide to Books for Backward Children*. 3rd ed. Victoria, Australia: Australian Council for Educational Research, 1966.

HILL, MARGARET. *A Bibliography of Reading Lists for Retarded Readers*. Extension Bulletin. College of Education Series, No. 37. Iowa City: State University of Iowa, 1953.

HOBSON, CLOY, and OSCAR HAUGH. *Materials for the Retarded Reader*. Kansas State Department of Public Instruction, 1954.

HOWARD, VIVIAN. *Books for Retarded Readers*. Illinois State Library, 1954.

JULITTA, SISTER MARY, and SISTER MICHAELLA. "A List of Books for Retarded Readers," *Elementary English* 45 (1968):472-477.

KOTTMEYER, WILLIAM. *Teacher's Guide for Remedial Reading*. Manchester, Mo.: Webster Publishing, 1959, pp. 189-201.

KRESS, ROY. *A Place to Start: A Graded Bibliography for Children with Reading Difficulties*. Reading Center, Syracuse University, 1963.

KUGLER, LORNA et al. *Choosing the Right Book*. California Library Association, 1955.

LAZAR, MAY, ed. *The Retarded Reader in the Junior High School*. Bureau of Educational Research Bulletin No. 31, New York Board of Education, 1952.

ORR, KENNETH. *Selected Materials for Remedial Reading*. Division of Special Education, Indiana State Teachers College.

ROSWELL, FLORENCE et al. *Selected Materials for Children with Reading Disabilities*. Rev. ed. New York: Remedial Reading Service, School of Education, The City College, 1966.

RUE, ELOISE. *America Past and Present*. New York: H. W. Wilson Co., 1948.

SHOR, RACHEL, and ESTELLE A. FIDEL. *Children's Catalog*. 11th ed. New York: H. W. Wilson Co., 1966.

SPACHE, GEORGE. *Good Reading for Poor Readers*. Rev. ed. Champaign, Ill.: Garrard Publishing Co., 1970.

STRANG, RUTH et al. *Gateways to Readable Books*. 4th ed. New York: H. W. Wilson Co., 1966.

WILLARD, CHARLES B., and HELEN I. STAPP. *Your Reading*. Champaign, Ill.: National Council of Teachers of English, 1966.

WITTY, PAUL A.; ALMA M. FREELAND; and EDITH H. GROTBERG. *The Teaching of Reading*. Chicago: D. C. Heath and Co., 1966, p. 66.

WOOLF, MAURICE, and JEANNE WOOLF. *Remedial Reading*. New York: McGraw-Hill Book Co., 1957, pp. 385-394.

WRIGHT, JOSEPHINE. *Library Resources*. Salt Lake City, Utah: Exemplary Center for Reading Instruction, 1968.

APPENDIX E3
HIGH INTEREST AND LOW VOCABULARY BOOKS

Title	Difficulty Grade Level	Interest Grade Level
Dan Frontier Books Series	1-3	1-7
Cowboy Sam Books Series	1-3	1-4
The Button Books Series	1-3	1-4
Sailor Jack Books Series	1-3	2-7
Space Age Books Series	2-3	2-6
What Is It Series	2-4	4-8
Pioneer Series	4	4-7

Published by Benefic Press, 10300 W. Roosevelt Road, Westchester, Ill. 60153.

✷ ✷ ✷

Childhood of Famous American Series	4-5	4-9

Published by Bobbs-Merrill Co., 4300 W. 62nd St., Indianapolis, Ind. 46268.

✷ ✷ ✷

All About Books Series	2-4	2-8
The True Books Series	2-3	2-8
Frontiers of America Series	3	3-8
Middle Grade Books Series	4	3-7

Published by Children's Book Centre, 140 Kensington Church St., London W 8, England.

✷ ✷ ✷

Jim Forest Readers Series	1-3	3-6
Checkered Flag Series	2	6-11
The Deep Sea Adventure Series	2-4	3-9
The Morgan Bay Series	2-4	4-9
The Wildlife Adventure Series	2-4	3-8
Americans All Series	4	4-7
The Reading-Motivated Series	4-5	4-10

Published by Field Educational Publications, Inc., 609 Mission St., San Francisco, Calif. 94105.

✷ ✷ ✷

The Interesting Reading Series	2-3	4-11

Published by Follett Educational Corp., 1010 W. Washington Blvd., Chicago, Ill. 60607.

✷ ✷ ✷

Basic Vocabulary Series	1-3	2-4
Discovery Books Series	2-4	3-6
Folklore of the World Books Series	3	2-8
Pleasure Reading Series	3-4	3-5

Title	Difficulty Grade Level	Interest Grade Level
Junior Science Books Series	3-4	3-6
Pleasure Reading Books	4	3-6

Published by Garrard Publishing Co., Champaign, Ill. 61820.

✿   ✿   ✿

Simplified Classics Series	4-6	4-10

Published by Globe Book Co., 175 Fifth Ave., New York, N. Y. 10010

✿   ✿   ✿

We Were There Books Series	4-5	5-9
Getting to Know Books Series	4-5	5-9

Published by E. M. Hale and Co., 1201 S. Hastings Way, Eau Claire, Wis. 54701

✿   ✿   ✿

American Adventure Series	2-6	4-9
Modern Adventure Stories Series	4-6	4-11

Published by Harper and Row, Publishers, Inc., 49 E. 33rd St., New York, N. Y. 10016.

✿   ✿   ✿

Teen Age Tales	4-6	6-11
Strange Teen Age Tales Books	5-6	5-11

Published by D. C. Heath and Co., 285 Columbus Ave., Boston, Mass. 02116.

✿   ✿   ✿

Beginner Books Series	1-2	1-4
Gateway Books	2-3	3-9
Step-Up Books Series	2-3	3-9
Allabout Books Series	4-6	5-11
Landmark Books Series	5-7	5-11

Published by Random House, 457 Madison Ave., New York, N. Y. 10022.

✿   ✿   ✿

Simplified Classics Series	4-5	4-10

Published by Scott, Foresman and Co., Glenview, Ill. 60025.

✿   ✿   ✿

Junior Everyreaders Series	2-4	2-7
Everyreader Series	4-5	4-10

Published by Webster Division of McGraw-Hill Book Co., Manchester Rd., Manchester, Mo. 63011.

APPENDIX G
PUBLISHERS OF TESTS AND OTHER
READING MATERIAL

List of Publishers or Manufacturers of Reading
Tests, Textbooks, Materials and Devices

The following alphabetically arranged list contains the names and addresses of publishers or manufacturers of reading tests, textbooks, materials, and devices mentioned in this book. Because of the rapidity of change in publishers' names and addresses, some of these entries will be out of date.

Addison-Wesley Publishing Co., Inc., Sand Hill Road, Menlo Park, Calif. 94025.

Alcock, Dorothea, 107 N. Elspeth Way, Covina, Calif. 91722.

American Book Co., Division of Litton Educational Publishing, Inc., 450 W. 33 St., New York, N. Y. 10001.

American Teaching Aids, P. O. Box 1652, Covina, Calif. 91722.

Appleton-Century-Crofts, see Meredith Corp.

Audio-Visual Research Co., 1317 Eighth St., S. E., Waseca, Minn. 56093.

Barnell Loft, Ltd., 11 S. Centre Ave., Rockville Centre, New York, N. Y. 11571.

Beckley-Cardy Co., 1900 N. Narragansett Ave., Chicago, Ill. 60639.

Bell and Howell Co., Audio Visual Products Divisions, 7100 McCormick Road, Chicago, Ill. 60645.

Better Reading Program, Inc., 8 South Michigan Ave., Room 303, Chicago, Ill. 60603.

BFA Educational Media, 2211 Michigan Ave., Santa Monica, Calif. 90025.

The Bobbs-Merrill Co., Inc., 4300 W. 62nd St., Indianapolis, Ind. 46268.

Milton Bradley Co., 74 Park St., Springfield, Mass. 01102.

Bureau of Publications, Teachers College, Columbia University, New York, N. Y. 10027.

California Test Bureau, Monterey, Calif. 93940.

Cenco Educational Aids, 2600 S. Koster Ave., Chicago, Ill. 60623.

Chicago Press, University of, 5750 Ellis Ave., Chicago, Ill. 60637.

Coast Visual Education Co., Inc., 5610 Hollywood Blvd., Hollywood, Calif. 09928.

Committee on Diagnostic Reading Tests, Mountain Home, N. C. 28758.

Craig Research Inc., 3410 S. La Cienago Blvd., Los Angeles, Calif. 09916.

Creative Teaching Press, 514 Hermosa Vista Ave., Monterey Park, Calif. 91754.

Dick Blick, P. O. Box 1267, Galesburg, Ill. 61401.

Dowlings, Inc., 3017 N. Stiles, Oklahoma City, Okla. 73105.

Educational Aids, 845 Wisteria Drive, Fremont, Calif. 94538.

Educational Development Laboratories, Inc., a Division of McGraw-Hill Book Co., Huntington, N. Y. 11743.

Educational Electronics, Inc., 609 W. Sheridan, Oklahoma City, Okla. 73102.

Electronic Futures, Inc., 57 Dodge Ave., North Haven, Conn. 06473.

Encyclopaedia Britannica Educational Corp., 425 N. Michigan Ave., Chicago, Ill. 60611.
Essay Press, Box 5, Planetarium Station, New York, N. Y. 10024.
Expression Co., Publishers, P. O. Box 11, Magnolia, Mass. 01930.
Fearon Publishers, 2165 Park Blvd., Palo Alto, Calif. 94306.
Follett Educational Corp., 1010 W. Washington Blvd., Chicago, Ill. 60607.
Garrard Publishing Co., 1607 N. Market St., Champaign, Ill. 61820.
Ginn and Company, Statler Bldg., Back Bay, P. O. 191, Boston, Mass. 02117.
Grolier Educational Corporation, 845 Third Ave., New York, N. Y. 10022.
Hammond Educational Sales, a Division of McGraw-Hill Book Co., 330 W. 42nd St., New York, N. Y. 10036.
Harcourt Brace Jovanovich, Inc., 757 3rd Ave., New York, N. Y. 10017.
Harper and Row, Publishers, 49 E. 33rd St., New York, N. Y. 10016.
D. C. Heath and Co., 125 Spring St., Lexington, Mass. 02116.
Hoffman Information Systems, 5623 Peck Road, Arcadia, Calif. 91006.
Holiday House, Inc., 18 E. 56th St., New York, N. Y. 10022.
Holt, Rinehart and Winston, Inc., 383 Madison Ave., New York, N. Y. 10017.
Houghton Mifflin Co., 2 Park St., Boston, Mass. 02107.
Ideal School Supply Co., 11000 S. Lavergne Ave., Oak Lawn, Ill. 60453.
Imperial Productions, Inc., 247 W. Court St., Kankakee, Ill. 60901.
Initial Teaching Alphabet Publications, Inc., 20 E. 46th St., New York, N. Y. 10017.
International Reading Association, 6 Tyre Ave., Newark, Del. 19711.
The Judy Co., 310 N. 2nd St., Minneapolis, Minn. 55401.
Kenworthy Educational Service, Inc., P. O. Box 3031, 138 Allen St., Buffalo, N. Y. 14205.
Keystone View Co., Meadville, Penn. 16335.
Kohner Brothers, 200 5th St., New York, N. Y. 10012.
Lafayette Instrument Co., North 9th Street Road and 52 By-Pass, Lafayette, Ind. 47902.
Lakeshore Curriculum Materials, 5369 W. Pico Blvd., Los Angeles, Calif. 90619.
Learning Through Seeing, Inc., 8138 Foothill Boulevard, Sunland, Calif. 91040.
J. B. Lippincott Co., E. Washington Square, Philadelphia, Penn. 19105.
Listen and Learn, Americana 600 Tower Dr., Mundelein, Ill. 60060.
Lyons and Carnahan, Inc., 407 East 25th St., Chicago, Ill. 60616.
McCormick-Mathers Publishing Co., Inc., P. O. Box 2212, Wichita, Kans. 67201.
McGraw-Hill Book Co., 330 West 42nd St., New York, N. Y. 10036.
The Macmillan Co., 866 Third Ave., New York, N. Y. 10022.
Meredith Corp., 750 Third Ave., New York, N. Y. 10016.
Milliron Co., 1198 S. LaBrea Ave., Los Angeles, Calif. 90019.
Milton Bradley Co., 74 Park St., Springfield, Mass. 01101.
Open Court Publishing Co., Box 599, La Salle, Ill. 61301.
F. A. Owen Publishing Co., 7 Bank St., Dansville, N. Y. 14437.
Parker Brothers Inc., Salem, Mass. 01971.
Perceptual Development Laboratories, Box 1911, Big Springs, Texas 79720.
Phonics, 30690 Providence Rd., Cleveland, O. 44124.
Phonovisual Products, Inc., Box 5625, Washington, D. C. 20016.
Prentice-Hall, Inc., 521 Fifth Ave., Englewood Cliffs, N. J. 07632.

Psychotechnics, Inc., 7433 N. Harlem Ave., Chicago, Ill. 60648.

G. P. Putnam's Sons, 200 Madison Ave., New York, N. Y. 10016.

Random House/Singer, School Division, 457 Hahn Road, Westminster, Md. 21157.

Reader's Digest Services, Inc., Educational Division, Pleasantville, N. Y. 10570.

The Reading Laboratory, Inc., 55 Day St., South Norwalk, Conn. 06854.

Remedial Education Press of the Kingsbury Center, 2138 Bancroft Place, N. W. Washington, D. C. 20008.

Rheem Califone, 5922 Bowcroft St., Los Angeles, Calif. 90016.

The Ronald Press Co., 79 Madison Ave., New York, N. Y. 10016.

Scholastic Magazines and Book Services, 50 W. 44th St., New York, N. Y. 10036.

Science Research Associates, Inc., 259 East Erie St., Chicago, Ill. 60611.

Scott, Foresman and Co., 900 E. Lake Ave., Glenview, Ill. 60025.

Society for Visual Education, Inc., 1345 Diversey, Chicago, Ill. 60614.

Steck-Vaughn Co., P. O. Box 2028, Austin, Tex. 78767.

Study-Scope Co., P. O. Box 689, Tyler, Tex. 75701.

Syracuse University Press, Box 8, University Station, Syracuse, N. Y. 13210.

Teachers' Supplies, 6571 Beach Blvd., Buena Park, Calif. 90620.

Teaching Technology Corp., Box 505, 5520 Cleon Ave., North Hollywood, Calif. 91603.

3 M Visual Products, 2501 Hudson Rd., St. Paul, Minn. 55119.

Visualcraft, Inc., 12842 S. Western Ave., Blue Island, Ill. 60406.

Webster Division of McGraw-Hill Book Co., Manchester Rd., Manchester, Mo., 63011.

Winston. See Holt, Rinehart and Winston.

Winter Haven Lions Research Foundation, Inc., Box 112, Winter Haven, Fla. 33880.

Wordcrafters Guild, St. Albana School, Mass., and Wisc. Ave., N. W. Washington, D. C. 20016.

Author Index

Subject Index